Plywood Projects Illustrated

Plywood Projects Illustrated

Kenn Oberrecht

Charles Scribner's Sons New York

Library of Congress Cataloging in Publication Data

Oberrecht, Kenn.
Plywood projects illustrated.

1. Plywood craft. I. Title.
TT191.024 1983 684'.08 83-14142
ISBN 0-684-17972-5

This book published simultaneously in the United States of America and in Canada—Copyright under the Berne Convention.

1 3 5 7 9 11 13 15 17 19 H/C 20 18 16 14 12 10 8 6 4 2

Printed in the United States of America.

For Chet Fish

Acknowledgments

For this and all of my workshop books and articles, my closest business associates for the better part of a decade have been Roger Conrad and the staff of the W. J. Conrad Lumber Co. of Coos Bay, Oregon. As home-improvement centers go, there's none better. Conrad's, as it's known locally, is a do-it-yourselfer's delight, where I can always find courteous and friendly service, able assistance, expert advice, and hot coffee.

My special thanks go, of course, to Roger, and to the following folks who have helped make my job easier and more enjoyable:

Matt Budiselich
Don Carlson
Larry Carpenter
Kathy Cook
Eddie Griggs
Greg Gulseth
Darwin Guye
Don Jackson
Steve Jeter
Curt Monsebroten
Vickie Pihlak
Glen Robertson
Clayton Smith
Darrell Smith
Gary Smith
Curtis Schwarze
Cliff Washburn

Contents

Part I	**Materials, Tools, and Techniques**	1
Chapter 1	Plywood: An Introduction	3
Chapter 2	Building Materials for Plywood Projects	9
Chapter 3	Tools for Plywood Projects	15
Chapter 4	Building with Plywood	21
Chapter 5	Finishing Plywood Projects	28
Part II	**Half-Sheet Projects**	33
Chapter 6	Record Album Bin	35
Chapter 7	Stackable Storage Boxes	38
Chapter 8	Executive's Wastebasket	41
Chapter 9	Card and Game Table	46
Chapter 10	Lighted Dictionary Stand	49
Chapter 11	Stacking Storage Bins	53
Chapter 12	File 13	56
Chapter 13	Stack-and-Bundle Boxes	60
Chapter 14	Covered Bridge for Newspapers	63
Chapter 15	Wall-Mounted Magazine Rack	67
Part III	**One-Sheet Projects**	71
Chapter 16	Basic Workbench with Shelves	73
Chapter 17	Paperback Shadowbox	79
Chapter 18	Decorative Cedar Chest	82
Chapter 19	Two-Drawer File Cabinet	87
Chapter 20	Firewood Crib	93
Chapter 21	Modern Accent Tables	96
Chapter 22	Desktop Organizer and Light	100
Chapter 23	A Pair of Nightstands	104
Chapter 24	A Roll-Around Utility Cabinet	111
Chapter 25	WORKMATE Workshop	118
Part IV	**Major Projects**	123
Chapter 26	Platform Bed	125
Chapter 27	Easy-up Bookshelves	130
Chapter 28	Home Video Center	134
Chapter 29	A Case for Magazines	140
Chapter 30	Elegant Butcher-Block-Style Tables	144
Chapter 31	Four-Drawer Chest	149
Chapter 32	Bookcase / Entertainment Center	155
Chapter 33	Four-Drawer File Cabinet	160
Chapter 34	Modern Pedestal Desk	165
Chapter 35	Base-Cabinet Workbench	171

Part V	**Projects from Leftovers**	181
Chapter 36	Workshop Helpmates	183
Chapter 37	Bulletin Board	186
Chapter 38	Once-Around Cribbage Board	189
Chapter 39	Quick and Simple Magazine Rack	192
Chapter 40	Handy Lap Desk	194
Chapter 41	Correspondence Trays	198
Chapter 42	Small-Bird Chalet	201
Chapter 43	Large-Bird Nesting Box	204
Chapter 44	Handy Tool Tote	207
Chapter 45	Desktop Book Trough	210
Chapter 46	Triangle Game	213
Chapter 47	Pair of Bookends	216
Chapter 48	Simple Wine Rack	218
Chapter 49	Easy-up Utility Shelves	221
Chapter 50	Workshop Plan Stand	223
Chapter 51	Stereo Speaker Elevators	226
Chapter 52	Spice or Small-Parts Rack	229
Chapter 53	Space-Efficient Corner Table	232
Chapter 54	Sturdy Step Block	235
Chapter 55	Shoeshine Box	238
	Customary to Metric System Conversion Table	241

Plywood Projects Illustrated

Part

I

Materials, Tools, and Techniques

Before starting to work on any of the projects in this book, you should familiarize yourself with the materials, tools, and techniques that will ensure success. If you're a veteran home-workshop enthusiast, you're probably already familiar with much of what appears in Part 1, but you will likely find a few tips and pointers that will prove valuable. If you're a beginning do-it-yourselfer, you'll find these first five chapters an essential introduction to the basics of woodworking.

1 Plywood: An Introduction

Although plywood, as we know it today, can be considered a product of modern technology, it has been around in one form or another for as long as man has been crafting in wood. Laminated woods, in fact, predate Columbus's landing on American soil by some three thousand years.

It wasn't until the nineteenth century, however, that plywood was found to be a strong and versatile product that could be used in the manufacture of various furniture, fixtures, and implements where other wood products proved inferior. Veneered wood, as it was known then, was used in the construction of such disparate items as desks, pianos, train seats, trunks, carriages, and cabinets of all sorts.

The plywood industry was shaped and organized during the first four decades of the twentieth century. Standards of manufacture and application were established, and countless uses for the material found. Today, plywood is the most common wood product in use. It is an integral material in the construction of our homes, apartment buildings, warehouses, barns, sheds, and virtually every kind of building one can imagine.

While plywood is better understood and more widely used by designers, architects, engineers, and building contractors than by do-it-yourselfers, its popularity among home craftsmen is growing rapidly as more and more of them discover the product's durability, versatility, and countless applications. For those who have made these discoveries already, plywood is their first choice for many home workshop projects.

Plywood—from Forest to Workshop

Because of the demands placed on our forests by the building trades for the past century, there is little old-growth timber left in the contiguous states. Most of our timber is now scientifically planted and grown on tree farms, where it is harvested when it reaches sufficient size for its intended use.

Those trees that are to be turned into plywood are felled, limbed, loaded aboard log trucks, and hauled to nearby plywood mills. There they are sorted and classified according to such criteria as species and intended use.

Logs are then barked and cut into lengths slightly longer than eight feet. These shortened logs, known as peeler blocks, are then heated—usually by a steam-and-hot-water process—to facilitate veneer cutting. Once properly heat-treated, they're moved to the peeler lathes, where they're chucked and turned against full-length blades that cut away a continuous veneer from each block until all that remains of the original log is a small core only a few inches in diameter.

Face veneers, particularly in the hardwoods, are usually sliced instead of peeled, which allows for superior grain characteristics in the finished panel and reduces the tendency of the veneer to curl, as peeled veneers often do. Veneers are then cut or clipped to the desired length and are dried to reduce moisture content, usually in kilns or special veneer dryers.

In simplest terms, layup is the stacking and gluing of veneers to roughly form sheets that will eventually become finished panels. Alternating plies are glued to one another with the grain running at right angles, which is what makes plywood unique among all wood products and gives it the strength and durability for which it is known.

From layup, the partially completed and slightly oversized panels move to the hot press, where heat and pressure are combined to cure the glue. Panels are then trimmed to finished dimensions and are sanded according to the grades that will be assigned to them. Sanding might range from a mere touching down of high spots to complete face-sanding of one or both sides of the panel.

Panels are then inspected and repaired as necessary. Finally, they are graded, stamped, stacked, bundled, and sent to their various destinations by truck, rail, or ship. Ultimately, some of these bundles find their way to your nearby lumberyard or home-improvement center, where they're stacked in ricks to await your next building project.

Of course, there are different processes, machinery, special layups, and finishing techniques used at the various mills throughout North America, the details of which are not as important to the home handyman as are the facts that follow. But, in simple terms, this is how plywood makes it from the forest to the workshop.

Types of Plywood

Broadly, there are two different types of plywood: softwood and hardwood. Softwood plywood (fir, pine, and so forth) is mainly manufactured from coniferous trees, under the auspices of the American Plywood Association (APA). The hardwood plywoods (birch, oak, and so forth) are largely made from broadleaf trees, according to the specifications of the Hardwood Plywood Manufacturers Association (HPMA). You will find, however, that some hardwoods are used in making some softwood plywoods, and vice versa.

The vast bulk of plywood used by the building trades is softwood, and most of that is Douglas fir. So too in the home workshop: Softwood plywood will be the type to use for most projects and certainly for any project that will be painted. Softwood plywood is the cheaper of the two and the most readily available in the greatest number of sizes and widest range of grades and applications.

There are three general types of softwood plywood—marine, exterior, and interior—which differ from one another mainly in the type of glue used to bond the veneers and to some extent in the manufacturing processes. Of the three types, marine plywood is the toughest and most expensive, and important only to the do-it-yourselfer involved with marine-type projects (boats, boathouses, pontoons, and so forth).

Exterior plywood is the type to use for any project exposed to the elements, where relative humidity is high, or where moisture is a threat. In some instances, it's a better choice than the cheaper interior plywood for indoor projects, simply because it's better made, with higher quality inner plies. Consequently, it lies flatter and exhibits fewer gaps and holes in the edges.

Although interior plywood is sometimes manufactured with interior glue or a water-resistant intermediate glue, most of it today is made with completely waterproof exterior glue. Such plywood differs from exterior-type primarily in the lower-grade interior plies. Nevertheless, interior plywood should never be used for permanent outdoor projects. For most indoor projects, interior plywood is the type you'll want, mainly because it will fill your needs and is cheaper than exterior.

In addition to the various types of plywood already mentioned, there are plywoods designed and manufactured for siding, flooring, sheathing, and roofing. There are special layups and special surfaces, as well. In short, there is a plywood to meet practically any building need.

One specialty plywood that should be of some interest to the home-workshop enthusiast on a tight schedule is an exterior-type panel with a special resin-based fiberboard overlay on one or both sides. Such panels are classified as High Density Overlay (HDO) or Medium Density Overlay (MDO); they are extremely tough and are perhaps the most weather-resistant of all plywoods. They are readily available in most areas, as they are widely used for making highway signs and for other industrial purposes.

HDO and MDO plywood comes with grooved, textured, or perfectly smooth surfaces. Although such panels are considerably more expensive than conventional plywood, they require little or no surface preparation, as the overlays will be virtually blemish-free. Consequently, they're great time-savers on any project that will be painted.

A number of do-it-yourself books and magazines have touted the qualities of Finnish or Baltic plywood, which, because of special layup processes and a higher number of superior-quality interior plies, is one of the strongest plywoods made. Moreover, the nearly perfect interior laminations make it possible, by merely sanding the edges, to produce a smooth finish free of the usual gaps and holes associated with plywood edges.

One problem with this product, however, is that it is one of the highest-priced plywoods on the market; it is considerably more expensive than top-grade hardwood plywood and not nearly as suitable for a natural finish. Unless you have a specific need for a product with great load-bearing capacity, you should pass this one by in favor of a more suitable and less expensive hardwood or softwood product.

Plywood Sizes

Plywood is manufactured in a wide variety of dimensions for special purposes, but the product most commonly available everywhere is the standard 4 × 8′ sheet. Many lumberyards and home-improvement centers are now stocking smaller panels as well—usually 4 × 4′ or 2 × 4′—for projects requiring less than a full sheet.

There are special plywoods manufactured as thin as ⅛″ or as thick as several inches, but the standard thicknesses most widely available are ¼″, ⅜″, ½″, ⅝″, and ¾″. You will probably find ¼″, ½″, and ¾″ plywood suitable for most home-workshop projects.

Another commonly stocked product is 1⅛″ plywood flooring, which either comes tongued and grooved or with squared edges. This plywood is heavy (120 pounds per sheet) and extremely strong; it is quite useful for a variety of projects, particularly workbench, desk, and table tops.

Softwood Plywood Grades

With nearly three dozen grades and grade trademarks in softwood plywoods alone, the grading system, at first, might seem confusing. It's not all that difficult to grasp, though, and many of the different grades and aspects of the grading system can be ignored by the do-it-yourselfer. This is not to say, however, that grades are unimportant. Quite the contrary, a rudimentary knowledge of plywood grades and what they mean is essential if you are to buy wisely and pick the right product for your particular needs.

Broadly, softwood plywoods come either in engineered or appearance grades. The engineered-grade panels are grade-stamped on the back face of each panel; appearance-grade plywood is grade-stamped along the edges.

While the grade stamp will provide such information as species group, type (exterior or interior), product standard number, and mill number, the most prominent and important mark for the bulk of your projects will be

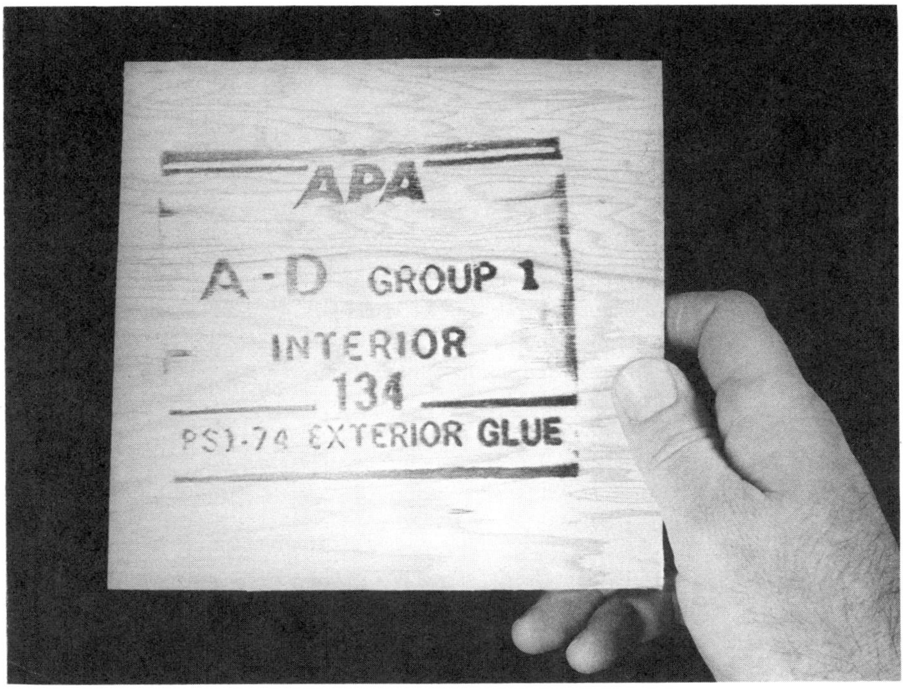

Typical grade stamp found on the back face of engineered grades of plywood

that which indicates the quality of the veneers on the panel face and back. Ranging from highest to lowest quality, these veneers will be graded N, A, B, C, or D. The first letter of the grade refers to the face veneer and the second to the back veneer. For example, a sheet marked A-C would have a grade-A face and a grade-C back.

Incidentally, common among those who buy and sell plywood are the terms "good-one-side" and "good-two-sides," written as G1S and G2S. A G1S sheet might be graded A-C or A-D, while a G2S sheet would be A-A or A-B.

Following are the letter grades for softwood plywood and the quality standards for each, as well as some specific recommendations:

Grade N

A plywood face graded N is a top-quality surface veneer that is consistent and without noticeable defects of any kind. According to standards, small defects may be filled with synthetic fillers. All surface repairs must be made of wood, and the maximum number of repairs per face is held to six per 4 × 8′ sheet. N-grade plywood, which usually must be special-ordered, should only be used where a natural finish is desired, as lower, less expensive grades are adequate for painted projects.

Grade A

An A-grade face is smooth and neatly repaired with either wood or synthetic filler. According to APA standards, no open imperfections—such as knots, holes, and pitch pockets—are permitted, and a maximum of eighteen repairs per 4 × 8′ sheet are allowed. A-grade plywood is ideal for projects that will be painted as it is completely sanded and requires a minimum of surface preparation.

Grade B

Plywood veneers graded B are smooth and solid, though they might exhibit tight knots as large as one inch in diameter, as well as wood or synthetic repairs. Repairs might consist of plugs and these need not run with the grain. Standards allow for minor splits and surface blemishes easily filled by the do-it-yourselfer. The surface is sanded, but not as smoothly and consistently as a grade-A veneer. Although B-grade veneers require a bit of extra preparation and finishing, they are excellent for most projects that will be painted.

Grade C-Plugged

While C-grade veneers are considered by some to be too rough for anything but utility-type projects, they're cheaper than the higher grades and can be easily patched, filled, and finished for painting. The C-Plugged sheets are a cut above C-grade and should not be overlooked by the handyman in search of an economical building material. Standards allow for splits up to ⅛″ wide and tight knots up to 1½″. These faces will exhibit synthetic repairs, stitching, wood-borer holes, and other surface imperfections. Sanding is comparable to that found in a B-grade veneer. For the woodworker who has the time for finishing chores, this grade might prove the best buy. Properly filled and sanded, it is certainly adequate for most painted projects.

Grade C

A C-grade surface will likely have knots as large as 1½″ in diameter and knotholes up to 1″, as well as splits to ⅛″, wood-borer holes, and other open defects. Repairs might be in the form of plugs, synthetic patches, and shims. Visible repairs might be numerous, although there are limitations. The surface is sanded but might exhibit rough spots and loose splinters. C-grade is best suited to utilitarian-type projects and special applications, such as tabletop underlayment—but for the do-it-yourselfer who has the time for extensive patching and sanding, it can prove to be a cheap material adaptable to most painted projects.

Grade D

A D-grade face will usually have knots and holes up to 2½″ in diameter and a variety of other surface imperfections. Splits might be present and stitching is permitted. Veneers graded D are rough and unsuitable for exterior surfaces, as too much filling and sanding would be required to bring them up to a quality necessary for painting. A D-grade surface is adequate as an underlayment, however, and can often be used as the second side of a good-one-side panel when the D surface will be concealed.

Hardwood Plywood Grades

Hardwood-veneer plywood is graded, best to worst, as *A* (premium), 1 (good), 2 (sound), 3 (utility), and 4 (backing). For the projects contained in this book, only premium and good hardwood veneers should be considered. If you plan to paint any given project, there is no sense in spending the extra money for a hardwood veneer. If, on the other hand, you plan to finish a project naturally and desire the characteristics associated with a particular hardwood, you'll want an unblemished surface, free of open defects.

Why Use Plywood?

Because of manufacturing processes that position grain at right angles in alternating plies, plywood is stronger than lumber and other wood products of like thickness. And the thicker the plywood is, the greater the burdens it will support. It will not check, cup, or bow as dimensional lumber often does; and it will not split when nailed or screwed, although it will sometimes splinter when nailed or screwed too near the edges.

Shrinkage, although a problem in most dimensional lumber (even the so-called dry lumber), is nonexistent in plywood. Consequently, you won't have to worry about panels pulling apart and joints failing after a project is completed.

Plywood is widely available in an array of thicknesses, types, and grades to fit numerous needs and a great variety of applications. In fact, it is sometimes the only feasible material to use, especially when large panels are required for such projects as cabinets, chests, drawer faces, doors, and table tops.

Although the higher grades of plywood are often more expensive than other lumber and wood products, in the final analysis they often prove cheaper to use. It's usually necessary to buy as much as 25 percent more lumber than required for any particular project to allow for waste caused by serious imperfections. By carefully planning cuts, however, there is little waste with plywood, and leftovers can almost always be put to use in other projects.

Plywood is not without faults, but most of its shortcomings pale in comparison with those of other products. Moreover, the woodworker who is aware of the pitfalls and knows how to deal with them is going to end up ahead in time and money on his plywood projects.

Selecting the Right Plywood

By now, you have a good basic understanding of plywood, its uses, how it's graded, and what to expect from the material. You still must face the problem of picking the right plywood for any given project, but this is not as difficult a task as it might seem. A trip or two to your local lumberyard and a hands-on inspection of the various types and grades of plywood at your disposal will provide you with a wealth of practical plywood knowledge.

Don't be afraid to ask questions when you're shopping for building materials. The people at the counter and those who load your lumber, plywood, and materials usually have the expertise to answer any questions you might have. If one salesperson can't help you, there will be someone else who can. They deal with building problems day in and day out, from the simplest and most basic questions of the beginning do-it-yourselfer to complex queries from master craftsmen and building contractors. If you don't tap their knowledge, you won't get your money's worth.

Picking the right plywood for any project is, to some extent, a personal matter that depends largely on individual requirements. If you're on a tight schedule and don't want to spend a lot of time finishing a project, you would do well to buy the highest-quality product, as it will require a minimum of surface preparation. If, on the other hand, your funds are limited and you have the time to spend patching and filling, you can get by quite well with a lower-grade product.

Choosing the best plywood for the job often amounts to being able to make a quick decision or change of plans at the lumberyard. Even though plywood is manufactured according to stringent requirements, you might find that a given batch is not quite up to the quality of the same type and grade you bought previously. Perhaps it was poorly repaired or erroneously graded at the mill, mishandled in shipping, or improperly stored at the warehouse or lumberyard. If stock is low, you might find an abundance of sheets that were used on the tops and bottoms of shipping bundles that exhibit scratches, gouges, and damage caused by the banding straps. These sheets should be culled, downgraded, and sold at a discount. Don't accept them if they do not meet the standards of quality set forth by APA or HPMA or if they simply don't look good enough to you.

If any particular type or grade seems to be less than what you expect or need, take a look at something comparable. If, for example, all the ½″ A-C interior plywood in stock appears too rough, has an abundance of gaps in the laminations, or simply won't lie flat, check the same grade of exterior plywood. Although you'll pay a few dollars more, you'll be getting a better product, since the inner plies of exterior plywood are of a higher grade and the panels are not as likely to exhibit the problems you found in the interior type.

You should watch for plywood sales, and examine any plywood that has been substantially discounted because of defects or damage. In fact, rejects are often stamped "shop grade" and are carried as regular inventory at many lumberyards and home-improvement centers. While some of these can be quite rough and not worth the trouble it would take to get them up to sufficient quality, often you can find sheets with only minor defects that are easily remedied.

For example, you might find a sheet of plywood that has been crushed along one edge and is thus marked down to half-price. If you can cut away twelve inches along the damaged edge and end up with a 3 × 8′ panel of good plywood, you'll have 75 percent of a full sheet for which you paid 50 percent of the full price.

Storing Plywood

Few do-it-yourselfers have the room to store large quantities of plywood properly, so it's a good idea to buy only as much as you'll use in a short span of time. If you must store plywood for an extended period, either lay it flat and stack sheets one on top of another, or stand it on one of its long edges as near the vertical as possible.

If you want to equip your workshop with a plywood storage rack, you can build a vertical rack with sections to allow for upright storage. For horizontal storage, overhead racks are best, but panels should be supported at least every twenty-four inches—and better yet, every sixteen inches—to keep them from bowing. In such racks, store the thicker sheets on the bottom and stack thin sheets on top.

2 Building Materials for Plywood Projects

One problem with projects built entirely of plywood is that they usually look like projects built entirely of plywood. That is, they often look cheap and tacky, because the designer or builder has failed to combine plywood with other suitable materials to create attractive and functional furnishings and fixtures.

Of course, selecting the right plywood for a particular project and finishing it properly will go a long way toward assuring the project's success in terms of beauty as well as function. But the first secret to success is knowing where to use plywood in conjunction with other materials.

It's important, too, to understand that plywood has limitations, and that the use of other lumber, moldings, and the like is often essential. Moreover, it is usually cheaper and easier to use other materials in some phases of construction in many plywood projects.

Again, my best recommendation is that you spend some time at your local lumberyards, home-improvement centers, and hardware stores, learning what is locally available. There is truly no substitute for hands-on experience. Meanwhile, a few pointers and a brief introduction to some of the essential materials should help you determine what you will need for any plywood project.

Lumber

As with plywood, the two types of lumber you will encounter are softwood and hardwood, the former always in greater supply and the latter always more expensive. The species locally stocked will vary from region to region.

Although there are dozens upon dozens of softwoods and hardwoods indigenous to North America, only a few are abundant enough to be regularly stocked at retail outlets. Pine, fir, spruce, hemlock, and cedar are some of the softwoods most readily available. Birch, maple, oak, and walnut are popular hardwoods that are stocked by many retailers or can be special-ordered from nearby distributors.

You will want to use softwood lumber for the bulk of the projects in this book, and most others as well. Indeed, the only time you should pay the extra money for hardwood is when you're matching exterior trim pieces and moldings with hardwood plywood that you plan to finish naturally.

Of course, you should always use the lumber best suited to a particular project, but, as with plywood, this does not mean you must always use the highest grade. Often, lower grades will prove totally adequate.

Why a 2 × 4 Isn't a 2 × 4

During the lumber-manufacturing process, logs are cut into strips, boards, dimensional lumber, and timbers. As the wood is dried, either by air or in a kiln, it shrinks. Its size is further reduced in milling. Consequently, wood that was originally 2″ thick and 4″ wide will finish out to actual dimensions of 1½ by 3½″, but will still be called a 2 × 4.

With few exceptions, we refer to most lumber by its original or nominal dimensions, even though its actual dimensions will be smaller. Inch-thick lumber is actually ¾″ thick, yet we still call it "one-by . . ." Similarly, 2″ lumber is really 1½″ thick, and 4″ lumber is 3½″ thick.

Widths are similarly affected. What we call a 1 × 4 actually measures ¾ by 3½″. A 2 × 12 checks out to 1½ by 11¼″.

Pieces of inch-thick lumber with a nominal width of at least 2″ but less than 6″ are called strips. Those from 6 to 12″ in nominal width are called boards. Wood in nominal thicknesses of 2 to 5″ is known as dimensional lumber, and pieces thicker than 5″ are timbers.

In most places, hardwoods are now being sold by actual rather than nominal dimensions. Hardwood and softwood strips narrower than 1½″ are also referred to by their actual dimensions. For example, a strip that actually measures ¾″ by ¾″ is not called 1 × 1, but is referred to by its actual dimensions or is called ¾-square.

Nominal and Actual Sizes of Strips, Boards, and Lumber

NOMINAL SIZE	ACTUAL SIZE
1 × 2	¾ × 1½″
1 × 4	¾ × 3½″
1 × 8	¾ × 7¼″
1 × 10	¾ × 9¼″
1 × 12	¾ × 11¼″
2 × 2	1½ × 1½″
2 × 4	1½ × 3½″
2 × 8	1½ × 7¼″
2 × 10	1½ × 9¼″
2 × 12	1½ × 11¼″
4 × 4	3½ × 3½″

Grading of Lumber

A lumber-grading system does exist, one that we're told is consistent, reliable, and was not conjured up only to confuse us; the opposite, however, often seems the case. Although there have been attempts made to standardize the grading system and eliminate the confusion of seemingly arbitrary grades and overlapping terminology, the fact remains that lumber is still graded numerically, alphabetically, or literally—or by all of the above. Moreover, regional or local preferences might lean toward government standards or those of a particular trade association, or a combination of the two. The grades might also be affected by local terminology.

To illustrate, among the so-called board grades, the best are called Select, and the top grade in the Select category might be labeled B & Better, or #1 & #2 Clear. In descending order, the lower select grades are C Select and D Select. In the Finish category, boards are graded from best to worst as Superior, Prime, and E. (E? They could as easily and logically have been graded 1, 2, and Q; or A, B, and 13.)

Under board grades in the Board category we find some semblance of a system, as grades there run from #1 Common to #5 Common. But it is simply inconsistent to have any portion of this mishmash make sense, so I will dispense with that forthwith by telling you that, not long ago, I stopped by a local lumberyard to buy such a board and headed home with a hunk of hemlock graded Select-Common, whatever that is.

Among the framing grades, which include 2″ and larger dimensional lumber, you'll find such categories as Light Framing, Studs, Structural Light Framing, Appearance Framing, and Structural Joists and Planks.

In the Light Framing category, 2 × 2, 2 × 4, and 4 × 4 lumber is graded best to worst as Construction, Standard, Utility, and Economy. The same size lumber in the Stud category is graded either Stud or Economy, while in the Structural Light Framing category it will be Select Structural #1, #2, #3, and Economy. The Appearance category includes lumber from 2 to 4″ thick and 2″ or wider in width, and the only grade is Appearance. The Structural Joists and Planks category, which includes lumber from 2 to 4″ thick and widths of 6″ or greater, is graded the same way as the Structural Light Framing category.

If all of this is beginning to confuse you, don't despair; I don't think anyone completely understands it. The fact that no retailer stocks all grades of lumber anyway makes the grading system even less valuable to the do-it-yourselfer. The best thing to do is learn to rely on your own visual inspection and the expertise of your local lumber salesperson to get the right wood for any given job.

As with plywood, the best grades are the most expensive, but they also require the least preparation and finishing. On the other hand, some of the lower grades can be patched and sanded to meet most needs.

Most important, you should make sure that any lumber you buy is either air-dried or kiln-dried to a moisture content of 19 percent or less. If you buy so-called green wood or only partially dried lumber—no matter how great the savings—you'll probably regret the purchase. In the dry interior of your home, the wood will eventually lose much of its moisture, and as it does it will shrink, twist, split, and pull joints apart, ruining any project in which it was used.

Buying Lumber

Most lumber is sold by the board foot, linear foot, or piece. Although prices on large quantities are often quoted in board feet, most of the lumber you buy for the home workshop is priced by the linear foot or by the piece, which eliminates the need for any complicated mathematical exercises.

Should you every encounter board-foot pricing, here is what you need to know to figure your cost. A board foot is simply one square foot of lumber one (nominal) inch thick. A 1 × 12, 8′ long, would contain eight board feet. A 1 × 6 the same length would contain four board feet. The same size 2 × 12 would contain sixteen board feet. But other dimensions don't translate so easily; for that operation you need a formula: thickness (nominal inches) X width (nominal inches) X length (actual feet) ÷ 12 = board feet. To determine how many board feet are in a 16′ 2 × 8, for example, you would multiply 2 (thickness) × 8 (width) × 16 (length) for a product of 256. Dividing 256 by 12 tells you there are 21.333 board feet in that single piece.

Most lumber is stocked in lengths of 8, 12, and 16′. The eight-footer is the most common, and is the easiest length for the average do-it-yourselfer to handle and haul. Occasionally the better grades of softwood and most hardwoods are stocked in shorter lengths, so whenever you need only a small amount, be sure to ask. Most obliging lumber salesmen will agree to cut you a four-footer from a 12′ piece, as this leaves them with a salable eight-footer.

An old rule of thumb for buying lumber is to get 25 percent more than you actually need to allow for waste. While this is a useful guide to follow when buying the lower grades that might have loose knots, holes, pitch pockets, and other imperfections you'll have to cut around, it doesn't apply to the higher grades of clear lumber, hardwoods, moldings, and the like. Plan your purchases of these expensive materials to allow for a minimum of waste, and demand the right to inspect and refuse any piece that isn't up to standards.

Be watchful for sales, especially on the sizes of lumber you use often and might wish to stock in small quantities. I use a lot of 1 × 2, 2 × 2, and 2 × 4 lumber, and I remain alert for sales on these. Truckload and boxcar sales often allow me to lay in a supply of lumber at substantial savings.

When mill rejects go on sale, I make it a point to sort through the stacks and pick out lumber I can put to use. Often I save as much as 50 percent on these pieces, and at that price I can well afford to cut away damaged portions, or finish-sand a rough side, or correct any of the other flaws that caused the lumber to be culled.

Moldings

Moldings are made from small-dimension, clear lumber. Most have been run through a shaper or planer to give them their characteristic shapes, and all can be considered finish quality—that is, they require little or no sanding.

In terms of the amount of wood you end up with, moldings are probably the most expensive of all wood products. But they are essential to many projects and often mean the difference between furnishings that look homemade and those that appear custom-built.

Some moldings are functional, while others are largely decorative, but even the latter serve a useful purpose when they're employed to conceal the unsightly portions of a project or to cover cosmetic flaws or mistakes.

You will find $\frac{3}{4}$″-square molding and parting bead ($\frac{1}{2}$ × $\frac{3}{4}$″) to be among the most useful moldings for small framing jobs, drawer-bottom cleats, gluing blocks, and the like. Many of the decorative moldings are ideal for concealing plywood edges, as are outside-corner moldings and some picture-frame moldings.

Most moldings are available in a variety of lengths, from 3′ up to about 16′, and the well-stocked home-improvement center will carry dozens of different sizes and types. Familiarize yourself with the moldings that are locally available, and keep them in mind for any projects you design yourself.

Manufactured Wood Products

In addition to plywood, two other manufactured wood products you will find useful for some jobs are particleboard and hardboard.

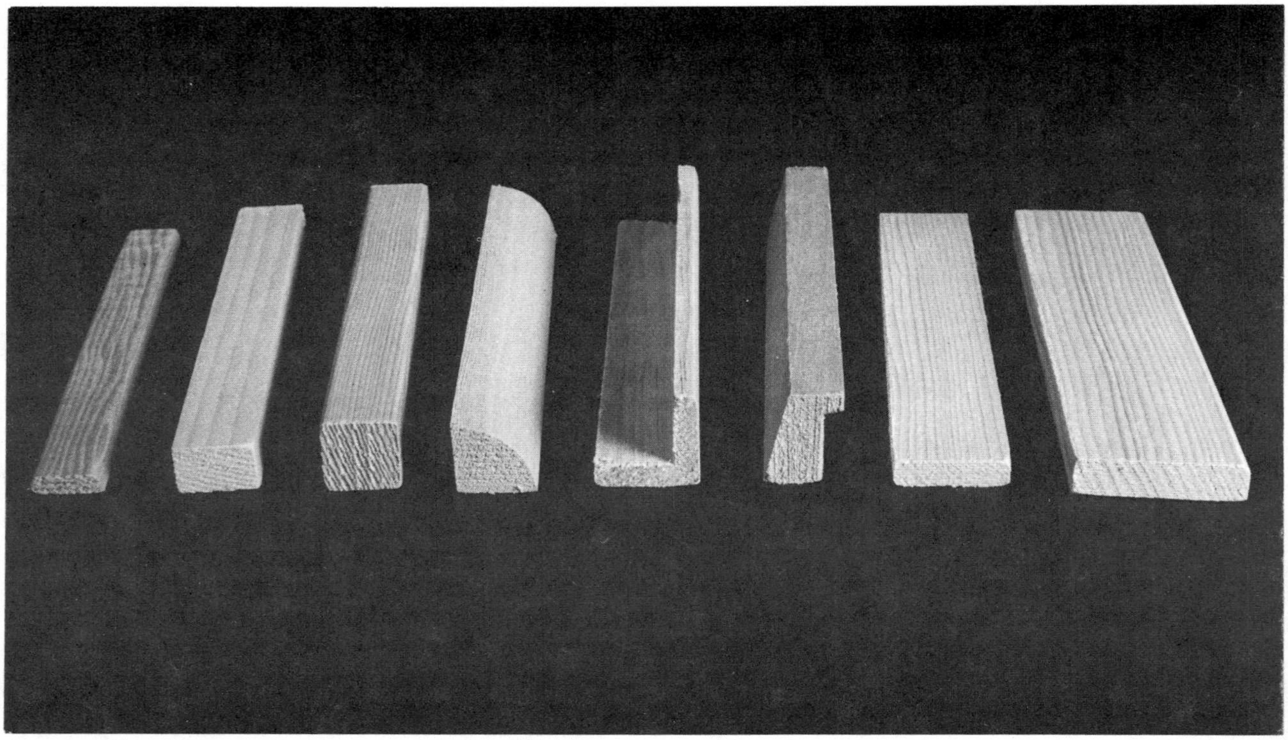

Some useful moldings for plywood projects include (from left) screen molding (¼ × ¾″), parting bead (½ × ¾″), ¾″-square, quarter-round, outside corner molding, picture-frame molding, lattice, and bullnose stop

Particleboard is made of wood chips combined with a bonding agent and pressed into shelving or sheets. The most common thicknesses are ¼″, ½″, and ¾″, the last the most widely stocked in various sizes. At most retail outlets, you'll find particleboard available in 4 × 8′ sheets, 12″ shelving, and 25″-wide sheets made for counter tops. Common lengths for shelving and counter tops are 8′, 10′, and 12′.

Although particleboard is considerably cheaper than plywood of like thickness, it is also heavier and weaker. If used for shelving, it requires more support than plywood or even dimensional lumber. Particleboard will also quickly dull power tools, so it's a good idea to cut it with carbide-tipped saw blades and use only carbide-tipped bits when routing it.

Hardboard is made of tiny wood fibers bonded into sheets by heat and pressure to form a dense, dent-resistant product that is useful for a variety of do-it-yourself projects. It is usually available in ⅛″ and ¼″ thicknesses, either tempered or untempered.

Although tempered hardboard is a bit more expensive than untempered, it will prove the better choice for most purposes. Tempered hardboard is stronger, more rigid, and moisture resistant. The tempered surface will also accept latex paints without absorbing excess water.

There are textured, grooved, and filigreed hardboards, but the two types most widely stocked are smooth-surfaced and perforated (pegboard). Standard, smooth-surfaced hardboard is an excellent material for making drawer bottoms, cabinet and chest backs, small shelves, and other items that need not support much weight. And nothing is better than perforated hardboard, used with the various pegboard hooks and fixtures, for organizing a workshop, sewing room, or hobby area.

Wall paneling is another manufactured wood product you should be familiar with. All-wood paneling is very similar to plywood; indeed, some types of paneling *are* plywood. Most paneling is ¼″ thick, although some panels are as thin as ⅛″, and on-stud paneling is 7/16″.

Paneling can sometimes be substituted for plywood in building projects, and it's often possible to increase the beauty of an item and decrease the cost by making such a substitute. Attractive ¼″ paneling, in fact, will usually run from 25 to 50 percent cheaper than hardwood plywood of the same thickness and might well prove to be as good or better for making sliding doors, chests, cabinet shells, and other items.

Fasteners

For putting your projects together, there are two types of fasteners that are indispensable: nails and screws. You will want to stock a ready supply of the sizes most commonly used.

The nails I normally keep on hand are ¾″, 1″, 1¼″, and 1½″ brads; ⅞″ wire nails; 6d and 8d finishing nails; and 6d and 8d box nails.

Technically, any finishing nail shorter than 1″ should be called a brad, but small wire nails up to 1½″ with finish-type heads are normally labeled brads. Finishing nails have small heads that are meant to be countersunk and concealed with some type of filler. Wire nails and box nails have broad, flat heads and offer greater holding power than brads and finishing nails.

Tacks, brads, and small wire nails are normally sold by the box or come in small plastic containers. Larger nails are sold in bulk by the pound or box, according to their "penny" size, which is designated by a number and the letter d. The larger the number, the larger the nails: a 4d nail is 1½″ long; a 6d is 2″; an 8d measures 2½″.

The rule of thumb for matching nail length to material thickness is to use nails at least three times the size of the material, so that for ½″ stock you would need 1½″ nails, or for 1½″ stock you would need 4½″ nails. For several reasons, though, I seldom follow this rule and can't recommend it for the projects and techniques used in this book.

Generally, the longer the nail, the greater its diameter. Thicker nails are more difficult to drive, and the greater the force required, the less accurate you'll be. Moreover, thicker nails are more likely to split wood. If I'm attaching ½″-thick molding, for example, the rule dictates the use of 1½″ brads, but I normally use ¾″ or 1″ brads to prevent splitting.

What's most important, here, is that I invariably use glue in conjunction with nails. Consequently, I only need nails long enough to hold the material in place until the glue sets and creates a bond stronger than the wood itself.

One other type of nail I have been using lately with excellent results is the ring-shanked or threaded paneling nail. The ringed shanks have excellent holding ability and the small heads are easily countersunk and concealed. Although in terms of holding power they aren't as stong as screws, they often prove the better choice when the joint will be glued.

With paneling nails, there's no need to lay out, punch, drill, and countersink pilot holes as you must with screws. Furthermore, the narrower-gauge nails are less likely to separate plywood laminations, particularly when thin stock is being joined. And the smaller holes that are left require less filling and sanding.

Screws come in a great array of head configurations and sizes to fit every conceivable need. By far the most common type used for woodworking projects is the flathead wood screw, which is designed for countersinking. Other useful screws for specific applications are roundhead and ovalhead wood screws, and panhead sheet-metal screws. Most of the screws you use will be slotted, although hinges, pulls, and other hardware often come packaged with Phillips screws.

Screws are sized according to their length and diameter, and most are labeled in that order. That is, 1½″ screws, size 8, will normally be labeled 1½ × 8. Some manufacturers reverse these elements, but that causes no problem, as it's easy to look at the screws and determine which number is which.

Screws are normally sold in small packets or by the 100-count box. For unusually large or small screws required for any particular project, it only makes sense to buy as many as you'll need, and this often means buying in small quantities. But screws are cheaper by the 100-count box, and you will save money if you buy commonly used sizes this way. I normally keep a good supply of ¾″, 1″, 1½″, and 2″ flathead wood screws on hand, in sizes 4 to 10.

Although I have lately begun using paneling nails in place of screws wherever possible, I still use screws when I need a superior joint, when I'm working with thick and heavy stock, or when a joint will be subjected to stress and I need the extra holding power afforded by screws. Screws are also the best choice for pulling joints together and holding them in place when the material being joined is warped.

As for matching screw length to material, the rule states that at least two-thirds of the screw shank should be driven into the base material. Again, though, I almost always use glue in conjunction with screws for wood joinery and mainly need screws just long enough to hold the pieces together until the glue sets.

For some projects, you'll want to use nuts and bolts, lag screws, corner braces, flat irons, toggle bolts, anchor screws, or any of dozens of different kinds of fasteners. Such items required for any of the following projects will be covered more fully in the appropriate chapters.

Adhesives

The variety of adhesives available today boggles the mind. Some are highly specialized in their applications, while others are broadly useful. Some are waterproof; others aren't. Some set hard, while others cure to a resilient consistency. There are adhesives that come ready to use and some that must be mixed. They come in cans, bottles, jugs, tubes, and sticks that must be melted. Some are odorless and harmless, while others produce noxious or even explosive fumes. There are those that can be used with only a narrow range of materials and those that glue practically anything to anything else. Some cure in minutes, while others take days to set.

The best way to learn about adhesives is to spend some time at your local home-improvement center reading labels on adhesive containers. If you have a special problem, ask one of the experts behind the counter.

For purposes of the projects in this book, the glue used most often is a polyvinyl resin adhesive that is white or off-white in color and is commonly called white glue. This is one of the fastest-setting glues available and is among the safest to use. It dries clear, thins and cleans up with water, and can be used with a variety of materials. It is a superb wood glue when used with nails or screws.

White glue comes in pint, quart, and gallon containers. It's cheaper in large containers, but you will also need a small applicator bottle that's easy to use on most jobs and can be refilled from the larger stock container.

One drawback with white glue is that it isn't waterproof. Consequently, it should only be used on indoor-type projects that will not be subjected to excessive moisture. For outdoor projects and any others that might get wet from time to time, use one of the waterproof adhesives, such as plastic resin glue.

The instructions for these projects will specify the type of adhesive needed whenever something other than white glue is called for. For projects of your own design, check at your local home-improvement center for the best adhesive to use. But always be particularly mindful of the label warnings, read them carefully and heed them. Wear rubber gloves with any adhesive that irritates the skin, and make sure there is adequate ventilation when using any that produce harmful fumes.

3
Tools for Plywood Projects

Probably every do-it-yourselfer dreams of someday having that perfect workshop, well stocked with all the fine tools necessary to see to any needs that might arise. We browse through tool catalogs, examine the displays at hardware stores and home-improvement centers, drop unsubtle hints at Christmastime, and wonder what it would be like to have the money to buy, at once, all the tools we'll ever need.

Most of us, however, start out with a few basic tools and gradually add others as our needs arise and our budgets allow. In retrospect, I'm glad that I had to build my own tool collection piece by piece, giving careful consideration to every purchase. I'm convinced that this approach enabled me to get the most out of the tools I owned at any given time and forced me to buy wisely. Moreover, I have come to realize that there is no such thing as the ultimate workshop. As our skills improve, our needs and desires change. We find greater challenges and discover new or different tools to meet them.

If you're just getting started as a do-it-yourselfer, I recommend that you do as I did. Buy the basic tools and learn to use them skillfully; then add others according to the requirements of the projects you're planning.

When you find that you need a particular tool you don't own for a project, you must determine whether the project justifies its purchase. If it doesn't you might consider renting the tool. This is an excellent and inexpensive way to get a good introduction to tools of potential value, and it is how I got acquainted with belt sanders and routers. What I was able to learn from a few days' rental was enough to lead to later purchases.

You must consider, also, that by building your own furniture and fixtures you save a great deal. For example, if it's possible to purchase fifty dollars' worth of material and build an item that would cost you two hundred dollars at a retail outlet, it should be easy to justify the purchase of a particular tool that will help you with that project and many more to come. Good tools, properly cared for and competently used, are among the best investments you will ever make.

What follows is an introduction to some of the tools useful for constructing plywood projects. A few of them are essential for nearly all projects; some simply make many tasks easier; others are fairly specialized and suited to specific tasks. Their particular uses will be covered more fully in the construction steps for the projects themselves.

Measuring and Marking Tools

Layout is one of the most important phases of any building project, and measuring and marking tools are essential. Some will be used on every job, while others are needed less often.

First, you'll need a steel tape rule. These are available in lengths from 3 to 20′, but you'll probably find a twelve-footer best. It will handle most measuring jobs, yet is compact and easy to use. Get one that clips to your belt or pocket. The locking type is most useful.

Squares are handy, if not absolutely essential, and come in a number of designs. There are carpenter's squares in several sizes that are good for scribing straight lines and right angles. T-squares are even easier to use, but for working with large sheet stock you'll want a four-footer. For starters, invest in a combination square that will perform a number of tasks.

Combination squares come with sliding square heads, protractor heads, and center heads. The most useful is the square head, with which you can scribe 90° and 45° angles. You can also set the head flush with one end of the rule and use the tool as a try square to check the squareness of inside corners; slide the head up the rule and you can check outside corners. The combination square can also be used as a depth gauge, and it's a great time-saver on many repetitious steps, such as marking for screw-starter or drill-starter holes along a scribed line.

A yardstick is a handy ruling instrument for many jobs. Invest in a good aluminum one that will last a lifetime.

As for the actual marking of lines, you have several choices. Carpenter's pencils are commonly used and are fine for scribing lines for freehand sawing and other imprecise work, but for accuracy you'll want something that makes a finer line. I prefer a mechanical pencil and thin lead for scribing light pencil lines that I'll later remove before finishing a project.

For freehand cutting, in which the saw blade will eradicate the line, and on parts of a project where layout lines will not be visible, I prefer to scribe a fine ink line, which is much easier to see. I have tried a number of felt-tipped and fiber-tipped pens, and the only one that will hold up in the workshop is the Pilot Ball Liner with a fine point. You'll find these at your local office-supply outlet.

Here's a tip that will save sweat and sandpaper: Keep an art gum eraser in your tool box and use it to remove pencil layout lines from your projects prior to finish sanding. The lines disappear quickly under the eraser's touch, yet take an inordinate amount of sanding to remove.

You should have a compass on hand for when you need to scribe circles. And for scribing arcs, a 6″ protractor is useful.

Screwdrivers

A few screwdrivers are essential in any workshop, and the main rule that applies to their use is to match the blade to the screw slot. Standard screwdriver blades range from ¼″ to ½″ in widths to fit the screws most often used.

You'll need a Phillips screwdriver for attaching hinges and other hardware; a medium-size driver is fine for most jobs.

There are several types of screwdrivers designed for working in tight quarters. Stubby screwdrivers have small handles and short shafts. You should be able to get by with two medium-size models, one standard and one Phillips. An offset screwdriver, with blades at right angles to the handle, is sometimes the only one that will work where space limitations prohibit the use of a conventional screwdriver. For holding screws in place where your free hand won't fit, use a screw-holding screwdriver.

Whether you buy your screwdrivers one at a time or by the set, get the best you can afford, with top-quality shafts and comfortable handles. For jobs requiring numerous screws, you can save a lot of time and energy with screwdriver attachments that fit an electric drill. These come with blades to fit various size screws and can be bought individually or in sets.

Hammers

Of all the various hammers and mallets available, there's one type to buy first: the claw hammer. A good claw hammer can be used for all the projects in this book and many more as well.

A tack hammer is better for driving small brads and tacks, and the ball-peen hammer is a good general-purpose tool recommended for striking chisels and punches. But a claw hammer will get almost any job done.

Punches and Chisels

The two types of punches you will use most often are the nail set and center punch. Each is used similarly, in conjunction with a hammer, but for different purposes.

The nail set is used for setting nail heads beneath the surface of wood so they can be concealed with filler. This is also the tool with which to punch most screw-starter holes, although some craftsmen prefer a scratch awl for this purpose.

The center punch, with its blunter, conically shaped point, is the tool to use for punching drill-starter holes, which keep the drill from "walking" off its intended mark.

Wood chisels come in an assortment of blade widths, the most common being from 1/4" to 1 1/2". You can buy them one at a time as your needs dictate or by the set.

You'll need chisels for making certain joints by hand and for other wood-removal chores. For the projects in this book, you should be able to get by with two or three chisels, with 1/2" to 1 1/2" widths.

Handsaws

The handsaw I use more than all the others, and the one that I emphatically recommend, is a backsaw, which I almost always use with a mitre box. Backsaws come with blades ranging in length from 12 to 26" or more and should be matched with the type of mitre box you buy.

A hacksaw is good to have for metal-cutting jobs, although if you own a sabre saw you can fit it with a metal-cutting blade for most such tasks.

If you do not own any power tools, you should think about getting some (see "Portable Power Tools," page 19). If, for some reason, you must work with hand tools only, you will need several other handsaws to do the jobs most of us leave to our "electric blades." For example, you'll need a good panel saw for the bulk of your sawing jobs. For cutting arcs, circles, and irregular designs, you should have a coping saw. For cutout work, you'll need a keyhole saw.

Before rushing off to buy an assortment of handsaws, however, give careful consideration to the advantages of power saws. Ask other woodworkers and seek the advice of professionals. I think you'll opt for the power tools and be glad you did.

Planes, Rasps, and Files

If you're careful during the layout and cutting processes for most plywood projects, you won't often need a plane or rasp to remove excess wood. By their design, however, a few projects in this book call for the use of such tools.

A small block plane is handy for minor wood-removal jobs and should be fine for most plywood projects. You'll need a wood rasp or two for cleaning and smoothing out some joints, particularly those made with a chisel.

In recent years I've come to use the Stanley Surform® tools for most of my wood-removal jobs. These tools come in a variety of configurations, and their sharp and efficient blades are replaceable. The Surform Pocket Plane is a good substitute for a block plane. The Surform File Type and Mini File take care of most tasks I would normally perform with rasps, and they do a better job. The little Surform Shaver, though, is my favorite all-purpose wood-shaping tool.

Pliers and Wire Cutters

Although pliers and wire cutters come in numerous sizes and designs, you can get by with a couple such tools for most plywood projects and other woodworking jobs. When you shop for tools, you'll find displays that include slip-joint pliers; lineman's pliers; pump pliers; longnose, needlenose, and bentnose pliers; as well as wire cutters and strippers of several different designs.

Either slip-joint or lineman's pliers are good all-purpose tools. You should also have a pair of longnose pliers for working in hard-to-reach spots and holding brads and tacks that are too small for your fingers. Make sure at least one pair is capable of cutting wire, unless you plan to buy wire cutters as well.

Wrenches

As with so many other tools, the kinds and number of wrenches you'll need depend on the types of projects you normally undertake. Certainly, the do-it-yourselfer who wants to be totally equipped for home and auto maintenance and repair as well as woodworking will need a large selection of open-end and box-end wrenches, socket wrenches and their various attachments, Allen wrenches, nut drivers, and a few special-purpose wrenches. But most of us acquire these gradually, as we need them.

You will need wrenches only occasionally for the projects in this book. If you have a set of box-end or open-end wrenches, you won't need anything else. If you do not own any wrenches, I suggest you start with two or three adjustable (crescent) models that can be adapted to most simple jobs.

Clamps

For some reason, many beginning do-it-yourselfers underrate the importance of clamps. I want to state emphatically that clamps are among the most important tools you'll ever buy. Although you can get by with a few different types and sizes in the beginning, most likely you will want to invest in new and different clamps, periodically, for years to come.

An in-depth report on clamps and their various applications would fill a volume larger than this one. Space limitations here permit only a brief look at clamps and a few recommendations. Their uses will be covered more fully in the later chapters.

You will need clamps of some sort for almost every project in this book, as well as for most other woodworking jobs you'll be involved with. Clamps are used to secure material for sawing, drilling, routing, sanding, and other operations. They help in making joints, in repairs, and in both simple and complicated setups. Clamps, in fact, are among the greatest aids to workshop safety and professional-quality craftsmanship. A woodworker without clamps is like an accountant without a calculator: He will be able to get most jobs done, but without the essential speed and accuracy.

Spring clamps are the simplest and cheapest and will serve well as light-duty clamps. They're faster and easier to use than C-clamps, but don't possess as much holding power. They come with jaw openings from about 1″ to 4″. Spring clamps with plastic-covered jaws are best, as they need no additional cushioning. You should have at least two medium-size spring clamps.

The most universally popular clamps are C-clamps, which come in several designs, with jaw openings ranging from a ½″ to 12″. Although you might later wish to add several pairs of smaller, larger, and specially designed C-clamps, start with a pair of 6″ clamps.

Bar clamps come in a wide array of sizes and designs. Because of their sliding heads, they are quicker to use than C-clamps, and the smaller ones are good substitutes. Larger bar clamps are ideal for gluing jobs that call for a big reach, and they are essential for some projects. Bar clamps are relatively expensive, though, so you might want to put off their purchase until you need them for a particular chore.

Among the extensive line of top-quality clamps made by the Adjustable Clamp Company are "Pony"® pipe-clamp fixtures, with which you can make your own clamps with any length of ½″ or ¾″ black iron pipe. Such clamps will prove cheaper than comparable bar clamps and are more versatile, since all you need to do is switch to a different length of pipe to change the size of the clamp. Like bar clamps, they're excellent for jobs that are too wide for other clamps.

Corner clamps, also known as mitre clamps, are sold singly or in sets of four and are available for a wide range of framing and gluing jobs. Although these clamps are most often used for making mitre joints, they're equally useful for making butt joints and others. They also make it possible for one person to handle large and unwieldy objects, such as cabinet shells and chests. You'll need at least one, but I recommend investing in a set of four that will greatly increase your speed and efficiency on many of the projects in this book.

When no other clamp will get the job done, a band clamp or two usually will. This type consists of a head fixture to which a length of strap—usually nylon web—is attached to form a loop that is adjustable and will conform to large and odd shapes. It will hold round and irregular shapes as well as square ones. Most come with 15′ straps. You needn't rush out and buy band clamps, but you will need a pair for several of the projects that follow.

Always use some sort of cushioning material with clamps to keep them from marring wood surfaces. Small scraps of wood work well, as do paint-stirring paddles. Some clamp manufacturers also offer plastic cushions to fit their clamps.

Other Useful Tools

Several years ago, Black & Decker introduced its first WORKMATE® Work Center and Vise, and the line has since grown to several different models and an assortment of accessories. I got my first WORKMATE shortly after its introduction and found it indispensable for the various projects I worked on in the confines of an apartment. When I later moved into a house with a large garage and shop, I didn't get rid of my WORKMATE; rather, I bought a larger model and now use the two as often as any other tools I own.

The various models of the WORKMATE serve as sawhorses, portable workbenches, and layout tables. They also function as the most useful of all vises, with wide jaws that are made even more versatile by use of the swivel grips that come as standard equipment. Jaws are equipped to hold round or cylindrical objects and move independently to secure odd shapes. The units also fold for easy storage.

You'll need a pair of sawhorses, particularly for working with plywood and other awkward sheet stock. And, even if I do say so myself, the best sawhorses you'll find for plywood projects are the Helpmates that you can make yourself by following the plans in Chapter 36.

Another essential tool for giving your woodworking projects a professional appearance is a mitre box. Mitre boxes come in many sizes and designs, from inexpensive plastic or wood boxes made for cutting 90° and 45° angles to large all-metal tools that adjust to any setting from 45° to 90°. I recommend that you get a top-quality, large-capacity mitre box immediately—the best you can afford.

Too many do-it-yourselfers think of a mitre box only as a tool for cutting molding and making mitre joints. However, I use mine on any material that will fit for perfect square cuts as well as mitres. Perfect cuts mean perfect joints, and perfect joints are what make furnishings and fixtures look as if they've been built by a craftsman. Anyone who can operate a handsaw can use a mitre box and backsaw as well as any professional finish carpenter or cabinetmaker. All it takes is careful measuring, double-checking of measurements, and proper use of the tools.

Make sure your mitre box is firmly secured. You can attach it to a bench top with stove bolts and wing nuts that allow for easy removal; you can mount it permanently where you have room; or you can mount it temporarily with C-clamps. I have mine mounted on a plywood base that clamps between the jaws of a WORKMATE.

It's equally important to clamp material you are cutting in a mitre box. Some of the better models come with a holddown clamp, but spring clamps and C-clamps work as well or better.

Portable Power Tools

I could proudly proclaim that all the projects in this book can be built without the aid of power tools and wouldn't be lying. I could also suggest that you mow your lawn with a push mower or that you cook all your meals over an open fire. But we live in an age of electricity and machinery and might as well take advantage of what's available to us. Moreover, most of us are busy people who don't have the time to spend weeks on woodworking projects that should take only hours, or a few days at most.

The most important considerations for the person looking to stock a workshop with tools are: (1) some portable power tools prove cheaper, in the long run, than the hand tools they can replace; and (2) power tools not only increase speed but efficiency and accuracy as well.

For many projects, you will need to drill holes. Of course, you could buy a hand drill for small-diameter holes and a bit brace for bigger jobs. But a good electric drill will do the jobs of both and more. Additionally, you should be able to find a good-quality 3⁄8″, variable-speed electric drill for less than what you'd pay for the manual models it replaces.

Such is also the case with portable power saws. Most handsaws are relatively specialized and aren't as cheap as one might think. On the other hand, a good circular saw and a sabre saw with an assortment of blades will see to any job in this book and most others as well. Moreover, with them you'll save time and energy and will produce better results, as long as you use the tools correctly. Buy the best 7¼″ circular saw you can afford, and a variable-speed sabre saw.

The bulk of your plywood-panel cutting will be done with the circular saw, and for that purpose you'll want a fine-tooth plywood blade. In fact, the same blade, though slower than a combination blade, is a good choice for making fine cuts in most woods and wood products.

For the sabre saw, you will want an assortment of blades ranging from coarse to extra-fine, and suited to a wide variety of materials from softwoods to plastics and metals.

Sanding is one of the most time-consuming and (for me) boring of all woodworking chores. Although I always do some hand-sanding, especially when I'm working for the finest possible finish, there are few jobs I would care to tackle without the aid of an electric sander. If you're out to buy your first, get the best pad sander you can afford. Also known as orbital, vibrating, or finish sanders, these tools are made for producing medium to fine finishes and are adequate for most plywood jobs.

For some jobs and for fast removal of material, you might later wish to invest in a good belt sander. A belt sander can take a coarse or rough finish down to a medium finish in a fraction of the time it would take with a pad sander. If you find you don't need a belt sander very often, you can rent one when you do want it for a few dollars a day.

A router is another tool that you'll find valuable for a broad range of jobs. Only a few of the projects in this book call for a router, and for those you could certainly rent the tool. But once you've had a chance to work with a router, you'll probably want to own one. Again, though, it's a purchase you can put off for now.

There are also a few inexpensive accessories that improve safety and accuracy with power tools and should be top-priority items on your shopping list.

Trying to make a straight cut with a circular saw or a straight pass with a router without the aid of some sort of guide is more difficult than drawing a straight line without a ruler. Although freehand cuts are okay for some projects, if you want to be assured of square fits, tight joints, and that seemingly elusive professional appearance, use a saw guide. You can fashion your own guides with straight pieces of wood, metal straightedges, and the like, or you can do as I did a couple of years ago and invest in an accessory made for that purpose. The one I have is an aluminum saw and router guide consisting of two 51″ sections, either of which is perfect for crosscutting a sheet of plywood. Connected, the two sections become a 102″ guide, with which I can rip-cut the entire length of plywood and other sheet stock.

My saw guide came with two C-clamps and clamp cushions, but I most often use a pair of quicker-acting bar clamps with vinyl cushions attached.

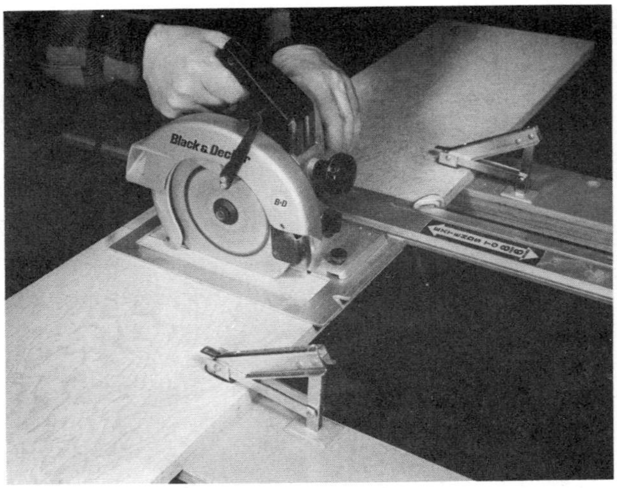

The Strate-Cut saw guide will keep your circular saw on course, whether you're crosscutting or ripping the full length of a plywood sheet

Another simple tool that's a great aid for the do-it-yourselfer working on plywood and other sheet stock is the KerfKeeper. Made by the Adjustable Clamp Co., this ingenious device fits into the saw kerf to keep plywood and similar products from sagging and causing the saw to bind. When used with power saws, KerfKeepers prevent dangerous kickback. (For tips on using both KerfKeepers and saw guides, see page 22.)

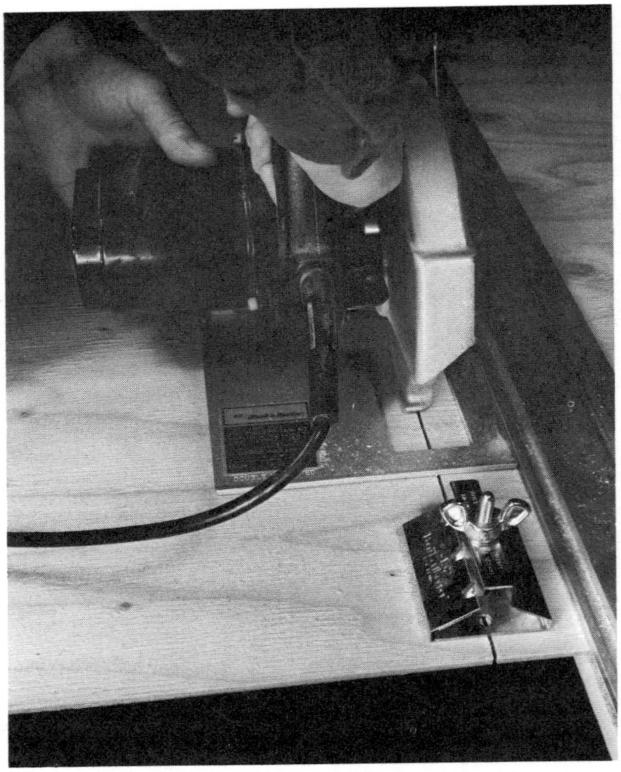

Kerf Keepers improve accuracy while preventing dangerous kickback. You should have a pair for plywood projects

Sometimes it's necessary to drill an absolutely straight hole, so you should consider buying an inexpensive drill-press attachment for your electric drill. Not only will such an attachment ensure accuracy, but with it you can adjust the depth of penetration and speed up repetitive drilling. Several manufacturers are now offering so-called portable drill presses that are relatively inexpensive and do a fine job.

4 Building with Plywood

Plywood is one of the most useful of all building materials, but it takes a certain amount of skill and craftsmanship to turn these slabs of laminated wood into functional and attractive furnishings. That is not to say you need be a veteran woodworker to successfully complete plywood projects; you simply must be aware of potential problems and their solutions and must be familiar with the techniques that will assure success.

Learning by doing is an excellent way to gain experience and expertise with tools and building materials. That's one reason why I have put the bulk of instructional information into the construction steps and illustrations found in the projects themselves, rather than devote several extra chapters to general woodworking methods. Nevertheless, there are some basic pointers applicable to most projects that should be outlined here.

Layout and Cutting

The first step in any plywood project is the layout and cutting of the sheet or sheets into assembly panels. This is also one of the most important steps, because careful layout prevents needless waste, and careful cutting ensures the snug joints necessary for structural strength and pleasing appearance. For all but the simplest projects in this book, I have provided cutting diagrams that will enable you to lay out and cut your plywood with a minimum of waste. When you build projects of your own design, you would do well to prepare similar diagrams to aid you in this important first step.

For layout, use the measuring and marking tools discussed in Chapter 3. Scribe your layout lines carefully, and *always double-check your measurements*. The old rule of thumb is "measure twice and cut once." This goes for drilling and routing as well.

There will always be some splintering on surface veneers when you cut plywood, particularly in crosscutting (cutting across the grain). But there are some precautions you can take to keep splintering to a minimum. First, always use a fine-tooth saw blade. If you're cutting with a handsaw, position the plywood with the *good face veneer up,* and keep the blade at a low angle to the plywood surface. You will also want the good side up when you cut with a table saw or radial-arm saw. With a circular saw or sabre saw, however, lay the plywood *good face down*.

Positioning the plywood this way will keep the good side relatively splinter-free. There will be some splintering on the opposite face veneer, but this is inconsequential in projects where only the good side of the plywood will show. Where both sides of the panel will be visible, you might want to take extra steps to reduce splintering, particularly with hardwood plywood, which tends to splinter more drastically. On rip cuts (with the grain), you shouldn't have much of a problem. But on crosscuts you can run a strip of masking tape across the plywood, on the side that will tend to splinter, and along the path the saw blade will take.

One way to nearly eliminate splintering is to clamp the plywood to a cutting board, which can be a sheet of shop-grade ¾″ or thicker plywood. Lay the cutting board atop your sawhorses and the good plywood atop the cutting board. With your circular saw properly set so that the blade will cut the good plywood while only penetrating the cutting board about ⅛″ or so, you can make nearly splinter-free cuts every time. Use a cutting board only when necessary, though, because the added wear on your blade will cause it to dull a bit faster. Friction will also be increased during cutting, so you should progress more slowly than normal.

Always make sure that the plywood is adequately supported on each side of the cut. In the case of full sheets being cut into large panels, this often means using additional sawhorses or using sawhorses in conjunction with a workbench or cutting table. The material should be securely clamped so that it will not move during the cut or at the termination of the cut. Improperly supported panels will put an uneven strain on one side of the cut, which can lead to damage or even personal injury.

The "Pony"® KerfKeepers, mentioned in Chapter 3, are excellent aids in maintaining even support of plywood during the cutting operation. To use them, start by making your cut until the rear edge of the base plate on your circular or sabre saw is several inches beyond the edge where you started the cut. Slide a KerfKeeper into the saw kerf and tighten the wing nut to secure it.

For short cuts of less than 3′, one KerfKeeper should suffice. You can stop the saw midway through the cut and slide the Kerfeeper to the center position if you wish, or you can support the far end of the panel with your hand if that's possible. For cuts longer than 36″, use two KerfKeepers. Stop the saw as necessary, and slide one or both KerfKeepers along the kerf to provide even support for the length of the cut.

KerfKeepers will handle material up to 1″ thick, so they should see to most of your needs. For thicker material, such as plywood flooring and solid-core doors, you'll have to take different measures. On the thicker material, stop your saw after you have cut about 12″ beyond the starting point. Then use one or two clamps and two large scraps of wood (¾″ plywood works well) to support the panels on each side of the kerf. Place one scrap on top of the plywood and the other on the underside and clamp them firmly in place. If you use only one clamp, center it on the kerf. With two clamps, put one on each side of the kerf. Deep-throated C-clamps or deep-reaching bar clamps work best; in their absence, use the largest C-clamps you have.

If you're ripping narrow strips the entire length of a large panel or full sheet, you can use two or more deep-throated C-clamps or deep-reaching bar clamps and wood scraps to provide support along the entire kerf.

For accuracy, a saw guide is very important, as mentioned in Chapter 3. The guide should be clamped to the piece being cut, with one clamp at each end, and it should be parallel to the path the blade will take. Since the edge of the saw's base plate will run along the guide, the guide must be positioned a distance from the cut line that is equal to the distance from the base-plate edge to the blade. This will vary from one saw to another, so you must measure your own base plate to determine how to place your guide. Remember, though, that blade teeth are offset, and you must account for this when measuring.

When using a saw guide with a sabre saw, you can put the guide on whichever side of the cut is convenient. With a circular saw, however, make sure that the clamps will not get in the way of the saw motor. It's best to plan your cuts so that the guide can be clamped to the right of the cut line or on the side opposite the motor. Keep in mind, though, that your circular saw should be adequately supported on the motor side by the material being cut.

When using a power saw—or any power tool, for that matter—don't force it. Let the tool do the work, at its own speed. Proceed only as fast as you can without causing the motor to lug. This will not only keep you from putting undue stress on the motor, but will reduce the chance of splintering and splitting at the exit point. If your saw will not progress adequately without being forced, or if the motor is lugging and the blade overheating, chances are your blade has become dull, and it's time to switch to a new one.

Whenever possible, hold portable power saws with both hands. If you're clamping and supporting your work as you should, you'll be able to use two hands most of the time, and this will improve accuracy, particularly on freehand cuts.

If you don't own or have access to a table saw, a circular saw is the tool you will want for the bulk of your cutting. Use it for turning sheets of plywood into assembly panels, as well as on other sheet stock and on broad lumber. For complicated and irregular cuts, the sabre saw is the best tool. Properly set up and used, these saws will be every bit as accurate as their table-type or bench-top counterparts.

With a circular saw, table saw, or radial-arm saw, cutting depth is important for keeping the blade moving freely, without unnecessary friction, while making a clean and complete cut. For best results, set the blade so that no more than three or four teeth will penetrate the material at one time.

The most accurate and fine-cutting tool at your disposal is a mitre box and backsaw. Use it for cutting all molding and any lumber and plywood that will fit. Make all your measurements carefully, and mark them with a thin-lead pencil. Then align each piece in the mitre box so that one of the extreme offset teeth of the saw just barely touches your mark. Secure the piece with one or two clamps and saw with light and even strokes, keeping the saw as perfectly horizontal as possible.

When framing out a project, whether you are using mitre joints or butt joints, it's best to measure and cut each piece of the frame individually, rather than cut all the pieces at once according to the dimensions of the object being framed. With one end of a piece of framing material mitre-cut or square-cut, lay it into position and use the object as a guide to mark the framing piece for the cut at the opposite end. Attach the piece and measure and mark the next piece the same way. This is sometimes a slow and tedious process, but it's the best way I know to get the perfect joints that are the mark of fine craftsmanship.

Drilling

Much of what I've said about sawing applies to drilling as well. You should use every technique at your disposal to assure accuracy and keep potential damage to a minimum. And you should proceed carefully and cautiously.

If you get into the habit of double-checking your measurements, you won't end up with spare holes in your woodworking projects. Sure, it takes a bit of extra time to remeasure, but not as much as it does to fill errant holes, or, worse, to lay out and cut a new panel.

You need to guard against splintering with drills, too. Wood will tend to splinter on the exit side, but there are precautions you can take to reduce the chances. First, proceed slowly, without forcing the tool. As you feel you're approaching the opposite side of the wood, back off the pressure on the drill until it is very light. This is all you'll need to do on any project where the exit-hole side will be concealed. To prevent splintering altogether, clamp a piece of scrap wood tightly to the underside of the piece being drilled.

Specially designed wood-boring bits normally make clean and splinter-free entry holes, but standard twist-drill bits tend to splinter wood on entry, particularly thin face veneers. Use wood bits whenever possible, especially for larger-diameter holes. If you must use twist-drill bits, though, you can reduce chances of splintering by starting with the lightest possible pressure and proceeding slowly until the bit tip has entered the wood.

Hole saws, which come in an assortment of diameters up to several inches and attach to an electric drill, make perfect splinter-free holes. They're worth considering, especially for making large-diameter holes that would otherwise have to be cut with a sabre saw, which is slower and not nearly as accurate.

When extreme accuracy is called for, you should use some sort of a drill guide, drill press, or drill-press attachment for your electric drill. A number of guides are available commercially, some of which allow for angle drilling as well as horizontal and vertical drilling with a fairly high degree of accuracy.

It is sometimes necessary to control for depth while drilling. For this, nothing beats a drill press or drill-press attachment. Some drill guides also allow for depth settings, and there are special drill stops that fit over the bit and are sold by the set. In the absence of any such attachment, you can measure the drill bit and mark it with a fine-pointed, felt-tip, or fiber-tip pen for the desired depth. I have found red to be the best color for such marking. Proceed slowly and use good illumination so the bit mark is easily seen.

You'll also improve accuracy and assure the safe operation of a hand-held drill by clamping your material to a solid surface. This frees both hands for holding and guiding the drill and keeping it on a true course. It also allows for the delicate touch so often required.

Basic Wood Joints for Plywood Projects

By and large, wood joinery is what woodworking is all about, especially in projects such as those that follow. After all, once the wood is cut, building is mainly a matter of putting the pieces together. How they're joined depends to one degree or another, upon the builder's skill, time, available tools, and recommended techniques.

Butt Joint

The simplest and most frequently used joint is the butt joint. As the name implies, the joint is made by simply butting one piece of wood to another, usually at right angles to each other. No special tools are needed to make butt joints, although corner clamps often make the job easier, especially if large panels are being joined.

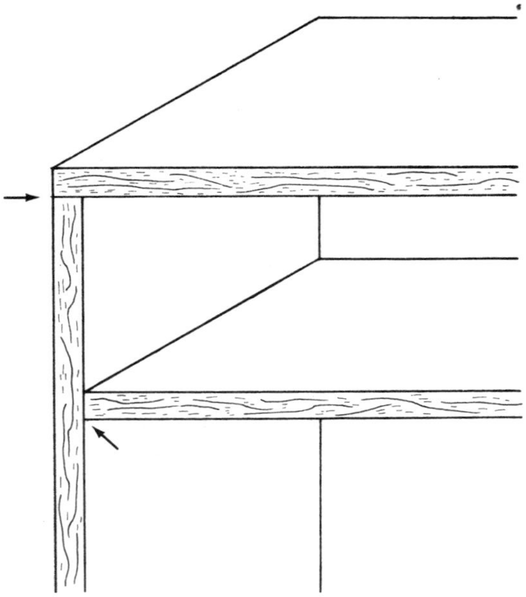

Butt joints

Rabbet Joint

The rabbet joint is similar to the butt joint but stronger and better in appearance, especially in naturally finished furnishings. It is mainly used for joining pieces and panels at right angles to one another. The rabbet is a notch cut in one end of a piece or along one edge of a panel to the width of the piece it will be joined to.

Rabbet joints are easily made with a router equipped with a rabbeting bit or with a straight bit and router guide. They also can be made with a jointer, or with a table or radial-arm saw equipped with a dado head. You can make them with a circular saw by setting the blade for a partial cut and removing the material with a wood chisel. On stock that's narrow enough, you can use a mitre box and backsaw to cut partway through the wood and finish with a wood chisel.

If you want to spend the extra time, you can use rabbet joints in nearly any of the following projects calling for butt joints, but you'll have to alter dimensions to compensate.

Dado Joint

A dado is a U-shaped notch or channel cut across a piece of lumber or plywood, into which the end of another piece will fit. This is an ideal joint for shelving, but it has other applications as well. Long dadoes are sometimes called grooves.

Dadoes are easy to make with a router and straight bit. Straight bits are commonly available in diameters up to 5/8". For wider dadoes you can make more than one pass with the router. Be sure to use a guide to keep the router running on course.

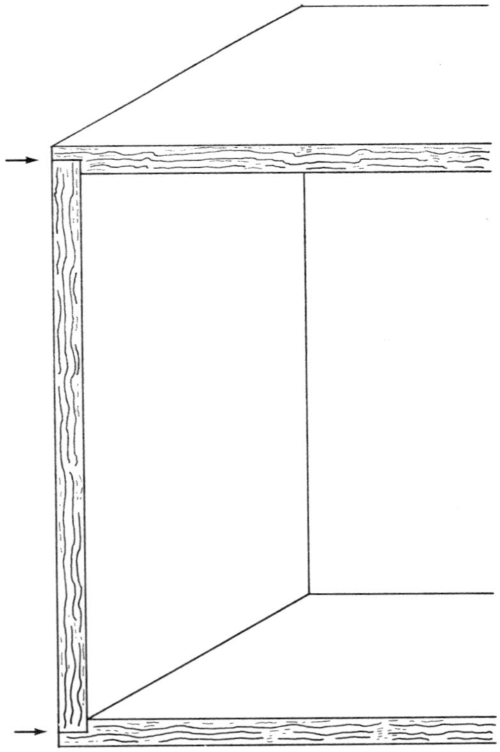

Rabbet joints

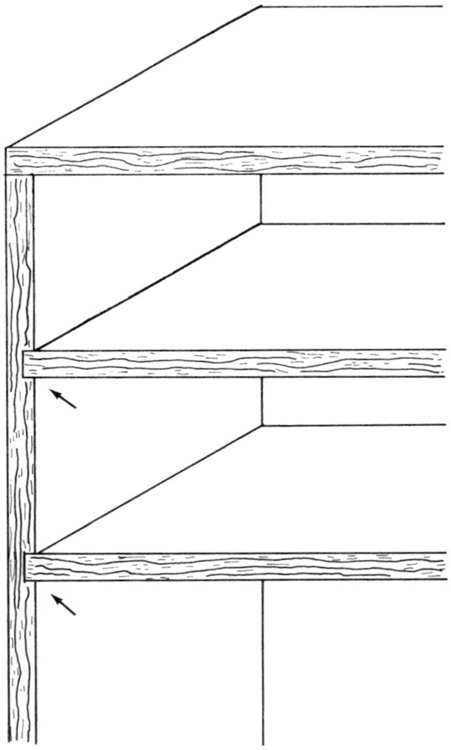

Dado joints

You also can make dadoes with a table or radial-arm saw equipped with a dado head. To make a dado with a circular saw, set the blade for the required depth and make two cuts with the distance between them equal to the thickness of the piece that will fit into the dado. Remove the material between the cuts with a wood chisel and hammer. Use the same technique for making a dado with a mitre box and backsaw.

Lap Joints

When one board or strip crosses another, a lap joint is formed. The simplest of these is the overlap, in which one piece is merely attached to the other with no prior alterations to either piece having been made. In a full lap joint, a notch is cut in one piece to a width and depth that matches the width and thickness of the other piece; sometimes both pieces are notched. The full lap is frequently used to join pieces of different thicknesses. The half lap or end lap, resembling a large rabbet, is a notch cut in the end of each of two pieces that are to be joined broadside at right angles.

As with rabbets and dadoes, lap joints can be made with a router and straight bit by making several passes with the tool. Or you can use a jointer, or a table or radial-arm saw equipped with a dado head. Similarly, you can use a circular saw or mitre box and backsaw to make initial cuts and remove material with a wood chisel.

Full-lap joint

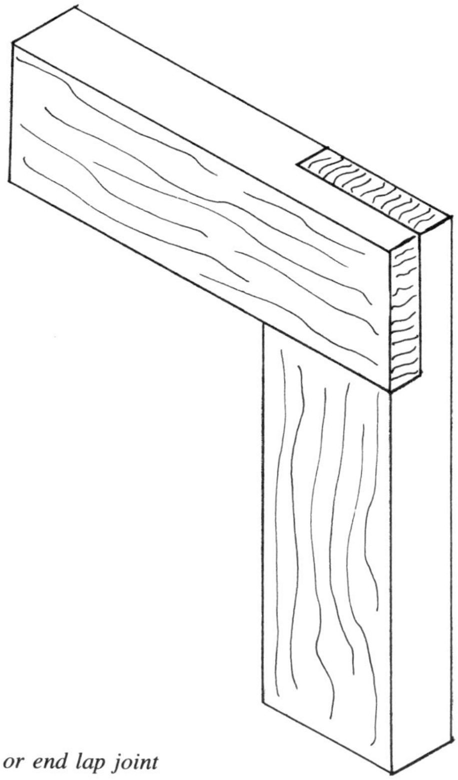

Half-lap or end lap joint

Lap joints are among the strongest joints and are ideal for most heavy-duty applications, such as the leg-and-frame assembly for a workbench.

Mitre Joint

The mitre joint is the familiar 45° angle, cut at the end of two pieces that are then joined to form a right-angle corner. Different angles are sometimes used in mitre joints for hexagons, octagons, and other shapes, but 45° is the angle most frequently used for framing and trimming.

Next to the butt joint, the mitre is the easiest to make with a radial-arm saw, table saw, or portable power saw and saw guide set for the angled cut. For small-dimension lumber and molding, a mitre box and backsaw are the best tools for making mitre cuts.

The mitre is one of the weakest joints and should be considered a finishing and trimming joint that is used mainly for appearance. It should not be used where structural strength is important.

You might want to be able to dismantle some projects (for moving, storage, and the like), in which case you should make joints with screws or nuts and bolts. In some cabinets and bookcases you might want shelves to be movable, so you would not fasten them permanently. But in most instances, you will want your joints to be

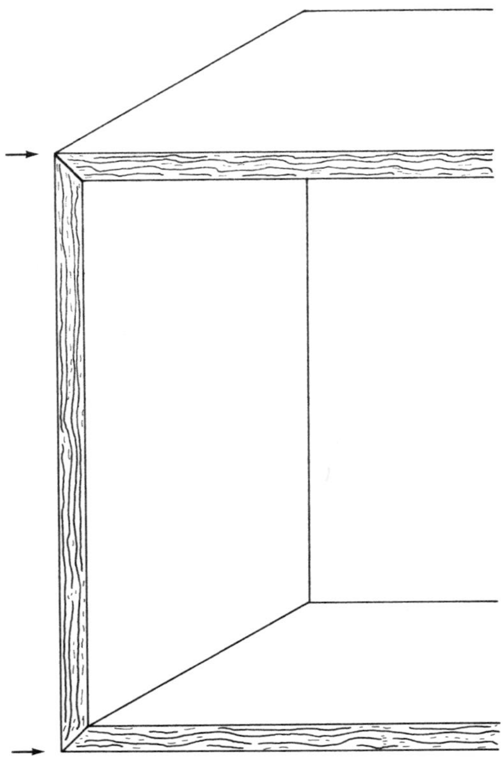

Mitre joint

permanent and as strong as possible. This means they must be glued and normally either nailed or screwed.

When using corner clamps for making joints, dry-clamp the pieces before gluing and fastening them. That is, join the pieces and hold them in place with corner clamps. Make all necessary adjustments of clamps and materials until a perfect fit is achieved. Then loosen only one side of each clamp and move the piece it was holding only enough so that glue can be applied. Rejoin the pieces and tighten the clamp and the pieces will be ready for nailing or screwing together to form a perfect joint.

Keep a damp sponge handy whenever you're assembling projects with white glue. As glue seeps from joints, wipe it away while it is still wet. When it dries, excess glue is much harder to remove and is sometimes impossible to reach.

Twenty-One Tips on Shop Safety

I have already cautioned you against several harmful or dangerous practices, but there are other potential hazards you ought to be aware of. Some time ago, I started compiling a list of safety tips to include in all of my workshop books, and I think it's appropriate to put it here, so you can review the tips before you set to work on the projects.

1. Keep your tools stored safely out of the reach of children, and keep children away from workshop projects unless you are teaching them. In that case, be sure to instruct them in the rules of shop safety before you start any construction.
2. Keep your work area uncluttered. Tools that aren't being used should be kept in their proper places, away from the project at hand.
3. Use clamps or a vise to secure your work. Not only will this ensure maximum safety, but it will allow you to do a more professional job of sawing, routing, drilling, or whatever you're engaged in.
4. Make sure that such tools as handsaws, power-saw blades, drill bits, chisels, planes, and knives are sharp. A dull tool is a dangerous tool and one that won't function properly. Dull bits and blades also overwork power tools and can cause expensive damage to motors.
5. Always carefully read instruction manuals for tools with which you are unfamiliar before attempting to operate them. It helps to review your instruction manuals occasionally to make sure you haven't developed any bad habits.
6. Always wear some kind of safety glasses when working with power tools. If you are working outside on a sunny day, wear sunglasses with impact-resistant lenses.
7. Wear ear protectors when operating dangerously noisy power tools; any tool that causes your ears to ring for ten minutes or more is probably causing permanent damage to your ears that might go unnoticed until your hearing has been seriously impaired. Don't simply stuff your ears with cotton; use approved protectors, such as those designed for target shooting.
8. Proper tool maintenance is essential to long life—for the tool as well as the operator. Keep tools clean and lubricated. Check electric cords frequently for signs of wear and replace damaged ones.
9. Make sure power tools are switched off before plugging them in. Always unplug a power tool before changing bits or blades or making any sort of adjustments to the tool.
10. Power tools should always be properly grounded. If the tool is equipped with a three-conductor cord and three-prong plug, make sure that the outlet is a proper, grounding-type receptacle. Extension cords should be properly grounded, too, and any used outdoors should be designed for that purpose and so labeled.
11. Always check tool cords and extension cords to make sure they are out of the way and will not interfere with the operation of the tool.
12. Any power tool that has a two-prong plug should be labeled "double insulated."

13. Avoid wearing jewelry and loose-fitting clothing when operating any tools or machinery that might entangle it and cause personal injury. Remove rings, watches, and the like before operating any portable power tool that isn't double insulated.

14. When working for prolonged periods with sanders and other tools that create dust, wear a face mask, especially if you suffer from any sort of respiratory ailment.

15. If a power tool stalls during operation, release the trigger or switch the machine off immediately. Then unplug the tool and work it loose in safety.

16. Always grip a portable power tool firmly before switching it on, as the torque of the machine could cause you to lose your grip.

17. When working with acids, solvents, chemicals, and adhesives that can cause skin damage, always wear rubber or plastic gloves.

18. Lacquers, thinners, cleaners, solvents, and glues that produce toxic or explosive fumes should only be used in a well-ventilated area, away from sources of excessive heat or open flame.

19. Read labels on all materials used in the workshop. Pay special attention to bold CAUTION and WARNING notices.

20. Protect yourself against severe strain when working with heavy lumber, plywood, masonry, and other objects. Don't assume the weight of any object. Test its weight by moving it slightly or lifting a corner. Then be conscious of possible injury before you attempt to lift it. Get help if you need it. Then keep your back straight while lifting, bend your legs instead of stooping over, and let your legs do all the work.

21. Most important of all, use common sense on every workshop project.

By following these simple rules of workshop safety and reviewing them from time to time, you will keep your shop a safe and enjoyable place.

5 Finishing Plywood Projects

There are two basic ways to finish plywood projects: you can paint them or finish them naturally. Finish is largely a matter of the builder's choice, but it is a decision that must be made at the onset of any project, as the kinds of materials used and the ways they are prepared for finishing depend upon the desired final appearance.

There is no great mystique about the finishing process, and anyone who wants to work at it can produce the finest of finishes on all projects. The tools, materials, and techniques are simple and easily mastered. So final appearance depends mainly on the care and preparation the builder puts into it.

Finishing Plywood Edges

On most projects, you'll want to conceal the unsightly edges of the plywood. During assembly, some edges will be concealed, and some joints are better than others for this purpose. For example, rabbet joints hide edges better than butt joints do. But no matter what kind of joints you use, there will generally be some edges to cover.

There are a number of ways to trim or finish plywood edges. On projects that are to be painted, you can use some sort of molding to trim the edges, or dress them with filler and sand them down to a smooth finish.

There are various decorative moldings on the market that work well for trimming, but standard moldings are cheaper and often preferable. Outside corner molding is a good choice for some jobs and comes in sizes to fit ½″ and ¾″ plywood. Screen molding, which is ¼″ thick and ¾″ wide, is comparatively inexpensive and serves well for trimming ¾″ plywood. For trimming the edges of bench tops, table tops, and other items made of plywood flooring, 1⅛″ bullnose stop is a good choice. You can cut costs, though, by using the same width of lath or lattice instead. Quarter-round is good for trimming some cabinet doors and drawer faces and for making inserts for notched corners.

On table tops, some cabinet faces, and other projects, you can give the appearance of heft and massiveness by using oversized trimming materials. For example, a table top made of ¾″ plywood can be trimmed with 1 × 2, 1 × 3, or 1 × 4 to make the top appear thicker than it actually is. The front edges of ¾″

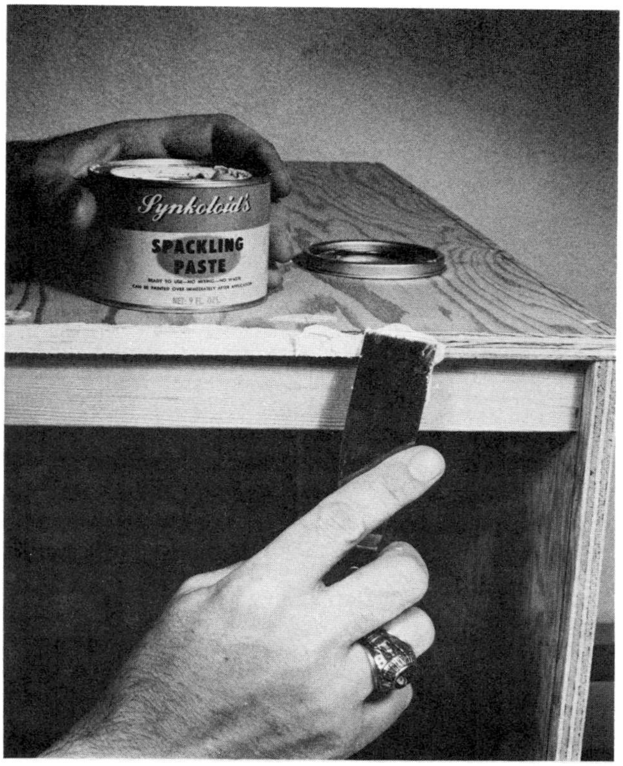

On projects that will be painted, use spackling paste to conceal plywood laminations

plywood shelving can be trimmed with 1 × 2 to give the appearance of 2″-thick dimensional lumber.

When trimming table tops, desk tops, bench tops, doors, drawer faces, and the like, you will normally want to make mitre joints at the corners. In some projects, such as the firewood crib (Chapter 20) and the home video center (Chapter 28), butt joints are best for face framing. No matter what type of joint you use, make sure all pieces fit together snugly to form a nearly invisible line. Tiny gaps can be filled, but if you end up with large and noticeable gaps, you should cut a new piece of trimming material.

On some projects, the trimming material should be attached with countersunk screws and glue and the screw holes plugged with wood pegs or covered with wood buttons sold for that purpose. Most molding and other trim, though, can be attached with glue and brads. The brads should then be countersunk and the holes filled.

If you prefer not to use fasteners, you can attach trimming material with glue and clamps, but this is a more time-consuming process and certainly unnecessary on any project that will be painted. It also requires bar, pipe, or special edge clamps.

Another alternative on projects that will be finished naturally, mainly those made of hardwood plywood, is to use edging tape to conceal the plywood edges. Edging tape is actually a very thin wood veneer, sold in rolls of various widths, and available in most popular hardwoods. It comes with or without a self-adhesive backing. It is cut to the desired length and applied to a smoothly sanded edge. One problem with edging tape, though, is that it's nearly as expensive as wood molding.

The cheapest and easiest way to conceal edges that will be painted is with spackling compound or paste. The compound that comes in powder form is cheaper, but it must be mixed with water, and leftovers usually go to waste. The paste, on the other hand, comes in a can, is ready to use, keeps well, and there is little waste.

Use a flexible putty knife to spread the spackling paste along the edges in a thin, even layer. It cures faster than other fillers and is much easier to sand down to a fine finish.

You can use spackling paste to fill nail and screw holes, tiny gaps at joints, small splits and holes in the plywood surface, and all but the largest and deepest open defects and gaps in the laminations. Large knotholes and deep gaps in the plywood laminations should be filled first with a plastic-resin wood filler (such as Duralite® Wood Dough or Plastic Wood®), or with a plastic surfacing putty, and allowed to cure. Then cover with a thin coating of spackling paste, let dry, and sand smooth.

On projects that are to be finished naturally, you can fill brad holes, tiny joint gaps, and minor surface imperfections with wood filler before staining and varnishing, or you can use a color-matched wax filler stick or putty afterward. The colored putties available today are superior products for such tasks.

Surface Preparation

To prepare surfaces for final finishing, abrasives are needed. Appearance-grade plywoods are normally sanded at the mill to a medium or better surface, so you won't usually need to coarse-sand them. If you're patching and filling a D-grade surface to bring it up to finish quality (and some C-grade surfaces as well), you will have to do some coarse sanding, as you will with any rough lumber or uneven surfaces that need to be smoothed out.

The fastest way to remove material and bring a rough surface up to standards is to use a belt sander and coarse belt. When the surface is smooth and even, switch to a medium-grit belt and sand it down further, until the surface is consistent, making sure you always sand with the grain.

If you don't own a belt sander, you can use coarse paper in your pad sander, but it will take more time and effort to prepare a rough surface. Even if you do have a belt sander, though, you will want to do the bulk of your finish sanding with a pad sander.

Sheet abrasives are graded numerically—the higher the number the finer the grit. For example, #50 sandpaper is a coarse grit, #100 and #150 are medium grits, #220 is fine, and #320 is extra-fine. Most plywood projects call for more medium-grit and fine-grit paper than the other grades, but you should stock some coarse-grit abrasives for rough work and some extra-fine and finer abrasives for preparing surfaces to take natural finishes.

Coarse sanding means fast removal of material. As the finish-preparation process progresses from medium to fine to extra-fine and beyond, however, less and less material is removed, and preparation during those phases primarily amounts to removing the sanding marks left by the previous sanding.

To keep from wasting time and energy and removing more material than necessary, it's important to pay attention to the transformation that takes place during sanding operations. That is, when a surface has been taken down to a consistent medium finish, further sanding with medium-grit paper would not only be a waste of time and energy, but would unnecessarily remove material without improving the quality or overall smoothness of the surface. That's the point at which you must switch to a fine-grit paper and take the surface down to a fine finish and no further. If you want a finer finish yet, switch to extra-fine-grit paper, and continue this process until you have achieved the desired smoothness.

During sanding operations, scratches, small dents, and other surface blemishes will fill with dust, so you must periodically clean the surface to remove dust and locate areas that need additional sanding. I have a 3″-wide pure-bristle paint brush that I use only for this purpose, and I keep it handy in a back pocket whenever I'm sanding. I clean and check potential problem areas frequently, and I always brush all dust away from the entire surface and examine it carefully before switching to a finer abrasive. This keeps me from having to go back later to sand out spots I've missed.

Projects that are to be painted normally require less preparation than naturally finished furnishings and fixtures. The reason is that modern paints will fill any sanding marks left by fine-grit paper, so it's unnecessary to sand beyond a fine finish. For special purposes, though, you might wish to take the surface down to an extremely fine finish before painting. For example, you can achieve the appearance of plastic by taking a wood surface down to the finest finish and painting with glossy enamel. Burnish all but the last coats with #000 steel wool, then buff the last coat with #0000 steel wool to remove brush marks. Apply a coat of paste wax, then polish to a glossy shine with a soft cloth.

The surface preparation required for naturally finished projects depends upon whether the item will be varnished or oil-finished. If you plan to varnish, take the surface down to an extra-fine finish with #320 sandpaper in a pad sander. Do final sanding by hand with #400 wet-or-dry paper or use #000 steel wool. For oil finishes, follow the same procedure, but also polish the surface to an ultra-fine sheen with #0000 steel wool prior to oiling.

Some craftsmen prefer steel wool to sandpaper for burnishing and polishing, as it will not clog as badly as sandpaper does. The grades you will find most useful are #00 fine, #000 Extra Fine, and #0000 Finest.

Painting Plywood Projects

Before painting any project, clean it thoroughly to remove all dust. Use a vacuum cleaner in hard-to-reach areas. Then wipe all surfaces down with a slightly damp sponge or tack cloth.

Large surfaces—such as cabinet shells, doors, and drawer faces—can be painted with a roller or with a wide brush. On smaller surfaces, match the brush width to the area being covered. For trim work, the poly-foam brushes are ideal, as they enable you to apply a smooth and even coat without running paint over the edges.

Latex flat or semi-gloss paints are best, I find, for most purposes. These paints are easy to apply with rollers or brushes, they conceal fine sanding marks, and dry quickly to a smooth and even finish that is relatively free of brush marks. They can be thinned and cleaned up with water.

Whether you use a roller or brush, always apply paint in a smooth, even, and relatively thin coat. On most jobs, you should be able to get by with two coats. When it is time to repaint an object, one coat will normally suffice, if you use the same color. If you switch colors, try to avoid applying a light color over a dark one, as it might take three or more coats to conceal the previous paint.

Finishing Plywood Projects Naturally

As with painting, before applying any natural finish you must thoroughly clean the item to remove all dust. If you plan to stain and varnish, be sure to try the stain on a scrap of the wood you used on the project. If it seems satisfactory, stain the item according to the manufacturer's directions.

Most of the plywood projects I finish naturally are ones I've built with hardwood plywood. When I stain them I usually only want enough stain to bring out the character of the wood. Consequently, I like transparent stains that do not overly darken the wood. I apply the stain liberally but leave it on for no more than fifteen minutes; then I wipe it away with paper towels and let it dry overnight. I seldom need to apply another coat, but when I do I follow the same procedure. With this method, I am able to control the accenting of grain and the level of overall darkening, and I can always apply additional coats until the desired effect has been achieved.

The decision whether to varnish or finish with oil is largely a personal one, but should be guided somewhat by the type of project being finished and the use it will be put to. A varnished surface is more durable and less susceptible to wear than an oiled finish. So table tops, desk tops, and other areas that will get much use are better varnished than oiled. However, I personally prefer the appearance of a finely polished and oiled finish, and use oil whenever possible.

Modern polyurethane varnishes are relatively easy to apply and produce a remarkably tough yet attractive finish. With these products you have a choice of finishes: high gloss, satin sheen, or dull. If you can't decide which is best, go with the glossy finish. Then if you don't like it, you can take it down to a dull finish by buffing with #0000 steel wool. If that proves too dull, apply a couple of coats of paste wax, buff with a soft cloth, and you'll end up with a satin-sheen finish.

Although polyurethane varnish can be applied to clean, dry, stained or unstained raw wood, I prefer to start with a coat of fast-drying sanding sealer, which dries much more quickly than varnish and serves as a good base coat. When the sealer has dried, I lightly burnish all surfaces with #000 steel wool until the gloss is gone. I then clean surfaces with a tack cloth and apply a light, even coat of varnish.

Sometimes this is all that's necessary. But for a deeper finish, I apply additional coats of varnish, allowing at least twenty-four hours for each to dry (more time during damp weather or when humidity is high), and burnishing with steel wool between coats.

There are numerous oils and oil-resin finishes on the market, and I've used many different kinds over the years. The one I now use almost exclusively is Watco Danish Oil, which is a deep-penetrating oil-and-resin sealer that comes in natural, medium-dark, and dark finishes.

You can finish wood naturally with the Watco natural oil, which will slightly darken and deepen the character of the wood as any clear finish does, or you can stain and oil simultaneously with the medium-dark and dark oils. I have had excellent results with all three, but I most often use a transparent stain to achieve the effect I want and follow that with applications of the natural Watco Danish Oil.

I suggest that you use several types of oil finishes to find the one you prefer, but do be sure to try Watco. It's a versatile product that can be put to use on a variety of projects.

I apply the oil according to the manufacturer's directions and have found no special handling or additional techniques required. After letting the project stand for twenty-four hours, I then apply a liberal coat of light carnuba wax on light woods, or dark carnuba wax on dark woods, and work it in with #600 wet-or-dry sandpaper. I then remove excess wax with paper towels and let dry for about fifteen minutes, after which I buff with a soft cloth.

Sometimes no further finishing is required. But if the object is a piece of furniture that will be subjected to wear, I apply two thin, even coats of Johnson's Paste Wax for durability, allowing each coat to dry for fifteen minutes, and buffing each with a soft cloth. I then rewax as required—usually every three to six months.

If you opt for the oil-and-wax finish instead of varnish on furnishings that will get a lot of use, as I'm so often tempted to do, it's important to keep them waxed and polished to protect the wood. Don't set glasses on such surfaces without using coasters, and wipe up any spilled liquids immediately. Water will stand in beads on the waxed surface and won't cause any problems if removed right away. Alcohol, some soft drinks, and other liquids, however, can dissolve the wax right down to bare wood. If you wipe up a spill and find a dull spot, that's a good indication that the wax has been removed. Rewax at your first opportunity.

Part

II

Half-Sheet Projects

Each of the ten projects in this section can be built from a half-sheet or less of plywood.

6
Record Album Bin

Record albums should always be stored vertically to prevent warping. This simple and inexpensive bin will take about eighty albums, and can be stored on a shelf unit, in a stereo cabinet, or on the floor. Although the partitions increase the unit's structural stability, they were included in the design mainly for convenience in keeping albums organized.

Construction Steps

1. Along the top 13'' edge of each side panel, measure in 6″ from the front corner and make a mark. Measure down the front edge 6″ from the same corner and make another mark.
2. Along the top $12^3/_4$″ edge of each partition, measure in 6″ from the front corner and make a mark. Measure down the front edge 6″ from the same corner and make another mark.

Step 5

3. On each side panel and partition, scribe a diagonal line connecting the marks made in **Steps 1** and **2.**
4. Clamp each side panel and partition to a bench top or other solid surface and remove the top corners by cutting with a circular saw along the lines scribed in **Step 3.**
5. Align rear and bottom panels side by side and clamp to a bench top or other work surface. Then with a router and ½″ straight bit, rout ¼″-deep dadoes 8″ from each end.
6. Sand the routed faces of the rear and bottom panels and both faces of the side panels and partitions with medium-grit and fine-grit sandpaper.
7. Run a bead of glue along the bottom edge of the rear panel and butt it to the bottom panel. Clamp each end with a corner clamp, and join the panels with 1″ ring-shank paneling nails, spaced about 6″ apart.
8. Prenail each side panel with three 1″ paneling nails along and ¼″ inside the bottom edge and three more along and ¼″ inside the rear edge.
9. Run a bead of glue along the left edges of the rear and bottom panels and attach the left side panel with paneling nails. Attach the right side panel the same way, and countersink the nails.

Step 9

10. Run a thin bead of glue along the dadoes in the rear and bottom panels, and slide the partitions into the dadoes.
11. Drive a 1″ paneling nail through the rear panel, about 1″ from the top edge, into each partition. Drive another nail through the bottom panel, about 1″ from the front edge, into each partition, and countersink nails.
12. Fill nail holes and conceal plywood laminations with spackling paste and let dry.
13. Hand-sand the spackled areas with fine-grit sandpaper; then clean the unit to remove dust.
14. Apply two coats of interior latex paint and let dry.

Required Tools

Steel tape rule	Paint brush
Pencil	Circular saw
Claw hammer	Saw guide
Nail set	Pad sander
Two C-clamps	Router and ½″ straight bit
Two corner clamps	
Putty knife	

Required Materials

Half-sheet of ½″ plywood, G2S
White glue
1″ ring-shank paneling nails
Spackling paste
Medium-grit and fine-grit sandpaper
Interior latex paint

Plywood Panels

From a half-sheet of ½″ plywood, graded A-C or better, cut the following panels:

QUANTITY	SIZE	NOMENCLATURE
1	12 × 24″	Rear panel
1	13 × 24″	Bottom panel
2	12½ × 13″	Side panels
2	12¼ × 12¾″	Partitions

7
Stackable Storage Boxes

These simple but sturdy crates were designed to replace the ubiquitous cardboard boxes we're inclined to use for storage and utility purposes. They're great in the workshop, utility room, garage, and anywhere else where odds and ends need to be boxed. Use them for storing wood scraps and kindling, hauling groceries, collecting bottles and cans for the recycling center, or anything else you can think of. They're also ideal for camping and will keep a lot of gear organized.

You can build two boxes with a half-sheet of $\frac{1}{2}''$ plywood, and any grade will do. If you want to take them outdoors, use exterior plywood and waterproof glue.

Step 7

Construction Steps

1. On each of two 12 × 12″ end panels, scribe a line 2″ from and parallel to the top.
2. Mark for drill-starter holes on each line 4¼″ from the left and right side edges.
3. Use a center punch to make drill-starter holes at the marked spots.
4. Stack a marked and punched panel atop an unmarked end panel and those two pieces atop a scrap of wood. Clamp them together and secure them to a workbench with two C-clamps.
5. Use a 1½″-diameter bit to drill through two end panels at each marked spot. Drill end panels for the second box the same way.
6. On each end panel, scribe a line from the top of one hole to the top of the other, and another line from the bottom of one hole to the bottom of the other.
7. Use a sabre saw to cut along the scribed lines, removing the piece of plywood between each hole in each panel, creating an oblong hand hole in each.
8. Run a bead of glue along an end edge of a bottom panel and butt to the bottom of an end panel. Secure panels with two corner clamps, and attach the end panel to the bottom panel with three 1″ brads.
9. Attach the other end panel to the opposite end of the bottom panel the same way.

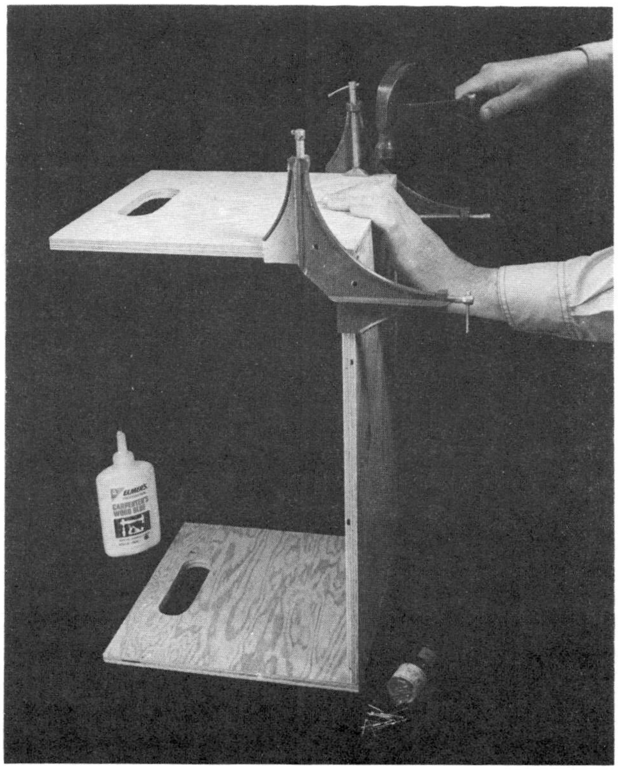

Step 9

10. Turn the unit on its side and run a bead of glue along the upright edges of each end panel and the bottom panel; then attach a side panel with 1″ brads.
11. Rotate the unit 180° and attach the remaining side panel with glue and brads.
12. Use a nail set to countersink all brads.
13. For each box, cut two pieces of 1 × 2 to 11⁵⁄₁₆″. Then prenail each piece with four 1¼″ brads in a staggered pattern.
14. Attach two of these pieces with glue and brads to the bottom of each box—one at each end, just inside the bottom edge of each end panel. Then countersink brads with a nail set.
15. Lightly sand each box with medium-grit paper, being careful to remove any splinters and rough edges in the hand holes.

Step 14

Required Tools

Steel tape rule	Two C-clamps
Combination square	Two corner clamps
Pencil	Electric drill and 1½″ bit
Claw hammer	Circular saw
Nail set	Saw guide
Center punch	Sabre saw
Mitre box and backsaw	

Required Materials

Half-sheet of ½″ plywood, any grade
4′ of 1 × 2, utility or better
White glue
1″ brads
1¼″ brads
Medium-grit and fine-grit sandpaper

Plywood Panels

From a half-sheet of ½″ plywood, any grade, cut the following panels:

QUANTITY	SIZE	NOMENCLATURE
4	12 × 12″	End panels
4	12 × 21″	Side panels
2	12 × 20″	Bottom panels

8
Executive's Wastebasket

Here's an attractive and functional conversation piece, loaded with reverse snob appeal. This classy trash can is perfect for the office, den, or study, and it makes a great gift.

Although it can certainly be built with softwood plywood and painted in contrasting colors, the effect is best if it's built in a rich hardwood and beautifully finished.

Construction Steps

1. Sand front, rear, and side panels with medium-grit, fine-grit, and extra-fine-grit sandpaper.
2. Sand rough edges off wooden letters.

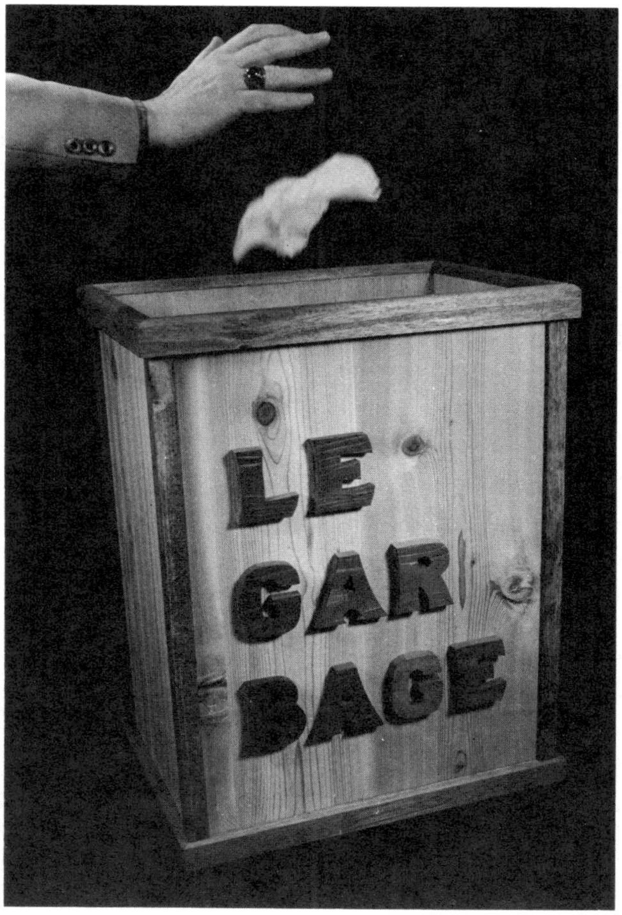

3. Apply dark or contrasting stain to the letters and let dry.
4. Arrange letters on front panel to spell out "LE GAR BAGE" in three lines. Use a T-square or straightedge to align letters and space them properly.
5. Apply a thin film of glue with a paper towel to the back of the letter L and press it in place. Continue doing the same to the rest of the letters, one at a time.
6. Put a heavy object (e.g., can of motor oil, box of screws) on each letter to create sufficient bonding pressure, and let stand until the glue sets.
7. Cut four pieces of ¾″-square to 20″ (glue blocks), two to 14″ (cleats), and two to 8″ (cleats).
8. Run a bead of glue along one edge of a 14″ cleat and center it flush with the bottom edge on the side of the front panel, 2″ from each end. Carefully turn the panel over and attach with four ¾″ brads.
9. Attach the other 14″ cleat the same way along the inside bottom edge of the rear panel.
10. Similarly, attach the 8″ cleats along the inside bottom edges of the side panels.
11. Make two or more marks along the inside of and ¼″ from each 24″ edge of the front and rear panels.
12. Run a bead of glue along one edge of a 20″ glue block and center it along the inside of a 24″ edge of

Step 5

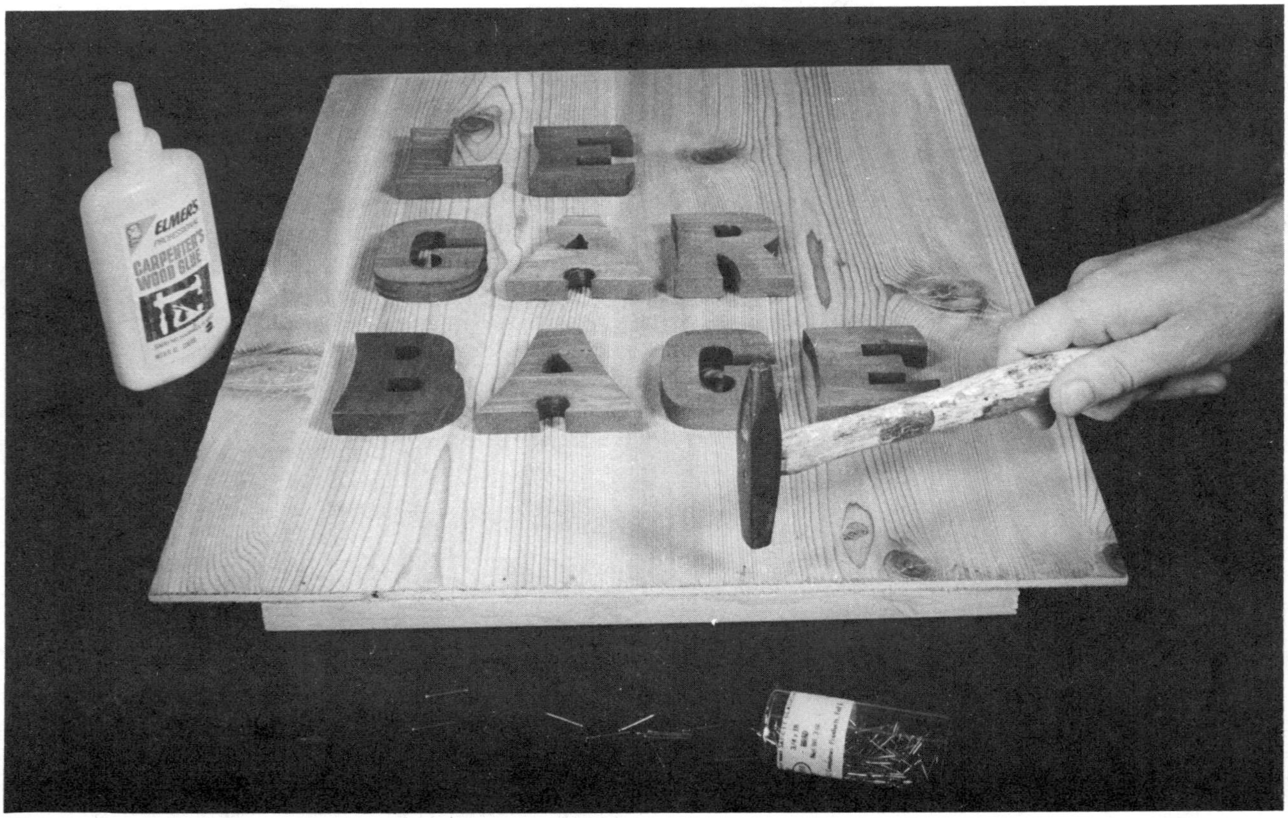

Step 9

the front panel, aligned with the $\frac{1}{4}$" marks made in **Step 11.**

13. Hold the glue block in place with two spring clamps or small C-clamps. Use a scrap piece of $\frac{1}{4}$" plywood to check the distance of the glue block from the edge of the panel; adjust as necessary.

14. Turn the panel over and attach the glue block to the panel with seven $\frac{3}{4}$" brads.

15. Attach another glue block, the same way, along the opposite 24" edge.

16. Using the same techniques, attach the remaining two glue blocks to the inside of the rear panel.

17. Scribe a line on the outside face of each side panel along and $\frac{1}{4}$" inside each 24" edge.

18. Hold the front panel and one side panel upright, with the side panel butted to the front panel to form a corner. Mark for five screw holes along the line scribed on the side panel, making sure the screw holes are located between the brads in the glue block.

19. Butt the side panel to the rear panel and mark for screw holes the same way along the other line.

20. Mark the other side panel in the same manner.

21. Use a center punch and hammer to make a drill-starter hole at each mark; then drill a $\frac{9}{64}$"-diameter hole at each spot and countersink for #6 flathead screws.

22. Run a bead of glue along the glue block inside the front panel and another along the butting edge of the side panel.

23. Butt the side panel to the front panel and hold the two pieces together by hand. Insert a $\frac{3}{4} \times 6$ flathead wood screw in the top hole and tap lightly with a hammer to start. Drive with a screwdriver.

24. Insert a screw in the bottommost hole and drive into the glue block.

25. Drive the remaining three screws along this corner. Wipe away any glue seepage with a damp sponge. Then use the same techniques to attach the side panel to the rear panel.

26. Before attaching the remaining side panel, run a bead of glue along the surface of the bottom cleats. Lay the bottom panel atop the cleats and secure with $\frac{3}{4}$" brads driven through the bottom panel into the cleats.

27. Run a bead of glue along each glue block and each butting edge of the remaining side panel as well as along the top edge of the cleat on the side panel. Then attach the side panel with screws, and nail the bottom to the remaining cleat.

28. Carefully measure the top and bottom of the basic unit to make sure dimensions are $18 \times 12\frac{1}{2}$".

29. Assuming final dimensions are right, use a mitre box and backsaw to mitre-cut four pieces of frame

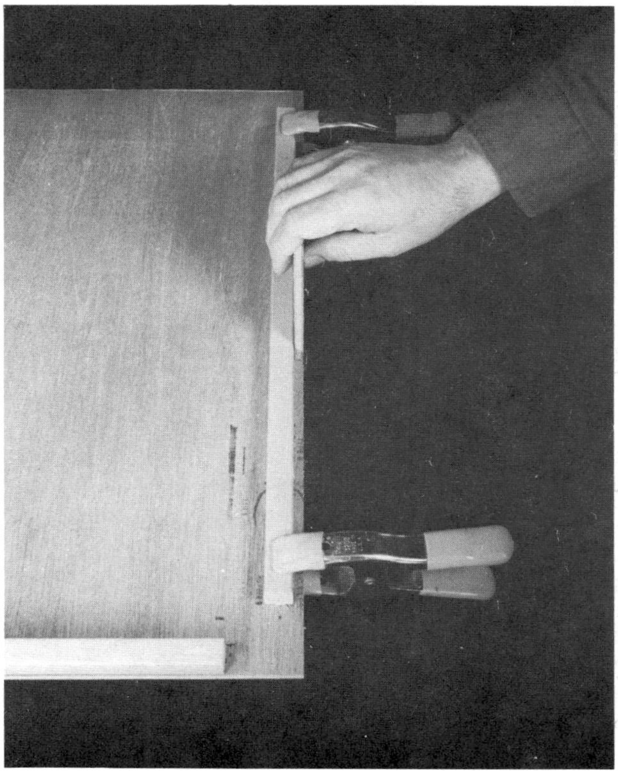

Step 13

Step 23

Step 26

molding to $18\frac{1}{32}''$ and four more to $12\frac{17}{32}''$—or just slightly over 18″ and $12\frac{1}{2}''$. (If dimensions are slightly different on the unit, adjust accordingly.)

30. With four corner clamps, assemble a frame measuring $18\frac{1}{32}'' \times 12\frac{17}{32}''$, gluing each mitre joint.

31. Hammer and countersink a 1″ brad through the short frame piece into the long piece at each corner of the frame.

32. Assemble another identical frame, using the same techniques.

33. Stain frames to match the letters, and let stand until glue sets and stain dries (several hours or overnight).

34. Run a bead of glue along the bottom edge of the unit, and push one frame into place. Set unit upright.

35. Run a bead of glue along the inside of the other frame, and press it into place on the top edge of the unit.

36. Carefully measure the distance along each corner of the unit, between top and bottom frames, and cut four pieces of 1″ outside corner molding to fit snugly.

37. Stain molding to match frames and lettering, and let dry.

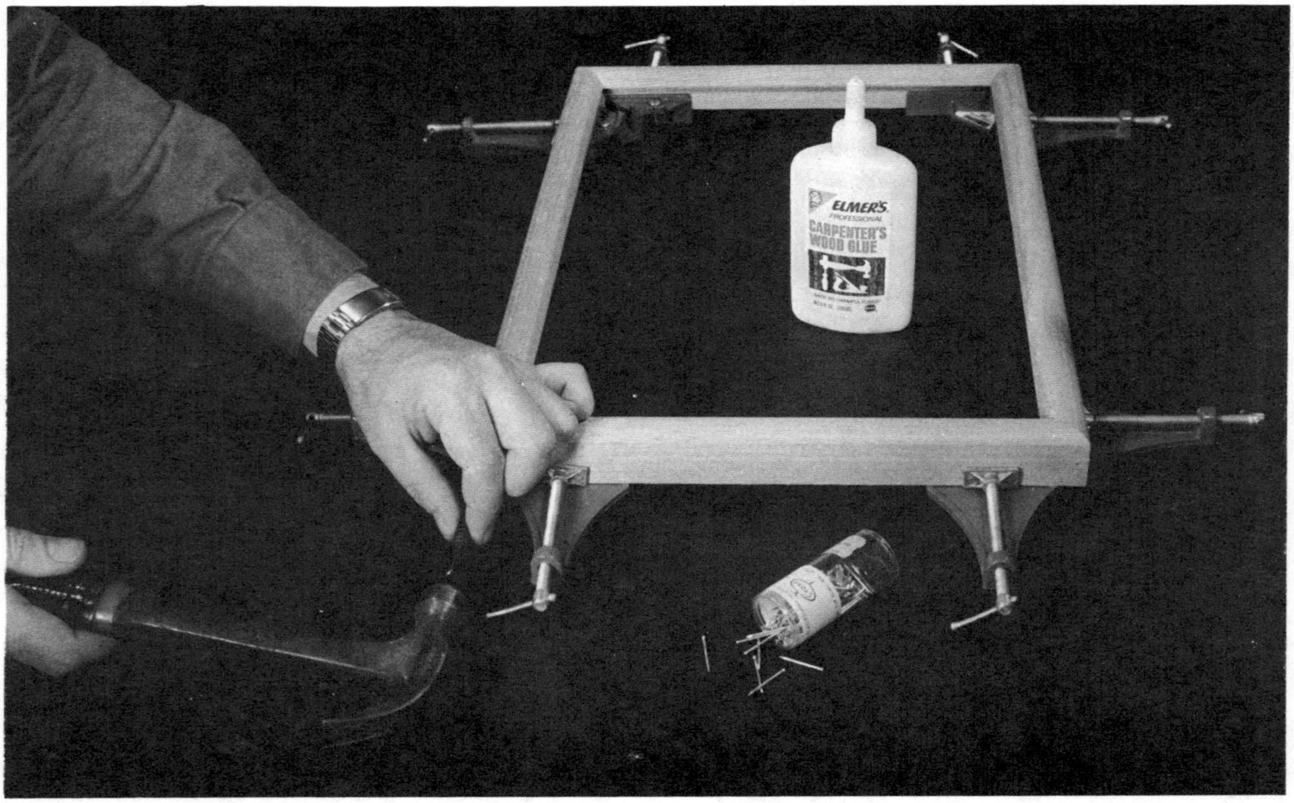

Step 30

38. Run a narrow bead of glue along the inside of the corner molding, and press each piece in place to conceal corners of the unit. Lightly clamp, if necessary, with bar clamps or band clamps, and let stand until glue sets.

39. Apply the finish of your choice (oil or polyurethane varnish), and let unit stand until dry.

Required Tools

- Steel tape rule
- Straightedge
- Pencil
- Claw hammer
- Nail set
- Center punch
- Screwdriver
- Mitre box and backsaw
- Two C-clamps or spring clamps
- Two 36″ bar clamps or band clamps
- Four corner clamps
- Paint brush
- Electric drill and 9/64″ and #6 countersink bits
- Circular saw
- Saw guide
- Pad sander

Required Materials

- Half-sheet of 1/4″ hardwood plywood, premium or superior grade
- 8′ of 1″ O.S. corner molding
- 12′ of 3/4″-square molding
- 12′ of picture-frame molding
- White glue
- 3/4″ brads
- 1″ brads
- 20 3/4 × 6 flathead wood screws
- Medium-grit, fine-grit, and extra-fine-grit sandpaper
- Stain of choice
- Varnish or oil finish
- 9 wooden letters to spell "LE GARBAGE"
- Paper towels
- Colored putty or wax filler sticks

Plywood Panels

From a half-sheet of 1/4″ hardwood plywood or suitable all-wood paneling without grooves, cut the following panels:

QUANTITY	SIZE	NOMENCLATURE
2	12 × 24″	Side panels
2	18 × 24″	Front and rear panels
1	12 × 17½″	Bottom panel

9
Card and Game Table

This card-and-game table can be made from any scrap of $\frac{3}{4}$" plywood that measures at least 36 × 36". Not only does it comfortably seat up to four persons for card and board games, but it will also double as a dining table for two—ideal for the apartment or small house.

You can follow the same directions and alter dimensions slightly to make a larger table if you wish. A full half-sheet of plywood will render a surface area of 48 × 48", or you can trim it to any size that fits your needs. A 4'-square table will seat four persons for dinner.

Assembly is quite simple and requires no more than about two hours of actual construction time, although additional time will be needed for glue, stain, and varnish to dry.

For the top covering you'll need a piece of cloth-backed vinyl upholstering material, which can be found at a local upholstery shop. A 36 × 36" table needs a piece of vinyl about 40 × 40". For a larger top, allow an extra 4" in length and width. Such material is usually stocked in a variety of patterns and colors, and you'll save some money if you can find what you need among the remnants and roll ends.

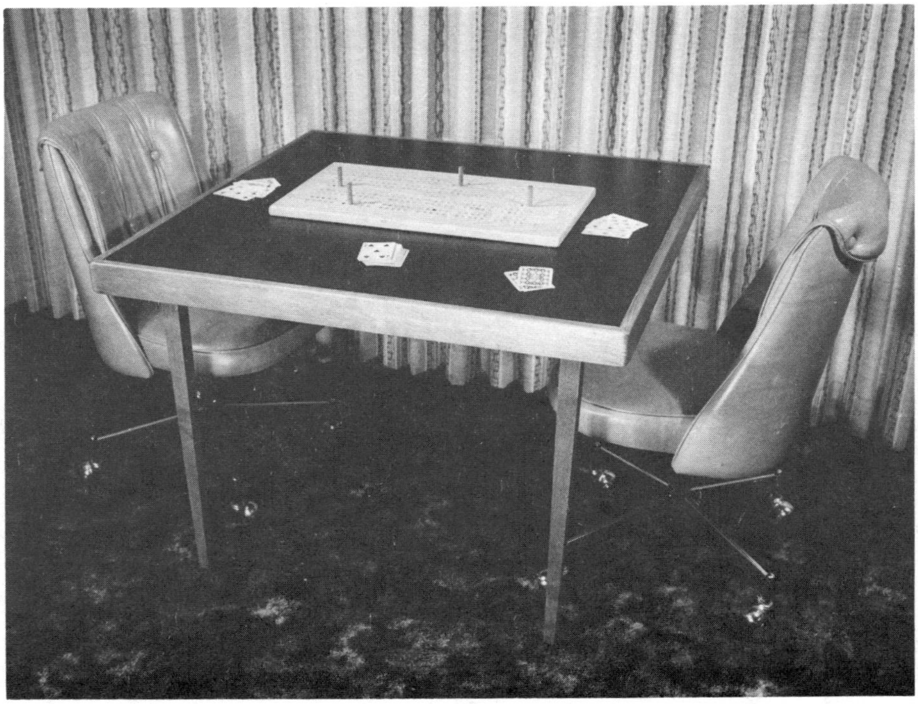

For easy storage in a closet, beneath a bed, or elsewhere, simply unscrew the table legs. The table will set up quickly whenever you need it. The vinyl top will wipe clean with a damp cloth or sponge, but it should be cleaned periodically and polished with STP® Son Of A Gun! or any good vinyl cleaner.

Construction Steps

1. Trim a half-sheet of 3/4″ plywood to 36 × 36″, or desired dimensions.
2. Pour about a half-cup of white glue into a jar and thin with water to the consistency of latex paint.
3. With a paint brush, apply a thin and even coat of glue to one side of the plywood top.
4. Spread the vinyl, cloth side up, on a workbench or other flat working surface. Then center the plywood top on the vinyl, glued surface down.
5. Pull one end of the vinyl up and around one edge of the plywood, stretch tightly, and staple to the bottom side of the plywood, spacing staples about two inches apart.
6. Continue stretching and stapling the vinyl along the remaining edges of the plywood.
7. At each corner, fold and tuck the vinyl and cut away excess with scissors. Staple folded vinyl at each corner.
8. Restretch each edge of the vinyl by hand, and drive another staple between each staple driven in **Steps 5** and **6.**
9. Use a utility or X-Acto knife to trim excess vinyl away, about 1/2″ inside the staple line along each edge.
10. Use four or more C-clamps, bar clamps, or spring clamps to clamp the table top, vinyl surface down, to a flat surface, and let stand overnight.
11. Run a strip of 1″-wide vinyl tape along the underside edge of the vinyl covering material to conceal staples.
12. With a mitre box and backsaw, mitre cut a piece of 1 × 3 to fit one edge of the table.
13. Stand the table top on one edge, and apply glue to the top edge. Then attach the 1 × 3 trim with 1 5/8″ ring-shank paneling nails, spaced about 6″ apart.
14. Measure, mitre-cut, and attach 1 × 3 trim to the remaining three edges the same way.
15. At each corner, drive two 1″ ring-shank paneling nails through the mitre joint. Then countersink all nails with a nail set.
16. Fill nail holes with wood filler, let dry, and hand-sand all trim with medium-grit and fine-grit sandpaper.

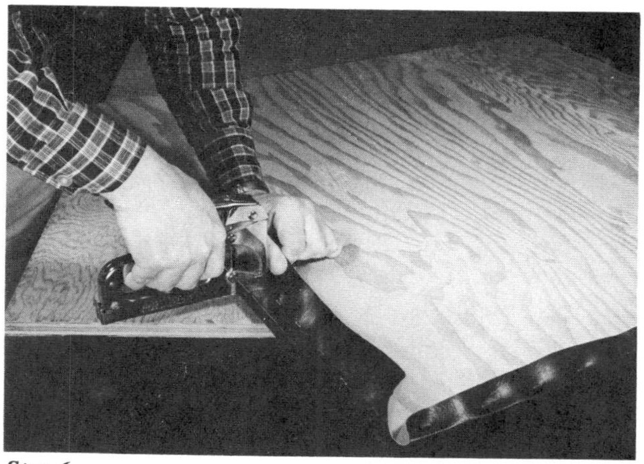

Step 6

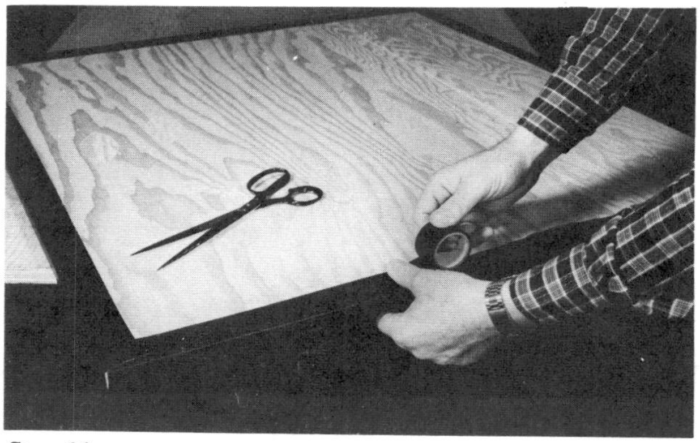

Step 11

Step 15

17. Lay table top on a working surface, face down. Position a leg plate 2″ inside each corner; then, using the plate as a guide, mark for and punch screw-starter holes. Mount leg plates with screws provided.
18. Turn table top over and clean to remove all dust. Then use masking tape and newspaper to cover the vinyl surface only.
19. Turn table top over and set atop two sawhorses. Screw legs into leg plates.
20. Apply the stain of your choice to the legs and 1 × 3 trim to achieve desired effect. Let stand overnight.
21. Apply a coat of fast-drying sanding sealer to legs and trim and let dry. Burnish with #000 steel wool; then apply a thin and even coat of polyurethane varnish to legs and trim, and let dry. Apply additional coats if necessary, and burnish between coats.
22. When varnish has dried, remove masking tape and newspaper. Clean away any gum and tape residue with a cloth slightly dampened with lighter fluid. Then clean and polish vinyl with a good vinyl cleaner, and the table is ready for use.

Step 17

Required Tools

Steel tape rule	Paint brushes
Pencil	Putty knife
Claw hammer	Staple gun
Nail set	Scissors
Screwdriver	Utility knife
Mitre box and backsaw	Circular saw
Four C-clamps, spring clamps, or bar clamps	Saw guide
Paint brushes	

Required Materials

Half-sheet of $\frac{3}{4}$″ plywood, G1S
14′ of 1 × 3, clear
Four 28″ table legs
Four leg plates with mounting screws
White glue
Wood filler
1$\frac{5}{8}$″ ring-shank paneling nails
1″ ring-shank paneling nails
$\frac{3}{8}$″ staples
Medium-grit and fine-grit sandpaper
Sanding sealer
Stain of choice
Polyurethane varnish
40 × 40″ piece of cloth-backed vinyl upholstery material
Roll of 1″ vinyl tape to match
Roll of 2″ masking tape
Several sheets of newspaper
Small can of lighter fluid
Vinyl cleaner

10
Lighted Dictionary Stand

Large dictionaries and other reference volumes are often unwieldy and difficult to use. Atop a specially designed stand, however, such a large book can be kept ready for easy use.

The built-in fluorescent light fixture makes this book stand doubly convenient. The unit is easy to build and can be painted to match or contrast its surroundings.

Construction Steps

1. On the inside of each 14 × 18″ side panel, measure up the rear edge and mark spots at 5″ and $6\frac{1}{2}$″ from the bottom (Points B and C on the cutting diagram).
2. Measuring from the bottom edges of the panels, mark spots along the front edges at 1″ and $2\frac{1}{2}$″ (Points H and G on the cutting diagram).
3. On each panel, scribe a line connecting Point B with Point H and Point C with Point G.

4. At the top of each panel, starting at Corner D, measure 6″ to Point E and mark a spot. Do likewise along the bottom edge, marking Point J 6″ from Point A.
5. Using these marks as guides, scribe a vertical line from Point E to Line CG, terminating at Point F.
6. Use a sabre saw to make a cut on each panel from Point E to Point F. Make another cut from Point G to Point F.
7. Cut two pieces of ¾″-square molding to 12″; then prenail each piece with three 1″ brads.
8. Run a bead of glue down each piece of molding. Align each along Line BH, ½″ from the rear edge of the panel; then drive and countersink the brads.
9. Cut a piece of 1″ lattice to 24″; then prenail with four ¾″ brads.
10. Run a bead of glue along one long edge of the 13⅜ × 24″ bottom panel and attach the lattice with brads, making sure the bottom edge of the lattice is flush with the underside of the panel, creating a ½″ lip.
11. Run a bead of glue along the right edge of the 18 × 24″ back panel. Butt the right side panel to it and attach with five 1″ brads; countersink brads (use corner clamps to hold pieces if necessary).
12. Turn unit over and attach the other side panel with glue and brads.
13. Scribe a centered line lengthwise along the underside of the top panel; then mark for screw-starter holes on the line 6½″ from each end (for standard

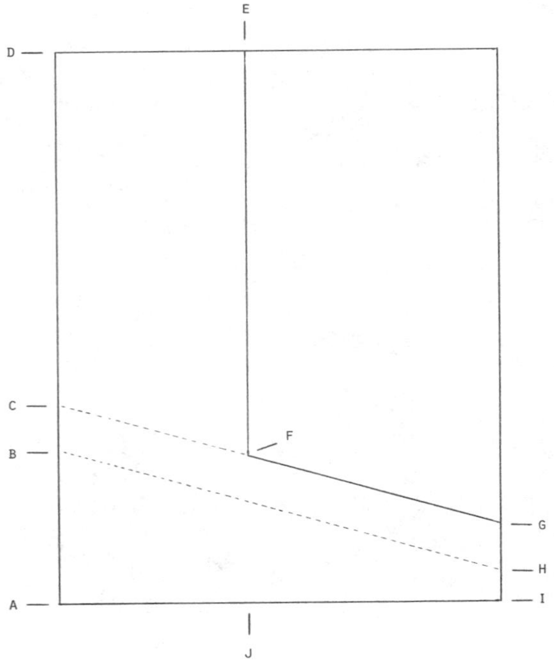

Side-panel cutting diagram

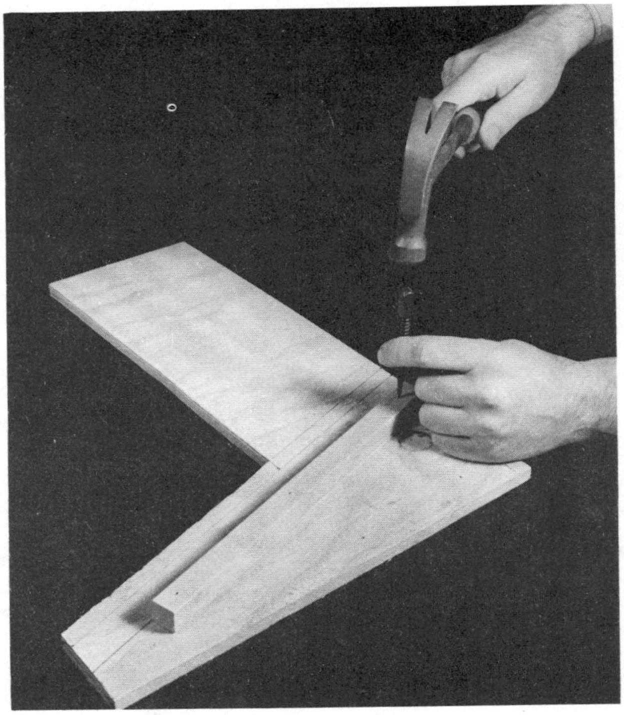

Step 8

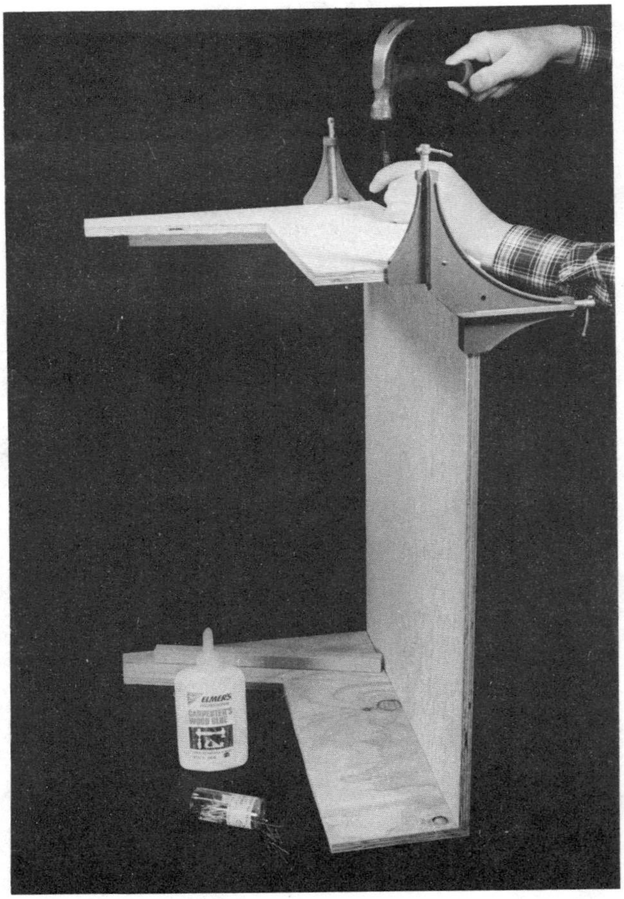

Step 12

under-cabinet light fixture). Use a nail set to punch screw-starter hole.

14. Turn top panel over and prenail with three 1″ brads along each side edge and five along the back edge.

15. Run a bead of glue along the top edges of the unit, and lay top panel in place; then drive and countersink brads.

16. Prenail the bottom panel with three 1″ brads along each side edge.

17. Run a bead of glue along each ¾″-square cleat on the side panels. Lay the bottom panel atop the cleats, attach with brads, and countersink.

18. Depending on which side of the under-cabinet light the cord exits, drill a ¼″-diameter hole in the back panel, 2″ from the side and as near the top as possible.

19. Conceal all plywood laminations, fill brad holes, and patch any surface imperfections with spackling paste and let unit stand for several hours or overnight.

20. Sand entire unit with medium-grit and fine-grit sandpaper. Clean to remove dust, and apply two coats of latex interior paint.

21. Drive light-mounting screws into holes punched in **Step 13.**

22. With wire cutters or wire-cutting pliers, cut the plug off the light-fixture cord.

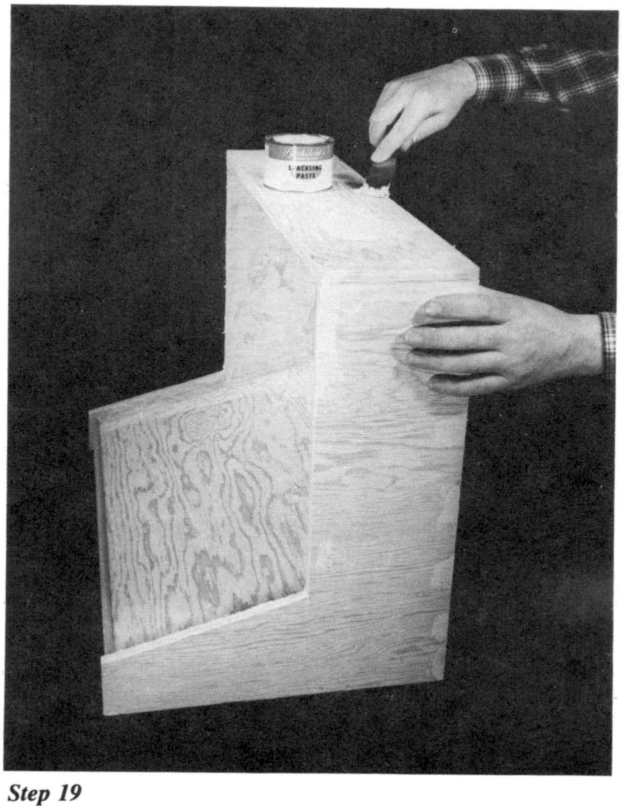

Step 19

23. Attach the light fixture to the mounting screws in the top of the unit and run the cord through the hole in the back panel.

24. Attach a snap-on plug to the end of the light cord and the unit is ready to plug in and use.

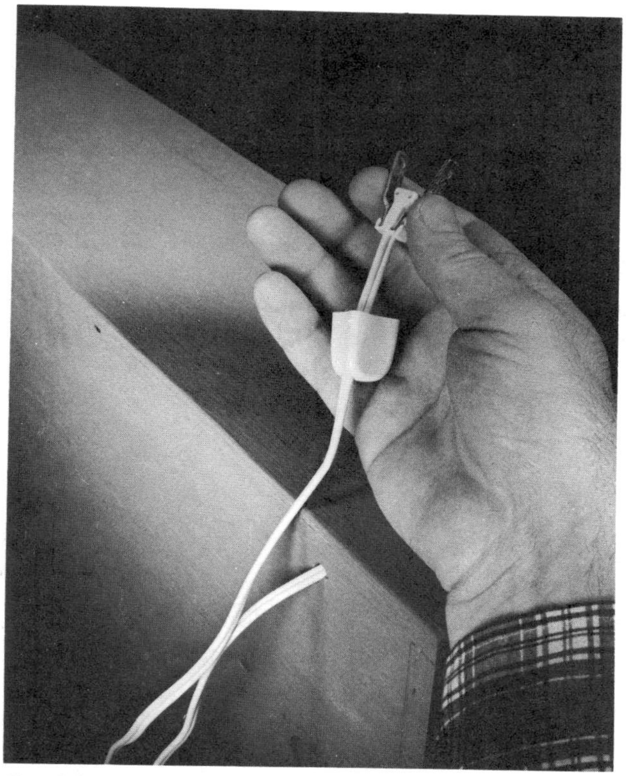

Step 24

Required Tools

Steel tape rule	Wire cutters
Yardstick	Paint brush
Pencil	Putty knife
Claw hammer	Electric drill and 1/4″ bit
Nail set	Circular saw
Screwdriver	Saw guide
Mitre box and backsaw	Sabre saw
Two corner clamps	Pad sander

Required Materials

- Half-sheet of 1/2″ plywood, A-C or better
- 2′ of 1″ lattice
- 2′ of 3/4″-square molding
- White glue
- Spackling paste
- 1″ brads
- Medium-grit and fine-grit sandpaper
- Interior latex paint
- 18″ undercabinet fluorescent light fixture
- Snap-on electrical plug

Plywood Panels

From a half-sheet or available scraps of 1/2″ plywood, cut the following panels:

QUANTITY	SIZE	NOMENCLATURE
2	14 × 18″	Side panels
1	18 × 24″	Back panel
1	6 × 25″	Top panel
1	13 3/8 × 24″	Bottom Panel

11 Stacking Storage Bins

With these simple and easy-to-build stacking storage bins you can quickly organize the hardware, small parts, hobby and craft materials, toys, and even kitchen items that seem to accumulate throughout the house. The bins can be set individually or stacked, one atop another, on a desk, workbench, or table. They will also fit inside cabinets or on top of shelves.

Although you can make three bins with a half-sheet of $\frac{1}{4}''$ plywood, you might want to assess your needs before heading for the lumberyard. You can probably find uses for a half-dozen or more in the workshop alone.

This project calls for the use of Weldwood®Touch-n-Glue®, instead of the usual white glue. The reason is that this is a fast-acting adhesive, similar to contact ce-

ment, and requires no clamping. If you own an electric glue gun, you can substitute hot-melt glue, in which case staples aren't necessary. Whichever one you use, make sure you apply enough to slightly bead over the edges when panels are joined. When glue sets, trim away excess with a pocket knife or utility knife.

Construction Steps

1. Measure up the front edge of two 10 × 14″ side panels and mark a spot (A) at 5″. Now, measuring from one of the front corners down a 14″ edge, mark a spot (B) at 3″. Mark a corresponding spot (C) on the opposite 14″ edge.
2. Scribe a line from Point A to Point B and another from Point A to Point C.
3. Stack each of the marked side panels atop two more side panels, and align them carefully; then clamp the stacked panels to the edge of a workbench or cutting board, and cut away the front corners along the lines scribed in **Step 2.**
4. Clean all panels with a tack cloth to remove dust. Then run an ample bead of Touch-n-Glue down each 11″ edge of each 10 × 11″ bottom panel. Press each glued edge firmly to the bottom inside edge of a side panel, pull the pieces apart, and allow the glue ten minutes to get tacky. (Apply more glue wherever blank spots occur.)
5. Butt a bottom panel to the bottom edge of a side panel and press firmly together. Carefully press the opposite side panel in place along the opposite edge of the bottom panel. Then set each partially assembled unit up on its rear edges and adjust panels for a square fit.
6. Use a staple gun to drive three or more 3/8″ staples through each side panel into the bottom panel.
7. Use a hammer to tap all staples flush with the plywood surfaces.
8. Tip each unit up on a front edge; then run a bead of glue along the rear edges of the side and bottom panels.
9. Press a rear panel firmly in place on each unit; then remove the panels and allow ten minutes for glue to get tacky. Apply more glue as necessary.
10. Press rear panels in place and staple. Hammer staples flush with surface.
11. Stand each unit up on its rear panel, and use the same techniques to attach a front panel to each on the "lower" front edges of the side panels.
12. Cut six pieces of 3/4″-square molding to 10½″, and sand any rough edges with medium-grit sandpaper.
13. Run a bead of glue down one edge of each piece of molding. Then press two pieces of molding in place on the underside of each bottom panel, with each piece located just inside the bottom edges of the rear and side panels. Then remove the molding and let stand until glue gets tacky.
14. Press molding in place and let units stand overnight until glue cures.

Step 2

Step 6

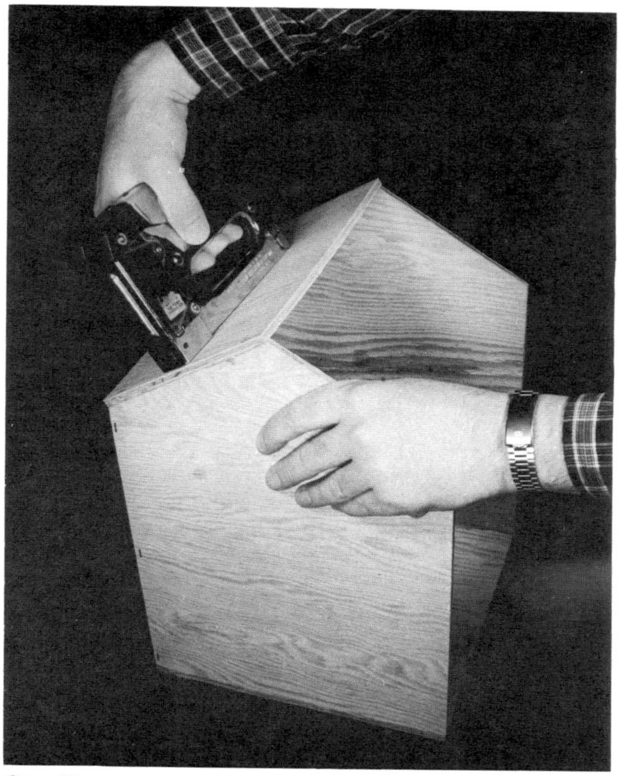

Step 11

Required Materials

Half-sheet of 1/4" plywood, any grade
6' of 3/4" square molding
Tube of Weldwood Touch-n-Glue
3/8" staples
Medium-grit sandpaper
Tack cloth

Plywood Panels

From a half-sheet of 1/4" plywood, cut the following panels:

QUANTITY	SIZE	NOMENCLATURE
6	10 × 14"	Side panels
3	10 × 11"	Bottom panels
3	10 × 10½"	Rear panels
3	5⅞ × 10½"	Front panels

Required Tools

Steel tape rule
Carpenter's square or yardstick
Pencil
Claw hammer
Mitre box and backsaw
Two C-clamps
Staple gun
Utility knife or pocket knife
Circular saw

12
File 13

Here's another whimsical wastebasket that is sure to make your friends smile. Everyone relegates material to File 13, but nobody owns one. If you plan to build any of the other office or den furnishings in this book, you can match hardware and paint to make your File 13 part of a coordinated set.

Although the plans call for assembly with glue and screws, you can do just as well with glue and one-inch paneling nails and save time in the process.

Construction Steps

1. From 1 × 2 stock, cut two cleats to 14″ and two more to 13″.
2. Cut two pieces of parting bead to 14½″.
3. Lay the right side panel on a flat working surface, outside face up, and scribe a line from top to bottom ¾″ from the front edge and another ¼″ from the rear edge. Do likewise on the left side panel.

4. Mark for screw holes along each line at 1″, 7″, 13″, and 19″ from the top.
5. With a hammer and center punch, make drill-starter holes at each spot along the scribed lines.
6. Drill a $^9/_{64}$″-diameter hole at each spot, and countersink for #6 flathead screws.
7. In each 13″ and 14″ cleat, drill two $^9/_{64}$″-diameter holes, each located an inch or so from each end; then countersink for #6 screws.
8. Turn side panels over and scribe a line on each, from top to bottom, ½″ from the front edge.
9. Run a bead of glue down the underside of a 14″ cleat and position it along the bottom of one side panel, 1″ from the front edge and ½″ from the rear edge. Lightly clamp in place with two spring clamps or C-clamps. Then do likewise with the other side panel.
10. Insert a 1 × 6 flathead screw into each hole in the cleats, tap lightly with a hammer to start, and drive with a screwdriver.
11. Similarly, attach a 13″ cleat to the front panel and another to the rear panel, centered along the bottom edges, ¾″ from the left and right edges.
12. Run a bead of glue down the left edge of the rear panel and butt the rear panel to the left side panel. Lightly clamp at the top with a corner clamp and screw panels together with ¾ × 6 flathead screws, starting at the bottom hole and working up.
13. Attach the right side panel to the rear panel the same way.
14. Run a bead of glue along the top edges of the cleats and lay the bottom panel in place atop the cleats. Affix the bottom to the cleats with 1″ brads, using longnose pliers to hold the brads while hammering. Countersink brads.
15. Lay the front panel face up on a working surface and scribe vertical lines ¼″ from the left and right edges. Then scribe horizontal lines 1½″ from the top edge and 2½″ from the bottom edge.

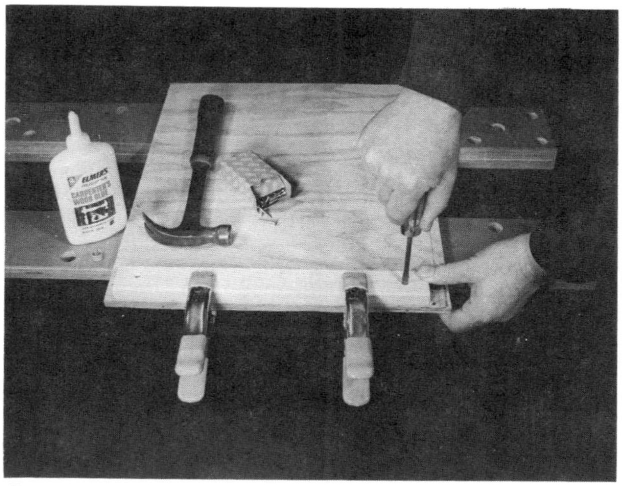

Step 10

Step 12

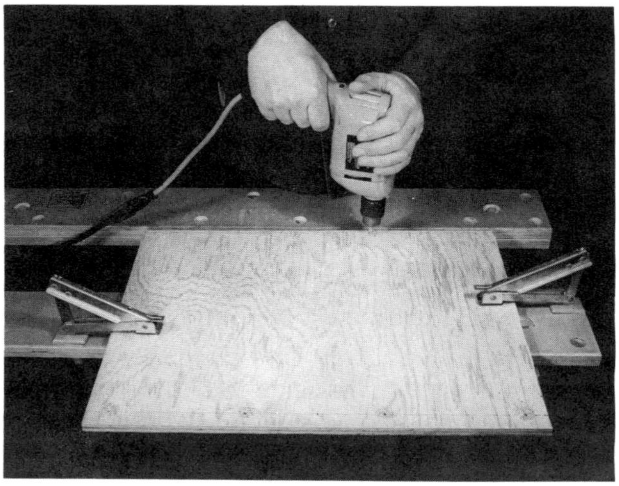

Step 6

16. Lay the drawer face on a work surface and scribe a vertical center line. Intersect that line with a horizontal line 5″ from the bottom edge.
17. For a standard drawer pull, mark the drawer face for screw holes on the horizontal line 1½″ on each side of the vertical center line. Then punch a drill-starter hole at each spot.
18. Lay the drawer face atop the front panel, aligned

with the lines you scribed in **Step 15.** Lightly clamp the two pieces together with C-clamps, and double-check to make sure the drawer face is $1\frac{1}{2}''$ from the top and $2\frac{1}{2}''$ from the bottom, centered $\frac{1}{4}''$ from each side.

19. Drill screw holes through both pieces at the spots marked and punched in **Step 17.** (Measure drawer pull to determine drill-bit size.)

20. As standard $\frac{3}{4}''$-long mounting screws are too short for the two panels, turn clamped pieces over and use a $\frac{3}{8}''$-diameter bit to countersink each hole $\frac{1}{4}''$ deep.

21. Remove C-clamps and put drawer face aside. Now, run thin beads of glue down the left and right edges of the front panel, align panel edges along the lines scribed on the inside front edges of the side panels in **Step 8,** and clamp each top corner with a corner clamp. Then attach sides to front with $\frac{3}{4} \times 6$ flathead screws.

22. Run a bead of glue along one $\frac{3}{4}''$ face of a $14\frac{1}{2}''$ piece of parting bead and lay it in place on the front panel along the bottom edge. Temporarily clamp with two spring clamps or C-clamps; then attach with three $\frac{3}{4}''$ brads. Attach another piece of parting bead along the top edge in the same way and countersink brads.

23. Use a putty knife and spackling paste to fill all screw holes, brad holes, and imperfections. Conceal plywood edges with spackling paste, and let stand until paste cures.

24. Sand unit and drawer face to a smooth, even finish with medium-grit and fine-grit sandpaper. Sand wooden numerals as required.

25. Use a vacuum cleaner to remove dust from unit; then wipe clean with a damp sponge.

26. Apply two coats of latex paint to the unit. On front panel, paint only slightly inside the scribed lines, leaving plenty of raw wood surface for gluing drawer face.

27. Apply two coats of paint in a contrasting color to the front and edges of the drawer face.

28. Paint numerals to match the unit and contrast the drawer front. If numerals are ridged to allow easy application of a second color, paint the face surface to match the color of the drawer face.

29. After paint has dried, and with unit lying on its back, apply an ample amount of glue to the unpainted portion of the front panel.

30. Lay the drawer face atop the front panel so screw holes align. Then attach the drawer pull with mounting screws.

31. Lightly clamp the top edge of the drawer face to the front panel with two C-clamps, using clamp cushions. Leave clamps in place until glue sets.

32. Center the numerals $1\frac{3}{4}''$ from the top edge of the drawer face. Then, one at a time, put a couple of pieces of double-sided tape on the back of each and press numerals in place. Permanently attach with $1\frac{1}{4}''$ brads driven through the holes predrilled by the manufacturer and countersink the brads.

33. Fill brad holes in numerals with spackling paste and smooth over with a wet finger. When paste dries, conceal the filler with paint, and the unit is ready for filing appropriate material.

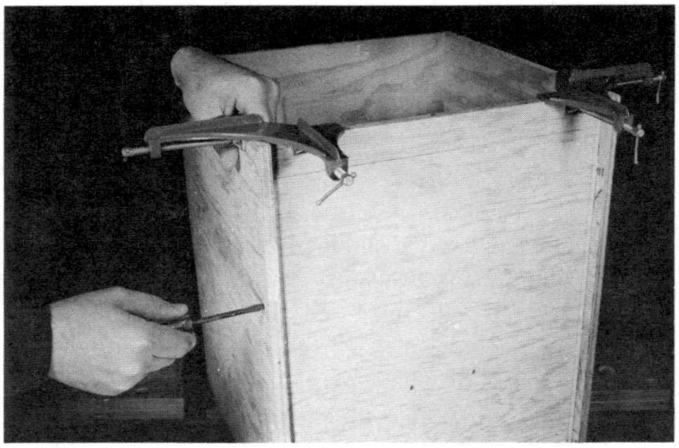

Step 21

Step 22

Required Tools

- Steel tape rule
- Pencil
- Claw hammer
- Nail set
- Center punch
- Screwdriver
- Mitre box and backsaw
- Two C-clamps
- Two corner clamps
- Paint brush
- Putty knife
- Electric drill and assorted bits
- #6 countersink bit
- Circular saw
- Saw guide
- Pad sander

Plywood Panels

From a half-sheet of ½″ plywood, cut the following panels:

QUANTITY	SIZE	NOMENCLATURE
2	15½ × 20″	Side panels
2	14½ × 20″	Front and rear panels
1	14 × 14½″	Bottom panel
1	14 × 16″	Drawer face

Required Materials

- Half-sheet of ½″ plywood, G1S
- 5′ of 1 × 2, clear
- 3′ of parting bead
- White glue
- Spackling paste
- ¾″ brads
- 1″ brads
- 1¼″ brads
- 16 ¾ × 6 flathead wood screws
- Eight 1 × 6 flathead wood screws
- Medium-grit and fine-grit sandpaper
- Interior latex paint
- Roll of double-sided tape
- Drawer pull
- Two wooden numerals ("13")

13 Stack-and-Bundle Boxes

It doesn't take long for newspapers and magazines to accumulate in untidy heaps that clutter the garage or basement. When the spirit finally moves us to get rid of them, we still have to stack them and tie them into manageable bundles. Just thinking about the job is enough to justify canceling subscriptions.

With a pair of stack-and-bundle boxes that you can make from a half-sheet of $\frac{1}{2}''$ plywood, old newspapers and magazines practically package themselves. All you have to do is tie the knots, toss the bundles into the car, and drop them at the recycling center the next time you drive by.

Construction steps are the same for each box. The only difference between the two are dimensions. Build either from available scraps or both from a half-sheet. Run pieces of twine through the bottom channels in each box, and when a box gets full, tie off the bundles and remove them.

Construction Steps

1. For each box, prenail two side panels with three 1″ brads each, located ¼″ from the bottom edges.
2. Run a bead of glue down one long edge of a bottom panel. Butt the side panels to it, leaving a 1″ gap between them, and drive and countersink the brads.
3. Prenail the remaining side panels and attach them the same way to the opposite edge of the bottom panel.
4. Prenail two end panels with two 1″ brads each along the bottom edges and three along each edge that will be butted to a side panel.
5. Run a bead of glue along a short edge of the bottom panel and up the edge of each adjacent side panel.
6. Butt the end panels to the bottom and side panel edges, leaving a 1″ gap between them; then drive and countersink the brads.
7. Turn the box over and attach the remaining two end panels the same way.
8. Apply an ample amount of glue to the underside of one of the inlay panels and press it into position on the box floor, butted into one corner. Install the remaining three inlays the same way, creating two 1″-wide channels that intersect in the center of the box floor.
9. Let boxes stand until glue sets.

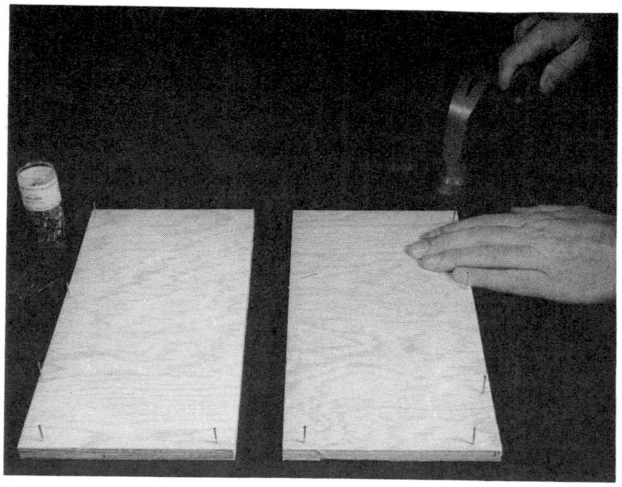

Step 4

Step 7

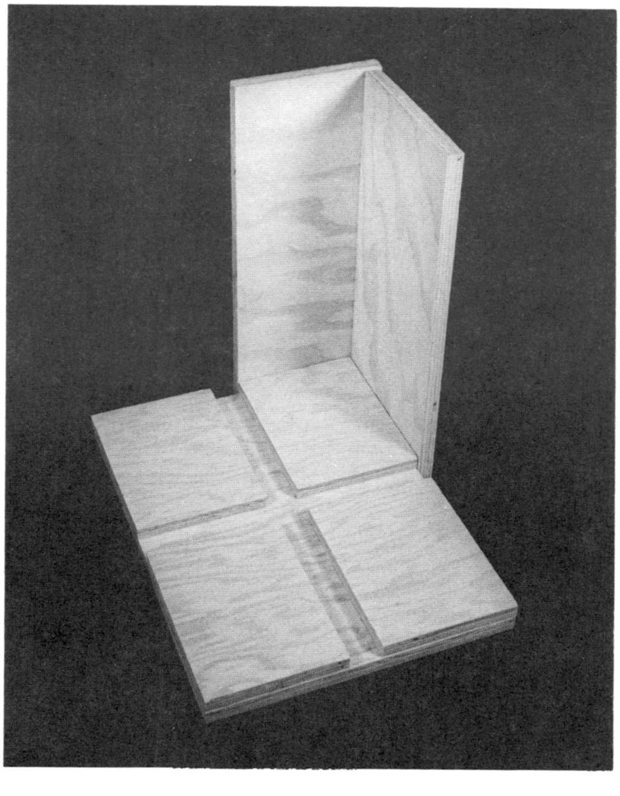

Required Tools

Steel tape rule	Claw hammer
Yardstick or straightedge	Nail set
Pencil	Two C-clamps
	Circular saw

Required Materials

Half-sheet of ½″ plywood, any grade
White glue
1″ brads
Medium-grit sandpaper

Plywood Panels

For the newspaper-size stack-and-bundle box, cut the following panels from ½″ plywood:

QUANTITY	SIZE	NOMENCLATURE
4	6 × 12″	End panels
4	7 × 12″	Side panels
4	5½ × 7″	Bottom inlays
1	12 × 15″	Bottom panel

For the magazine-size stack-and-bundle box, cut the following panels from ½″ plywood:

QUANTITY	SIZE	NOMENCLATURE
4	4½ × 12″	End panels
4	5½ × 12″	Side panels
4	4 × 5½″	Bottom inlays
1	9 × 12″	Bottom panel

14
Covered Bridge for Newspapers

If you're tired of having your newspapers blown around on windy days or being turned into papier-mâché when it rains, here's the perfect project for you. This little covered bridge can be painted and trimmed to match your house or set off in contrasting colors. It can be easily mounted to a porch or deck railing, set atop a post, or fastened to a fence.

Construction Steps

1. Measure in $4\frac{1}{2}''$ from a $12''$ edge on each $9 \times 12''$ end panel and make a mark at the center of the top $9''$ edge.
2. Measure down each $12''$ edge and make a mark $4\frac{1}{2}''$ from each top corner.
3. Scribe a line from the mark on each side edge to the mark on the top edge.
4. Scribe a light pencil line across each end panel $5''$ from and parallel to the bottom edge.

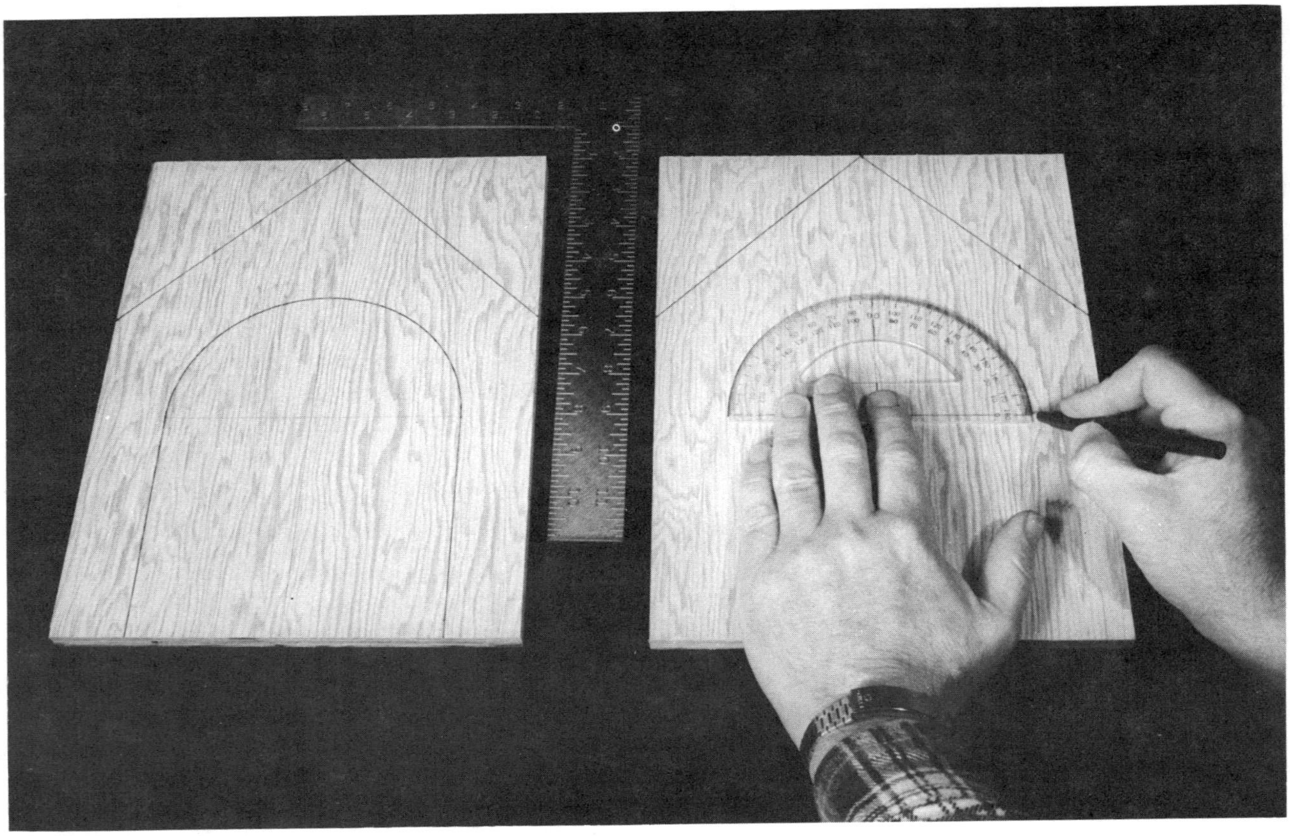

Step 6

5. Scribe another light pencil line that runs vertically from the bottom edge up 8″ and is centered 4½″ from each side.
6. Align a 6″ protractor with the base guideline along the horizontal pencil line and the 90° mark on the vertical pencil line. Now scribe an arc from 0° to 180°.
7. On each end panel, carefully measure the distance from each arc end to the nearest side edge and make corresponding marks at the bottom edge of each panel. Now connect the arc ends to those marks with vertical lines.
8. Use a circular saw to cut away the top corners from the end panels along the lines scribed in **Step 3.**
9. Use a sabre saw to cut the archway out of each panel, using as guides the lines laid out in **Steps 6** and **7.**
10. Turn the 9 × 20″ bottom panel upside down and prenail with five 1″ brads along each long edge.
11. Run a bead of waterproof glue down one long edge of a side panel, butt it to the bottom panel, and drive and countersink the brads.
12. Attach the other side panel the same way.
13. Prenail each end panel with three 1″ brads along each side.

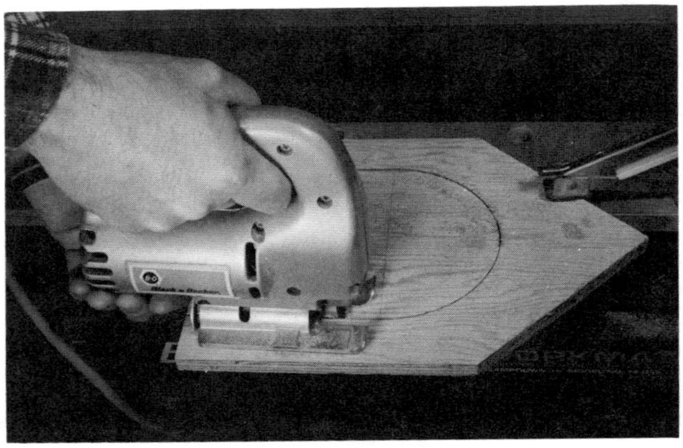

Step 9

14. Run a bead of glue along the ends of the side panels and bottom panel and attach the end panels. Countersink the brads.
15. With a mitre box and backsaw, cut four pieces of 1″ outside-corner molding to fit the four corners of the unit. Tops should be mitred to fit roof slope and bottoms cut square.
16. Attach corner molding with ¾″ brads and glue. Then countersink brads.

17. Measure the distance between the corner molding along the bottom edges of the unit (should be 19½"). Then cut a piece of 1" lattice to fit and attach it along the bottom edge with ¾" brads. Similarly, attach another piece on the opposite side of the unit.

18. Cut six more pieces of lattice to 6 ⅜", squared at the bottom and mitred at the top to accommodate roof slope.

19. Prenail each piece with two ¾" brads; then apply glue to the opposite side.

20. Attach three pieces to each side: the first piece located 10¼" from each end, the next 5 ⅛" from one end, and the other 5 ⅛" from the other end. Countersink brads.

21. File the points down on any brads that have come through the side walls.

22. Scribe a pencil line parallel to and 1¼" inside each end of each roof panel.

23. Prenail the 7½ × 23" roof panel with three 1 " brads along each line.

24. Run a bead of glue down one side of each roof support (the upper, angled edges of the end panels).

25. Lay the roof panel in place atop the supports, with the top edge of the panel flush with the peaks of the end panels; then drive and countersink the brads.

26. Prenail the 8 × 23" roof panel with two brads along each line scribed in **Step 22** and five more along and ¼" inside the top edge.

27. Run a bead of glue along each remaining roof support and along the top edge of the attached roof panel.

28. Position the remaining roof panel atop supports, butted to the top edge of the attached panel; then drive and countersink the brads.

29. Cut a piece of 1" outside-corner molding to 25", mitred 45° at each end.

30. Run a bead of glue along the inside of the corner molding and attach to the roof peak with ¾" brads. Countersink brads.

31. Fill all brad holes and any open defects with spackling paste and let dry. Then sand unit with medium-grit and fine-grit sandpaper.

32. Vacuum all dust from the unit. Then apply two coats of exterior flat latex paint. When paint dries, paint trim in a contrasting color, and let dry.

33. Attach the unit to a post, fence, or porch or deck railing with four 1" corner braces and wood screws.

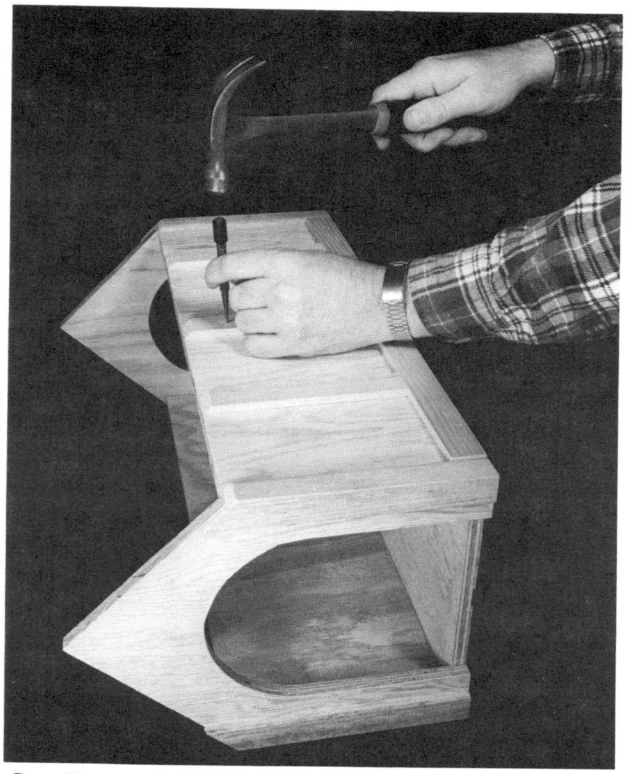

Step 20

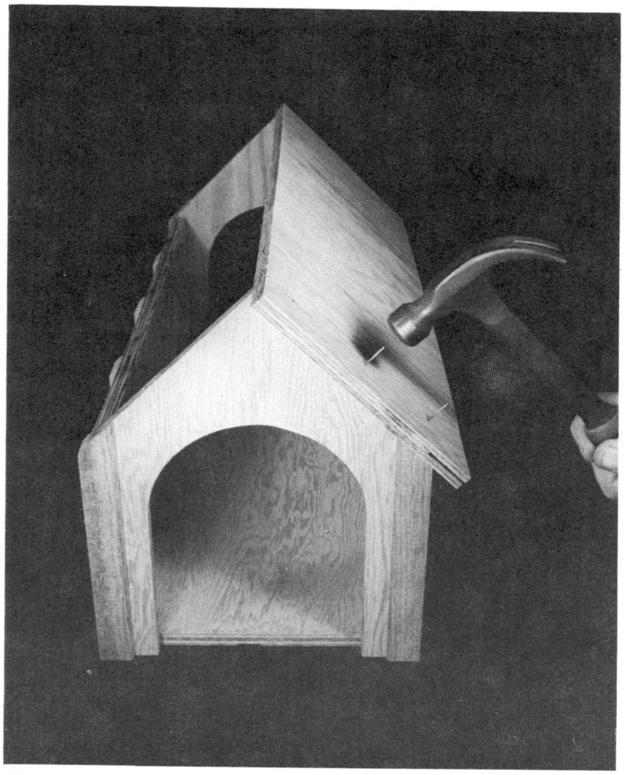

Step 25

Required Tools

- Steel tape rule
- 6″ protractor
- Carpenter's square
- Pencil
- Claw hammer
- Nail set
- Mitre box and backsaw
- Paint brushes
- Putty knife
- Circular saw
- Saw guide
- Sabre saw
- Pad sander

Required Materials

- Half-sheet of ½″ exterior plywood, G1S
- 4′ of 1″ O.S. corner molding
- 7′ of 1″ lattice
- Tube of urethane waterproof glue
- Spackling paste
- ¾″ brads
- 1″ brads
- Four 1″ corner braces with screws
- Medium-grit and fine-grit sandpaper
- Exterior latex house paint

Plywood Panels

From a half-sheet of ½″ plywood, cut the following panels:

QUANTITY	SIZE	NOMENCLATURE
2	9 × 12″	End panels
2	7 × 20″	Side panels
1	9 × 20″	Bottom panel
1	8 × 23″	Roof panel
1	7½ × 23	Roof panel

15
Wall-Mounted Magazine Rack

Magazine racks are functional furnishings that come in an endless variety of sizes, shapes, and designs. This one was designed to hold a large assortment of magazines while attractively adorning a wall. It should be painted to match or contrast with the room's color scheme and can be trimmed in a coordinating color.

Construction Steps

1. Trim a half-sheet of ¼″ plywood to 30 × 48″.
2. With a steel tape rule, measure down each 48″ edge of the plywood and make pencil marks at 8″, 24″, and 40″.
3. Align a yardstick or square with the set of marks at 8″ and mark for drill-starter holes 4″ from each 48″ edge. Do likewise at the 24″ and 40″ marks.
4. With a hammer and center punch, make a drill-starter hole at each spot marked.

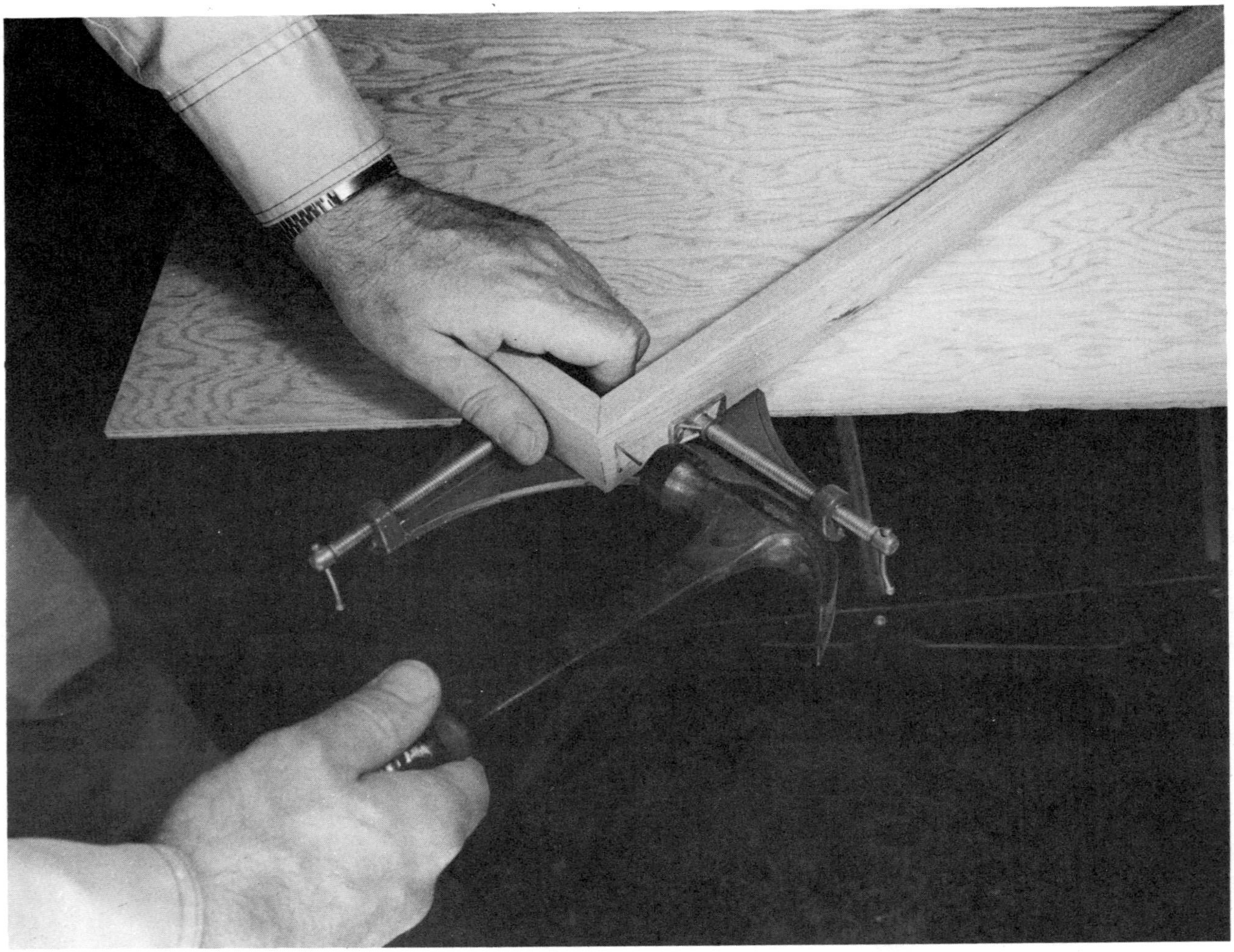

Step 8

5. Drill a $^{13}/_{64}$″-diameter mounting-screw hole at each spot.
6. Sand surface of the plywood smooth with medium-grit and fine-grit paper.
7. With a mitre box and backsaw, mitre-cut two pieces of 1 × 2 to 48″ (outside measurement). Cut two more to 30″ (outside measurement).
8. Apply glue to the end of a 30″ piece, joint it to the end of a 48″ piece, and secure with a corner clamp. Then drive and countersink two 1″ brads at the joint.
9. Glue, clamp, and nail remaining pieces the same way, creating a 30 × 48″ frame.
10. Measure from one corner up one of the 30″ sides of the frame and make a mark at 15″. Do the same on the other 30″ side.
11. Use a combination square to scribe a line across the inside of each 30″ side at the 15″ marks.
12. Measure along a 48″ side from the inside of one corner to the inside of the opposite corner, and cut a 1 × 2 shelf to that length.

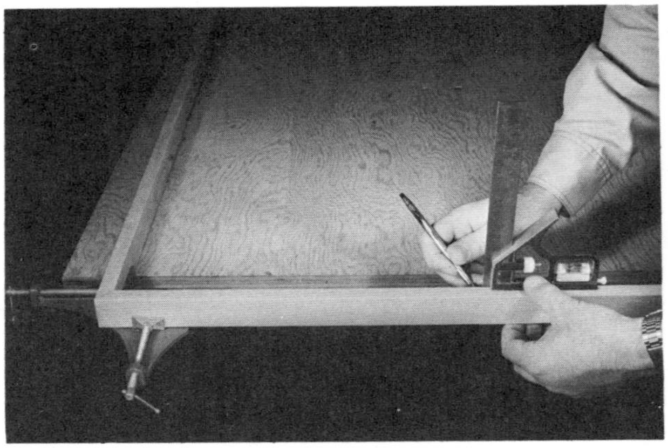

Step 11

13. Apply glue to each end of the shelf and butt the ends to the 30″ sides, with the bottom edges of the shelf aligned with the lines scribed in **Step 11.**
14. Drive two 1″ brads through each 30″ side into the 1 × 2 shelf ends.

15. Measure 10″ in from each bottom corner and make a mark on the top edge of the bottom frame piece. Make corresponding marks on the bottom edge of the shelf.
16. Use a combination square to scribe lines across the inside edge of the bottom frame piece and the underside of the shelf at the 10″ marks.
17. Measure the distance between the bottom inside of the frame and the underside of the shelf; then cut two pieces of 1 × 2 to that length.
18. Measure in 19″ from each side edge and scribe a line across the top of the shelf and underside of the top frame piece.
19. Measure the distance between the shelf and the top frame piece and cut two pieces of 1 × 2 to fit.
20. Apply glue to the ends of the 1 × 2 uprights and position them between the shelf and frame, aligned inside the lines scribed in **Steps 15** and **18**. Drive two brads through the shelf or frame piece into each end of each upright.
21. Apply glue to the rear edges of the 1 × 2 uprights, lay the rear panel on the framework, and attach with ⅞″ wire nails, spaced about 6″ apart.
22. Cut picture-frame molding to fit the outside edges of the unit, and attach with glue and 1″ brads. Countersink brads.
23. Fill all brad holes with spackling paste and let dry. Then apply two coats of interior latex paint to partially assembled unit.
24. Measure the distance between each side piece of frame molding, and cut four pieces of decorative molding or 1″ lattice to fit.
25. Lay two pieces of molding or lattice across the unit beneath the shelf and the other two above the shelf. Mark each where it intersects the vertical center of an upright. Then punch a drill-starter hole at each spot with the narrow point of a nail set. *(Do not use a center punch.)*
26. Drill a $\frac{1}{16}$″-diameter pilot hole at each spot.
27. Apply two coats of paint to both sides of the molding, being careful to avoid the areas on the rear side that will come in contact with the uprights.
28. Use glue and 1″ brads to attach one piece of molding or lattice flush with the bottom piece of frame molding.
29. Attach another piece so that the bottom of the molding is flush with the bottom edge of the shelf.
30. Attach the remaining two pieces of molding or lattice 5¼″ above the bottom piece and shelf piece.
31. Fill visible brad holes with spackling paste and let stand until the paste hardens. Then lightly sand with fine-grit paper as necessary.
32. Touch up paint as required. Then trim picture-frame and decorative molding with contrasting or coordinating color of paint.
33. Mount the unit directly to the wall studs with six 1½ × 8 ovalhead screws and finish washers. If you're unable to mount to the studs, use toggle bolts and finish washers.

Step 20

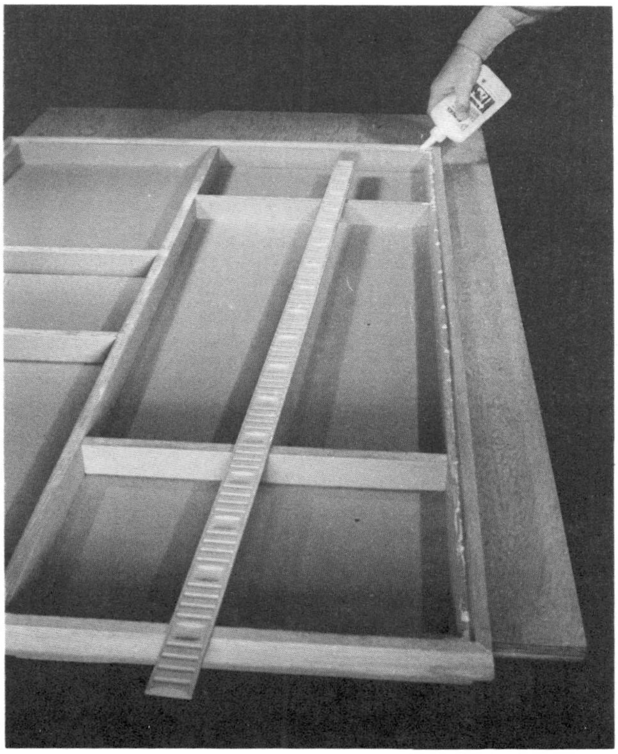

Step 28

Required Tools

- Steel tape rule
- Combination square
- Yardstick
- Pencil
- Claw hammer
- Nail set
- Center punch
- Screwdriver
- Mitre box and backsaw
- Two C-clamps
- Four corner clamps
- Paint brushes
- Putty knife
- Electric drill and 1/16″ and 13/64″ bits
- Circular saw
- Saw guide
- Pad sander

Required Materials

- Half-sheet of 1/4″ plywood, G1S
- 22′ of 1 × 2, clear
- 16′ of carved 1″ molding or 1″ lattice
- 14′ of picture-frame molding
- White glue
- Spackling paste
- 1″ brads
- 7/8″ wire nails
- Six 1 1/2 × 8 ovalhead wood screws
- Six #8 finish washers
- Medium-grit and fine-grit sandpaper
- Interior latex paint

Part III
One-Sheet Projects

Each of the following ten projects requires more than a half-sheet of plywood but no more than one full 4 × 8′ sheet.

16
Basic Workbench with Shelves

If you are a beginning do-it-yourselfer this is an excellent first project. You'll not only learn a number of useful techniques during the building process, but you'll end up with the sturdiest workbench you can build.

The bench bolts together so that it can be easily dismantled for moving. Even if you plan to build a more elaborate bench later, this one will serve you well until you need something larger, at which time you can keep it in the shop to provide additional bench space, use it elsewhere, or sell it for a profit.

If your local lumber yard stocks $1\frac{1}{8}''$ plywood with square edges, you need only buy a sheet and cut the top and shelves from it. If you can only find tongue-and-groove plywood flooring, however, you'll need to take a couple of extra steps to get the panels you need. Everything you need to know follows.

Construction Steps

1. Use a circular saw to rip 1″ from each 8′ side of a 4 × 8′ sheet of $1\frac{1}{8}''$ tongue-and-groove plywood flooring. (This removes the tongue and groove, leaving a 47 × 96″ sheet.)
2. Now make another lengthwise (rip) cut, rendering a 32 × 96″ piece and a $14\frac{7}{8} \times 96''$ piece ($\frac{1}{8}''$ is lost to the saw kerf).
3. Cut the 32″-wide piece to a length of 60″, creating the bench top.
4. Rip the $14\frac{7}{8}''$-wide piece to a width of 13″; then cut it in half, yielding two bench shelves.
5. Cut four pieces of 2 × 4 to 48″, four to $34\frac{7}{8}''$, and four more to 20″.
6. With the four $34\frac{7}{8}''$ pieces resting on their broad sides, mark a B (for "Bottom") on one end of each.
7. Scribe lines across the broad face of each $34\frac{7}{8}''$ leg at 10″, $13\frac{1}{2}''$, $21\frac{1}{2}''$ and 25″ from the bottom.
8. Now scribe vertical lines from the bottom to the first horizontal line and from the top to the last horizontal line $\frac{3}{4}''$ inside each vertical edge of each leg.
9. Turn the legs over and scribe vertical lines on the opposite broad faces, identical to those made in **Step 8.**
10. Rotate the legs 90° so they're standing on their narrow faces; then scribe a centered vertical line the length of each.
11. Rotate the legs 180° and scribe vertical center lines on the opposite narrow faces.
12. At this point, all four legs have identical lines. Now set them off in pairs, with the horizontally scribed sides up, and mark the bottom of one leg of each pair B-1 and the other B-2. Left of each designation, mark a small L and on the right a small R.
13. Set the legs on their narrow edges, left edge up on the B-1 legs and right edge up on the B-2 legs. Now scribe horizontal lines across each at $3\frac{1}{2}''$ and 7″ from the bottom and $3\frac{1}{2}''$ from the top. (Put legs aside for now.)
14. Stand the four 20″ pieces on their narrow edges and scribe centered lines along the length of each narrow face, as you did to the legs. Rotate 180° and scribe identical lines on the opposite narrow faces.
15. Now lay the pieces on their broad sides and scribe lines across each at $3\frac{1}{2}''$ from each end. (Put these pieces aside for now.)
16. Lay the 48″ pieces out, broad faces up, and scribe lines across each, $1\frac{1}{2}''$ from each end.
17. Rotate these pieces 90° and scribe centered lines along the narrow faces to points just over $1\frac{1}{2}''$ inside each end. Turn the pieces over and do the same on the opposite narrow faces.
18. Use a mitre box and backsaw to make initial joint

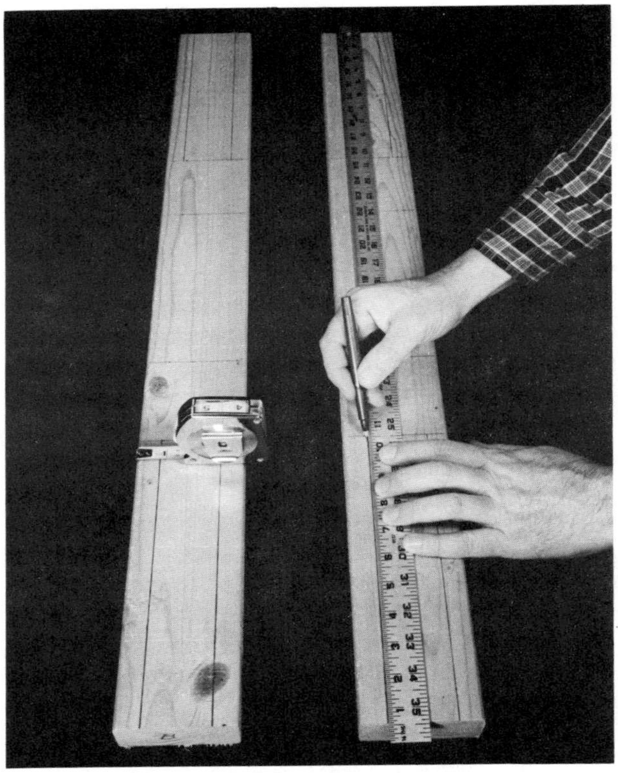

Step 8

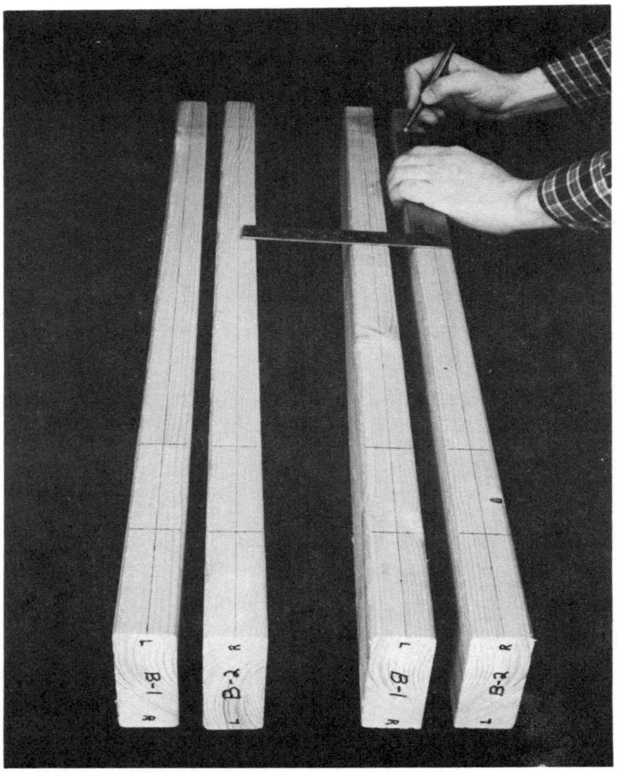

Step 13

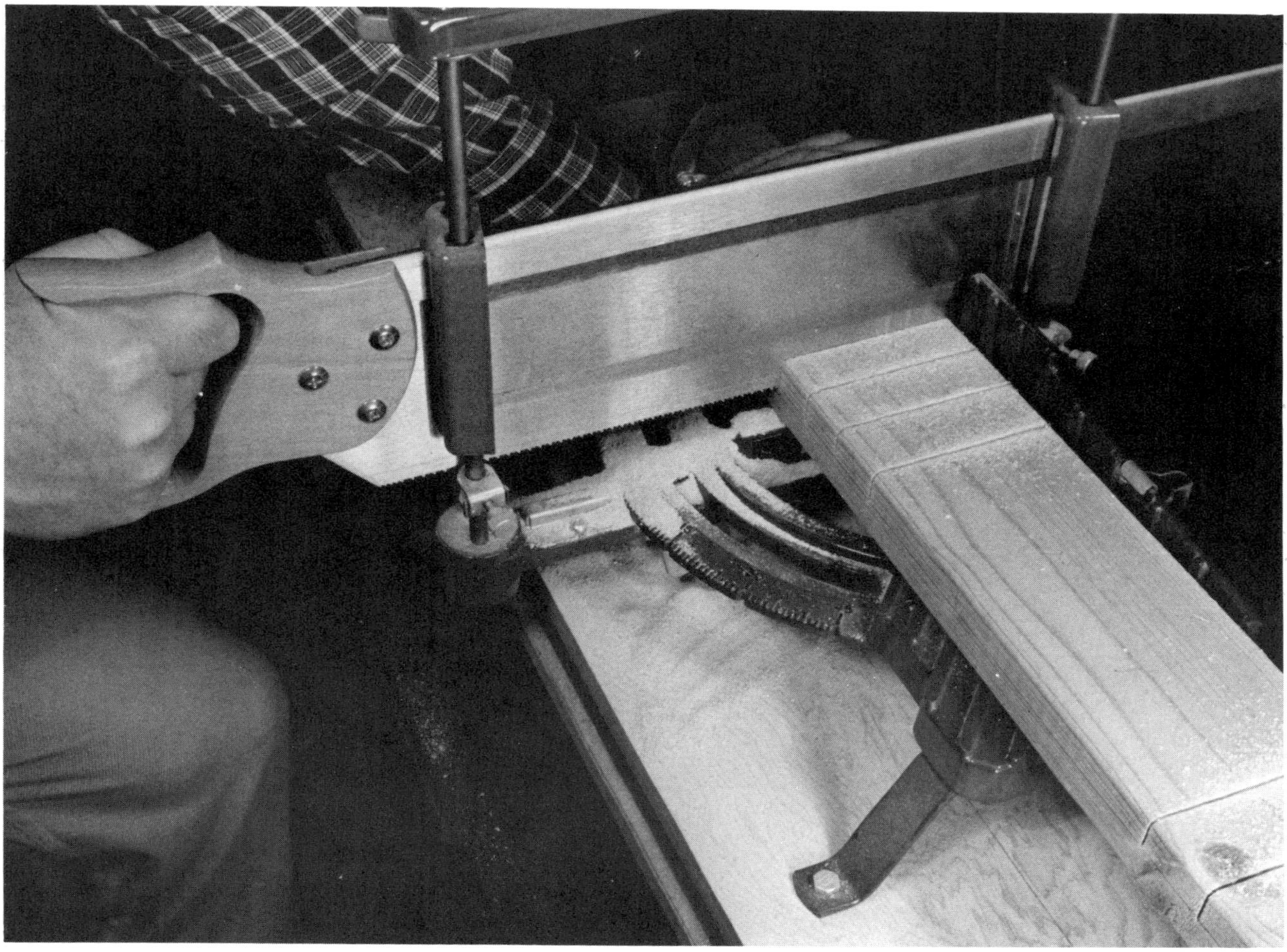

Step 18

cuts. Start by cutting across the legs at the lines made for the 3½″-wide dadoes. Cut to a depth of ¾″—down to the stop lines scribed along the narrow faces. Make two additional cuts inside the scribed lines to facilitate later removal of material.

19. Turn each leg onto a narrow edge in the mitre box and cut across the lines scribed 3½″ and 7″ from the bottom; make two more cuts between the lines—all to the ¾″ stop line. Make similar cuts at the line 3½″ from the top of each leg.

20. Make ¾″-deep cuts along the lines at each end of each 20″ leg span.

21. Makes ¾″-deep cuts along the lines at each end of each 48″ cross beam.

22. Use a 1½″ wood chisel to remove material and make the 3½″-wide notches in the broad faces of the legs. Start on one side and tap the chisel to a depth of about ⅛″. Turn the leg over and drive the chisel about ¼″ deep along the guide line. Continue slowly alternating from side to side until all material has been removed.

Step 22

23. Use the same techniques to make the notches on the narrow faces of the legs.
24. Clamp a leg upright in a vise and use a backsaw or panel saw to cut down to the cut made earlier $3\frac{1}{2}''$ from the top, removing a $\frac{3}{4} \times 3\frac{1}{2}''$ piece of the corner. Align your saw blade along the vertical guidelines. Repeat the process on the other three legs.
25. Use the same techniques to make $\frac{3}{4} \times 3\frac{1}{2}''$ end laps at each end of each 20″ leg span.
26. With the same techniques, make $\frac{3}{4} \times 1\frac{1}{2}''$ laps at the ends of each 48″ cross beam.
27. Use a wide rasp to smooth out all joint cuts.
28. Test fit legs, leg spans, and cross beams. Use a $\frac{1}{2}''$ rasp to widen any joints where pieces won't fit properly.
29. At each end of each 20″ leg span, scribe a diagonal line on the face opposite the end lap, running from one corner of the lap to the other. Then mark for drill-starter holes 1″ inside each end of each line.
30. With a combination square set for $\frac{3}{4}''$, mark for drill-starter holes at each end of each 48″ cross beam on the face opposite the cutout. Lines should intersect $\frac{3}{4}''$ from the end and $\frac{3}{4}''$ from the long edges of the beam.
31. Use a hammer and center punch to make drill-starter holes at each spot marked.

Step 24

Step 29

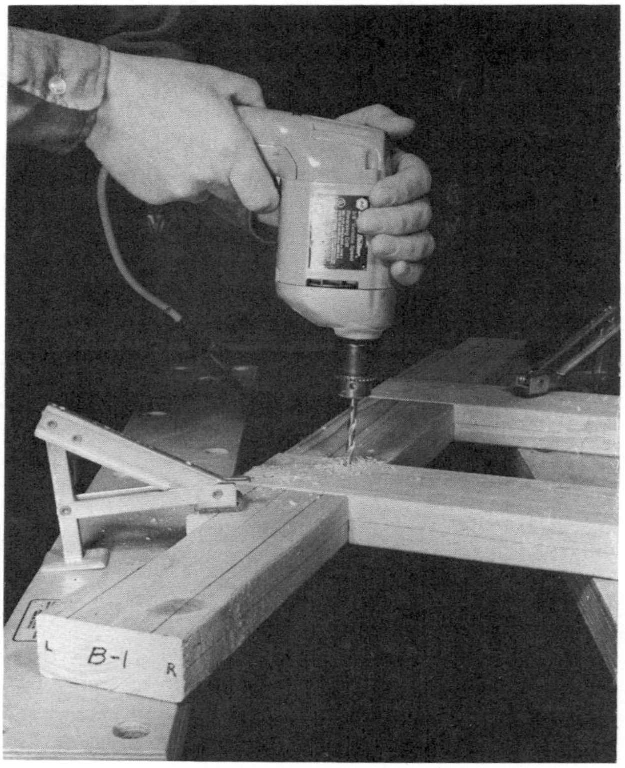

Step 32

32. Fit two leg spans into the notches cut in a B-1 leg with the spans extending from the R edge of the leg. Clamp to a solid surface and drill $\frac{1}{4}''$-diameter holes through the designated spots.
33. Bolt leg spans to legs, using a $\frac{1}{4} \times 2''$ bolt, two $\frac{1}{4}''$ flat washers, and a $\frac{1}{4}''$ nut at each hole.
34. Fit a B-2 leg to the other ends of the spans; then drill and bolt together the same way.
35. Drill and bolt the other leg assembly together in the same manner.

36. Drill a $\frac{9}{32}$"-diameter hole at each designated spot in the ends of the 48" cross beams.
37. Stand leg assemblies on the floor, 48" apart, with legs horizontal and spans vertical. Fit a 48" cross beam into the notches near the bottom of the two legs and drill $\frac{11}{64}$"-diameter pilot holes into the legs, through the $\frac{9}{32}$" holes at the ends of the cross beams.
38. Bolt the cross beam to the legs with four $\frac{1}{4} \times 2$" lag bolts and flat washers.
39. Attach another cross beam to the top of the leg assemblies using the same techniques.
40. Turn the unit over and attach the two remaining cross beams the same way.
41. Set the completed bench frame upright and, using a 3" corner brace as a guide, mark for bolt holes 3" inside each end of each top cross beam.
42. Make a drill-starter hole and drill an $\frac{11}{64}$"-diameter hole at each spot marked.
43. Mount four 3" corner braces with $\frac{1}{4} \times 1$" lag bolts.
44. Lay the bench top on the floor, good side down. Position the bench frame upside down on the underside of the bench top. Using the corner braces as guides, mark for drill-starter holes on the bottom of the bench top. Punch drill-starter holes and drill $\frac{11}{64}$"-diameter holes to a depth of $\frac{3}{4}$". (The simplest way to gauge the depth is to measure $\frac{3}{4}$" from the tip of the bit and mark the bit with a red felt-tipped pen. Then drill slowly and watch the bit carefully, stopping when the red mark reaches the plywood surface.)
45. Mount frame assembly to bench top with $\frac{1}{4} \times 1$" lag bolts and corner braces.
46. Set workbench upright. Then use a mitre box and backsaw to cut $1\frac{1}{8}$" lattice or bullnose stop to fit one edge of the bench top with a 45° mitre at each end. Prenail with $\frac{3}{4}$" brads and attach to the edge with glue and brads. Countersink brads.
47. Continue trimming the edges of the bench top the same way and countersink all brads. Then fill brad holes with wood filler and let dry.
48. Sand bench top and shelves with medium-grit and fine-grit sandpaper. Clean the unit and move it into place in your workshop. Slide the shelves into position atop the leg spans, and your bench is ready for use. Except for sanding, no further finishing is necessary.

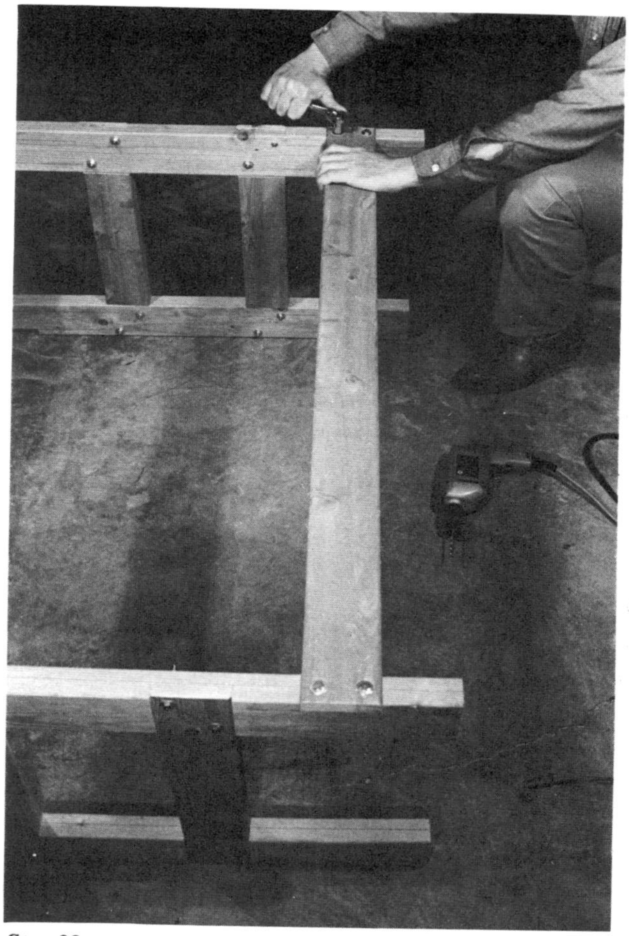

Step 38

Step 45

Required Tools

Steel tape rule
Combination square
Yardstick
Pencil
Claw hammer
Nail set
Center punch
Mitre box and backsaw
Two C-clamps
1″ or 1½″ wood chisel
1″ wood rasp
½″ wood rasp
Two 7/16″ or adjustable wrenches
Electric drill and 11/64″, ¼″, and 9/32″ bits
Circular saw
Saw guide
Pad sander

Plywood Panels

From a sheet of 1⅛″ shop-grade plywood flooring,* cut the following panels:

QUANTITY	SIZE	NOMENCLATURE
1	32 × 60″	Bench top
2	13 × 48″	Bench shelves

*If you're using tongue-and-groove flooring, read Construction **Steps 1** through **4** before cutting the plywood.

Required Materials

One sheet of 1⅛″ plywood flooring, shop grade
40′ of 2 × 4, graded standard or better
16′ of 1⅛″ lattice
White glue
Wood filler
¾″ brads
16 ¼× 2″ bolts
16 ¼″ nuts
16 ¼ × 2″ lag bolts
16 ¼ × 1″ lag bolts
48 ¼″ flat washers
Four 3″ corner braces
Medium-grit and fine-grit sandpaper

17 Paperback Shadowbox

Paperback books often look messy and out of place in bookcases and shelf units. The reason is that they are smaller than other books and conventional shelf units tend to overwhelm them. In a bookcase custom-made to hold these 4 × 7″ books, though, they can be attractively displayed and conveniently organized.

The paperback shadowbox is such a unit, designed to be mounted to a wall. And since it is shallow, it will go well in a hallway or along a staircase, where wall space often goes to waste.

Although the plans call for one sheet of $\frac{1}{2}$″ plywood, you can make all the 5″ strips from available scraps, if you prefer, and use $\frac{1}{4}$″ plywood or $\frac{1}{8}$″ or $\frac{1}{4}$″ hardboard for the rear panel.

Construction Steps

1. Clamp the $47\frac{1}{2}$″ horizontals securely, side by side, to a flat working surface, and use a router with a $\frac{1}{2}$″ straight bit to rout a $\frac{1}{4}$″-deep dado, $11\frac{3}{4}$″ from one end, across each piece simultaneously. Rout another

identical dado across each piece, $11\frac{3}{4}''$ from the opposite end.

2. Turn the horizontals over and simultaneously rout another dado across the center of each.
3. Rout a dado across the center inside surface of the top panel.
4. Rout a dado across the inside surface of the bottom panel, 12″ from the left end, and another 12″ from the right end.
5. Lay the left and right side panels side by side, clamp them, and rout dadoes simultaneously across each at 8″, $16\frac{1}{2}''$, and 25″ from the top.
6. Sand all surfaces with medium-grit and fine-grit sandpaper, and the unit is ready for assembly.
7. Run a bead of glue along the top edge of the right side panel. Butt it to the top panel and clamp the front corner with a corner clamp. Then drive three 1″ ring-shank paneling nails through the top panel into the side panel and countersink. (Leave the clamp in place.)
8. Attach the left side panel to the top panel the same way, and leave the clamp in place.
9. Lay the assembly on its back; then run a light bead of glue down each side edge of a horizontal and slide it into the top dadoes of the side panels with the center dado on the horizontal facing up. Dadoes on the bottom surface of the horizontal should align with the dadoes in the bottom panel below.
10. Clamp each front corner of the horizontal to a side panel with a corner clamp. Then drive two paneling nails through each side panel into the horizontal.
11. Remove the clamps from the horizontal only. (Leave bottom-panel clamps in place.) Then attach another horizontal the same way in the next set of dadoes in the side panel, this one with the center dado on the bottom surface of the horizontal to align with the horizontal below. Attach the remaining horizontal the same way but with center dado facing up.
12. Run a bead of glue across the bottom edges of the side panels, clamp the top panel to them with corner clamps, and nail each end with three paneling nails. Countersink nails and leave corner clamps in place at all four corners.
13. Run a thin bead of glue down the top and bottom edges of each $5 \times 8\frac{1}{2}''$ vertical, and slide each into dadoes in the horizontals.
14. Use two band clamps to pull horizontals in to tightly secure the verticals in their dadoes. Tighten clamps only enough for a snug fit, and let the unit stand until the glue sets.
15. Run a bead of glue along the rear edges of all horizontals and verticals. Lay the rear panel atop the unit, and nail down the corners; then continue driving and countersinking 1″ paneling nails along the

Step 1

Step 12

outside edges, spaced about 6″ apart. Lay one or several heavy objects on the back panel, and let the unit stand until the glue sets.

16. With a mitre box and backsaw, cut 3/4″ outside corner molding to fit the front edges of the top, bottom, and side panels, with 45° mitres at the ends of each piece.

17. Attach the molding to the front of the unit with glue and 3/4″ brads; countersink the brads.

18. Conceal all visible plywood laminations and fill nail holes and any imperfections with spackling paste.

19. Drill a 13/64″-diameter hole through the back, centered 4″ from the top. Drill another 8″ from the left and 13″ from the top, another 8″ from the right and 13″ from the top, another 8″ from the left and 30″ from the top, and one more 8″ from the right and 30″ from the top.

20. When spackling paste has hardened, sand with medium-grit and fine-grit sandpaper.

21. Clean the unit with a vacuum cleaner, and apply two coats of interior latex paint.

22. Mount the unit on a wall with five 2 × 8 ovalhead wood screws and #8 finish washers. Drive the screws directly into the wall studs, starting with the top center screw. Level the unit before driving the remaining screws. If you're unable to mount to the studs, use toggle bolts and finish washers instead.

Step 14

Required Tools

- Steel tape rule
- Pencil
- Claw hammer
- Nail set
- Center punch
- Screwdriver
- Mitre box and backsaw
- Four C-clamps or small bar clamps
- Two band clamps or long bar clamps
- Four corner clamps
- Paint brush
- Electric drill and 13/64″ bit
- Circular saw
- Saw and router guide
- Pad sander
- Router and 1/2″ straight bit

Required Materials

- One sheet of 1/2″ plywood, G2S
- 16′ of 1″ outside corner molding
- White glue
- Spackling paste
- 1″ ring-shank paneling nails
- Five 2 × 8 ovalhead screws
- Five #8 finish washers
- Medium-grit and fine-grit sandpaper
- Interior latex paint

Plywood Panels

From a sheet of 1/2″ plywood, graded A-C or better, cut the following panels:

QUANTITY	SIZE	NOMENCLATURE
1	34 1/2 × 48″	Rear panel
2	5 × 48″	Top and bottom panels
2	5 × 33 1/2″	Side panels
3	5 × 47 1/2″	Horizontals
6	5 × 8 1/2″	Verticals

18
Decorative Cedar Chest

A cedar chest is perfect for storing woolens, because the pleasant aroma of cedar repels moths. Consequently, there's no need to use chemicals to combat the voracious insect larvae.

This cedar chest can also double as a decorative accent table. If you have no need for a cedar chest, it can be left unlined and used for general storage. It makes a dandy firewood or kindling box.

Although you can build the chest from any kind of good-one-side plywood, I recommend hardwood plywood finished naturally. I used rough-sanded, cedar-faced paneling, which, though a softwood, was manufactured according to HPMA standards.

Whatever type of plywood you choose, it's important to lay it out and cut it so that corresponding lid and chest panels match exactly in grain and other features. Then mark the inside of each set of panels with a pen in the corners so they're easy to identify and match during construction.

The design calls for the use of picture-frame molding on the top and bottom of the chest, to conceal the plywood edges and add to the visual appeal. Pick a sim-

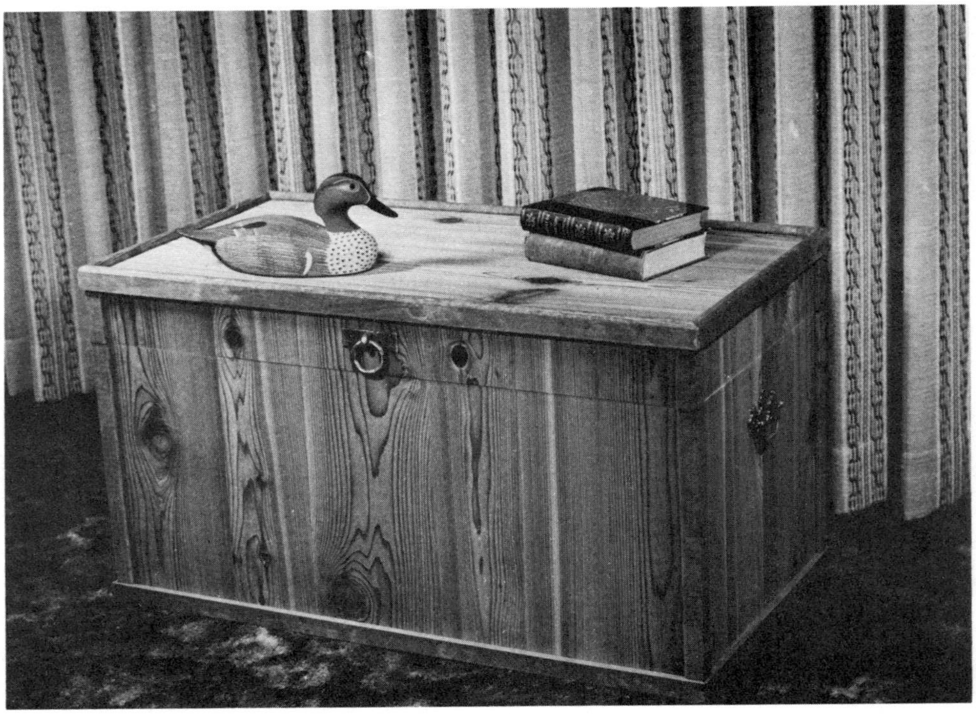

ple rounded, beveled, or squared molding, rather than one of the more expensive carved moldings.

You'll find a large assortment of suitable cabinet hardware available. I used antique brass drawer pulls for handles and a hammered antique brass pull for the lid lift. The hinges I chose were also brass. Manufactured lid supports are available, or you can do as I did and make your own.

The simple lid supports on my chest consist of two pairs of 1″ eye screws, two 14″ lengths of 1/8″ nylon rope, and two 1/2″ lengths of 1/4″-diameter pencil lead. You'll find pencil lead in the sporting-goods department at a local discount store or at tackle shops, where it is sold for fishing sinkers.

Do any necessary sanding of plywood panels before you begin construction. For a fine finish, simply follow the usual procedure outlined in Chapter 5. On my own chest, though, I wanted to retain the semirough appearance of the cedar face veneer, but I did not want any loose splinters showing. So I sanded with a pad sander and medium-grit sandpaper and finished the chest with Watco Natural Danish Oil to enhance the grain and bring out the rich character of the wood.

If you won't be using your chest for storing wool garments, simply skip the last construction step. If it will be a true cedar chest, though, you'll want to line it with aromatic cedar particleboard, which is made from Tennessee cedar and is normally stocked in 4 × 8′ sheets for use as closet lining. Sometimes it is available in smaller panels. You'll need less than a half-sheet for this project, so either use leftovers from a closet-lining job, or look for the smaller panels. If you have any difficulty finding the cedar lining locally, try your nearest Sears Catalog Store.

Step 4

Construction Steps

1. Cut four pieces of 1 × 4 to 32″ and four more to 14 1/2″.
2. Cut two pieces of 1 × 2 to 32″ and two more to 14 1/2″.
3. Prenail each end of each 32″ piece of 1 × 4 and 1 × 2 with two 1 1/2″ brads, about 3/8″ from the edge of the wood.
4. Put a dab of glue on one end of a 14 1/2″ piece of 1 × 2, butt it to one end of a prenailed 32″ piece, and clamp with a corner clamp. Drive the brads and countersink.
5. In the same way, attach the other 14 1/2″ piece of 1 × 2 to the opposite end of the 32″ piece and remove the corner clamps.
6. Similarly, butt-join the remaining 32″ piece to form a 16 × 32″ frame.
7. Using the same techniques, construct two identical 16 × 32″ frames with the 1 × 4 stock. Let all three frames stand for about an hour, or until glue sets.
8. Stand one 1 × 4 frame on end and apply a liberal amount of glue to the broad surface of one side piece. Lay a lid side panel in place, and clamp with two spring clamps or C-clamps. Attach the side panel to the frame with two 3/4″ brads at each end, and countersink. Leave clamps in place for thirty minutes, or until glue sets.
9. Rotate the frame and attach one of the 3 1/2 × 32 1/2″ panels to the adjacent side with glue and four clamps. Nail the ends, as in **Step 8,** and leave clamps in place until the glue sets. Attach remaining lid panels the same way. See page 84.
10. Run a bead of glue along the top edges of the lid frame, lay the top panel in place, and attach to the frame with 3/4″ brads, spaced about 6″ apart. Countersink brads.
11. Stand the other 1 × 4 frame on end and attach a chest side panel with glue and clamps. Then nail each end with two 3/4″ brads, and countersink.
12. Stand the 1 × 2 frame on end, and attach it to the other end of the chest side panel with glue and brads placed within 1/4″ of the edges. See page 84.
13. Rotate the unit and attach one of the 14 × 32 1/2″ panels the same way. Then attach the other side panel.

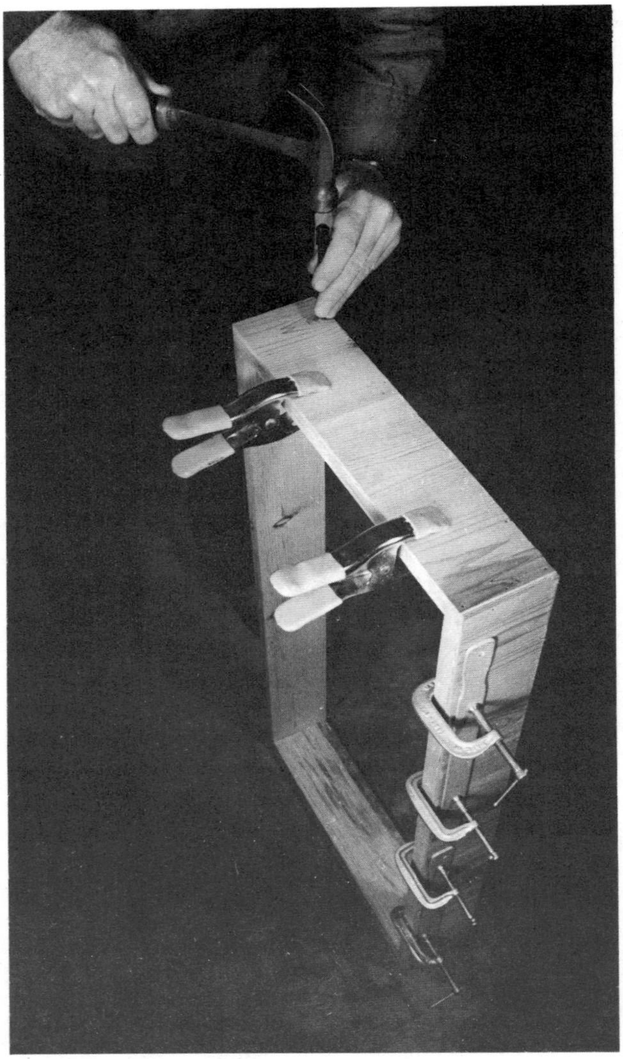

Step 9

14. Before attaching the remaining $14\frac{1}{4} \times 32\frac{1}{2}''$ panel, set the unit upright, with the 1 × 2 frame on the bottom, and run a bead of glue along the top edges of the 1 × 2.
15. Lay the bottom panel in place atop the 1 × 2 frame, and attach with $\frac{3}{4}''$ brads. Countersink brads.
16. Attach the remaining chest panel with glue and brads, and countersink the brads.
17. Double-check lid and chest dimensions; then use a mitre box and backsaw to mitre-cut four pieces of picture-frame molding to $16\frac{1}{2}''$ and four to $32\frac{1}{2}''$ (inside dimensions), or to fit lid and chest measurements.
18. Construct two $16\frac{1}{2} \times 32\frac{1}{2}''$ (inside diameter—I.D.) frames with glue and corner clamps. Drive one 1″ brad into each mitre joint, and countersink. Let frames stand until glue sets.

Step 12

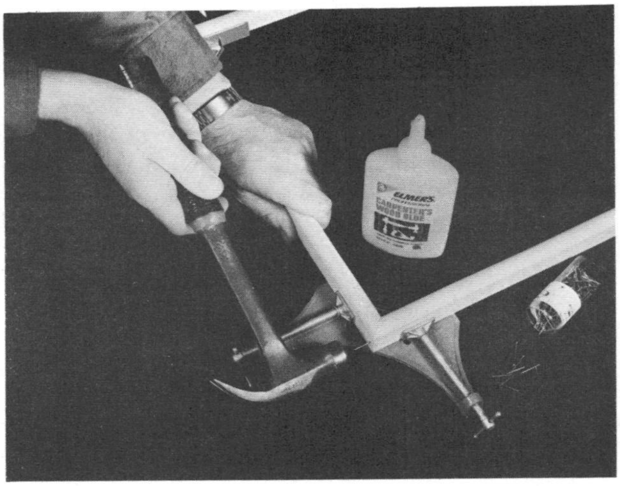

Step 18

19. Stain frames to match or contrast the plywood panels, and let dry.
20. Run a bead of glue along the inside of one frame and press it in place on the bottom of the chest. Secure it with two 1″ brads in each short frame section and three in each long section, and countersink.
21. Attach the other frame to the lid the same way.
22. Measure each corner edge of the chest and lid, and cut eight pieces of 1″ outside corner molding to fit.

Use medium-grit and fine-grit sandpaper to round over the bottom edges of the two rear lid pieces and the top edges of the two rear chest pieces.

23. Stain corner molding to match the frames, and let dry.

24. Attach corner molding with glue and ¾″ brads, and countersink.

25. In each chest end panel, drill holes for handles 3″ from the top. If mounting screws are too short, countersink the holes on the inside of the chest frame.

26. In the center of the front lid panel, drill holes for the lid lift the same way, and countersink from the inside if necessary.

27. Do any necessary final sanding and clean lid and chest to remove dust.

28. Apply the finish of your choice (sanding sealer and polyurethane varnish, or oil finish) and let dry.

29. Attach the lid to the chest with two hinges, each positioned 6″ from one end.

30. Attach handles and lid lift with mounting screws.

31. To make your own lid supports, start by measuring 6″ from the rear along each side piece of the lid frame and top chest frame and making a mark. Then measure 1″ inside the mark and punch a screw-starter hole with a nail set.

32. Drive a 1″ eye screw into each hole in each side frame piece.

Step 20

Step 33

33. Cut two pieces of ⅛″ nylon cord to 14″. Knot one end of each piece and run them through the screw eyes in the lid. Then, with the lid in a vertical position, run the cords through the eye screws in the chest, and knot the other ends. Trim away excess cord, then hold a burning match or cigarette lighter to the cord ends to fuse them and prevent fraying.

34. Cut two ½″ lengths of ¼″ pencil lead. Wrap each around one of the cords, just above the bottom knot, and crimp tight with pliers. (Lead weights will keep the cords running smoothly through the screw eyes as the lid is closed.)

35. Fill any visible brad holes with colored putty or wax filler stick to match the stain.

36. If you choose to line your chest with aromatic cedar, cut panels to fit the lid, bottom, and sides of the chest. Attach them with paneling adhesive or Weldwood Touch-n-Glue.

Required Tools

- Steel tape rule
- Pencil
- Claw hammer
- Nail set
- Center punch
- Mitre box and backsaw
- Four C-clamps or spring clamps
- Four corner clamps
- Paint brush
- Electric drill and bits
- Circular saw
- Saw guide

Required Materials

- One sheet of 1/4" hardwood plywood, graded good or better
- Half-sheet of 1/8" aromatic cedar particleboard
- 8′ of 1 × 2, graded standard or better
- 16′ of 1 × 4, graded standard or better
- 6′ of 1" outside corner molding
- 18′ of picture-frame molding
- White glue
- Paneling adhesive or Weldwood Touch-n-Glue
- 3/4" brads
- 1" brads
- 1 1/2" brads
- Medium-grit and fine-grit sandpaper
- Stain of choice
- Varnish or oil finish
- Three drawer pulls (handles and lid lift)
- Two 2 1/2" hinges
- Two lid supports (Optional—see text)

Plywood Panels

From a sheet of 1/4" hardwood plywood, graded good or better, cut the following panels:

QUANTITY	SIZE	NOMENCLATURE
1	16 1/2 × 32 1/2"	Lid top panel
2	3 1/2 × 32 1/2"	Lid front and rear panels
2	3 1/2 × 16"	Lid side panels
1	16 × 32"	Chest bottom panel
2	14 1/4 × 32 1/2"	Chest front and rear panels
2	14 1/4 × 16"	Chest side panels

19
Two-Drawer File Cabinet

Several years ago I needed three filing cabinets to store my business and personal files and records. After shopping around, I decided I could save money by building my own. I was right; the materials for the ones I built cost less than half of what I would have paid for the cheapest store-bought models, and I built the three cabinets over a weekend.

As my needs for file-storage capacity grew, I once again began looking at the commercially available cabinets, reasoning that I could afford to buy instead of build. So last year, when we moved into a new home and work complex, I bought four shiny, new, all-metal, full-suspension file cabinets. After a year's use, none of the drawers work smoothly, and two won't work at all without a lot of tugging and pounding.

Yet my old plywood cabinets continue to function perfectly. So, as you've probably guessed, I'm in the process of replacing my expensive cabinets with others I should have built in the first place.

I have improved the original design by including a full-face frame in the cabinet shell, and I have designed drawers that are easier to build. But the most important feature remains unchanged: the full-suspension, roller-bearing drawer slides used on each drawer. These are 24" channel-type slides with a load capacity of seventy-five pounds each. They're made by Knape & Vogt and should be available at your local home-improvement center. Ask for model 1300.

Should you experience any difficulty locating the slides, have a local dealer order them for you, or write the company for information:

Knape & Vogt Manufacturing Co.
2700 Oak Industrial Drive, NE
Grand Rapids, MI 49505

The hanging-file systems, such as Vertiflex and Pendaflex, are excellent for keeping file folders upright and organized. You should be able to find these at an office-supply outlet. Without them, you can keep standard file folders standing neatly in the drawers with inexpensive sheet-metal bookends, which you'll also find at an office-supply store and some discount department stores.

If you need greater capacity than this cabinet offers, consider the four-drawer model featured in Chapter 33.

Construction Steps

1. Cut six 2 × 2 verticals to 30½". Cut one 2 × 4 and two 2 × 2 horizontals to 14½".
2. Mark a line across two of the 30½" pieces 15½" from the bottom.
3. Prenail each of these verticals with two 8d finishing nails driven through the side, within 3½" of the bottom; two more above and within 1½" of the 15½" line; and two more within 1½" of the top.
4. Apply glue to the end of a 2 × 2 vertical, butt it to the top of one of the prenailed horizontals, and clamp in place with a corner clamp. Glue and clamp another 2 × 2 horizontal to the vertical with its bottom edge aligned with the 15½" line scribed in **Step 2.**
5. Apply glue to the end of the 2 × 4 horizontal; butt it to the vertical, flush with the bottom. Stand the assembly up on the verticals, then drive and countersink the nails.
6. Remove the clamps and attach them to the opposite ends of the 2 × 2 horizontals. Then clamp and glue the other prenailed vertical in place, and countersink the nails.
7. On the outside of each 25½ × 30½" side panel, scribe vertical pencil lines 1½" and 12¾" from the front edge and another 1¼" from the rear edge.
8. Turn the side panels over and on the inside of each scribe vertical lines ¾" and 12" from the front edge and another ½" from the rear edge.
9. Run a wavy bead of glue down one of the remaining 2 × 2 verticals, and clamp it to the inside of the side panel ½" inside the rear edge.
10. Glue and clamp another vertical 12" from the front edge.
11. Turn the panel over and nail it to the verticals with 1⅝" ring-shank paneling nails. To ensure a proper bond, stagger the nails ¼" each side of the guide lines scribed in **Step 7.**
12. Attach two verticals to the other side panel in the same way.
13. Scribe lines across each of these verticals at 3½" and 17" from the bottom.
14. Run a wavy bead of glue down the rear edge of the

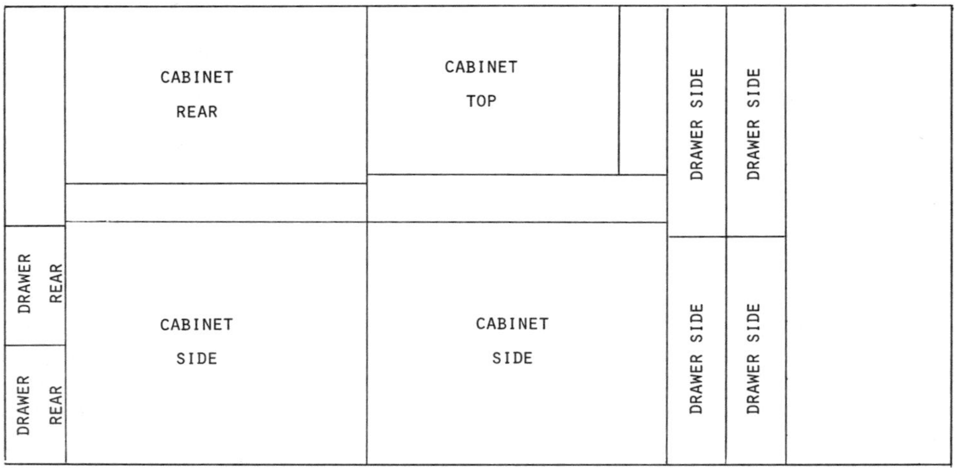

Cutting diagram for ½" plywood

rear vertical on each panel, and run another bead down the ½″ lip along the rear edge of each panel.

15. Fit the 17½ × 30½″ rear panel to the left side panel and clamp the top corner with a C-clamp or spring clamp. Do likewise with the right side panel.

16. Turn the unit to rest on its front edges, and clamp the bottom corners of the rear and side panels. Then nail the rear panel to the rear verticals with 1″ ring-shank paneling nails, spaced about 6″ apart. Countersink the nails.

17. Remove the clamps and set the unit upright. Clamp the top rear corners with corner clamps and leave them in place until the glue sets.

18. Apply a thin coat of glue with a paper towel to each side edge of the face frame. Spread the front of the side panels apart slightly and put the face frame in position between them. Align the face frame with the guide lines ¾″ from the front edges of the side panels, and clamp both sides top and bottom with C-clamps or spring clamps.

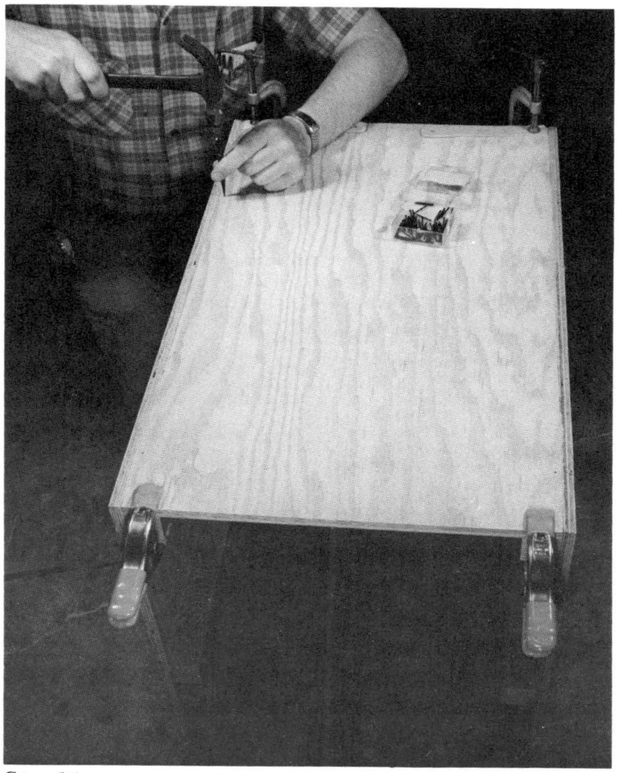

Step 16

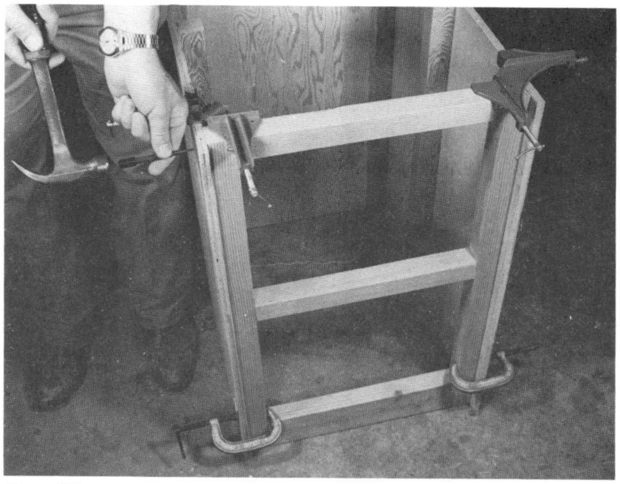

Step 19

Step 5

19. Attach the side panels to the face frame with 1″ paneling nails, spaced about 6″ apart and staggered along the guide lines scribed in **Step 7**. Countersink the nails.

20. Remove the clamps from the face frame; then clamp the top front corners with corner clamps and leave in place until the glue sets.

21. Turn the unit on its right side and lay a drawer channel marked C-R across the verticals, flush with the front of the face frame, resting against the 2 × 4 horizontal, and aligned with the lines scribed on the verticals in **Step 13.** Using the channel as a guide, mark each vertical for a screw-starter hole. Punch starter holes, and mount the drawer channel with screws provided.

22. Mount another C-R channel, the same way, at the center horizontal.
23. Turn the cabinet over and mount the C-L channels on the left side.
24. Stand the cabinet upright, remove the corner clamps, and apply glue to the top edges. Then attach the top panel with 1″ paneling nails along each edge and the top horizontal.
25. Cut six pieces of parting bead to 12½″ and four to 22½″.
26. Measure in 2″ from each end of four 12½″ pieces and mark for a centered hole. Punch a drill-starter hole at each spot. Then drill a 9⁄64″-diameter hole at each spot and countersink for #6 screws.
27. Prenail the remaining 12½″ pieces with three ⅞″ wire nails each. Prenail the 22½″ pieces with four ⅞″ wire nails.
28. Run a bead of glue down the back side of each prenailed 12½″ piece and nail it along the bottom edge of a 6 × 12″ drawer rear panel.
29. Run a bead of glue down the back side of each 22½″ piece of parting bead and nail along the bottom edge of a side panel, 1″ from the rear edge and ½″ from the front edge.
30. Run a bead of glue down the left edge of a drawer rear panel, butt it to the left side panel, and clamp the top corner with a corner clamp. Drive two 1″ paneling nails through the rear edge of the side panel into the rear panel, and countersink.
31. Attach the right side panel to the rear panel with glue, corner clamp, and paneling nails.
32. Apply glue to each end of a drilled 12½″ piece of parting bead. Slide it into position between the bottom front corners of the side panels, countersunk holes facing inside; attach it with one 1″ paneling nail at each end, and countersink.
33. Attach another drilled 12½″ piece with glue and paneling nails, flush with the top front corners.
34. Lay each assembly on its left side; then position drawer channel D-R on the right drawer panel, with the roller plate flush with the rear and bottom edges and the channel parallel with the bottom edge. Using the channel as a guide, mark for screw holes; then use a nail set to punch screw-starter holes, and attach the channel with screws provided.
35. Turn the drawer over and mount drawer channel C-L on the left side.
36. Drawer pulls should be mounted slightly below center. If you're using straight pulls, scribe a line

Step 23

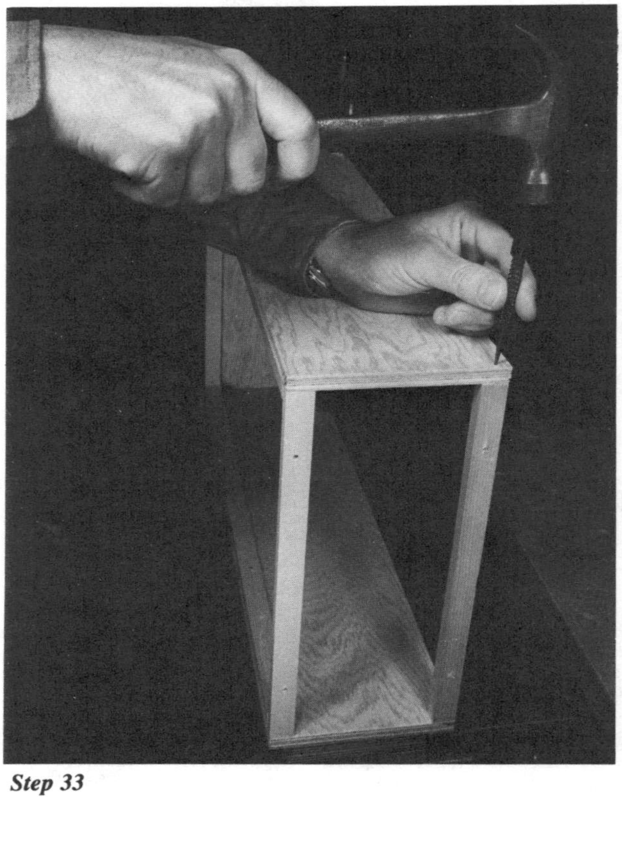

Step 33

Step 34

Step 40

across the front of each $13\frac{1}{2} \times 16\frac{1}{2}''$ drawer face 5″ from and parallel to the bottom edge. For offset pulls, line should be 6″ from the bottom.

37. Mark each line for drill-starter holes at $6\frac{3}{4}''$ and $9\frac{3}{4}''$ from one end. Center-punch a drill-starter hole and drill a hole at each spot large enough to accommodate drawer pulls.

38. Turn drawer faces over and scribe a line across each $\frac{9}{16}''$ from and parallel to the bottom edge. Measure in $1\frac{1}{2}''$ from each end and make a small perpendicular mark.

39. Run a bead of glue along the front edges of each drawer assembly; then lay it in place on the back of a drawer face, with the bottom parting-bead strip aligned with the horizontal line, between the vertical crossmarks. Clamp the parting bead to the drawer face with two spring clamps or C-clamps.

40. Insert a 1×6 flathead wood screw into each hole in the parting bead, tap lightly with a hammer to start, and drive.

41. For each drawer, cut a drawer bottom from $\frac{1}{4}''$ tempered hardboard to $12\frac{3}{8} \times 23\ \frac{3}{8}''$, or slightly under the inside dimensions of each drawer. Lay drawer bottoms atop the drawer cleats, or glue them to the cleats if you prefer.

42. Conceal plywood laminations, fill nail holes, and patch any imperfections with spackling paste, and let stand until paste cures.

43. Sand all exterior surfaces with medium-grit and fine-grit sandpaper.

44. Clean the cabinet and drawers with a vacuum cleaner to remove all dust. Then apply two coats of interior latex paint to the cabinet exterior and drawer faces. (Paint drawer faces with a contrasting color, if you wish.)

45. When paint has dried, install drawer pulls with mounting screws. Stick a self-adhesive drawer/door cushion (cork or felt) near each corner of each drawer opening on the face frame. Slide the drawers into the cabinet channels.

Required Tools

- Steel tape rule
- Combination square
- Pencil
- Claw hammer
- Nail set
- Mitre box and backsaw
- Four C-clamps
- Four corner clamps
- Paint brush
- Electric drill and bits, including #6 countersink
- Circular saw
- Saw guide
- Pad sander

Required Materials

One sheet of ½″ plywood, G1S
Two 13½ × 16½″ scraps of ¾″ plywood, G1S
Two 12⅜ × 23⅜″ pieces of ¼″ tempered hardboard
16′ of parting bead
18′ of 2 × 2, clear or patchable
3′ of 2 × 4, clear or patchable
White glue
Spackling paste
8d finishing nails
1″ ring-shank paneling nails
1⅝″ ring-shank paneling nails
⅞″ wire nails
Eight 1 × 6 flathead wood screws
Medium-grit and fine-grit sandpaper
Interior latex paint
Two sets of Model 1300 Knape & Vogt 24″ 75-pound-capacity drawer slides
Two drawer pulls
Eight self-adhesive drawer/door cushions

Plywood Panels

From a sheet of ½″ plywood, graded A-D or better, cut the following panels:

QUANTITY	SIZE	NOMENCLATURE
2	25½ × 30½″	Side panels
1	18½ × 25½″	Top panel
1	17½ × 30½″	Rear panel
4	6 × 24″	Drawer side panels
2	6 × 12½″	Drawer rear panels

20 Firewood Crib

Here's a simple and functional project that's attractive enough to display in any living room or family room. It holds an ample supply of firewood and doubles as an accent table.

Although my original plan called for the installation of a rear panel, I later decided to omit that piece. Since I planned to have the rear of the crib facing a wall, I did not need the rear panel for cosmetic purposes. Additionally, I decided that leaving the rear open would provide better ventilation to the firewood. Finally, eliminating the rear panel enabled me to build the crib with a half-sheet of plywood.

So, the rear-panel option is yours. If you prefer to include it, you'll need to buy eight extra corner braces. Mount the panel flush with the rear edges of the crib, using two corner braces on the top, bottom, and each side panel. Corner braces should be set $3/4''$ inside the rear edges of the unit.

If you want to duplicate the one I built, simply follow these steps.

Construction Steps

1. On the inside of each side panel, measure in 1½″ from each corner, along each 18″ edge, and scribe a 1½″-long line perpendicular to the 18″ edge.
2. Align a corner brace along each line, 1½″ from the front and rear edges, and use it as a guide to mark for screw-starter holes.
3. With a hammer and nail set, punch a screw-starter hole at each spot marked.
4. Mount four corner braces with screws on each side panel.
5. Lay the bottom panel on a bench top or other flat working surface. Butt a scrap of ¾″ plywood to each 18″ edge. Stand a side panel at one end of the bottom panel with the inside corner edges of the panels barely touching, so a ¾″ corner notch will be left when the scrap piece is removed.
6. Mark for and punch screw-starter holes; then attach the side panel to the bottom panel with screws and corner braces.
7. Attach the other side panel the same way.
8. Carefully invert the unit and stand it on the underside of the top panel. Attach the side panels to the top panel with screws and corner braces, leaving a ¾″ corner notch along each corner of the unit.

Step 6

Step 10

Step 15

9. Cut four pieces of ¾″ hardwood quarter-round to 18″.
10. Run a bead of glue down the flat edges of each piece of quarter-round and press each in place in one of the corner notches. Secure with two or three band clamps, and let the unit stand for an hour or until glue sets.
11. With a mitre box and backsaw, cut two pieces of hardwood 1 × 2 to 22″.
12. Mark each of these verticals for pilot holes 1½″ from each end and in the center. Marks should be located ⅜″ inside one edge of each vertical.
13. Use a hammer and center punch to make a drill-starter hole at each spot.
14. Drill a 5/64″-diameter pilot hole through the 1 × 2 at each spot.
15. Run a bead of glue down the front edges of each side panel. Lay the verticals in place with the outside edges flush with the unit's sides. Drive and countersink a 1¼″ brad at each pilot hole.

16. Measure the distance between the verticals and cut two hardwood 1 × 2 horizontals to fit.

17. Mark each horizontal for pilot holes 1″ and 10″ from each end and ⅜″ from one edge. Punch drill-starter holes and drill a pilot hole at each spot.

Required Tools

Steel tape rule	Two band clamps
Pencil	Electric drill and 5/64″ bit
Claw hammer	Circular saw
Nail set	Saw guide
Center punch	Pad sander
Mitre box and backsaw	
Two C-Clamps	

Required Materials

One sheet of ¾″ hardwood plywood, graded good or better
9′ of 1 × 2 hardwood to match plywood
12′ of ¾″ hardwood quarter-round molding to match plywood
White glue
Wood filler
1¼ brads
Medium-grit, fine-grit, extra-fine-grit, and #400 wet-or-dry sandpaper
#0000 Steel wool
Stain of choice
Varnish or oil finish
Paste wax (Optional—with oil finish)
Eight 1⅝″ brass corner braces

18. Run a bead of glue down the front edges of the top and bottom panels and apply a thin coat of glue to each end of each horizontal.

19. Press horizontals in place, flush with the unit's top and bottom surfaces, and attach with 1¼″ brads. Countersink brads.

20. Fill brad holes with wood filler and let stand until filler cures.

21. Use a pad sander to round over corners and sand all surfaces with medium-grit, fine-grit, and extra-fine-grit sandpaper. Then hand-sand with #400 wet-or-dry sandpaper and polish with #0000 steel wool.

22. Apply the stain of your choice according to the manufacturer's directions, or leave natural. Let stand until stain dries.

23. Apply two coats of polyurethane varnish, burnishing between coats with #0000 steel wool, or finish with Watco Natural Danish Oil.

24. If an oil finish is your choice, let the unit stand overnight; then apply two coats of paste wax to the exterior surfaces, and polish with a soft cloth.

Plywood Panels

From a sheet of ¾″ hardwood plywood, graded premium, cut the following panels:

QUANTITY	SIZE	NOMENCLATURE
2	18 × 30½″	Top and bottom panels
2	18 × 20½″	Side panels
1	20½ × 30½″	Rear panel*

*Rear panel is optional. Without it, the unit can be built from a half sheet.

21 Modern Accent Tables

If you're looking for a set of inexpensive accent tables for the living room or family room, stay away from the furniture stores and head for the lumberyard. There you can buy everything you'll need to make two end tables and a coffee table for less than a fourth of what you'd pay for comparable store-bought models. The tables can be built and finished in a single weekend with little effort.

A single sheet of plywood flooring is plenty for these three tables, with enough leftover for another table or two. Or you can enlarge the dimensions to fit your needs. If you don't need all three tables, perhaps you can build one or two from available scraps. One advantage of simple design is that it facilitates easy alterations. Decide what you need, make your own layout and cutting plan, and use the techniques described.

Finish preparations are a bit different for this project, mainly because the quality of the plywood is lower than what I have recommended for most other furnishings. But this design requires heavy, thick stock for the table tops and bases, and the only readily available plywood that fits the bill is flooring material, which is fairly

rough. It is, nevertheless, easy to bring up to furniture quality.

Most of the filling and sanding should be done prior to assembly. Use wood filler to plug large gaps in the laminations and other major open defects on the top surfaces of all panels. Then you should sand the panels and the legs to a fine finish *before* you build the tables.

Of course, the usual paint options are at your disposal, and if you will be using interior latex paint, there's no need to finish the tables beyond fine. For something different, though, you might wish to finish your tables as I did, with a plastic-smooth and lustrous appearance.

I took all surfaces down to an extra-fine finish with a pad sander, then hand-sanded with #400 wet-or-dry sandpaper. After assembly and additional sanding of filled areas, I cleaned the tables and applied three coats of flat black, oil-base enamel, burnishing between coats with #0000 steel wool to remove brush marks. After the final coat, I applied two coats of paste wax and buffed the tables to a semigloss finish with a soft cloth.

Finally, I stopped by the glass shop and bought two 18 × 18″ pieces and one 18 × 36″ piece of 1⁄4″ plate glass and had the edges seamed. I bought salvaged plate glass, by the way, which is considerably cheaper than new glass.

Construction Steps

1. Fill all open defects in the top surfaces and edges of all plywood panels with wood filler and let stand until filler cures.
2. With a mitre box and backsaw, cut six 1 × 2 coffee-table legs to 12¾″ and eight end table legs to 15¾″.
3. Use a pad sander to sand the tops and edges of plywood panels and legs with medium-grit and fine-grit paper. Sand undersides of plywood panels with medium-grit sandpaper to remove loose splinters and smooth the surfaces.
4. Set a combination square for ¾″; then measure in ¾″ from each corner on each plywood panel and mark for a drill-starter hole.
5. On the top and bottom coffee-table panels, measure 18″ down each 36″ edge, and make a mark ¾″ inside the edge.
6. Use a center punch to make a drill-starter hole at each spot; then drill a 13⁄64″-diameter hole at each. Countersink the tops of the holes in the top panels and the bottoms of the holes in the bottom panels for #10 screws.
7. Apply glue to the end of a 15¾″ leg and clamp it to the underside of an end table top panel, flush with the corner. Then attach the other three legs the same way, using corner clamps. See page 98.
8. Turn the unit over and drill a 9⁄64″-diameter hole through each existing corner hole, into the 1 × 2 legs. See page 98.
9. Attach each leg with a 2 × 10 flathead wood screw, and let the table stand, with clamps in place, for thirty minutes, or until glue sets.
10. Invert the table and attach the bottom panel the same way. See page 98.
11. Using the same tools and techniques, construct another end table.
12. Similarly, attach a 12¾″ leg to each corner of the coffee-table top panel and let stand, with clamps in place, until the glue sets.
13. Remove the clamps and use two of them to attach the center legs to the coffee-table top panel. Let stand for thirty minutes.
14. Invert the coffee table and attach the bottom panel the same way. As soon as the corner legs are secured with screws, remove two of the corner clamps and use them to attach the center legs. When those legs are secured, move those two clamps back to the

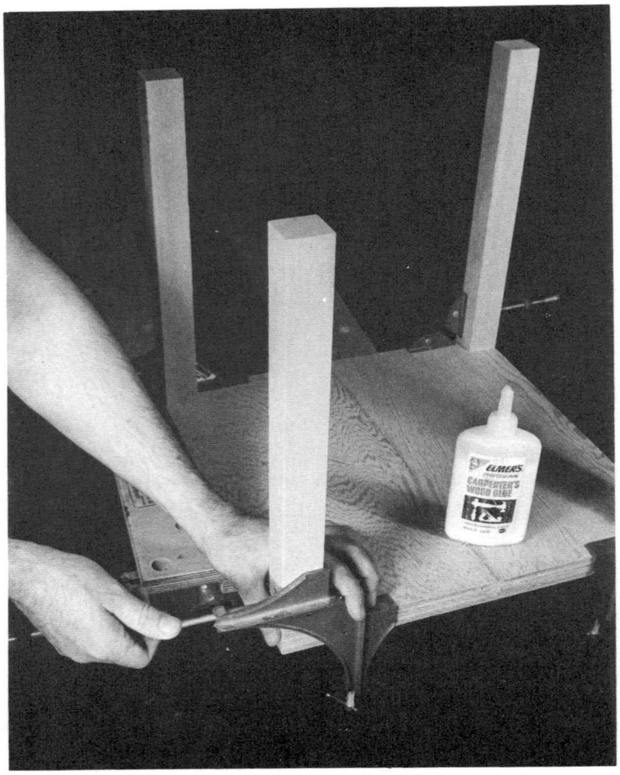

Step 7

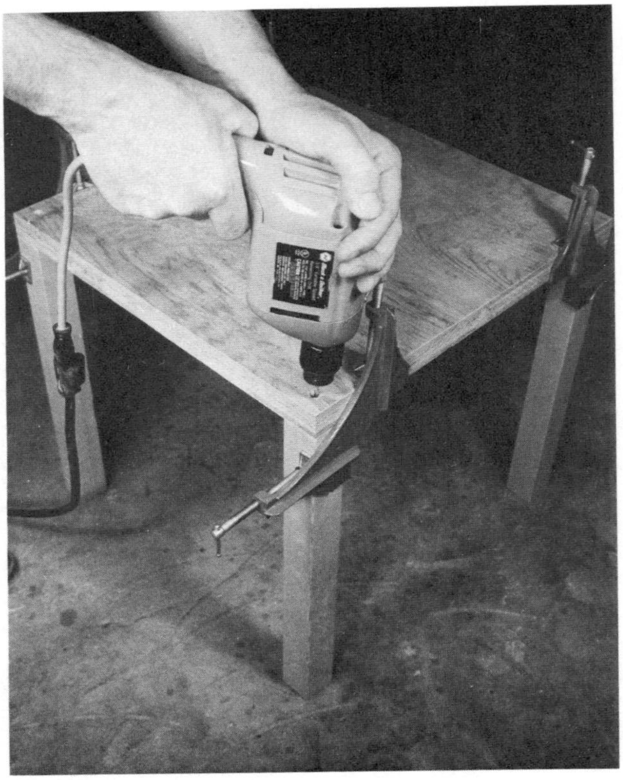

Step 10

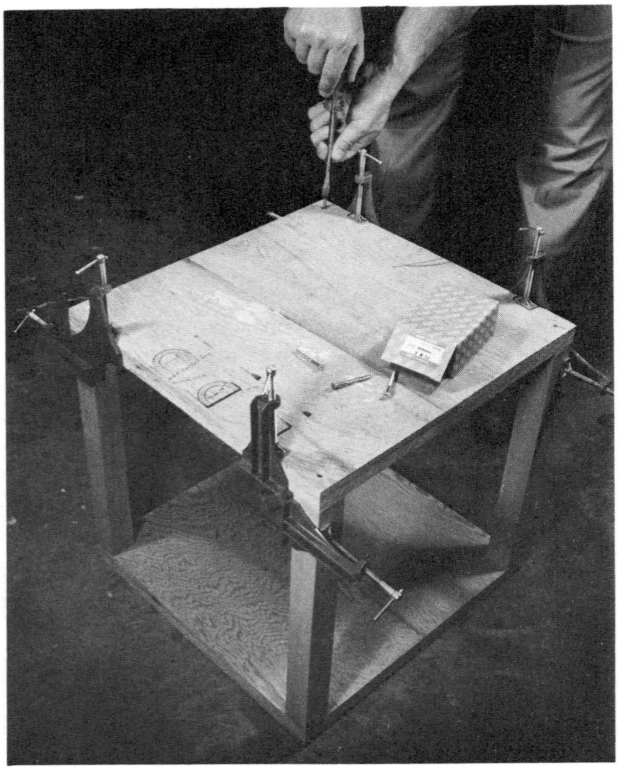

Step 8

corner legs and let the table stand with clamps at all corners until the glue sets.

15. Conceal the screw heads in the table tops and all leg joints with spackling paste and let tables stand until the paste hardens. Then sand with fine-grit sandpaper, and the tables are ready for cleaning and painting.

Required Tools

Steel tape rule	Four corner clamps
Combination square	Paint brush
Pencil	Electric drill and $^{9}/_{64}$", $^{13}/_{64}$", and #10 countersink bits
Claw hammer	Circular saw
Center punch	Saw guide
Screwdriver	Pad sander
Mitre box and backsaw	
Two C-clamps	

Required Materials

One sheet of $1\frac{1}{8}''$ plywood flooring, shop grade
18′ of 2 × 2, clear or patchable
White glue
Spackling paste
Wood filler
28 2 × 10 flathead wood screws
Medium-grit and fine-grit sandpaper
(Optional) Extra-fine-grit and #400 wet-or-dry sandpaper
(Optional) #0000 steel wool
(Optional) paste wax
Interior latex or paint or oil-base enamel
(Optional) Two 18 × 18″ and one 18 × 36″ pieces of $\frac{1}{4}''$ plate glass, with edges seamed

Plywood Panels

From a sheet of $1\frac{1}{8}$-inch shop-grade plywood flooring, cut the following panels:

QUANTITY	SIZE	NOMENCLATURE
4	18 × 18″	End table panels
2	18 × 36″	Coffee-table panels

22 Desktop Organizer and Light

Desk tops have a way of getting so cluttered that there often isn't enough surface space for the tasks at hand. One of the best ways to organize stationery, correspondence, notes, bills, labels, and tablets is to house them in a desktop organizer.

Such units are available from some office-supply outlets and mail-order companies. Most are made of sheet metal, and those that compare in size to the one featured here would cost you three or four times as much as what you'll pay for materials. Moreover, this desktop organizer has its own bulletin board and a built-in fluorescent light.

You have the option of making the small side shelves from the same ½″ plywood used for the rest of the unit or substituting glass or hardboard. If you decide on glass, use salvaged ¼″ plate; order four 9 × 12½″ pieces, and have one long edge on each seamed to remove sharp edges. If you have enough scraps of ¼″ hardboard they'll work as well.

You should note, however, that if you use something other than ½″ plywood for the side shelves, you will need only slightly more than a half-sheet for the rest of the panels. So you might want to take a look at some of the half-sheet projects (Part II) to see which ones are suitable for using up the leftovers.

Construction Steps

1. Use a router, router guide, and ½″ straight bit to rout a ¼″-deep groove across the front of the rear panel, 5″ from the top edge.
2. Rout another groove the same depth from the bottom to the first groove, 12½″ from and parallel to the right edge of the rear panel. Rout an identical groove from the first one to the bottom, 12½″ from the left edge.
3. Rout a ¼″-deep dado across the underside of the 47½″ shelf 12¼″ from the left edge and another 12¼″ from the right edge.
4. Clamp the two 9 × 24″ side panels side by side on a work surface, and rout a ½″-wide and ¼″-deep dado across both, simultaneously, 5″ from the top edge.
5. Now lay one of the 9¼ × 18¾″ uprights on each side of the two side panels and align the bottoms of all four panels until they're flush. Then, if you are using ½″ plywood for the side shelves, rout dadoes across all four panels at 11½″ and 15″ from the bottom. If you plan to use ¼″ plate glass or hardboard for the shelves, switch to a ¼″ straight router bit before making these last two passes.
6. Sand all surfaces with medium-grit and fine-grit sandpaper, and the unit is ready for assembly.
7. Run a bead of glue down the rear edge of the right side panel, butt it to the rear panel, and clamp with a corner clamp. Do the same with the left side panel.
8. Turn the unit over and nail the rear panel to each side panel with four 1″ ring-shank paneling nails. Countersink the nails.
9. Run a bead of glue along the inside of the top dado in the side panels and the groove in the rear panel. Slide the long shelf into the dadoes and push into the groove. Then drive and countersink a paneling nail through each side panel into the shelf, near the front edges.
10. Run a bead of glue down each dado on the underside of the shelf and the vertical grooves on the rear panel, and slide the uprights into them.
11. Drive and countersink a paneling nail through the top side of the shelf into the top edge of each upright, about ½″ from the front edge of the unit. See page 102.
12. Turn the unit over on its face, and drive and countersink a paneling nail through the rear panel into each upright, about 1″ from the bottom edge of the rear panel.
13. Turn the unit upside down, measure in 11″ from each upright, and scribe a centered line from front to rear on the underside of the shelf. Intersect that line with another centered horizontally on the shelf underside.

Step 2

Step 7

14. Measure the distance between the screw-mounting holes on the under-cabinet light fixture (usually 12″ or 13″ on an 18″ unit), and mark for screw holes on the centered horizontal line scribed in **Step 13.** Then use a nail set or scratch awl to punch screw-starter holes.
15. Drill a ¼″-diameter hole through the rear panel, near the shelf, and on the side where the light-fixture cord will be located.

16. Cut a piece of 1 × 2 to 22″ and apply a thin coat of glue to the top edge and sides. Fit it into position along the front underside of the shelf, between the uprights, clamp with three or four C-clamps, and let stand until the glue sets.
17. Conceal plywood laminations and fill nail holes and any imperfections with spackling paste and let the unit stand until the paste hardens.
18. Sand spackled surfaces with medium-grit and fine-grit sandpaper.
19. Scribe two horizontal lines across the center section of the rear panel 4″ and 16″ from the bottom.
20. Clean dust from all surfaces; then apply two coats of interior latex paint to all surfaces, except for the area between the lines scribed across the center section in **Step 19.** Also, avoid getting paint into the side-shelf dadoes.
21. When paint has dried, apply a thin, even coat of all-purpose adhesive to the unpainted area of the center section, and spread it with an adhesive spreader.
22. Trim a sheet of wall cork to 12 × 22″ and lay it in place on the center section. Use a J-roller or block of wood and hammer to firmly set the cork in the adhesive.
23. Drive the light-fixture mounting screws into the holes punched in the underside of the shelf.
24. Use wire cutters or wire-cutting pliers to snip the plug off the end of the light-fixture cord.
25. Mount the light fixture to the underside of the shelf and run the cord through the hole in the rear panel. Then attach a snap-on plug to the end of the cord.
26. Attach a self-adhesive cork cabinet-door cushion or self-adhesive felt at each front and rear corner of the bottom of the unit.
27. Slide the side shelves into the dadoes.

Step 16

Step 11

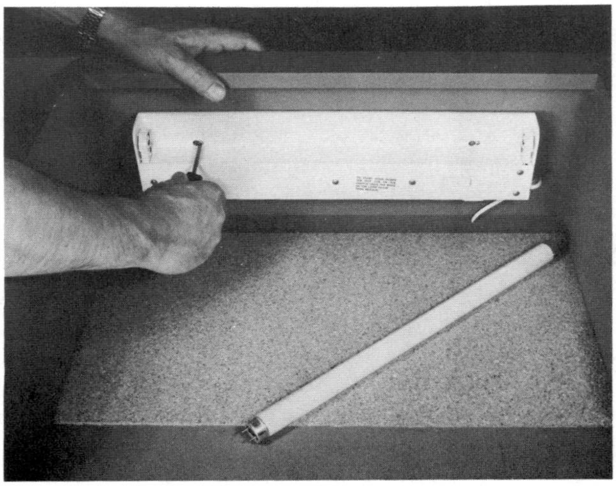

Step 25

Required Tools

- Steel tape rule
- Pencil
- Claw hammer
- Nail set
- Center punch
- Screwdriver
- Four C-clamps
- Two corner clamps
- Wire cutters
- Paint brush
- Adhesive spreader
- J-roller
- Electric drill and 1/4" bit
- Circular saw
- Saw and router guide
- Pad sander
- Router and 1/2" straight bit
- (Optional) 1/4" straight router bit

Required Materials

- One sheet of 1/2" plywood, G2S
- 2' of 1 × 2, clear
- White glue
- All-purpose adhesive
- Spackling paste
- 1" ring-shank paneling nails
- Medium-grit and fine-grit sandpaper
- Interior latex paint
- One 12 × 22" piece of wall cork
- (Optional) Four 9 × 12 1/2" pieces of 1/4" plate glass with one 12 1/2" edge seamed
- One 18" under-cabinet fluorescent light
- One snap-on electrical plug
- Four self-adhesive drawer/door cushions

Plywood Panels

From a sheet of 1/2" plywood, graded A-C or better, cut the following panels:

QUANTITY	SIZE	NOMENCLATURE
1	24 × 48"	Rear panel
2	9 × 24"	Side panels
2	9 1/4 × 18 3/4"	Uprights
1	9 1/4 × 47 1/2"	Shelf
4	9 × 12 1/2"	Shelves*

*Omit the four small shelves if you prefer to use glass or hardboard instead.

23
A Pair of Nightstands

These nightstands were designed with roomy tops and handy drawers. Each features a large shelf that will hold books, magazines, jewel chests, or other items. If you're in need of a chest of drawers for the bedroom, you might want to plan to build the one in Chapter 31, which was designed to match the nightstands.

The plan calls for ¾″ plywood drawer faces, and you should have no trouble finding suitable scraps. The plate-glass tops are optional, but they are handsome additions that improve the durability of the nightstand tops. Be sure to ask for salvaged ¼″ plate glass, and have all edges seamed to remove the sharp edges.

Although the instructions say to join the nightstand panels with glue and screws, you can substitute 1″ ring-shank paneling nails for the screws.

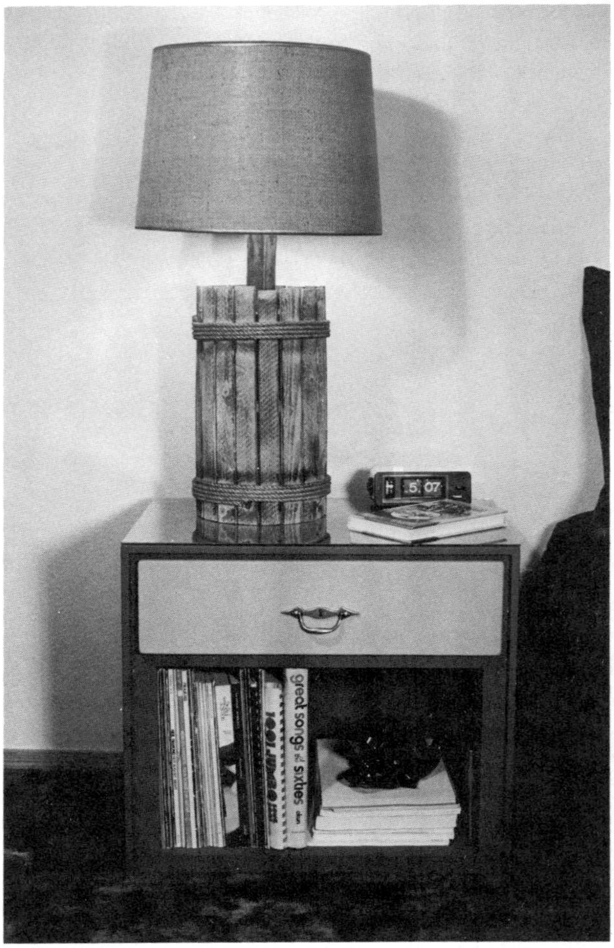

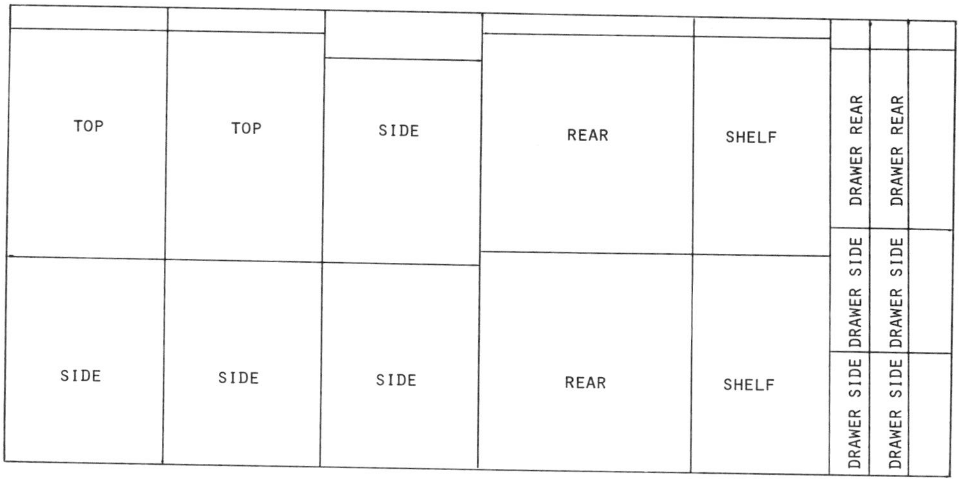

Cutting diagram for $\frac{1}{2}''$ plywood

Construction Steps

1. With a mitre box and backsaw, cut four 1 × 2 verticals to $21\frac{1}{2}''$ and six 1 × 2 horizontals to 20″.
2. Scribe a line across each $21\frac{1}{2}''$ piece 14″ from the bottom.
3. Apply glue to one end of a 20″ horizontal, butt it to the inside edge of a $21\frac{1}{2}''$ vertical (flush with the top edge of the vertical, to form an el), and staple the two pieces together with three staples.
4. Apply glue to the end of another horizontal and butt it to the inside edge of the vertical, with the bottom edge of the horizontal aligned with the line scribed in **Step 2;** then staple the two pieces together.
5. Glue, butt, and staple another horizontal to the bottom inside edge of the vertical to form a large letter E.
6. Gently rotate the vertical to lift the other ends of the horizontals and apply glue to those ends.
7. Butt another vertical to the ends of the horizontals and attach with glue and staples at each joint.
8. Lightly clamp the face frame with a bar clamp across the top and another across the bottom, and allow the glue to set for about an hour.
9. Construct another identical face frame with the remaining pieces of 1 × 2.
10. On the inside of each $21\frac{1}{2} \times 23''$ rear panel, scribe a line $6\frac{3}{4}''$ from and parallel to the top 23″ edge. Then make cross marks on the line at $8\frac{1}{2}''$, $11\frac{1}{2}''$, and $14\frac{1}{2}''$ from one end.
11. Measure $11\frac{1}{2}''$ down the top edge and make a mark; then scribe a line from that mark to the $11\frac{1}{2}''$ mark on the line scribed in **Step 10.**
12. Scribe another line parallel to and 1″ from the bottom edge of each rear panel.

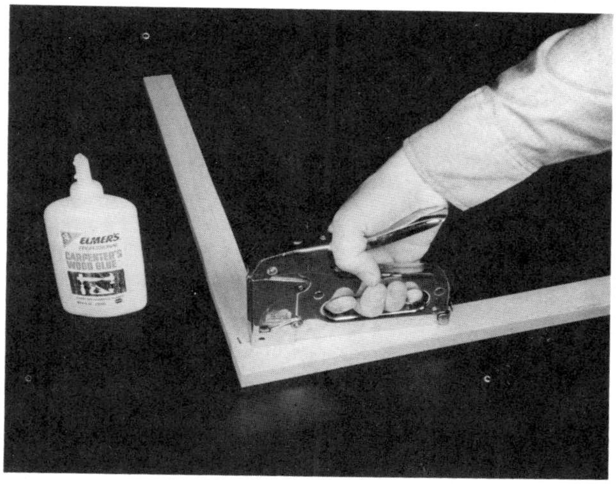

Step 3

13. Use a mitre box and backsaw to cut four drawer-guide supports to 6″ and four shelf cleats to 23″, all from ¾″-square molding.
14. For each rear panel, prenail a drawer-guide support with two 1″ brads and a shelf cleat with five.
15. Run a bead of glue down the underside of the drawer-guide support and press it in place immediately beneath the line scribed in **Step 10,** centered between the marks at 8½″ and 14½″. Drive and countersink the brads.
16. Similarly, attach the shelf cleat immediately beneath the line scribed in **Step 12.**
17. On the inside of each face frame, measure across the middle horizontal and make pencil marks at 8½″ and 14½″.
18. Scribe a line parallel to and 1″ from the bottom of the frame.
19. On each face frame, attach a drawer-guide support with glue and 1″ brads between the marks made in **Step 17,** flush with the bottom edge of the middle horizontal.
20. Prenail the remaining shelf cleats with 1″ brads; then attach each to the inside of a face frame with glue and brads, immediately beneath the line scribed in **Step 18.**
21. Use spackling paste to fill joint seams and any imperfections on the front of the face frames and let frames stand until paste sets up. Then sand with medium-grit and fine-grit sandpaper.

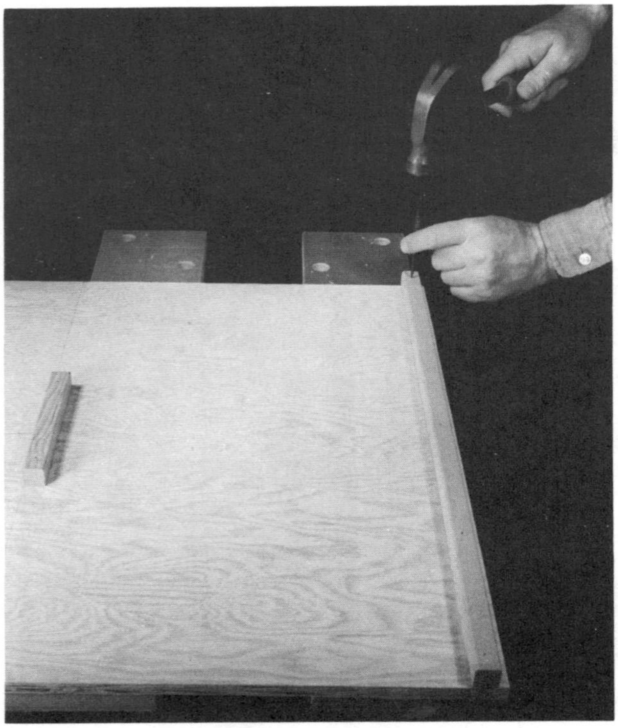

Step 16

22. On the inside of each side panel, scribe a line 1½″ inside and parallel to the front edge.
23. Turn each side panel over and scribe another line on each 1⅛″ inside and parallel to the front edge. Scribe another ¼″ from and parallel to the rear edge. Then mark each line at 1″, 7½″, 14″, and 20½″ from one end.
24. Center-punch a drill-starter hole at each spot marked in **Step 24.** Then at each spot, drill a 9/64″-diameter hole and countersink for #6 screws.
25. With a mitre box and backsaw, cut four pieces of parting bead to 19″. Prenail each with four ⅞″ brads.
26. Run a bead of glue down the underside of each piece of parting bead; then lay each in place on the inside of a side panel, along the inside of the line scribed in **Step 23,** one end flush with the top edge of the panel. Drive and countersink the brads.
27. Run a bead of glue down the front edge of one of the pieces of parting bead and down the inside of the side panel along the screw-hole line.
28. Fit one side of a face frame in place against the side panel and parting bead, and clamp the frame to the parting bead with a pair of spring clamps or C-clamps.
29. Insert a 1 × 6 flathead wood screw into each front hole in the side panel, tap lightly with a hammer to start, and drive.
30. Run a bead of glue down one side edge of the rear panel. Butt it to the rear edge of the side panel and turn the unit to stand with the side panel up. Clamp one corner of the rear and side panel with a corner clamp. While holding the opposite corner tightly, tap and drive a screw at the nearest hole. Drive the remaining three screws into the rear panel.
31. Set the unit upright, and run a bead of glue down the top of each shelf cleat. Lay the 14 × 23″ shelf atop the cleats and attach the shelf *to the front cleat only* with five 1″ brads.
32. Set the unit on its side and run a bead of glue down the remaining edge of the rear panel and another down the edge of the face frame, as well as the front edge of the parting bead on the remaining side panel.
33. Lay the side panel in place. Clamp the face frame to the parting bead with spring clamps or C-clamps and the top rear corner with a corner clamp. Attach the side panel with screws. Then assemble another nightstand the same way.
34. With a mitre box and backsaw, cut two pieces of 1 × 2 and two pieces of ¾″-square molding to 14″.
35. On the top of each end of each piece of ¾″-square molding, make a centered mark. Do likewise on a ¾″ edge of the 1 × 2 pieces.
36. Measure down the top edge of the rear panel of each

Step 29

Step 30

Step 31

unit and make a mark at 12″. Do the same on the top of each face frame. Then make another mark, top center, on the middle horizontal of the face frame.

37. Prenail each piece of $\frac{3}{4}$″-square molding with a 1″ brad at each end. Apply a spot of glue to the center of each drawer-guide support. Press a $\frac{3}{4}$″-square guide in place, using the pencil marks on the guide and the unit for alignment. Then drive and countersink the brads.
38. Apply a thin coat of glue to each end of a 1 × 2 and put it in place between the face frame and rear panel, flush with the top edges and centered on the pencil marks. Drive two $1\frac{1}{4}$″ brads through the face frame and two through the rear panel into the 1 × 2 ends and countersink. Do the same on the other unit.
39. On each top panel, scribe a line $1\frac{1}{8}$″ from and parallel to the front edge and another $\frac{1}{4}$″ from the rear edge. Mark each of these at 1″, $8\frac{1}{2}$″, $15\frac{1}{2}$″, and 23″.
40. Measure down each side of each top panel and make a centered mark $\frac{1}{4}$″ from the edge.
41. Center-punch each spot; then drill a $\frac{9}{64}$″-diameter hole at each and countersink for #6 screws.

Step 38

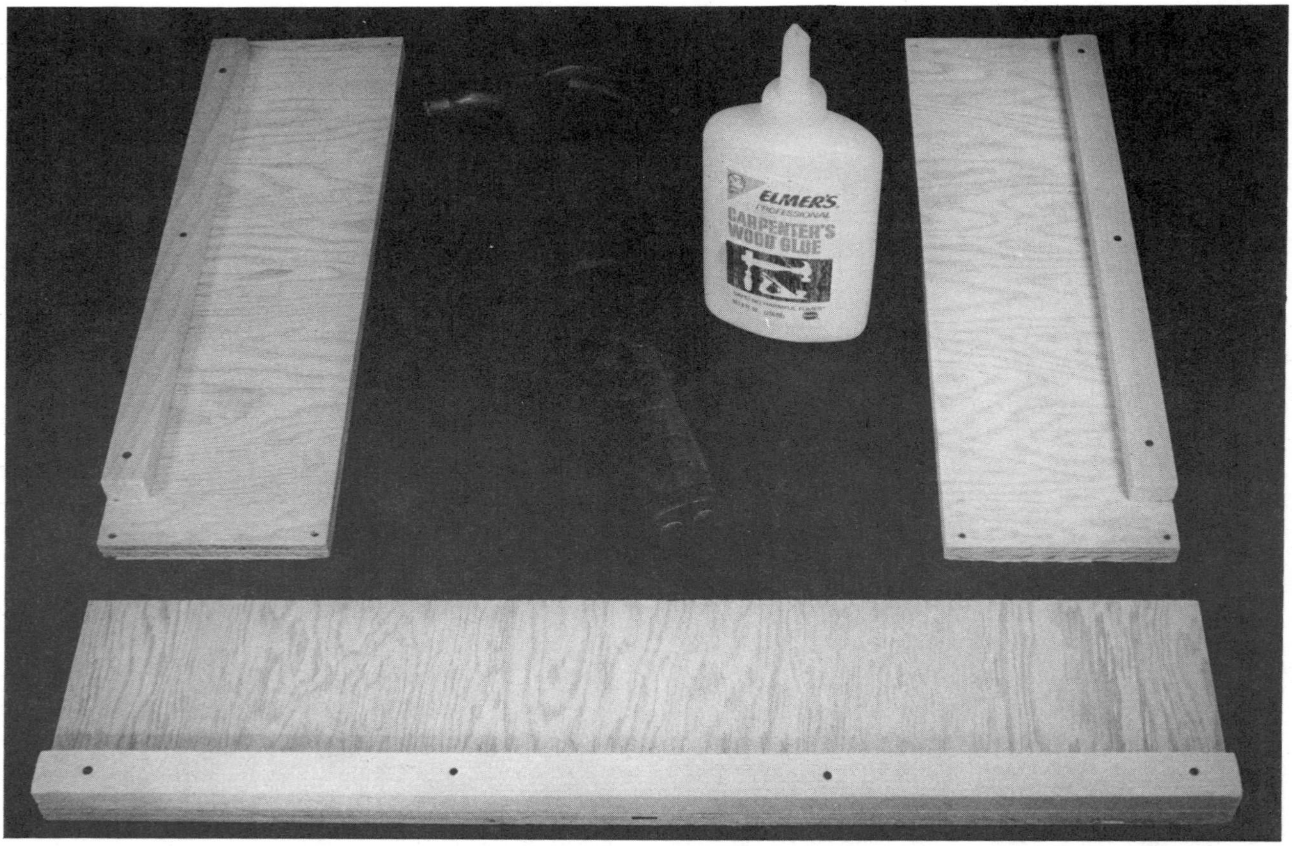

Step 47

42. Apply glue to the top edges of the units, and attach tops with 1 × 6 screws.
43. With a mitre box and backsaw, cut four pieces of parting bead to 12½″ and six to 18¾″. Use a combination square to scribe lines across four of the long pieces 2½″ from the ends. Then mark the centers of these lines for drill-starter holes.
44. Center-punch a drill-starter hole at each spot. Then drill a 9/64″-diameter hole at each spot and countersink for #6 screws.
45. Use a combination square to mark the outside of each 4 × 14″ drawer side panel for a drill-starter hole ¼″ inside each corner. Punch a starter hole at each spot; then drill a 9/64″-diameter hole and countersink for #6 screws.
46. Prenail each undrilled 18¾″ piece of parting bead with four ⅞″ wire nails and the four shorter pieces with three nails each.
47. For each drawer, glue and nail a long piece of parting bead along the inside bottom of the drawer rear panel. Then glue and nail a short piece along the inside bottom of each drawer side, 1″ from the rear edge and ½″ from the front edge.
48. Run a bead of glue down one side edge of a rear panel and butt a side panel to it, using a corner clamp to secure it if necessary. Then tap and drive a 1 × 6 flathead wood screw at each corner.
49. Apply a dab of glue to the end of one of the drilled pieces of parting bead, fit it into the notch at the bottom corner of the side panel, and tap and drive a screw into it. Then apply glue to the end of another piece and butt it to the top corner with a corner clamp. Tap and drive a screw into this piece. (Make sure countersunk holes face the drawer inside.)
50. Use corner clamps to hold the remaining side panel while you glue and screw it in place. Let the drawer stand with corner clamps attached until glue sets.
51. From available scraps of ¾″ plywood, cut two drawer faces to 6 × 22″ each.
52. On each drawer face, scribe a horizontal pencil line 3″ from the top and bottom edges. For standard pulls, mark that line at 9½″ and 12½″ from one end. Then center-punch drill-starter holes at the spots.
53. Drill a hole at each spot to fit the drawer-pull screws. (Standard: 11/64″-diameter.)
54. On the inside of each drawer face, scribe a line ⅝″ from and parallel to the bottom edge. Then scribe a perpendicular line 1⅛″ inside each end.
55. Run a bead of glue down each piece of parting bead on each drawer assembly; then lay the assembly on the back side of the drawer face, with the bottom strip aligned with the horizontal line on the drawer face, between the vertical marks. Then attach each drawer assembly to a face with four ¾ × 6 flathead wood screws.

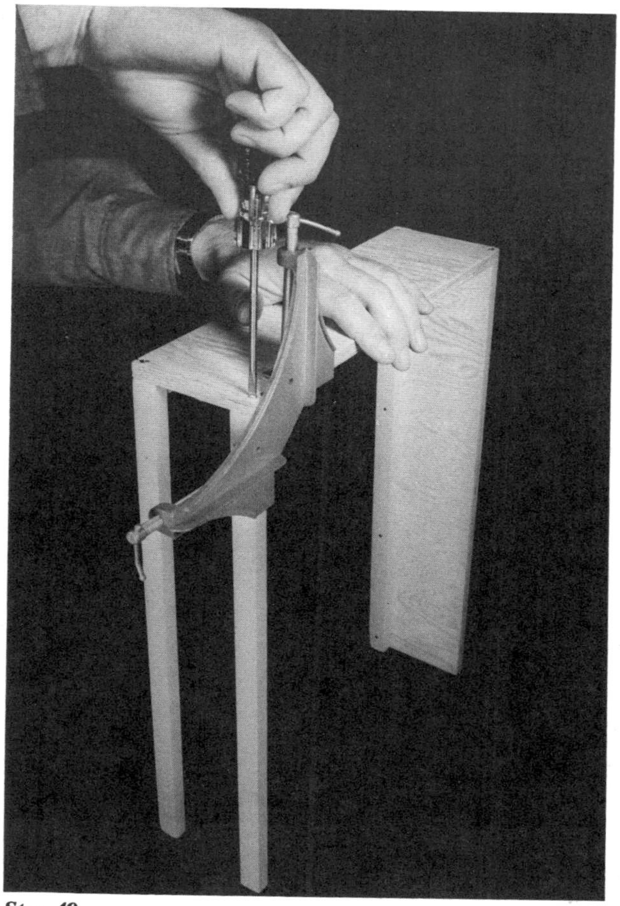

Step 49

Step 55

56. Use spackling paste to conceal all visible plywood laminations and imperfections and to fill screw and nail holes.
57. After spackling paste has cured, sand the units and drawer faces with medium-grit and fine-grit sandpaper. Clean the units and apply two coats of interior latex paint to all exterior surfaces. Use a contrasting color on drawer faces if you wish.
58. Double-check the inside dimensions of the drawers (should be 13½ × 18¾″), and cut two drawer bottoms from ¼″ tempered hardboard. If you plan to glue the drawer bottoms to the cleats, do so now. Otherwise, you can simply lay the bottoms atop the cleats later.
59. Install a Roll-eez™N roller on each side of the middle horizontal on each nightstand and another top center on each drawer rear panel. Install a Roll-eez M roller bottom center on each drawer rear panel.
60. Attach drawer pulls with screws. Then stick a self-adhesive cork drawer/door cushion near each corner of the drawer opening on each nightstand. Slide the drawers into the stands.

Step 59

Required Tools

Steel tape rule
Combination square
Yardstick
Pencil
Claw hammer
Nail set
Center punch
Screwdriver
Mitre box and backsaw
Two C-clamps
Two 24″ or larger bar clamps
Four corner clamps
Staple gun
Paint brush
Electric drill and bits, including #6 countersink
Circular saw
Saw guide
Pad sander

Plywood Panels

From a sheet of ½″ plywood, graded A-D or better, cut the following panels:

QUANTITY	SIZE	NOMENCLATURE
2	16 × 24″	Top panels
4	16 × 21½″	Side panels
2	21½ × 23″	Rear panels
2	14 × 23″	Shelves
4	4 × 14″	Drawer side panels
2	4 × 18¾″	Drawer rear panels

Required Materials

One sheet of ¼″ plywood, G1S
Two 6 × 22″ scraps of ¾″ plywood, G1S
Two 13½ × 18 ¾″ pieces of ¼″ tempered hardboard
22′ of parting bead
16′ of ¾″-square molding
22′ of 1 × 2, clear
White glue
Spackling paste
1″ brads
1¼″ brads
⅜″ staples
⅞″ wire nails
60 1 × 6 flathead wood screws
Interior latex paint
Eight self-adhesive door/drawer cushions
Two sets of Roll-eez ™ drawer rollers
(Optional) Two 16 × 24″ pieces of ¼″ plate glass with seamed edges

24
A Roll-Around Utility Cabinet

This roomy, sturdy cabinet on casters can be stored anywhere and wheeled to work whenever you need it. Inexpensive materials make it economical and the simple tools and techniques will allow you to build it over a weekend.

My own cabinet has experienced several incarnations since I first built it. I originally used it as an enlarger stand and cabinet that housed all my photographic papers, chemicals, easels, trays, and a wide assortment

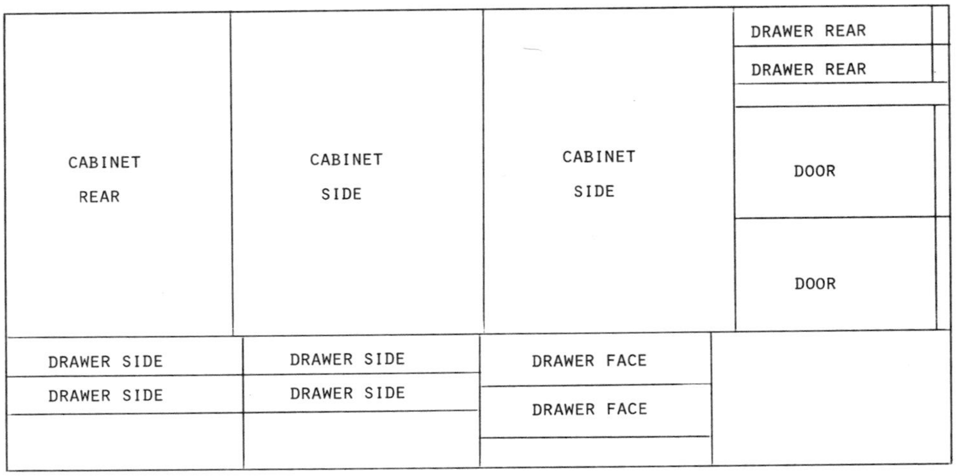

Cutting Diagram for ½" plywood

of darkroom accessories. It stood in the utility room when not in use, and I could easily roll it into the bathroom whenever I planned a day of printing. When we built a new home with a darkroom, I moved the cabinet to my workshop, where it functioned as a spacious tool cabinet. I am now repainting it to match my studio furnishings and it will be moved into that room to perform storage-cabinet duties.

If you will be using the unit on hard floors or concrete, buy rubber-wheeled casters. But if you'll be wheeling it over carpets, get the ball-type casters. Some of the latter come with removable nylon or plastic rim covers that permit their use on either hard or carpeted surfaces.

If you don't need a mobile cabinet, you can mount it instead on a base made of 2 × 4's. Two cabinets can be used as pedestals for a bench top, providing a sturdy, attractive workbench with plenty of storage space for tools and materials.

Construction Steps

1. From ¾" particleboard, cut a 23 × 25½" cabinet top, 23 × 25" cabinet bottom, and 23 × 24" shelf. (You can substitute ¾" plywood if you have suitable scraps available.)
2. Scribe lines across the inside of each cabinet side panel at 4⅝", 6¼", 10½", 12⅛", and 20" from the top and on the cabinet rear panel 20" from the top. Then on the side and rear panels, scribe lines ¾" from and parallel to the top and bottom edges.
3. Use a mitre box and backsaw to cut four 24¾" pieces, seven 20" pieces, and six 10" pieces of ¾"-square molding.
4. Prenail each piece of ¾"-square molding with 1" brads, spaced about 4" apart.

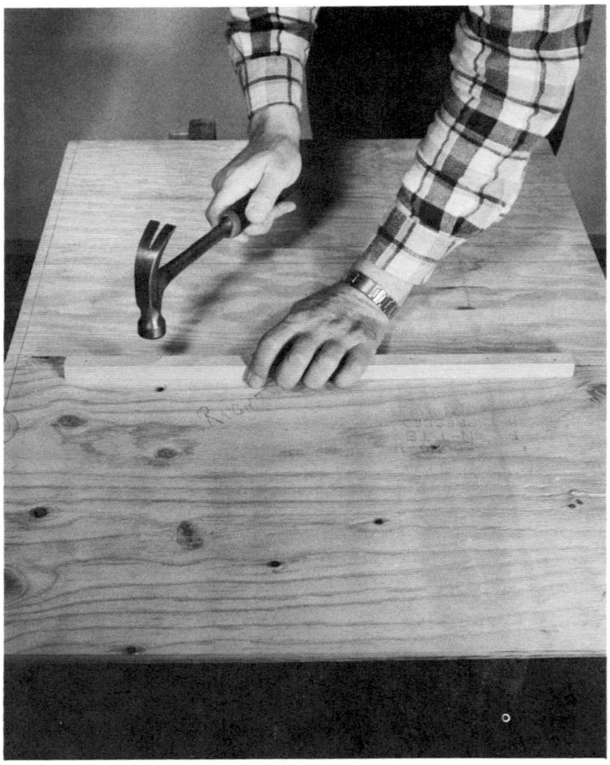

Step 5

5. Run a bead of glue along each of the 20" shelf cleats, center each immediately beneath one of the lines on the side and rear panels that are 20" from the top, and attach with brads. Countersink the brads.
6. To the inside of each cabinet side panel, attach the 24¾" drawer supports with glue and brads ⅛" inside the front edges of the panels and aligned immediately above the 6¼" and 12⅛" lines scribed in **Step 2.**

Step 7

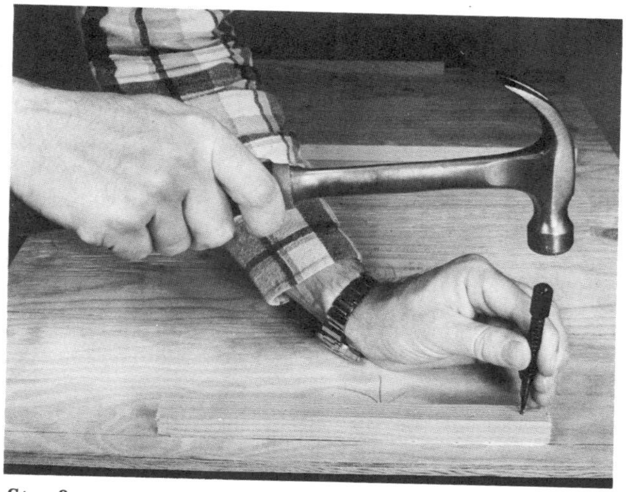

Step 8

Step 12

7. Attach the 20″ pieces of ¾″-square molding with glue and brads ⅛″ inside the front edges of the side panels, aligned just above the 4⅝″ and 10½″ lines scribed in **Step 2.**
8. On the rear panel and each side panel, attach a 10″ piece of ¾″-square molding immediately beneath and centered along the line that's ¾″ from the top, and attach another 10″ piece just above the line that's ¾″ from the bottom. Countersink all brads.
9. On the outside of the rear and side panels, scribe lines ⅜″ inside and parallel to the top and bottom edges. Scribe lines ¼″ inside and parallel to the rear edges of the side panels.
10. Mark for drill-starter holes about every 6″ along the lines scribed in **Step 9;** then center-punch a starter hole at each spot.
11. Drill a 9/64″-diameter hole at each spot, and countersink for #6 screws.
12. Run a bead of glue along the left edge of the rear panel. Butt it to the left side panel and clamp the corners with corner clamps. Then attach the panels with ¾ × 6 flathead wood screws. (It's easy if you stand the clamped panels up pup-tent style.)
13. Glue and clamp the right side panel to the rear panel the same way, and fasten with screws.
14. Apply glue to the 10″ top supports and to the left, right, and rear edges of the cabinet top. Lay the top on the supports, butted against the side and rear panels. Attach the top with wood screws; then turn the unit upside down and attach the bottom the same way.
15. Apply glue to the shelf cleats and lay the shelf atop the cleats. Let the unit stand until the glue sets.
16. Use a mitre box and backsaw to cut three pieces of 1 × 2 to 23″ and one to 19¼″
17. Run a bead of glue down one narrow edge of a 23″ piece of 1 × 2 and clamp it to the underside of the cabinet top, flush with the front edges of the side panels. (Note: Top overhangs ½″.)

18. Measure $4\frac{3}{8}''$ down each side panel from the piece of 1×2 installed in **Step 17** and make a pencil mark on the inside of each panel. Then, measure down from the top of each side panel and make marks at $7\frac{1}{8}''$ and $7\frac{3}{4}''$ from the top and $\frac{3}{8}''$ from the front edges.
19. Center-punch drill-starter holes at the marks on the outside of the side panels; then drill a $\frac{9}{64}''$-diameter hole at each spot and countersink for #6 screws.
20. Apply glue to each end of a 23″ piece of 1×2 and position it horizontally between the side panels, $4\frac{3}{8}''$ below the top piece, and attach with two $\frac{3}{4} \times 6$ wood screws in each end.
21. Measure in $11\frac{1}{8}''$ from each end of the last 23″ piece of 1×2 and mark for centered drill-starter holes on a narrow edge. Center-punch and drill an $\frac{11}{64}''$-diameter hole at each spot and countersink for #8 screws.
22. Apply glue to one end of the $19\frac{1}{4}''$ piece of 1×2, butt it to the center of the drilled piece opposite the holes, and clamp the pieces together with a corner clamp to form a T. Attach the two with two 2×8 flathead wood screws.
23. Lay the cabinet on its back; then mark for drill-starter holes $11\frac{5}{8}''$ from each end of the bottom panel and $\frac{3}{8}''$ inside the front edge. Drill a $\frac{9}{64}''$-diameter hole at each spot and countersink for #6 screws.

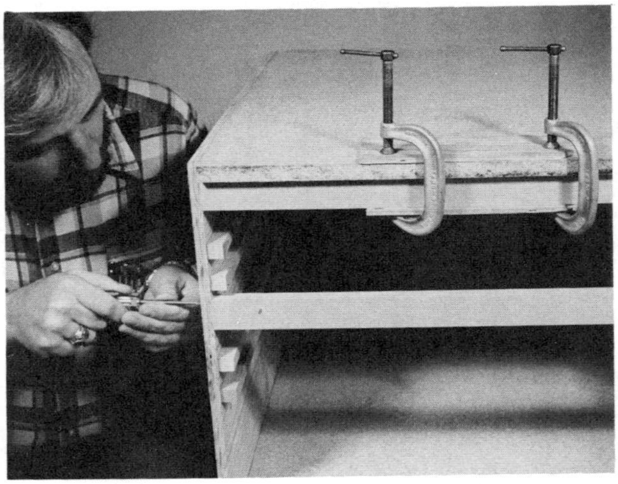

Step 20

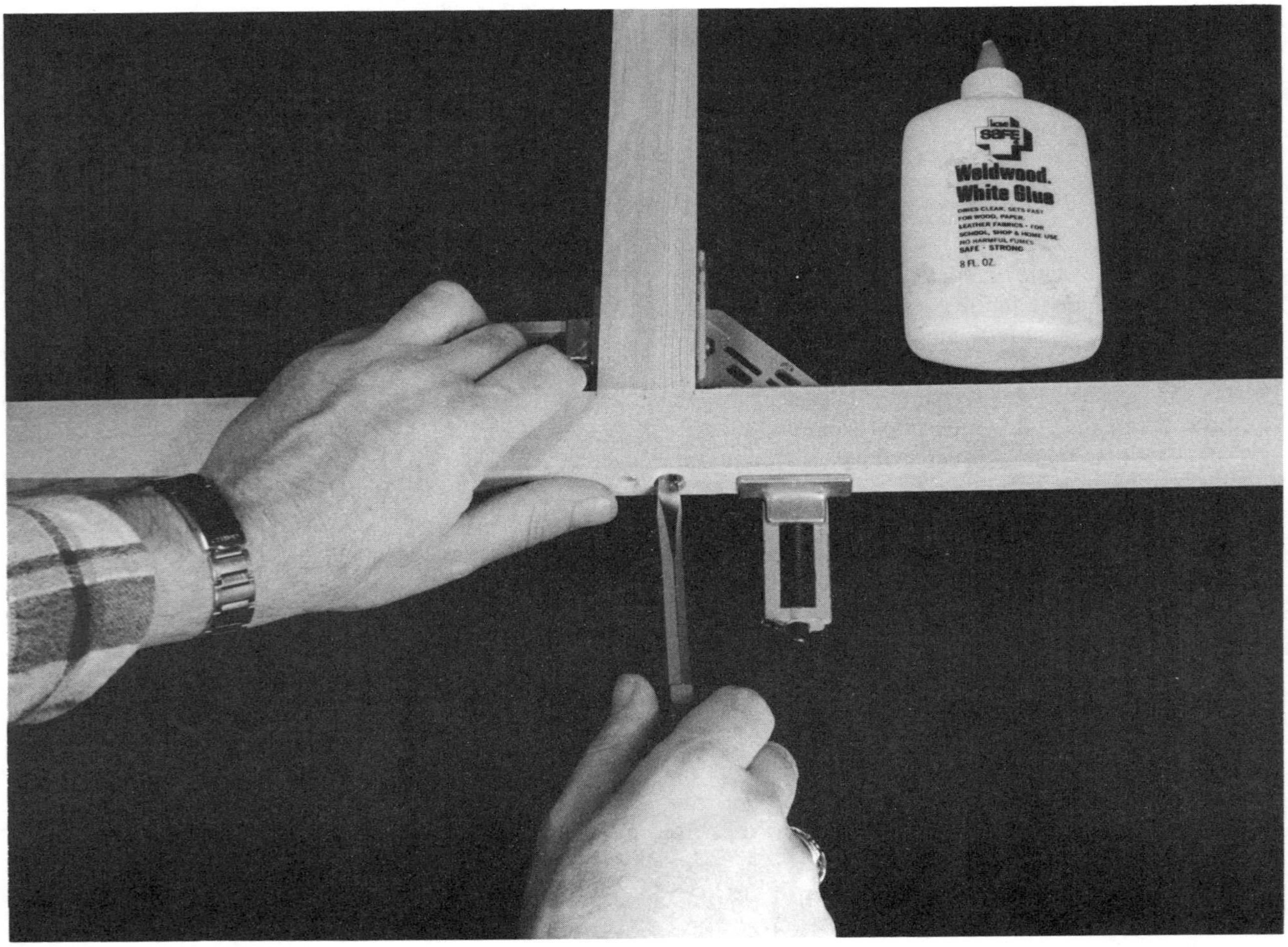

Step 22

24. Measure up the outside of each side panel and mark for drill-starter holes at 20⅜″ and 20¾″ from the bottom and ⅜″ inside the front edges. Center-punch and drill a $^9/_{64}$″-diameter hole at each spot and countersink for #6 screws.

25. Apply glue to the three ends of the 1 × 2 tee and clamp each end of the horizontal to a side panel with a corner clamp, with the horizontal aligned 4⅜″ from the one above.

26. Secure the stem of the tee to the cabinet bottom with two 1 × 6 flathead wood screws and each end of the horizontal to a side panel with ¾ × 6 screws.

27. Fill screw holes and conceal plywood laminations with spackling paste. Let paste harden while you assemble the drawers.

28. With a mitre box and backsaw, cut four pieces of parting bead to 21″, four to 20$^7/_{16}$″, and two to 18″.

29. Fasten a 21″ piece of parting bead along the inside bottom edge of each drawer side panel and an 18″ piece to each drawer rear panel with glue and 1 × 4 flathead wood screws. (Parting bead will support drawer bottoms on the ¾″ sides, so drill and countersink the $^7/_{64}$″-diameter holes through the ½″ sides.)

30. Mark the outside of each drawer side panel for drill-starter holes at each corner. Marks should be located ½″ inside the front and rear edges and ⅜″ inside the top and bottom edges.

Step 29

Step 26

31. Center-punch a starter hole at each spot; then drill a $^9/_{64}$″-diameter hole at each and countersink for #6 screws.

32. Run a bead of glue down one end of a drawer rear panel, butt it to a drawer side panel, and clamp with a corner clamp. Join the panels with two ¾ × 6 wood screws, and attach the other side panel the same way.

33. Mark for, center-punch, and drill four $^7/_{64}$″-diameter holes in each of the 20$^7/_{16}$″ pieces of parting bead, through the ½″ sides. Then countersink for #4 wood screws.

34. Attach two pieces of the drilled parting bead to each drawer, spanning the open drawer front from corner to corner, using glue and ¾ × 6 screws. See page 116.

35. Scribe a line ⅜″ above and parallel to the inside bottom edge of each drawer front. Run a bead of glue down the parting bead strips on the front of a drawer and stand the drawer assembly on the inside of the drawer face. Align the lower parting bead just above the line, making sure the drawer front extends 1″ beyond the left and right side panels, and secure with 1 × 4 wood screws. See page 116.

36. Finish the other drawer the same way, and leave the corner clamps in place at the rear corners of each drawer until glue sets.

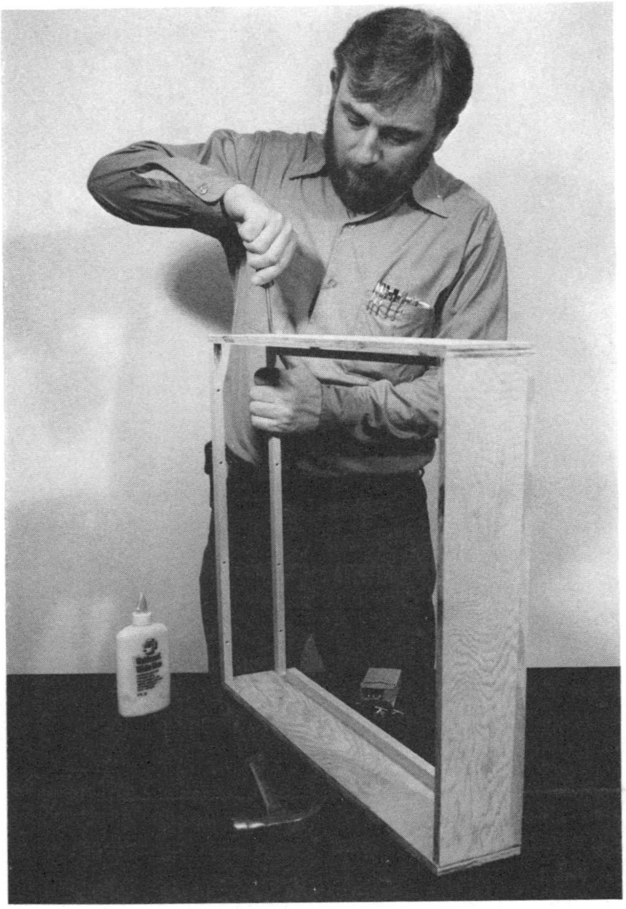

Step 34

37. Double-check the inside dimensions of the drawers, and cut two pieces of $\frac{1}{4}''$ tempered hardboard to fit (should be $23\frac{1}{2}'' \times 20\frac{7}{16}''$).
38. Apply a liberal amount of glue to the drawer-bottom cleats; then lay the drawer bottoms atop the cleats, and put several heavy objects (e.g., books, cans of paint) inside the drawers and let glue set.
39. On the outside of each drawer side panel, using glue and 1″ brads, attach a 24″ piece of $\frac{3}{4}''$-square molding, 1″ from and parallel to the bottom edges. Countersink brads and let glue dry. (When glue has dried, lubricate these drawer slides with paraffin wax or an aerosol dry lubricant.)
40. Sand cabinet, drawer faces, and doors with medium-grit and fine-grit sandpaper.
41. Turn the cabinet upside down and install a plate-type caster 1″ inside each corner, using the mounting screws supplied.
42. Mark each drawer face for a centered drawer pull; then center-punch and drill holes for the mounting screws.
43. Mark each door for a pull to be located $1\frac{1}{2}''$ from the inside edge and about 3″ from the top edge; then center-punch and drill holes for the mounting screws.
44. Clean cabinet, drawers, and doors to remove dust, and apply two coats of interior latex paint. Use a contrasting color on doors and drawer faces, if you wish.

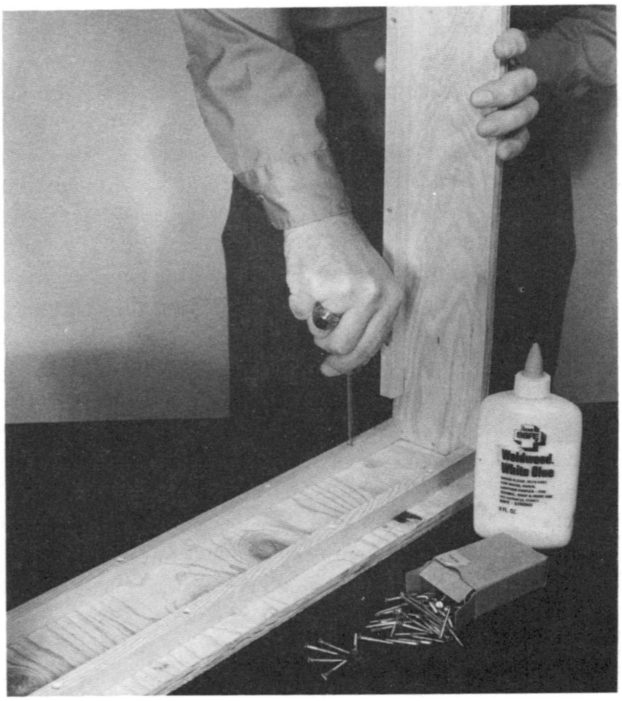

Step 35

Step 39

45. Install pulls with mounting screws. Then mount doors to the cabinet with hinges positioned 2″ from the top and bottom edges of the doors.

46. Install magnetic door catches on the vertical 1 × 2 and mount the catch plates to the inside of the doors with the screws provided.

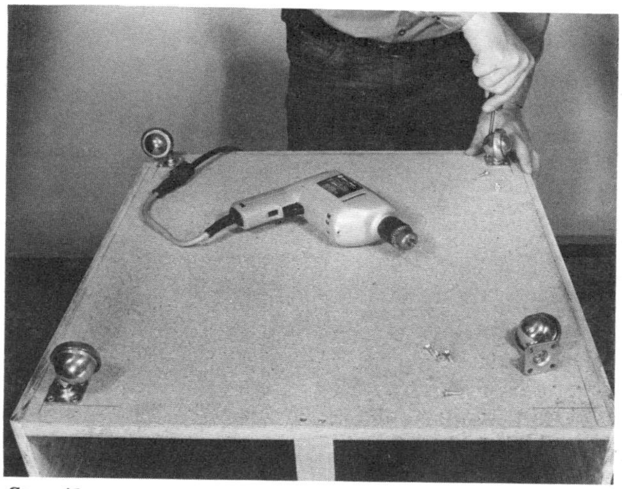

Step 41

Required Tools

- Steel tape rule
- Yardstick or large T-square
- Pencil
- Claw hammer
- Nail set
- Center punch
- Screwdriver
- Mitre box and backsaw
- Two C-clamps
- Four corner clamps
- Paint brush
- Electric drill and bits, including #6 and #8 countersink bits
- Circular saw
- Saw guide
- Pad sander

Required Materials

- One sheet of ½″ plywood, G1S
- Two 23½″ × 20⁷⁄₁₆″ pieces of ¼″ tempered hardboard
- 8′ of 25″-wide ¾″ particleboard
- 18′ of parting bead
- 8′ of 1 × 2, clear
- White glue
- Spackling paste
- 1″ brads
- 24 1 × 4 flathead wood screws
- One box (100-count) ¾ × 6 flathead wood screws
- Two 1 × 6 flathead wood screws
- Two 2 × 8 flathead wood screws
- Medium-grit and fine-grit sandpaper
- Interior latex paint
- Four drawer/door pulls
- Four plate-type casters
- Four 2″ utility hinges
- Two magnetic door catches

Plywood Panels

From one sheet of ½″ plywood, graded A-D or better, cut the following panels:

QUANTITY	SIZE	NOMENCLATURE
1	23 × 34″	Rear panel
2	25½ × 34″	Side panels
2	5½ × 23½″	Drawer faces
2	4 × 20⁷⁄₁₆″	Drawer rear panels
4	4 × 24″	Drawer side panels
2	11¾ × 20½″	Doors

25 WORKMATE Workshop

Each of the various models of Black & Decker's WORKMATE® Portable Work Center and Vise is a useful workshop accessory in its own right, but they can be made even more versatile with a few simple projects you can finish in an afternoon or evening. A single sheet of plywood, a length of 2 × 4, some molding, glue, and fasteners are all the materials you need. And each project goes together with simple tools.

From a sheet of shop-grade or G1S $\frac{3}{4}$″ plywood you can cut a spacious auxiliary bench top for use with your WORKMATE. With the scraps left over, you can fashion bases for various bench-type tools that can be stored out of the way and quickly secured to the WORKMATE whenever you need them.

Although you can make the bench top any size you want, one that's 3′ wide and 5′ long should prove most useful and easy to handle. As for the bench-tool bases, cut them to a length to fit whichever model WORKMATE you own—from 23 to 35″—and a width of 12″ for most tools. Even if you switch to a different model or add another WORKMATE later, the bases will work equally well with it.

I recommend using 2 × 4 stock to fashion the clamp-

ing block for the bench top, as it will keep the plywood from bowing when you lean it against a wall during storage. Clamping blocks for the bench-tool bases can be made of either 2 × 4 or 2 × 2 stock—whichever you have on hand. A single eight-foot 2 × 4, though, will provide enough material for the bench top and one 35″ bench-tool base.

Construction Steps (Auxiliary Bench Top)

1. Use a circular saw and saw guide to cut a 36″ × 60″ panel from a sheet of shop-grade or G1S $\frac{3}{4}$″ plywood.
2. Measure along each 36″ edge and make marks on the top surface of the panel at 17″ and 19″ from one corner. Measure across the center of the top surface and make identical marks.
3. Use a yardstick or large T-square to connect these marks, creating a pair of parallel lines running the length of the bench top.
4. Measuring from one end, make cross-marks on each line at 2″, 20″, 40″, and 50″.
5. Center-punch a drill-starter hole at each spot.
6. Cut a 2 × 4 clamping block to 60″. Turn the bench top upside down. Apply a liberal amount of glue to one broad side of the 2 × 4, lay the glued side down on the underside of the bench top, center it, and clamp each end with a C-clamp.

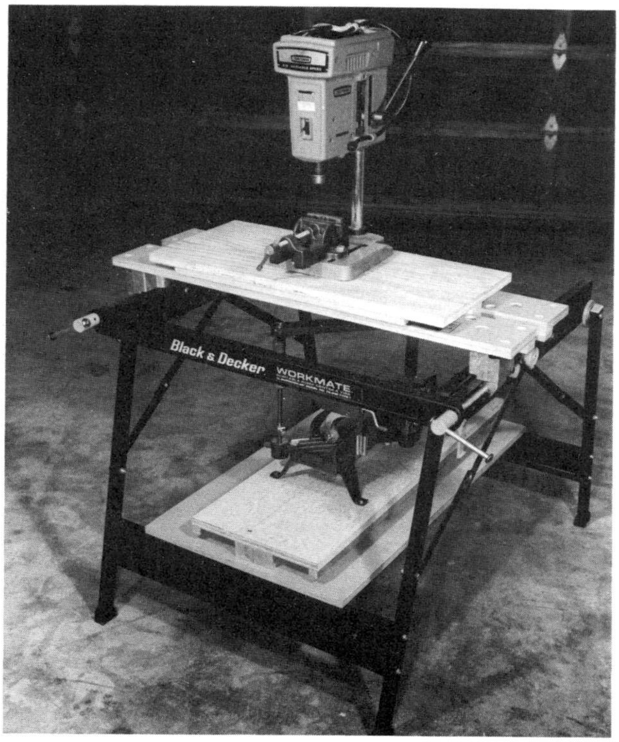

Step 6

7. Turn the bench top over, and drill a $\frac{1}{4}$″-diameter hole through the plywood and 2 × 4 at each spot punched in **Step 5.** Countersink holes for machine screws.
8. Insert a $\frac{1}{4}$ × $2\frac{1}{2}$ machine screw in each hole, and attach a $\frac{1}{4}$″ nut to each one. Tighten with a screwdriver and $\frac{7}{16}$″ or adjustable wrench.

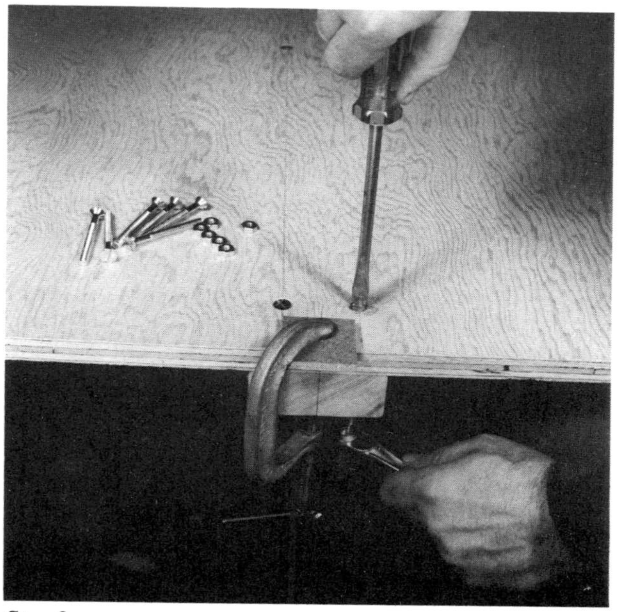

Step 8

9. Remove C-clamps and sand top and edges, as necessary, with medium-grit and fine-grit sandpaper. Your auxiliary bench top is now ready to be centered atop a WORKMATE and clamped between the unit's jaws.

Construction Steps (Bench-Tool Base)

1. Trim a scrap of ¾" G1S or shop-grade plywood to a width of 12" and maximum length of 35".
2. Measure along each 12" edge and make marks on the top of the panel at 5" and 7" from one corner.
3. Use a yardstick or large T-square to connect these marks, creating a pair of parallel lines running the length of the base.
4. Measuring from one end, make cross-marks on each line at 1", 11", 23", and 34" for a 35" base. (On shorter bases, adjust markings for even spacing.)
5. Center-punch a drill-starter hole at each mark.
6. Cut a scrap of 2 × 4 and two pieces of ¾"-square molding to 35" (or to base length).
7. Prenail each piece of molding with 1¼" brads, spaced about 6" apart.
8. Turn the base upside down. Run a bead of glue down each piece of molding; attach one piece along the front edge of the base and the other along the rear edge with brads, and countersink the brads. (Molding strips will keep the tool-mounting bolts from marring the WORKMATE surface.)
9. Apply a liberal amount of glue to one broad side of the 2 × 4 clamping block, lay the glued side down on the underside of the base, center it, and clamp each end with a C-clamp.
10. Turn the base over, and drill a ¼"-diameter hole through the base and 2 × 4 at each spot punched in **Step 5.** Countersink the holes for machine screws.
11. Insert a ¼ × 2½ machine screw in each hole, and attach a ¼" nut to each. Tighten with a screwdriver and 7/16" or adjustable wrench.
12. Remove C-clamps. Center the bench tool atop the base, and mark for mounting-bolt holes.
13. Center-punch a drill-starter hole, and drill a ¼"-diameter hole at each spot.
14. Sand the top and edges, as necessary, with medium-grit and fine-grit sandpaper.
15. Mount the tool to the base with ¼" × 1½" bolts, nuts, flat washers, and lock washers. The mounted tool can now be stored and easily mounted on the WORKMATE whenever needed.

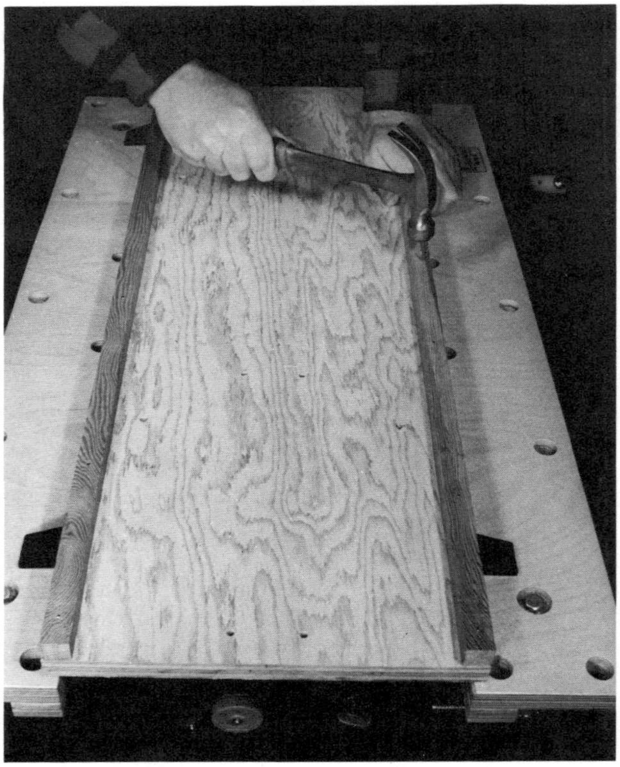

Step 8

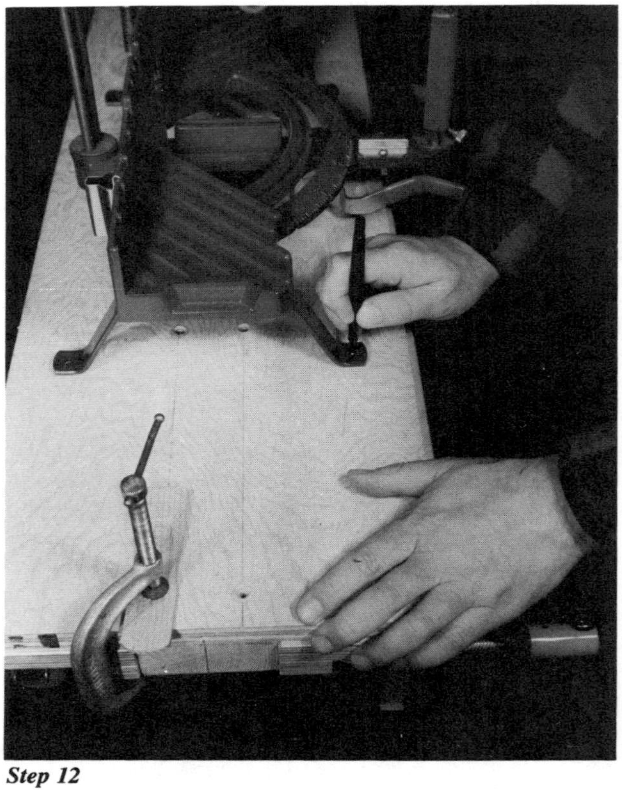

Step 12

Required Tools

- Steel tape rule
- Yardstick or large T-square
- Pencil
- Claw hammer
- Nail set
- Center punch
- Screwdriver
- Mitre box and backsaw
- Two C-clamps
- Two 7/16" or adjustable wrenches
- Electric drill with 1/4" and countersink bits
- Circular saw
- Saw guide
- Pad sander

Required Materials

- One sheet of 3/4" plywood, shop-grade or G1S
- 6′ of 3/4"-square molding
- 8′ of 2 × 4, economy or better
- White glue
- 1 1/4" brads
- 16 1/4 × 2 1/2 machine screws
- Four 1/4" × 1 1/2" bolts
- 20 1/4" nuts
- Four 1/4" flat washers
- Four 1/4" lock washers
- Medium-grit and fine-grit sandpaper

Part

IV

Major Projects

Each of the following ten projects requires more than one sheet of plywood, but none requires more than three sheets.

26 Platform Bed

The first time I built a platform bed, I did so mainly to save money. Not only was the bed far cheaper than any commercial model but, by design, it required only a mattress, instead of a mattress/box-spring set.

The second time I built a platform bed, I did so mainly for comfort and sound sleep. The fact that I saved a considerable amount of money by building instead of buying was a bonus.

The original bed served us well for more than five years and promises to keep on doing its job for many years to come. It is now in the guest room, and all who have spent a night on it have commented on how soundly they slept and how good they felt the next day.

Of course, the comfort of the bed is a product of the mattress's quality and firmness and the solidity of its foundation. Since you won't need a set of box springs for your own platform bed, you can afford to invest a little extra for the best-quality mattress available. We have found, as have our guests, that an extra-firm mattress provides maximum support and comfort, especially for anyone who suffers from back problems.

In building your own platform bed, you have several options. Although the construction steps that follow

Platform bed (the bedspread has been tucked under the mattress to show more of the platform; ordinarily it hangs to the floor)

are for a queen-size bed, you can easily adapt the plans to either a standard double-size or a king-size bed by simply cutting the plywood slabs to different dimensions. For a double bed you would need two panels cut to 37½ by 54″ each, for overall dimensions of 54 by 75″. For a king-size bed, cut each panel to 40 by 77″ for a bed that measures 77 by 80″.

You also have the choice of using either 2 × 10 or 2 × 12 stock for the frame, although the latter most closely approximates standard bed height, with a drop of about 21″ from the mattress edge to the floor. You can use butt joints at the frame corners instead of mitre joints. Additionally, if you opt for the mitre joints, you can assemble the frame with glue and 8d finishing nails at the joints instead of the corner braces and lag bolts called for in the plans. You can then conceal the corner joints with outside corner molding, or leave them exposed and simply fill the nail holes. The frame can be painted or varnished.

The slab edges can be trimmed and finished, or left untrimmed, as in the photo; if your bedspread will hang to the floor or nearly so, it matters little. If you plan to tuck in the bedding, however, I suggest you trim and finish the slabs to match the frame. You can use 1⅛″ bullnose stop or lattice for flush trim, or wider stock to give the impression of massiveness.

In trimming the slabs, if you have cut off the outside corners, as the plans dictate, you'll need to set your mitre box for a 22½° cut for proper mitre joints at the altered corners. Or you can leave the corners square and make the usual 45° mitre joints.

Your choices are many, but to duplicate the bed I built for our master bedroom, just follow these easy steps.

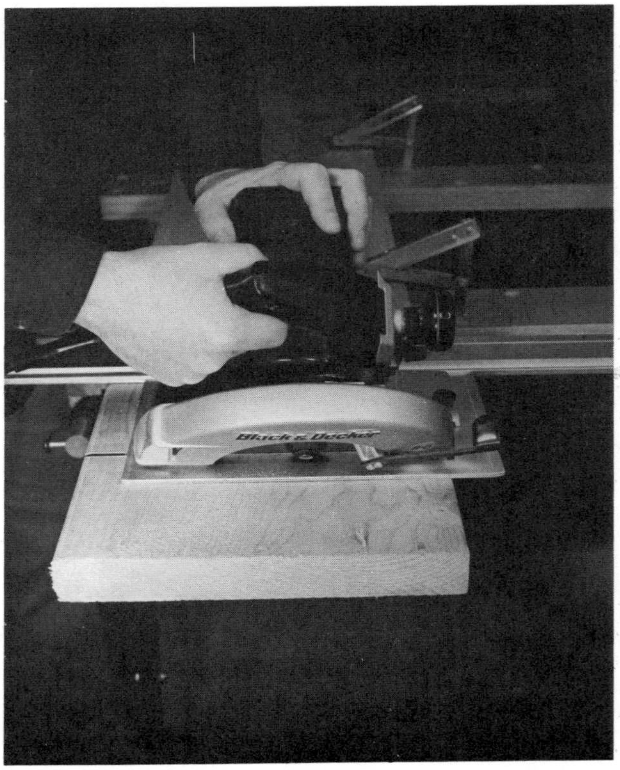

Step 2

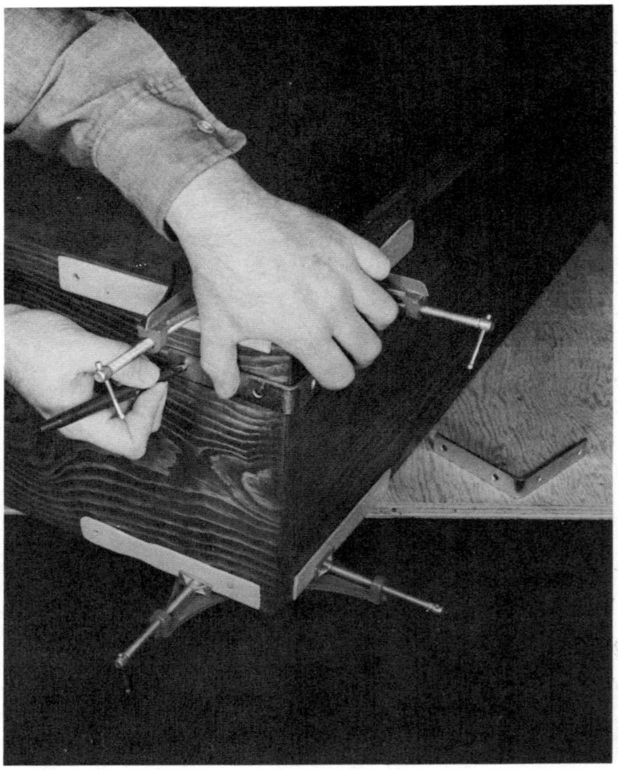

Step 8

Construction Steps

1. From two sheets of 1⅛″ plywood flooring, cut two identical slabs to one of the following dimensions: 37½ × 54″ (double), 40 × 60″ (queen), or 40 × 77″ (king). Set aside until later.
2. Use a circular saw set for 45° to mitre-cut two pieces of 2 × 12 to 60″ and two more to 40″ (outside measurements).
3. Fill any knots, pitch pockets, or other open defects with wood filler and let stand until filler hardens.
4. Sand outside faces of 2 × 12 with medium-grit and fine-grit sandpaper.
5. Wipe the surfaces of the 2 × 12 clean with a damp sponge or tack cloth and apply the stain of your choice according to the manufacturer's directions.
6. After stain has dried, apply two coats of polyurethane varnish to the 2 × 12 pieces, burnishing between coats with #0000 steel wool.

7. When varnish has dried, set a long piece and a short piece of 2 × 12 on their narrow faces on a flat working surface, and join at the mitres to form an el. Clamp top and bottom with corner clamps.
8. Position a 4″ corner brace 2″ from the top edge of the corner and mark for drill-starter holes. Do likewise with a corner brace 2″ from the bottom.
9. Center-punch a drill-starter hole at each spot.
10. Drill a $\frac{5}{32}$″-diameter hole at each spot, about $\frac{1}{2}$″ deep.
11. Mount each corner brace with four $\frac{1}{4}$″ × 1″ lag bolts.
12. Join the remaining three corners, using the same techniques and materials, creating a 40 × 60″ frame.
13. Position a 3″ corner brace inside each corner, about $1\frac{1}{2}$″ beneath the top edge of the frame, and mount with two $\frac{1}{4}$″ × 1″ lag bolts in the outside holes. (This step simply adds rigidity to the frame.)
14. Mask off each outside corner brace with 2″-wide masking tape.
15. Wipe corner hardware clean with a rag dampened with denatured alcohol to remove any dirt and grease or oily fingerprints.
16. Apply a light coat of metal primer spray paint. Let dry and apply a second coat. (You can speed the drying process by moving an electric hair drier over the painted surfaces.)

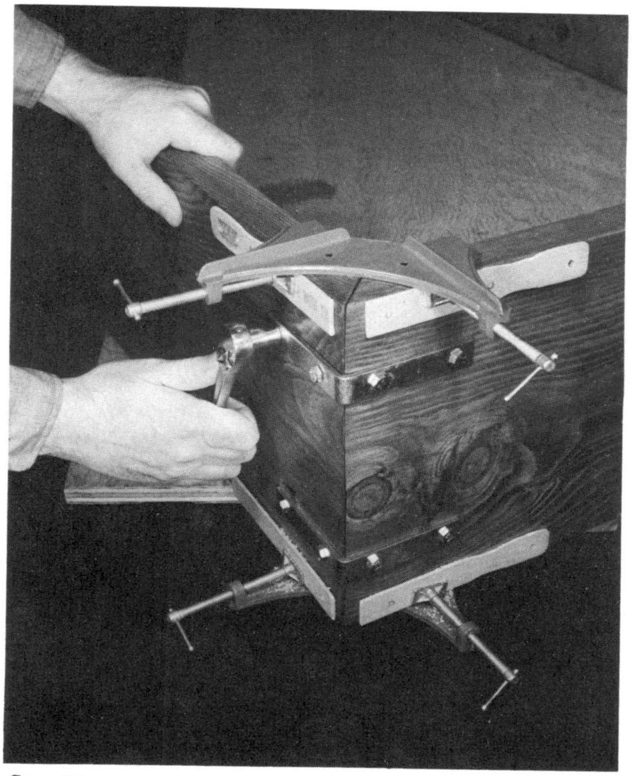

Step 11

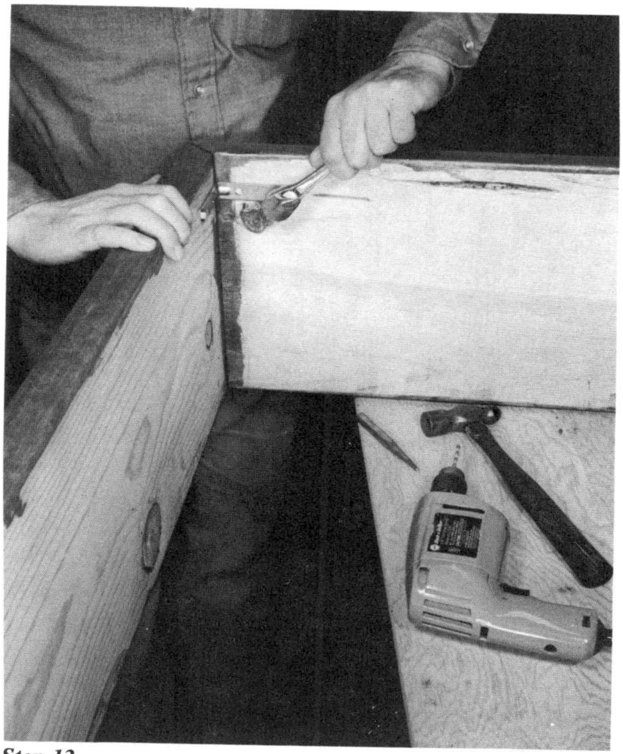

Step 13

Step 17

17. Apply at least two light coats of flat black spray paint—enough to adequately cover all primed surfaces. (Do not remove masking tape until later.)
18. Lay the bed slabs on the floor, underside up, butted together as they will be in use. Then scribe a line across the top slab 10″ from the top edge.
19. Lay the frame, upside down, atop the slabs, with the front edge lined up along the line scribed in **Step 18.** Carefully center the frame on the slabs, making sure its sides are equidistant (about 10″) from the edges of the slabs.

Step 20

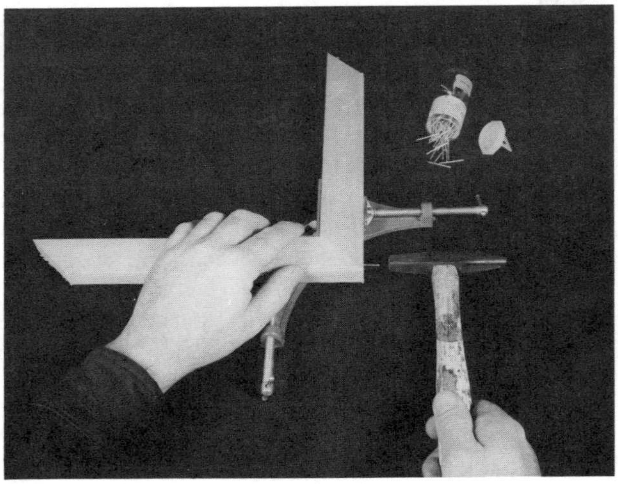

Step 23

20. Using the frame as a rule, scribe lines with a carpenter's pencil onto the slabs at each corner of the frame. Lines should be fairly heavy and about 10″ long. (You can now move the frame to the bedroom. Check the corner hardware for any nicks or scratches, and touch up the paint if necessary. Then remove the masking tape.)
21. Mark the edge of an 8′ length of 1 × 2 at 2″, 12″, 22″, 32″, 42″, 52″, 62″, 72″, and 82″.
22. With a mitre box set for 45°, make identical cuts at each mark on the 1 × 2, creating eight angle-cut pieces.
23. Glue and clamp two pieces together with a corner clamp, and drive a 1″ brad into the joint. Make three more identical pieces with the remaining 1 × 2 stock. Let stand until glue sets.
24. Mark each 1 × 2 assembly for drill-starter holes at 2″ and 9″ from the outside corners, centered on each leg of the L. Then center-punch a drill-starter hole at each spot.
25. Drill an $^{11}/_{64}$″-diameter hole at each spot and countersink for #8 screws.
26. Run a bead of glue along the underside of each 1 × 2 corner stop; then lay the stop in place on a plywood slab, aligned along the corner lines you scribed in **Step 20,** leaving the lines just visible along the inside edges of the corner stop.

Step 27

27. Insert a $1\frac{1}{2}$ × 8 flathead wood screw in each hole. Tap with a hammer to start, and drive. Install the remaining three stops at the other corner marks.
28. Measure 2″ up each edge from each outside corner of the plywood slabs and make a mark. Scribe a line connecting the two marks. Then use a circular saw to cut along those lines, removing the outside corners from the slabs.

29. Fill any splits, knotholes, or other open defects in the top sides of the slabs with surfacing putty or wood filler. Let the filler harden; then sand the slabs with medium-grit and fine-grit sandpaper. Trim and finish the slabs as desired, or leave unfinished.

30. Position the head of the bed frame about 11″ from the wall; then lay the head slab across it, fitting the corner stops around the corners of the frame. Slide the other slab into place, and the bed is ready for a mattress and bedding.

Required Tools

Steel tape rule
Combination square
Pencil
Claw hammer
Center punch
(Optional) Nail set
Mitre box and backsaw
Four corner clamps
Paint brush
Putty knife
Electric drill and $5/32$″, $11/64$″, and #8 countersink bits
Circular saw
Saw guide
Pad sander

Required Materials

Two sheets of $1\frac{1}{8}$″ plywood flooring, shop grade or better
8′ of 1 × 2, graded standard or better
20′ of 2 × 12, graded standard or better
(Optional) 24′ of 1 $\frac{1}{8}$″ bullnose stop or lattice
White glue
Wood filler
1″ brads
16 $1\frac{1}{2}$ × 8 flathead wood screws
40 $\frac{1}{4}$″ × 1″ lag bolts
Medium-grit and fine-grit sandpaper
#0000 steel wool
Eight 4″ corner braces
Four 3″ corner braces
One quart of polyurethane varnish
One roll of 2″ masking tape
One aerosol can of metal primer
One aerosol can of flat black paint
One bottle of denatured alcohol

27 Easy-up Bookshelves

This project is remarkably easy to construct and has the appearance of built-in shelving. The plan calls for two sheets of plywood and five shelf-support assemblies, for a floor-to-ceiling unit that spans 10′ of wall space. But you can easily reduce or increase the size to fit your requirements. For a 5′-wide unit, you would need one sheet of plywood and three shelf-support assemblies; a half-sheet and two shelf-support assemblies would suffice for a 30″-wide unit. For something larger, count on using a half-sheet of plywood and one more support assembly for each additional 30″ section.

These shelves are sturdy enough to serve as utility shelving in the workshop, garage, or basement. For such purposes, you can get by with cheaper grades of lumber and plywood and skip the edge trim on the shelves.

The unit can be painted or finished naturally. If you plan to paint, fill the holes and surface imperfections with spackling paste. Use wood filler if you want to finish it naturally.

There are no complicated cuts to make, but you have several cutting options. No matter what your plans are, you'll want to start by ripping each sheet of plywood into five 9½″-wide shelves. After that, you can crosscut these into 30″, 60″,or 90″ shelves, depending on your needs.

If you plan to erect the unit against a long wall with at least one end open, leave as many shelves as possible the full 90″, as the longer shelves are less likely to sag under heavy burdens. If you're working in tight quarters, however, where you don't have room to slide long shelves in from one open end, you'll find 30″ shelves easiest to install. Additionally, if you're not certain of how you want the shelves arranged, cut all to 30″; shelves of that length are fully adjustable.

Construction Steps

1. For each shelf-support assembly, trim two 2 × 2 verticals to 1″ less than floor-to-ceiling height (95″ for standard 8′ ceilings). For the 10′-wide unit, you'll need ten such verticals.
2. For each support assembly, cut two 2 × 4 horizontals and seven 2 × 2 horizontals—in all ten 2 × 4's and thirty-five 2 × 2's for the 10′ unit.

LE
GAR
BAGE

3. Measuring from the bottom of each 2 × 2 vertical, make marks at 15″, 26″, 37″, 48″, 59″, 70″, and 81″. Use a combination square to scribe a line across each vertical at each mark.
4. Using these lines as guides, scribe identical lines on the adjacent faces of the verticals.
5. Prenail one face of each vertical with two diagonally placed 8d finishing nails above and within 1½″ of each line scribed in **Step 4.** Drive two more above and within 3½″ of the bottom of each vertical, and two more below and within 3½″ of the top.
6. Apply glue to one end of a 2 × 4 horizontal. Butt it to the bottom of one vertical on the face opposite the nails, and drive two finishing nails into it to form a tall el. Attach a 2 × 4 horizontal to the top of the vertical the same way. Countersink the nails.
7. Apply glue to the end of a 2 × 2 horizontal, position it immediately above the 15″ line scribed in **Step 3**, and clamp it to the vertical with a corner clamp. Then drive and countersink two nails into it.
8. Continue attaching 2 × 2 horizontals to the vertical the same way—one immediately above each remaining line scribed in **Step 3.**
9. Turn the assembly over, with horizontals pointing up, and apply glue to the horizontal ends. Attach a prenailed vertical to the horizontals and countersink the nails.

Step 9

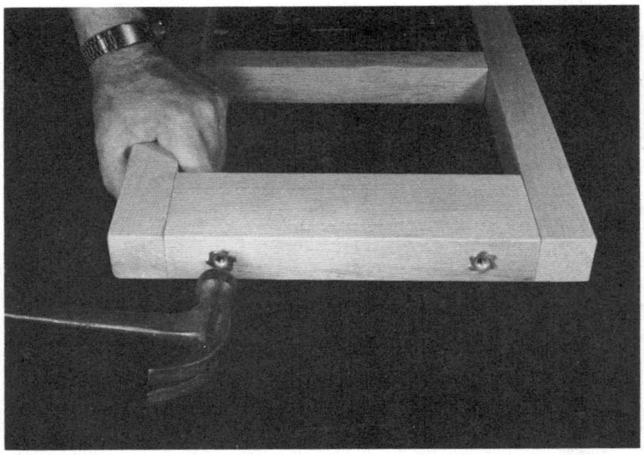

Step 18

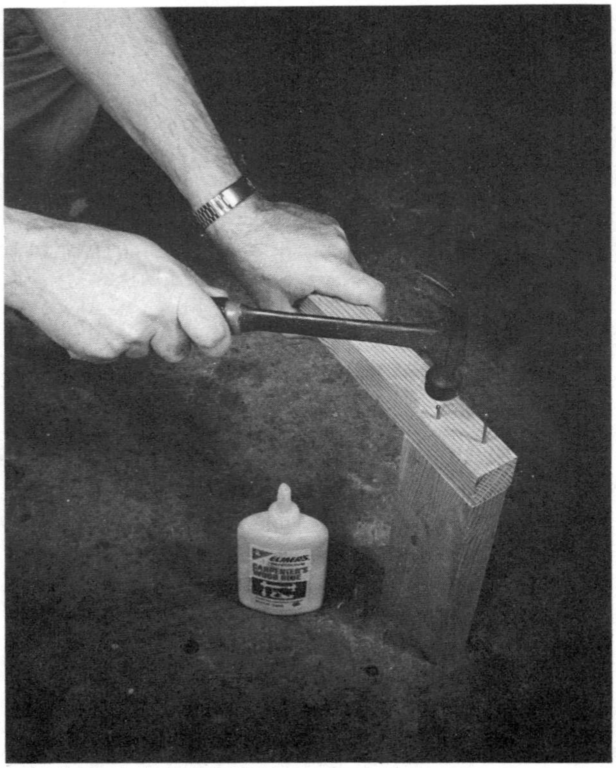

Step 6

10. Fill nail holes with spackling paste (if unit will be painted) or wood filler (for natural finish). Then let the assembly stand until glue sets.
11. Erect four more shelf-support assemblies the same way for a 10′-wide unit.
12. For each shelf, cut a piece of screen molding to fit the front edge. Prenail each piece with ¾″ brads, spaced about 6″ or 8″ apart.
13. Run a bead of glue down each piece of molding and attach each to the front edge of a shelf with brads. Countersink the brads.

14. Fill brad holes with spackling paste or wood filler.
15. Sand shelves and shelf-support assemblies, as required, with medium-grit and fine-grit sandpaper.
16. Measure in 3″ from the top front edge of each support assembly and 3″ from the top rear, and center-punch a centered drill-starter hole at each spot.
17. Drill a hole at each spot large enough to accommodate the female portion of a tension device.
18. Use a hammer to tap the female half of a tension device into each hole, and your unit is ready for the finish of your choice.
19. When the finish has dried, screw the male sections of the tension devices into the tops of the support assemblies. Stand one assembly against the wall where the unit will be erected, and screw tension devices up to the ceiling by hand.
20. Use a bubble level to make necessary adjustments of the assembly; then tighten the tension devices with an adjustable wrench.
21. Set up the next and each succeeding assembly the same way, 30″ apart, center to center. Slide shelves into position atop the supports.
22. When shelves are filled, retighten the tension devices for a snug fit against the ceiling. The support assemblies will settle under the weight, particularly on a carpeted floor. So it's a good idea to check them every few months and make sure the tension devices are secure.

Step 20

Required Tools

Steel tape rule	Bubble level
Combination square	Paint brush
Pencil	Putty knife
Claw hammer	Electric drill
Nail set	Circular saw
Mitre box and backsaw	Saw guide
Two C-clamps	Pad sander
Four corner clamps	

Required Materials

Two sheets of 3/4″ plywood, G1S
112′ of 2 × 2, clear or patchable
12′ of 2 × 4, clear or patchable
80′ of screen molding
White glue
Spackling paste or wood filler
3/4″ brads
8d finishing nails
Medium-grit and fine-grit sandpaper
Stain and varnish or paint of choice
10 tension devices

28
Home Video Center

If you have a portable or tabletop television in need of a place to rest, here's the perfect project. And if you have video accessories—such as a video cassette recorder (VCR) or disk player, or any of the popular video game consoles—all the better, because this cabinet is designed to house such equipment.

Ball-type casters provide all the convenience of a roll-around TV stand, but unlike a simple stand, this unit conceals all equipment, cassettes, game cartridges, and the like behind cabinet doors when not in use. And unsightly cables and cords are kept hidden from view.

The top section of the cabinet is large enough to hold televisions with screens up to 19″ diagonally. The lower section will hold any VCR or disk players and game consoles up to 25″ in width. Accessories currently available are considerably smaller that that, leaving plenty of room to store software.

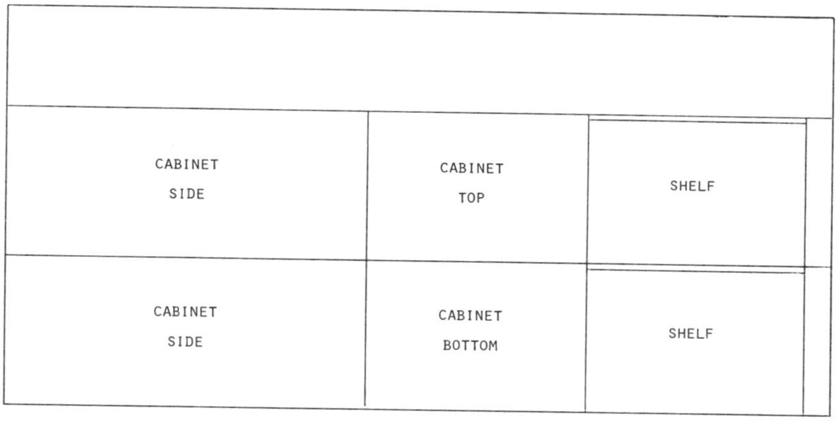

Cutting diagram for full sheet of $\frac{3}{4}''$ plywood

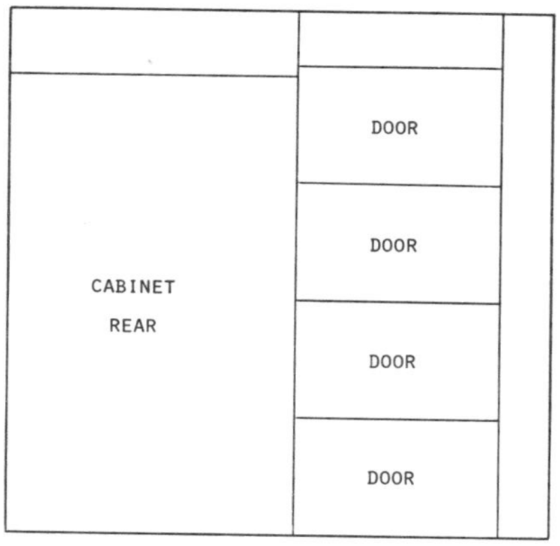

Cutting diagram for half-sheet of $\frac{3}{4}''$ plywood

Construction Steps

1. On the inside of the $25\frac{1}{2} \times 42''$ rear panel and each $18 \times 42''$ side panel, scribe lines $21\frac{1}{4}''$ and $31\frac{3}{4}''$ down from and parallel to the top edges.
2. On the rear panel only, measure down from the top and make pencil marks at $9\frac{1}{2}''$ and $17\frac{1}{2}''$, near the left and right edges. Then, with a yardstick or T-square flush with the left edge and aligned with the $9\frac{1}{2}''$ marks, scribe a line from the $5\frac{1}{4}''$ rule mark to the $20\frac{1}{4}''$ rule mark. Scribe an identical line with the yardstick aligned with the $17\frac{1}{2}''$ marks.
3. Connect the ends of these two parallel lines with vertical lines, creating an $8 \times 15''$ rectangle. (This will be the rear access window of the unit.)
4. On the rear panel, measure up from the center of the bottom edge and make marks at $1\frac{1}{2}''$ and $12\frac{1}{2}''$; then, with a center punch and hammer, make a drill-starter hole at each mark and another inside the rectangle.
5. Clamp a piece of scrap wood to the underside of the rear panel, and drill a $1\frac{1}{2}''$-diameter hole at each starter hole.
6. With a sabre saw and fine-tooth blade, cut the rear-access window out of the rear panel along the lines scribed in **Steps 2** and **3.**
7. Cut two shelf cleats from parting bead to $25\frac{1}{2}''$ and four to $16\frac{3}{4}''$.
8. Measuring from one end of each $25\frac{1}{2}''$ cleat, make marks at $1''$, $9''$, $16\frac{1}{2}''$, and $24\frac{1}{2}''$. On the $16\frac{3}{4}''$ cleats, make marks at $1''$, $8\frac{3}{8}''$, and $15\frac{3}{4}''$.
9. Center-punch a drill-starter hole, centered, at mark on the cleats. Then drill a $\frac{9}{64}''$-diameter hole at each and countersink for #6 screws.
10. Run a bead of glue down the underside of a $25\frac{1}{2}''$ cleat and attach it with four 1×6 flathead wood screws to the rear panel, aligning the top edge of the cleat with one of the lines scribed in **Step 1.** Attach the remaining $25\frac{1}{2}''$ cleat, the same way, along the other line.
11. Similarly, attach the $16\frac{3}{4}''$ cleats to the inside of the side panels, with the front of the cleats flush with the front edges of the panels and the rear ends of the cleats about $1\frac{1}{4}''$ from the rear edges of the panels.
12. Measure down $1''$ from the top corners of the rear panel and scribe a $1\frac{1}{2}''$ line parallel to the top edge. Scribe identical lines $1''$ inside each bottom corner.

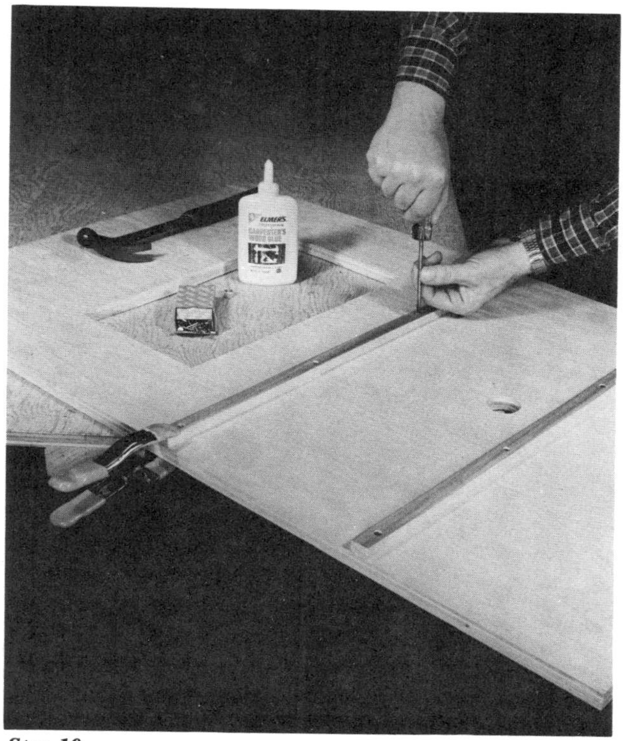

Step 10

13. Attach a $1\frac{5}{8}''$ brass corner brace 1″ from each corner, aligned with the lines scribed in **Step 12.**
14. Run a bead of glue down the right edge of the rear panel, butt the right side panel to it, and clamp the panels together with corner clamps top and bottom.
15. Attach the rear panel to the side panel with corner braces and screws.
16. Glue and clamp the left side panel in place the same way, and attach with corner braces and screws.
17. On the underside of the top panel, measure down each side edge about 1″ and scribe a line from the side edge $1\frac{1}{2}''$ toward the center and parallel to the front edge.
18. Mount a corner brace along each line with the rear of the brace flush with the side edge.
19. Scribe a line $\frac{3}{4}''$ inside and parallel to the rear edge of the top panel. Then measure in 2″ from each end of the line and scribe a $1\frac{1}{2}''$ perpendicular line from each point.
20. Position a corner brace at the intersection of each line, with one leg of the brace along the $1\frac{1}{2}''$ line and the rear of the brace aligned with the long line. Mark for and punch screw-starter holes, and attach braces with screws provided.
21. Position the top panel atop the partially assembled cabinet and carefully align front corners; then secure the front corners with corner clamps.

Step 15

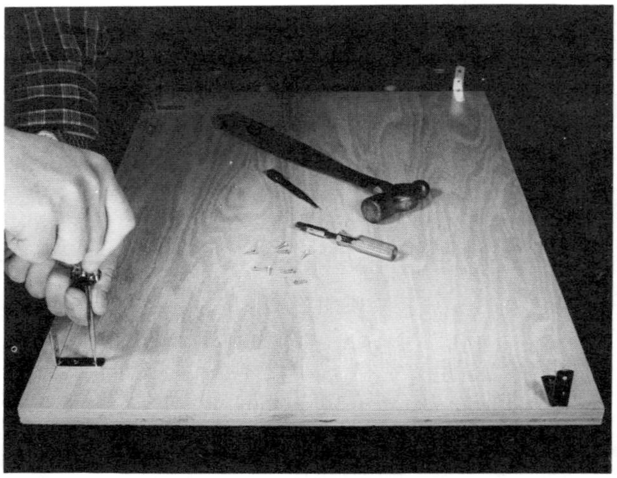

Step 20

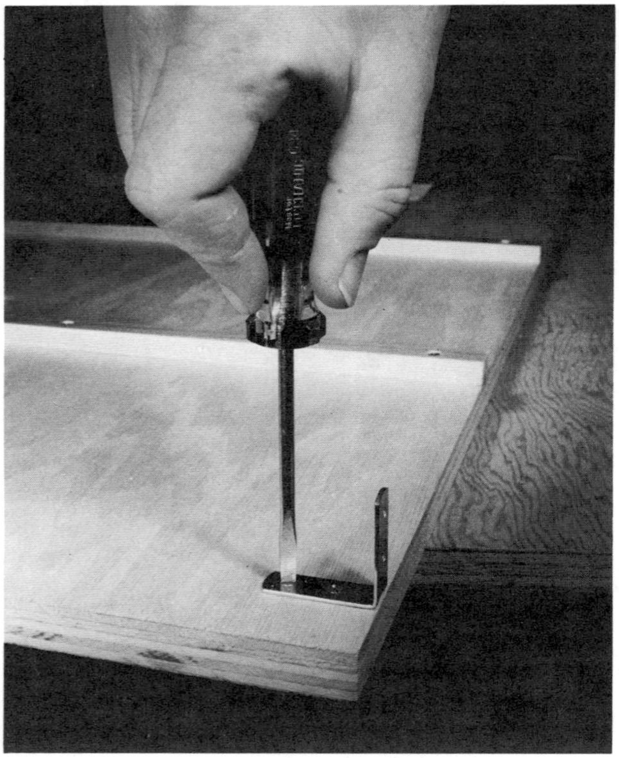

Step 13

22. Loosen the side screws only on the corner clamps, and remove the top panel, leaving the clamps attached to it.
23. Run a bead of glue down the top edge of the rear panel only. Replace the top panel and tighten the clamps. Then drive a $1\frac{1}{4}''$ brad through the top panel about $\frac{3}{8}''$ inside each rear corner into the rear panel and another centered $\frac{3}{8}''$ from the rear edge. Countersink the brads.

24. Lay the unit on its back and use a scratch awl to punch screw-starter holes for the rear-panel corner braces; then attach the braces to the rear panel with screws.
25. Turn the unit on its side and attach the corner brace to the side panel with screws. Turn the unit over and attach the other corner brace.
26. Remove the corner clamps and stand the unit on its top. Now attach the bottom panel as you attached the top panel in **Steps 17** through **25.**
27. Remove the clamps and set the unit upright. Run a bead of glue along the top shelf cleats and on the inside walls just above the cleats.
28. Lay the top shelf in place atop the cleats, making sure the front edge is flush with the front edges of the side panels. Use a pipe clamp or bar clamp to press the side panels into firm contact with the shelf sides.
29. Drive a 1″ brad through the shelf into the cleat just inside each front edge. Drive three more brads through the shelf into the rear cleat, and countersink brads.
30. Cut four pieces of hardwood quarter-round molding to 18″.
31. Lay the cabinet on its back. Then run a bead of glue down each flat edge of each piece of quarter-round and push each into position in one of the corner notches in the unit. Wrap two or three band clamps around the cabinet, and tighten to hold the quarter-round in place while the glue sets.
32. With a mitre box and backsaw, cut two verticals of hardwood 1 × 2 to 43½″.
33. Measuring from the bottom of each piece, make marks ⅜″ inside the outside edge of each at 1½″, 11½″, 21½″, 32″, and 42″. Then punch a small drill-starter hole at each spot with a nail set.
34. Drill a $\frac{5}{64}$″-diameter pilot hole at each spot on the 1 × 2's.
35. With the unit lying on its back, run a bead of glue down the front edge of each side panel. Lay the verticals in place, each flush with the cabinet sides, and attach them with 1¼″ brads, driven through the pilot holes and countersunk. (NOTE: outside corners of verticals that protrude will be rounded over later.)
36. Measure the distance between the verticals and cut three horizontals to fit from hardwood 1 × 2.
37. Mark the horizontals for pilot holes 1″ from each end and in the center. The top horizontal should have the holes located ⅜″ from the top edge, bottom horizontal ⅜″ from the bottom edge, and center horizontal ¾″ from each edge.
38. Run beads of glue down the front edges of the top and bottom panels and shelf. Apply a thin coat of glue to each end of each horizontal.
39. Attach the top horizontal flush with the cabinet top

Step 31

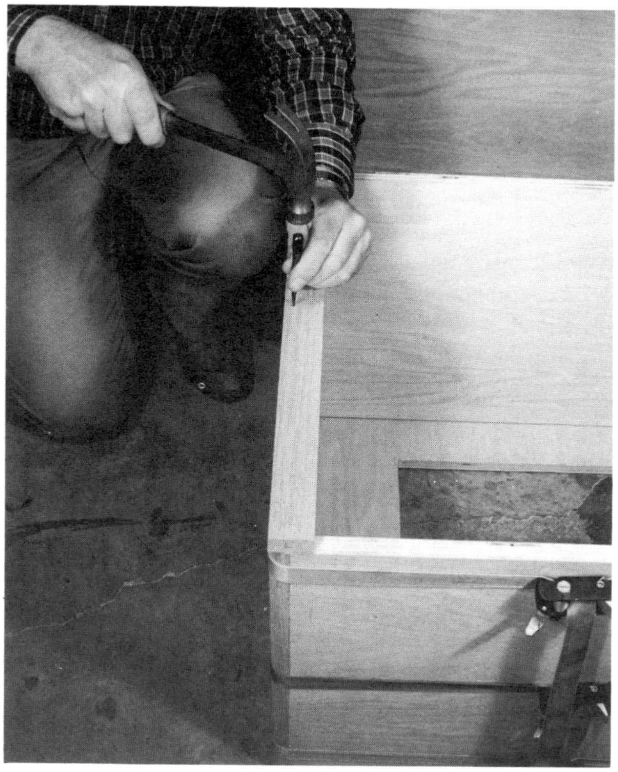

Step 35

and the bottom horizontal flush with the cabinet bottom. The center horizontal should be centered along the shelf front edge, creating a lip above and below the shelf. Fasten with $1\frac{1}{4}''$ brads and countersink.

40. Fill all visible brad holes with wood filler and let filler cure.
41. Carefully measure one edge of each door; then mitre-cut a piece of hardwood quarter-round molding to fit. Drill three $\frac{5}{64}''$-diameter holes in each piece, $\frac{3}{8}''$ from the rear edge, located $1\frac{1}{2}''$ from each and in the center. Attach the quarter-round to the doors with $1\frac{1}{4}''$ brads and countersink.
42. Mitre-cut one end of another piece of quarter-round for each door, fit to the attached piece, and mark for the mitre cut at the next corner. Drill, glue, and attach the same way as the first piece.
43. Continue attaching quarter-round to the doors until all four are trimmed.
44. Mark the doors for door-pull mounting screws $1\frac{3}{4}''$ in from the inside edges, and centered vertically. Punch drill-starter holes, and drill holes large enough to accommodate the mounting screws.
45. Fill the brad holes in the door trim with wood filler and let doors stand until filler hardens.
46. Using a pad sander, carefully round over the corners and sharp edges of the cabinet; and sand cabinet and door surfaces, as required, with medium-grit, fine-grit, and extra-fine-grit sandpaper.
47. Hand-sand all surfaces with #400 wet-or-dry sandpaper. Then polish with #0000 steel wool.
48. Clean all surfaces thoroughly and use a vacuum cleaner to remove dust from inside the cabinet. Then apply the stain of your choice according to the manufacturer's directions. (If you have built with oak and oak plywood and desire the English oak finish of the cabinet pictured apply Pen-Chrome #640-11 English oak stain with a brush, let penetrate for fifteen minutes, and wipe dry with paper towels.) Let cabinet and doors stand over night.
49. Finish with two or more coats of polyurethane varnish or Watco Natural Danish Oil, according to the manufacturer's directions.
50. Mount two self-closing hinges on the inside of each door, 2″ from the top and bottom outside edges.
51. Lay the cabinet on its back. Then lay the doors in place, and carefully adjust them so that their edges just barely touch and there is a $\frac{3}{4}''$ space between the top and bottom doors. Now, using the hinges as guides, mark the cabinet face frame for drill-starter holes.
52. Use a nail set to punch small drill-starter holes. Then drill pilot holes for the hinge screws.
53. Mount the door pulls on the doors. Then mount the doors on the cabinet with hinge screws.

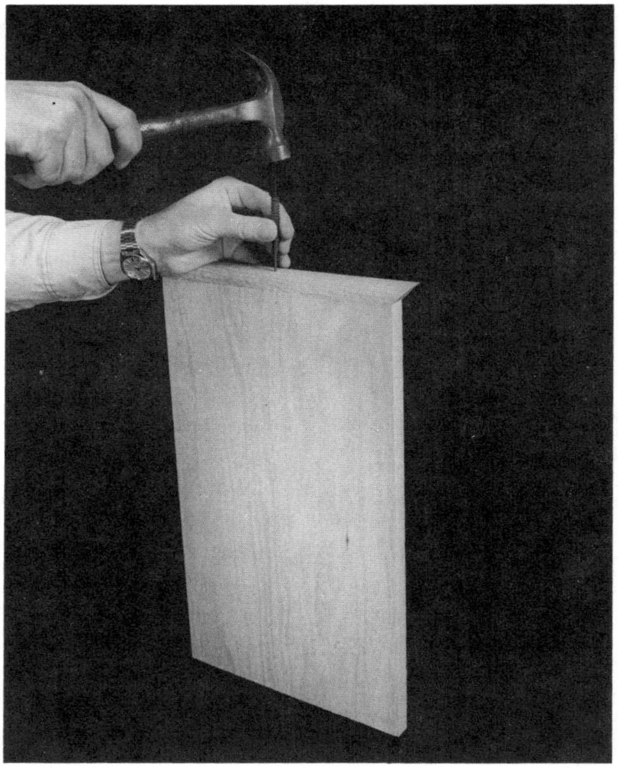

Step 41

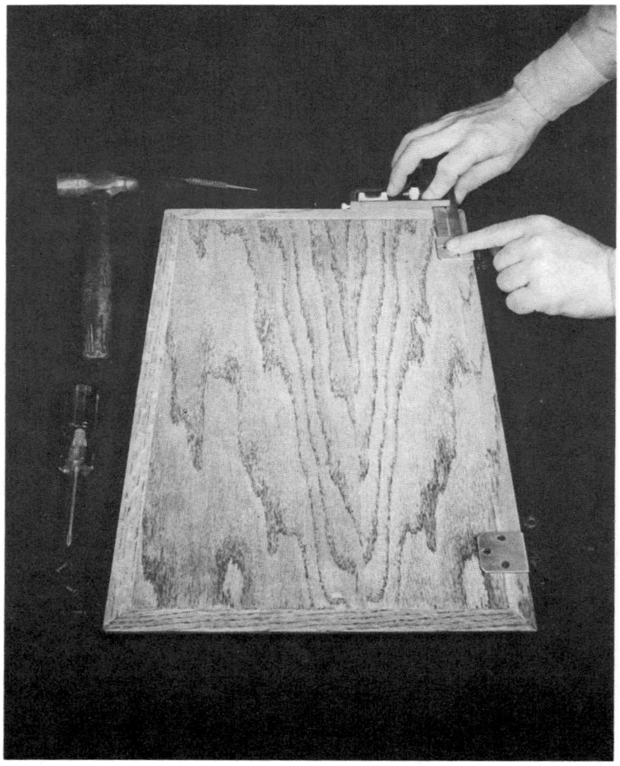

Step 50

54. Stick a self-adhesive cork door cushion on the cabinet face frame where each inside door corner touches.

55. Turn the cabinet upside down, and scribe a line 1″ from the front edge of the bottom panel and another 1″ from the rear edge. Scribe perpendicular lines 1½″ from the side edges.

56. Put a plate-type caster at each corner, aligned with the lines, and mark for drill-starter holes.

57. Center-punch drill-starter holes and drill 9/64″-diameter pilot holes ½″ deep.

58. Mount the casters with ¾″ × 12″ sheet metal screws.

59. If you have opted for the oil finish, apply a coat of paste wax to exterior surfaces, as well as to the inside of the doors. Buff with a soft cloth, apply a second coat, and buff to a sheen.

60. Move the cabinet to where it will be used and install equipment. Run accessory cords out through the 1½″-diameter holes in the rear panel. Use the rear-access window for TV cable hookup and the like.

Required Tools

Steel tape rule
Yardstick or large T-square
Pencil
Claw hammer
Nail set
Center punch
Screwdriver
Scratch awl
Mitre box and backsaw
Two C-clamps
36″ or larger bar or pipe clamp
Four corner clamps
Paint brush
Putty knife
Electric drill and 5/64″, 9/64″, 1½″, and #6 countersink bits
Circular saw
Saw guide
Sabre saw
Pad sander

Required Materials

One and a half sheets of ¾″ hardwood plywood, graded good or better
14′ of 1 × 2 hardwood to match plywood
35′ of ¾″ quarter-round molding, hardwood to match plywood
White glue
Wood filler
1″ brads
1¼″ brads
20 1 × 6 flathead wood screws
16 ¾ × 12 sheet metal screws
Medium-grit, fine-grit, extra-fine-grit, and #400 wet-or-dry sandpaper
#0000 steel wool
Stain of choice
Polyurethane varnish or oil finish
12 1⅝″ brass corner braces with screws
Eight self-closing hinges
Four door pulls
Eight self-adhesive cork door cushions
Four plate-type ball casters

Plywood Panels

From one and a half sheets of ¾" hardwood plywood, graded good or better, cut the following panels:

QUANTITY	SIZE	NOMENCLATURE
2	18 × 42"	Side panels
4	18 × 25½"	Top and bottom panels and shelves
4	10¾ × 18"	Doors
1	25½ × 42"	Rear panel

29
A Case for Magazines

We take a lot of magazines at our house, and although only a few of them are kept permanently, we often hold others until we've had a chance to clip and file articles of interest. It doesn't take long for them to accumulate into cumbersome and untidy stacks, so I designed a case specifically for storing and organizing these periodicals.

The shelves house the back issues we keep for reference, as well as others that will eventually be discarded. The slanted top holds current issues. You could systemize them even further by storing them in magazine boxes, which are sold through office-supply outlets and sometimes through the magazine publishers.

Even if you get only a few magazines, the top panel of this unit will hold them in an orderly fashion. The shelves can then be used to store books and other items.

The case is built quickly with simple tools and techniques, and can be painted to match the decor of any room.

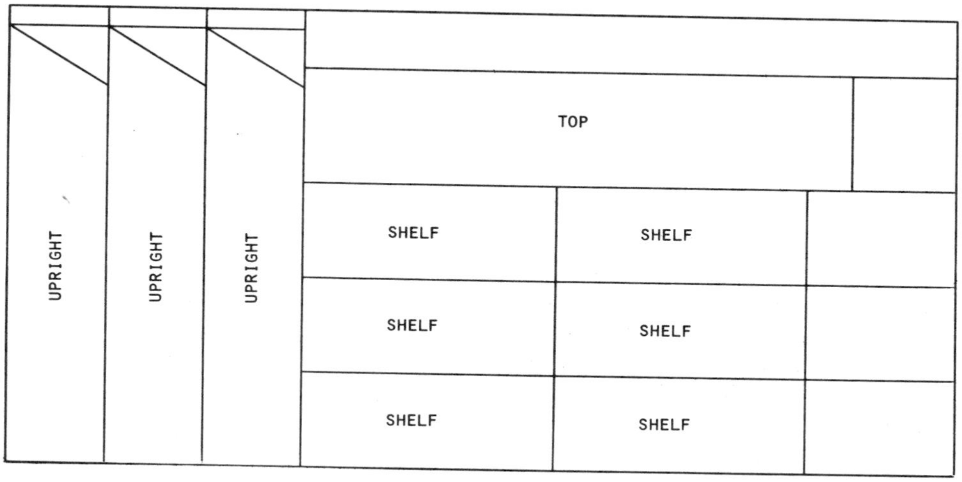

Cutting diagram for ¾″ plywood

Construction Steps

1. Measure 46″ up the rear edge of each 10 × 48″ upright panel, and make a mark. Measure 40″ up each front edge and make a mark. Connect the marks on each upright with a straight line.
2. Use a circular saw to cut away the front corner on each upright along the line scribed.
3. Sand all surfaces of all plywood panels, except for the back of the rear panel, with medium-grit and fine-grit sandpaper.
4. Lay the rear panel on a work surface, and scribe a centered vertical line from top to bottom, and two more ⅜″ from and parallel to the side edges.
5. Turn the rear panel face up and, measuring along the top edge, make marks at ¾″, 26⅜″, 27⅛″, and 52¾″. Make corresponding marks along the bottom edge; then connect all marks with vertical lines.
6. Between the vertical lines at ¾″ and 25⅜″, and between those at 26⅛″ and 52¾″, scribe horizontal lines at 2½″, 14″, and 27″ from the bottom.
7. On the inside of each side panel and both sides of the center panel, scribe horizontal lines at 2½″, 14″, and 27″ from the bottom. Then use a combination square to make a mark on each line ½″ from the rear edge.
8. From parting bead, cut six shelf cleats to 24$\frac{9}{16}$″ and twelve more to 8″.
9. Prenail the long cleats with four ⅞″ brads each and the short cleats with two 1″ brads.
10. Glue and nail one long cleat along and immediately beneath each horizontal line scribed on the rear panel in **Step 6,** aligned between the vertical lines; then countersink the brads.

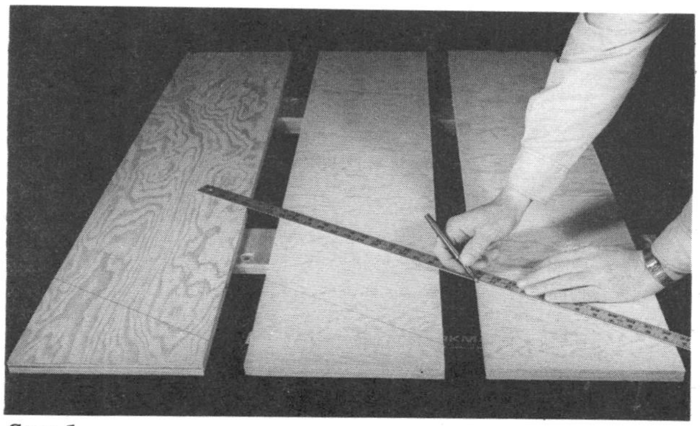

Step 1

Step 10

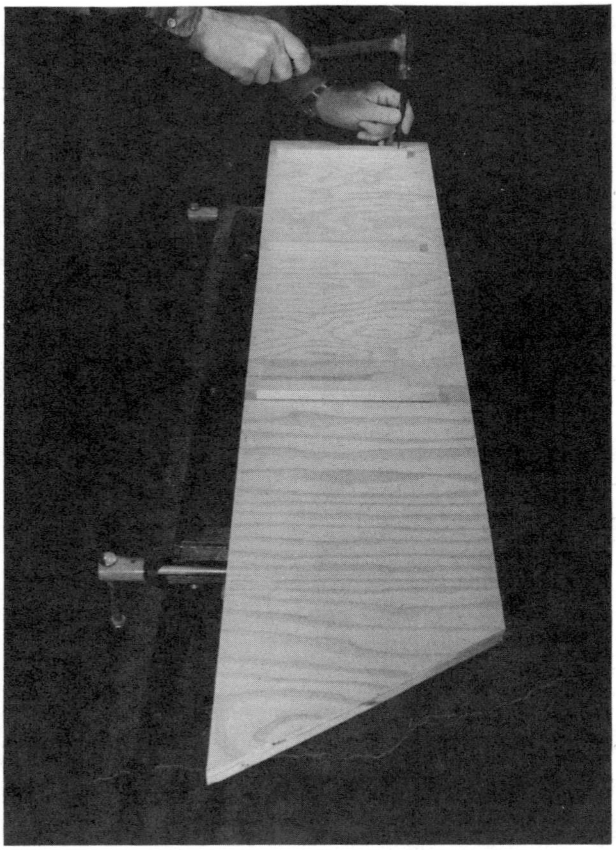

Step 11

Step 14

Step 15

11. Glue and nail each of the short cleats along and immediately beneath a horizontal line on each side panel and center upright, setting the cleats ½″ from the rear edges of the panels.

12. Run a bead of glue down the rear edge of each side panel and center upright, and butt them to the rear panel. Clamp each with a corner clamp top and bottom.

13. Carefully turn the unit over so it stands on the front edges, and nail the rear panel to the side panels and center upright with five 1⅝″ ring-shank paneling nails each, along each line scribed in **Step 4.** Let the unit stand with clamps in place until the glue sets.

14. Remove the clamps, and lay the unit on its back. Run a bead of glue along the bottom left shelf cleats. Press a shelf down onto the cleats and hammer two 1⅝″ paneling nails through the left side panel and two through the center upright into the shelf ends. Countersink the nails and install the other left shelves the same way.

15. Install the right shelves with glue and nails driven through the right side panel, but on the left side of the shelves, toenail a paneling nail through the front edges of the center upright into the end of each shelf. Countersink the nails.

16. Set the unit upright, and drive two 1″ brads through the left side of each right shelf into the shelf cleat, and countersink.

17. Scribe a vertical center line across the top panel; then scribe two more, each 1⅜″ from one end.

18. Cut a piece of 1⅝" bullnose stop and a piece of screen molding to 55½". Prenail each with seven 1" brads.

19. Run a bead of glue down the front edge of the top panel, attach the bullnose stop with brads, and countersink—making sure the bottom of the stop is flush with the underside of the panel, creating a ⅞" lip.

20. Run a bead of glue down the rear edge of the top panel; then attach the screen molding with brads and countersink.

21. Prenail the top panel with three 1⅝" ring-shank paneling nails along each line scribed in **Step 17.**

22. Run a bead of glue along each angled top of each upright panel. Lay the top panel in place with a 1" overhang at each end; then drive and countersink the nails.

23. Fill all nail holes and conceal plywood laminations with spackling paste, and let the unit stand until paste hardens.

24. Sand the spackled areas with medium-grit and fine-grit sandpaper.

25. Vacuum the unit to remove all dust, and apply two coats of interior latex paint. Let dry overnight.

Step 22

Required Tools

- Steel tape rule
- Yardstick or large T-square
- Combination square
- Pencil
- Claw hammer
- Nail set
- Mitre box and backsaw
- Two C-clamps
- Four to six corner clamps
- Paint brush
- Putty knife
- Circular saw
- Saw guide
- Pad sander

Required Materials

- One sheet of ½" plywood, G1S
- One sheet of ¾" plywood, G1S
- 24′ of parting bead
- 5′ of screen molding
- 5′ of 1⅛" bullnose stop
- White glue
- Spackling paste
- ⅞" brads
- 1" brads
- 1⅝" ring-shank paneling nails
- Medium-grit and fine-grit sandpaper
- Interior latex paint

Plywood Panels

From one sheet of ¾" plywood, graded A-C or better, cut the following panels:

QUANTITY	SIZE	NOMENCLATURE
6	10 × 25⅝"	Shelves
3	10 × 46"	Upright panels
1	12 × 55½"	Top panel

From one sheet of ½" plywood, GIS, cut the following panel:

QUANTITY	SIZE	NOMENCLATURE
1	46 × 53½"	Rear panel

30 Elegant Butcher-Block-Style Tables

Several years ago, I was browsing through the Bruce hardwood flooring display at a local home-improvement center, and it occurred to me that I might use parquet flooring to make relatively inexpensive but elegant table tops. After all, the parquet flooring squares are made of solid hardwood and come from the factory perfectly square for easy installation. If they can be laid atop a plywood floor underlayment, I reasoned, they should work equally well when glued to a plywood tabletop.

In my mind's eye I saw handsome and durable tables that could be built to any dimensions. The ones I built turned out better than my greatest expectations, and they were simpler to make than I had ever imagined.

I picked unstained oak flooring, because oak is my favorite furniture wood and the type we have selected for most of our naturally finished furnishings, and I knew I would want to stain the tables to match the English oak finish we favor. There are a number of other hardwoods available in parquet flooring, should you prefer something other than oak. All you need to do is find hardwood plywood and trim lumber to match.

As for size, you can make tables to any dimensions divisible by six, since these flooring parquets measure 6 × 6″. For example, you could make a large coffee table that would be 2′ wide and 4′ long before the edge trim was attached. Such a top would require four rows of eight parquets each. You could then add a pair of large

Step 3

end tables, measuring 2 × 3′ each. For each of these you would need four rows of six parquets.

I think the 6″ square parquets are the easiest to use and look the best. There are other sizes available, though, up to about 9 × 9″. You can use those by simply altering dimensions to fit your needs.

By shopping around you might be able to find parquet flooring available in less than case lots. Some home-improvement centers even sell them by the individual square. Even if you have to buy a full case, as I did, your tables will cost you far less than anything comparable in the furniture stores. And leftovers can be put to use in other projects.

The set of tables I built consists of a small coffee table, an end table (not pictured), and a large corner table that fits nicely between a couch and love seat. To duplicate them, just follow these easy steps.

Construction Steps

1. Set the 36 × 36″ corner table slab face up on a flat working surface and apply a thin, even coat of paneling adhesive with a notched spreader, carefully working the adhesive to the edges of the panel.
2. Starting at one corner of the slab, lay a 6 × 6″ oak flooring parquet atop the adhesive, aligning the edges of the parquet with the edges of the slab.
3. Lay another parquet next to the first, with the oak strips running perpendicular to the strips in the other parquet. Continue laying parquets in this alternating pattern until all 36 squares have been laid in place.
4. Press each parquet firmly into the adhesive by hand, adjusting them as necessary to keep their edges flush against one another.
5. Use a J-roller or rolling pin to apply pressure to the parquets and firmly seat them in the adhesive.
6. Attach parquets to the 18 × 36″ and 18 × 24″ slabs the same way. Then set all three aside in a warm, dry area until adhesive completely cures—twenty-four to seventy-two hours, depending on temperature.
7. To construct the pedestal for the corner table, start by laying one of the pedestal panels, inside up, on a flat working surface. Measure in 2″ from each corner along each 18″ edge, and scribe a 2″ line with a combination square perpendicular to the 18″ edge.
8. Align a 2″ corner brace inside each line, with the rear edge of the brace flush with the 18″ edge. Then mark for screw-starter holes, using the brace as a guide.
9. Use a nail set to punch two screw-starter holes for each corner brace. Then mount the braces with $\frac{1}{2}$ × 10 flathead wood screws.
10. Lay another pedestal panel, inside up, on the working surface; then stand the first on it by means of the corner braces so that the inside edges of the two panels just barely touch, creating a $\frac{3}{4}$″ corner notch on the outside corner of the panels. Attach the corner braces to the second panel with screws. See page 146.
11. Attach the remaining two pedestal panels the same way, creating a four-sided box with $22\frac{1}{2}$ × $22\frac{1}{2}$″ inside dimensions and a $\frac{3}{4}$″ notch at each outer corner.

12. Mount another 2″ corner brace with screws, top center on each panel of the pedestal, with the rear edges of the braces flush with the top edges of the panels.
13. With a mitre box and backsaw, cut four pieces of oak $\frac{3}{4}$″ quarter-round molding to 18″. Run a bead of glue down each flat edge of each piece, and press each into a corner notch on the pedestal.
14. Wrap two band clamps around the pedestal and tighten them with a wrench. Let the pedestal stand clamped until the glue sets.
15. Using the same techniques, build an end-table pedestal to $10\frac{1}{2}$″ by $16\frac{1}{2}$″ inside dimensions, and a coffee-table pedestal to $10\frac{1}{2}$″ by $22\frac{1}{2}$″.
16. For the end table, cut four pieces of oak quarter-round to 18″. For the coffee table, cut four pieces to $14\frac{1}{2}$″. Attach them with glue and band clamps, as in **Steps 13** and **14**.
17. Use a pad sander to sand all exterior surfaces of the pedestals with medium-grit, fine-grit, and extra-fine-grit sandpaper. Then hand-sand with #400 wet-or-dry sandpaper, and polish with #0000 steel wool.
18. When the adhesive has cured on the table tops, use a belt sander and medium-grit belt to carefully sand the edges of each top.
19. Check the edges for flatness with a flat board or scrap piece of $1\frac{1}{8}$″ plywood. Smooth out any high spots with a Stanley Surform Shaver or small block plane.
20. Use a belt sander and medium-grit belt to sand each table top to a smooth, even finish and to remove the factory finish.
21. Use medium-grit sandpaper or a flexible sanding block to remove small remaining traces of the manufacturer's finish as required.
22. Fill any nicks, gouges, or tiny gaps between parquets with wood filler and a putty knife. Let the table tops stand until the filler cures.
23. Cut a piece of oak 1 × 4 ($\frac{3}{4}$ × $3\frac{1}{2}$″) trim to 39″, mitred at one end.
24. Lay the oak trim along one edge of the 36 × 36″ table top. Carefully line up the mitred end at one corner and mark the opposite end for another mitre cut. Then cut that end at 45°.
25. Scribe two parallel pencil lines the length of the oak trim, $\frac{7}{8}$″ inside each of the long edges. Then, along each line, mark for drill-starter holes at $1\frac{1}{2}$″, 13″, $24\frac{1}{2}$″, and 36″ from one end.
26. Use a center punch to make a drill-starter hole at each spot.
27. Use a Stanley No. 05 wood-boring bit or similar bit to drill a $\frac{1}{2}$″-diameter hole to a depth of $\frac{1}{4}$″ at each spot. (You'll need a drill guide or drill-press attachment for your electric drill if you don't have access to a drill press.)

Step 10

Step 14

28. Use an $\frac{11}{64}$″-diameter bit to drill through the center of each $\frac{1}{2}$″-diameter hole *along the top line only.* (No further drilling will be done to the holes along the bottom line.) Then countersink top holes for #8 flathead screws.
29. Lightly but firmly clamp the oak trim to the edge of the table top with a pair of pipe or bar clamps; then drill through the holes along the top line with a $\frac{5}{32}$″-diameter bit.

30. Remove the clamps and trim and apply a thin, even coat of glue to the edge of the table top. Then attach the trim with 1 × 8 flathead wood screws.

31. Attach oak trim to the remaining three edges of the table top, using the same measurements, techniques, and materials.

32. In the same way, mitre-cut, drill, and attach a piece of oak trim to one of the long edges of the 18 × 36″ table top.

33. Now mitre-cut one end of a piece of oak trim and lay it along a short edge of the 18 × 36″ top. Mark the other end for a cut, and mitre-cut that end. (Piece should be 19½″ long.)

34. Scribe parallel lines the length of this piece, as you did on the other pieces. Now mark each line at 1½″, 9¾″, and 18″ from one end. Center-punch a drill-starter hole at each spot.

35. Drill and countersink holes in this piece as in the others, and attach with glue and screws. Then attach oak trim to the remaining two edges of the table top.

36. Similarly, attach a piece of oak trim to a short edge of the 18 × 24″ table top, locating the screw holes as in **Step 34.**

37. Measure and mitre-cut another piece of oak trim to fit a long edge of the table top, and scribe parallel lines as before. Mark for and punch drill-starter holes along each line at 1½″, 12¾″, and 24″ from one end.

38. Attach this piece and two others to the remaining edges of the table top.

39. With a mitre box and backsaw set for 90°, cut 84 screw-hole plugs approximately ½″ long from 7/16″-diameter dowel rod: 32 for the corner table, 28 for the coffee table, and 24 for the end table.

40. Pour wood glue into a small, plastic margarine tub or similar container to a depth of about ⅛″. Dip one end of each screw-hole plug into the glue and insert each into a screw hole in the oak trim. Firmly set each plug and twist while seating it to ensure a firm bond. The plugs will stick out about ¼″. Wipe away any seeping glue with a damp sponge, and let table tops stand for several hours or overnight.

41. Using the edge of the table top as a guide, cut off each plug with a small backsaw or dovetail saw. Cut off all top-row plugs first; then invert the table top and cut off the bottom-row plugs.

42. With a belt sander and medium-grit belt, take down any high spots in the table surfaces and edge trim.

43. Switch to a pad sander and sand table tops and sides with medium-grit, fine-grit, and extra-fine-grit sandpaper, rounding over sharp corners and edges while sanding.

44. Hand-sand all surfaces with #400 wet-or-dry sandpaper, and polish with #0000 steel wool.

45. Turn table tops upside down on a flat working surface. Center the pedestals on the undersides of the table tops, using a steel tape rule to make sure each is located an equal distance from the two opposite edges.

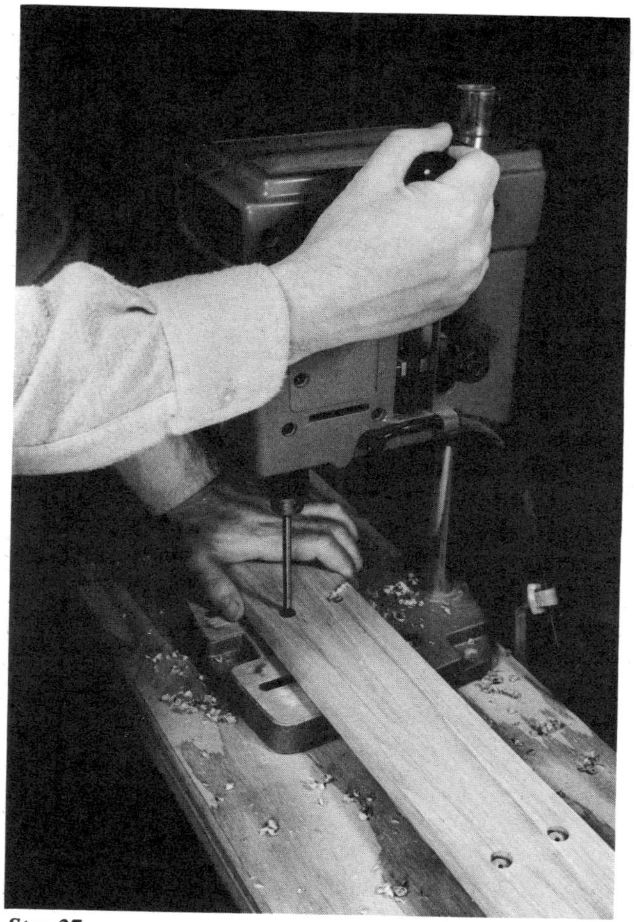

Step 27

Step 29

46. Mark the undersides of the table tops for screw-starter holes, using the corner braces on the pedestals as guides. Punch screw-starter holes with a nail set, and attach the pedestals to the tops with 3/4 × 10 flathead wood screws.

47. Use a vacuum cleaner to remove dust from the tables. Then wipe them down with a tack cloth or damp sponge, and they're ready for finishing.
48. For the oiled English oak finish, begin by using a paint brush to apply a liberal coat of Pen-Chrome English oak stain to each table, one at a time. Allow the stain to penetrate for no more than fifteen minutes; then wipe all surfaces dry with paper towels.
49. After the stain has dried overnight, use a soft cloth to apply a liberal coat of natural Watco Danish Oil to each table. Let oil penetrate for thirty minutes, applying more to any areas that appear dry.
50. Apply a second coat of Watco Danish Oil to all surfaces, and let it penetrate for fifteen minutes. Wipe all surfaces dry with paper towels and let the tables stand overnight.
51. To each table, apply a liberal amount of Watco Satin Oil with a soft cloth. Then, using more of the oil as a lubricant, lightly sand all surfaces with #600 wet-or-dry sandpaper.
52. Let the oil dry for ten minutes; then wipe dry with paper towels. Allow another thirty minutes drying time, and buff with a soft cloth.
53. Dampen a soft cloth or sponge with water, and wring out any excess. Use it to apply a thin and even coat of paste wax to each table top and trim. Let stand for ten minutes and buff with a soft cloth. Apply a second coat of paste wax, buff, and the tables are ready to use.

Required Tools

Steel tape rule
Yardstick or large T-square
Pencil
Claw hammer
Center punch
Screwdriver
Mitre box and backsaw
Two C-clamps
Two 40" or larger bar or pipe clamps
Stanley Surform Shaver or small block plane
Paint brush
Notched adhesive spreader
J-roller
Electric drill and 5/32", 11/64", and #8 countersink bits
Drill guide or drill-press attachment
Stanley No. 05 1/2" wood-boring bit
Circular saw
Saw guide
Belt sander
Pad sander

Required Materials

One sheet of 3/4" oak plywood, graded good or better
One sheet of 1 1/8" plywood flooring, shop grade or better
32′ of oak 1 × 4 (3/4 × 3 1/2")
One case of oak 6 × 6" parquet flooring. (If available by the parquet, 66 required)
5′ of 7/16" dowel rod
18′ of 3/4" oak quarter-round molding
White glue
One quart of paneling adhesive
42 1 × 8 flathead wood screws
120 1/2 × 10 flathead wood screws
24 3/4 × 10 flathead wood screws
36 2" corner braces
Medium-grit sanding belt
Medium-grit, fine-grit, extra-fine-grit, and #400 wet-or-dry sandpaper
#0000 steel wool

(Following optional for English oak finish)
One quart of Pen-Chrome English oak stain
One quart of Watco Natural Danish Oil
One pint of Watco Satin Oil
One can of Johnson's Paste Wax
#600 wet-or-dry sandpaper

Plywood Panels

From one sheet of 1 1/8" plywood flooring, shop grade or better, cut the following underlayment panels:

QUANTITY	SIZE	NOMENCLATURE
1	18 × 24"	End table panel
1	18 × 36"	Coffee table panel
1	36 × 36"	Corner table panel

From one sheet of 3/4" oak plywood, graded good or better, cut the following pedestal panels:

QUANTITY	SIZE	NOMENCLATURE
2	10 1/2 × 18"	End table panels
2	16 1/2 × 18"	End table panels
2	10 1/2 × 14 1/2"	Coffee table panels
2	14 1/2 × 22 1/2"	Coffee table panels
4	18 × 22 1/2"	Corner table panels

31
Four-Drawer Chest

This compact but roomy chest was designed to match the nightstands featured in Chapter 23. So if you're planning to build a coordinated set of bedroom furnishings, you'll want to paint this chest the same as the nightstands and install matching pulls. If you use glass tops on the nightstands, you might want to do the same on the chest. Order salvaged $1/4''$ plate glass cut to 16 by 32″, and have the edges seamed to remove sharp corners.

Other paint schemes and hardware can be substituted to give this chest a completely different look. If you have some scraps of $3/4''$ hardwood plywood lying about, you might prefer to finish the drawer faces naturally and paint the cabinet shell to match or contrast.

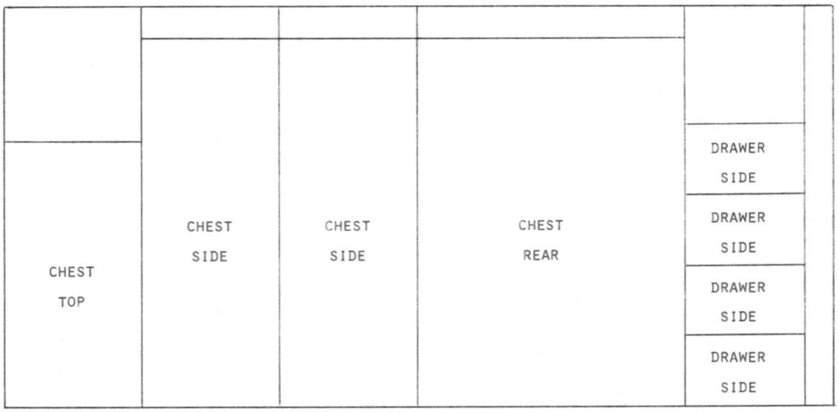

Cutting diagram for full sheet of ½" plywood

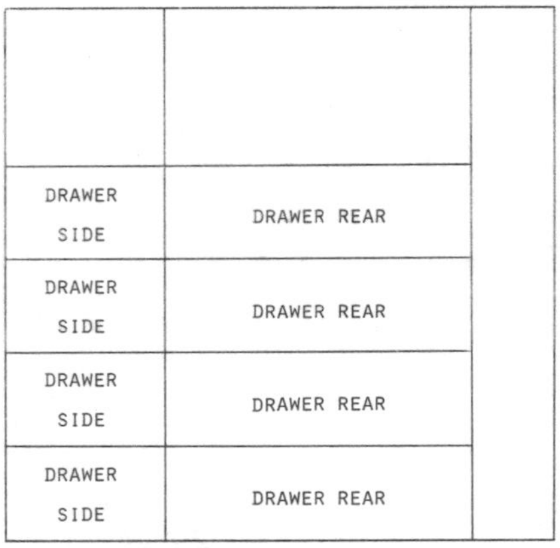

Cutting diagram for half-sheet of ½" plywood

Construction Steps

1. Cut two pieces of 1 × 2 to 44½", four to 28", and four to 14".
2. Cut a piece of 1 × 3 to 28" and another to 14".
3. Use a combination square to scribe lines across each 44½" vertical at 11½", 22", and 32½" from the bottom.
4. Apply glue to the end of the 28" piece of 1 × 3, butt it to the inside edge of one of the verticals—flush with the bottom—and staple the two pieces together with about five staples.
5. Apply glue to the end of a 28" piece of 1 × 2 and butt it to the inside of the vertical, with the bottom edge of the horizontal aligned with the line scribed nearest the bottom of the vertical; then staple together.
6. Continue gluing and stapling horizontals to the vertical the same way, with the last one flush with the top of the vertical.
7. Apply glue to the opposite ends of the horizontals, butt them to the other vertical, and staple them together.
8. Gently turn the face frame over and clamp top and bottom with bar or pipe clamps. Use corner clamps to tighten any loose joints on inside horizontals. Let the face frame stand until glue sets.
9. Scribe a line down the center of the inside of the 31 × 44½" rear panel. Then scribe short, intersecting, perpendicular lines at 11½", 22", and 32½" from the bottom.
10. On the outside of each 16 × 44½" side panel, scribe a line 1⅛" inside and parallel to the front edge. Scribe a parallel line ¼" inside the rear edge.
11. Turn each panel over and scribe a line 1½" inside and parallel to the front edge and another parallel to and ½" inside the rear edge.
12. Cut four pieces of parting bead to 44½" and prenail each with five ⅞" wire nails.

Step 8

13. Run a bead of glue down the underside of two strips of parting bead, lay on the inside of a side panel—aligned inside the lines scribed in **Step 10**—and drive the nails. Do likewise on the other side panel.
14. Turn the side panel over and prenail along each line scribed in **Step 11** with 1" ring-shank paneling nails, spaced about 6" apart.
15. On the left side panel, run a bead of glue down the front edge of the front parting-bead strip and the rear edge of the rear strip.
16. Run a bead of glue down the left edge of the face frame; then fit it into position against the parting-bead strip and clamp the side panel to it with two spring clamps or C-clamps.
17. Run a bead of glue down the left edge of the rear panel. Butt it to the rear of the side panel against the parting-bead strip, and clamp at the top and bottom corners with spring clamps or C-clamps.

18. Drive and countersink the nails and remove the clamps.

19. Attach the right side panel with glue and nails the same way.

20. Use a combination square to scribe center lines across the top and front edges of each face-frame horizontal. Similarly, scribe center lines across the top and bottom edges of the rear panel.

21. Scribe a short, centered guide line at each end of the top edge of each 14″ drawer guide (the 1 × 3's and 1 × 2's cut in **Steps 1** and **2**).

22. Lay the partially assembled chest on its back, and prenail the top horizontal of the face frame with two 1¼″ brads driven into the center line on the front edge. Apply a small amount of glue to each end of a 1 × 2 drawer guide and fit it into place between the face frame and rear panel, aligned with the guide marks scribed in **Step 20.** Drive and countersink the brads. Turn the unit over and drive two more brads through the rear panel into the drawer guide.

23. To each of the remaining 1 × 2 drawer guides, attach a 1⅝″ brass corner brace to the bottom edge, flush with the rear edge.

24. With the unit lying on its back, prenail each of the remaining horizontals with two brads, as in **Step 22.**

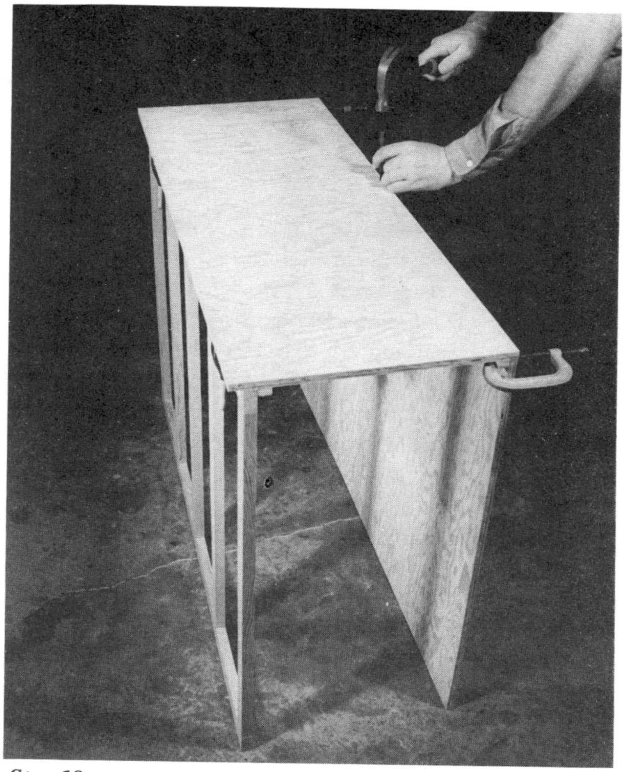

Step 18

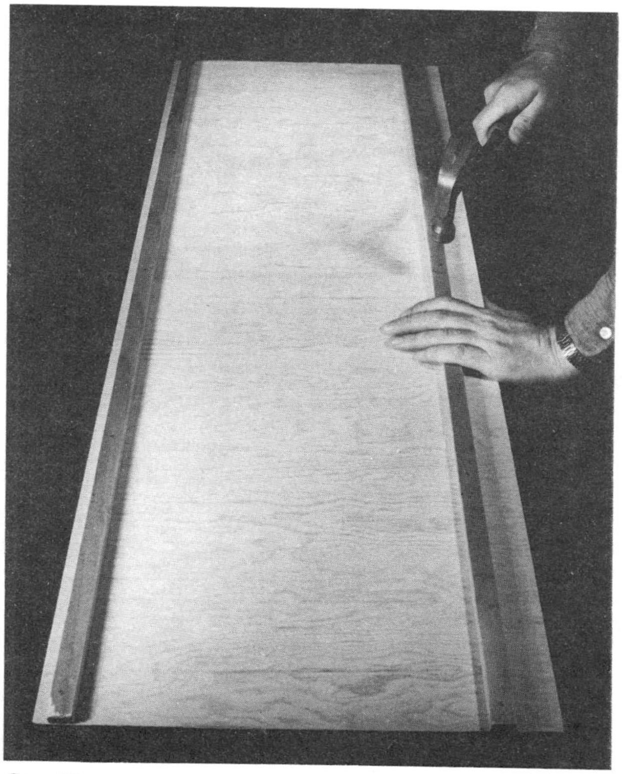

Step 13

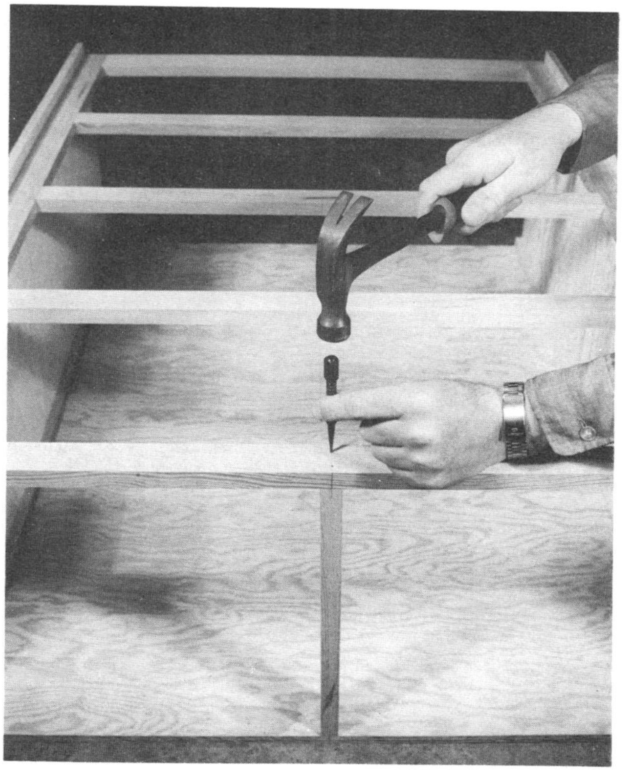

Step 22

25. Using the 1 × 2 drawer guides as templates, position each between the face frame and rear panel, with bottom rear edges aligned with the lines scribed in **Step 9,** and mark for screw-starter holes. Remove the guides and use a nail set to punch starter holes.

26. Install the 1 × 2 drawer guides with glue, brads (front), and screws (rear).

27. Install the bottom 1 × 3 drawer guide with glue and brads, the same way as the top guide.

28. On the top panel, scribe a line 1⅛″ from and parallel to the front edge and others ¼″ from and parallel to each remaining edge. Scribe another from front center to rear center. Then prenail the top panel with a 1″ ring-shank paneling nail ¼″ inside each corner.

29. Apply glue to all top edges of the partially assembled unit. Lay the top in place and nail down the corners. Now continue driving and countersinking 1″ paneling nails, about 6″ apart, along all lines on the top panel.

30. Conceal plywood laminations and fill nail holes and any imperfections with spackling paste.

31. Cut twelve pieces of parting bead to 26¾″ and eight pieces to 12½″.

32. Lay eight of the 26¾″ pieces side by side on a flat surface and use a combination square to scribe center lines across them simultaneously. Similarly, scribe other lines 2½″ from each end.

33. Set the square for ⅜″ and mark each of these lines for a centered screw hole.

34. Center-punch a drill-starter hole at each spot; then drill a 9/64″-diameter hole at each and countersink for #6 screws.

35. Sand the inside face of each drawer panel with medium-grit and fine-grit sandpaper to remove loose splinters and smooth the surfaces.

36. Prenail each of the undrilled 26¾″ pieces of parting bead with five ⅞″ wire nails, and each of the 12½″ pieces with three.

Step 26

37. Glue and nail each 26¾″ piece to the bottom inside of a drawer rear panel, flush with the bottom. Glue and nail each 12½″ piece to the bottom inside of a drawer side panel, flush with the bottom, 1″ inside the rear edge, and ½″ inside the front edge.

38. On the outside of each drawer side panel, scribe a line ¼″ inside and parallel to the rear edge and another ¼″ inside and parallel to the front edge.

39. Run a bead of glue down one side edge of a drawer rear panel, butt a side panel in place, and clamp the panels with a corner clamp.

40. Drive three 1″ paneling nails through the side panel into the rear panel, along the line scribed in **Step 38,** and countersink.

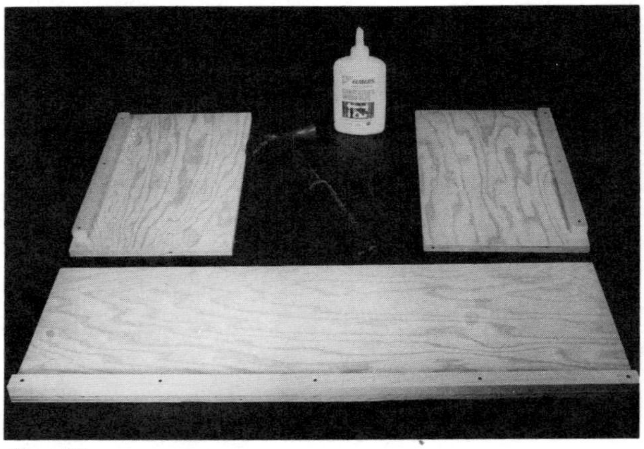

Step 37

Step 40

41. Attach the other side panel the same way.

42. Apply glue to each end of one of the drilled pieces of parting bead, and butt each end to a top front corner of the drawer; then clamp corners with corner clamps. Drive one 1″ paneling nail through a side panel into the parting bead at each end, and countersink. (Countersunk screw holes should face drawer inside.)

43. Apply glue to each end of another piece of drilled parting bead and to the front edges of the parting bead attached to the side panels. Press the parting bead into position at the bottom front corners of the drawer, and attach each end with a 1″ paneling nail.

44. Assemble the other three drawers the same way. Allow each to stand with at least two corner clamps in place while glue sets.

45. Scribe a centered horizontal line across the front of each drawer face. Then mark each line for screw holes at $4\frac{1}{2}''$ and 7″ from each end (for standard two-screw drawer pulls).

46. Center-punch a drill-starter hole at each spot. Then drill an $\frac{11}{64}''$-diameter hole (for standard pull screws) at each spot.

47. On the inside of each drawer face, scribe a line $\frac{5}{8}''$ from and parallel to the bottom edge. Then scribe a perpendicular line $1\frac{1}{8}''$ from the left edge and another $1\frac{1}{8}''$ from the right edge.

48. Run a bead of glue down the front edges of a drawer assembly and lay it atop the inside of a drawer face, aligning the bottom edge with the horizontal line and the sides inside the vertical lines. Tap and drive a $\frac{3}{4} \times 6$ flathead wood screw at each hole in the parting bead.

49. Attach the remaining drawer faces to the drawer assemblies the same way. Then conceal plywood edges with spackling paste.

50. From $\frac{1}{4}''$ tempered hardboard, cut four drawer bottoms to $13\frac{3}{8} \times 26\frac{5}{8}''$.

51. Drawer bottoms can be glued in place or simply laid atop the cleats. If they will be glued, apply glue to the drawer-bottom cleats and lay bottoms in place. Put a heavy object on each and let stand until glue sets.

52. Sand all exterior surfaces of the chest and drawer faces with medium-grit and fine-grit sandpaper.

53. Apply two coats of interior latex paint to all exterior surfaces of the chest shell and drawer faces.

54. Install a Roll-eez N roller at each bottom corner of the drawer opening and another top center on each drawer rear panel. Install an M roller bottom center on each drawer rear panel.

55. Attach drawer pulls with screws.

Step 43

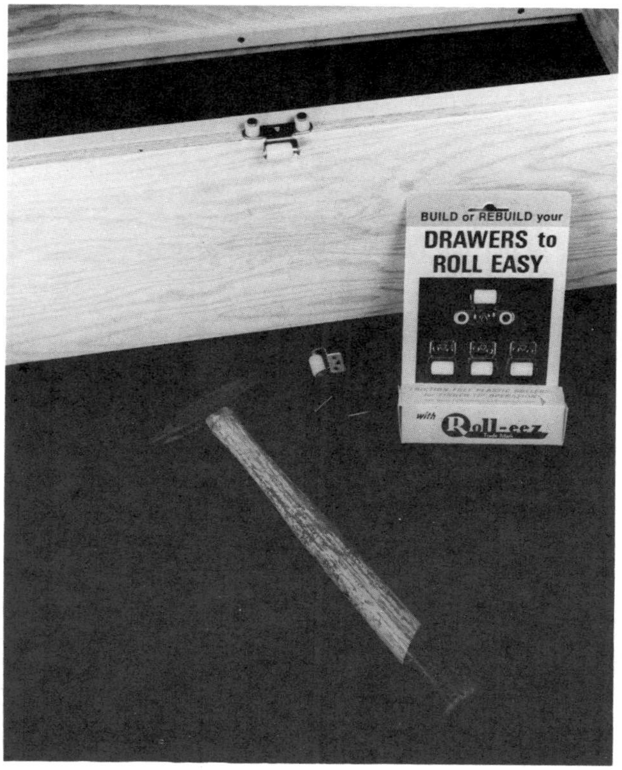

M roller is attached to bottom of rear drawer panel; N rollers are attached to drawer-supporting horizontals

Required Tools

Steel tape rule
Combination square
Yardstick or large T-square
Pencil
Claw hammer
Nail set
Center punch
Screwdriver
Mitre box and backsaw
Four C-clamps
Two 48″ bar or pipe clamps
Two to four corner clamps
Staple gun
Putty knife
Paint brush
Electric drill and $^{9}/_{64}$″, $^{11}/_{64}$″, and #6 countersink bits
Circular saw
Saw guide
Pad sander

Required Materials

One and a half sheets of ½″ plywood, G1S
Half-sheet of ¾″ plywood, G1S
Half-sheet of ¼″ tempered hardboard
18′ of 1 × 2, clear or patchable
4′ of 1 × 3, clear or patchable
40′ of parting bead
White glue
Spackling paste
1¼″ brads
⅞″ wire nails
Staples
1″ ring-shank paneling nails
24 ¾ × 6 flathead wood screws
Medium-grit and fine-grit sandpaper
Interior latex paint
Eight drawer pulls
Four sets of Roll-eez drawer rollers
Three 1⅝″ brass corner braces with screws

Plywood Panels

From a sheet and a half of ½" plywood, graded A–D or better, cut the following panels:

QUANTITY	SIZE	NOMENCLATURE
2	16 × 44½"	Side panels
1	16 × 32"	Top panel
1	31 × 44¼"	Rear panel
8	8½ × 14"	Drawer side panels
4	8½ × 26¾"	Drawer rear panels

From a half-sheet of ¾" plywood, graded A–D or better, cut the following panels:

QUANTITY	SIZE	NOMENCLATURE
4	10 × 30"	Drawer faces

32
Bookcase/ Entertainment Center

Here's a versatile unit that's handsome enough to use in the living room, family room, or anywhere else you might have a need for it. Since we needed something to house a small television set and stereo components in the master bedroom, that's where we put the one I built. With paint and trim to match our other bedroom furnishings, the unit looks made to order, which, of course, it was.

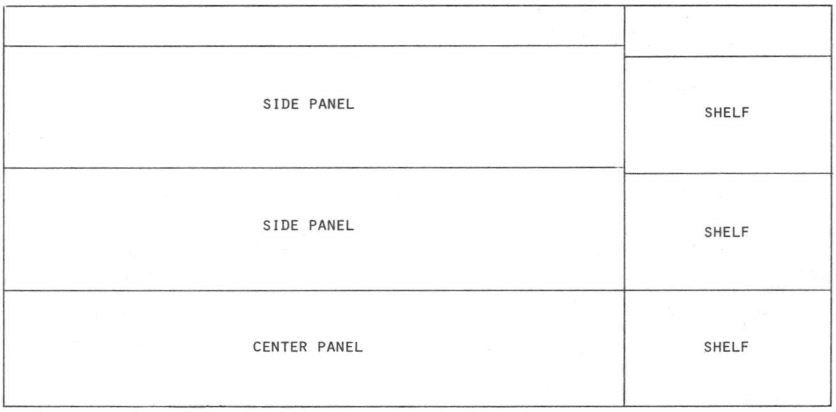

Cutting diagram for first sheet of 3/4" plywood

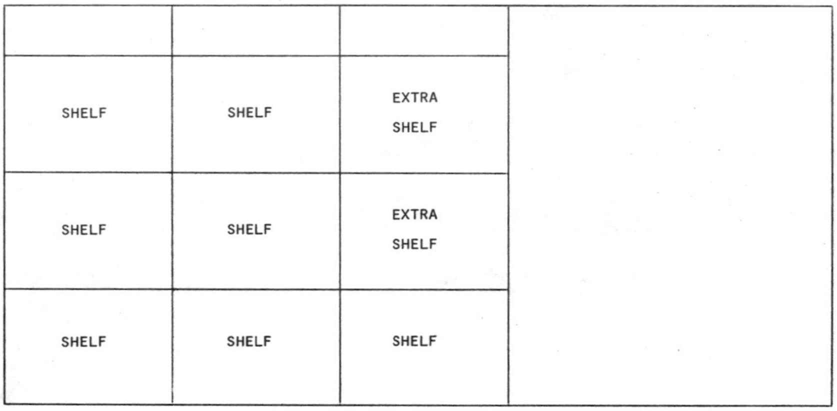

Cutting diagram for second sheet of 3/4" plywood

Fully adjustable shelves make this unit adaptable to a wide range of requirements. If you have no large items to store in it, you can make more than the ten shelves called for in the plan; there are sufficient leftovers of 3/4" plywood for as many shelves as you might want.

The rear panel adds stability to the unit and keeps unsightly electrical cords and speaker wires out of view. You will need to drill holes in the rear panel to run the wires through. So if you plan to keep any electrical equipment in your unit and know, beforehand, where it will be located, you should drill a 1"-diameter hole in the rear panel for each such apparatus before you paint. If you're not sure how you will arrange the shelves, you can drill the holes after the unit is finished and touch up the paint as required. These holes, incidentally, should be centered just above the shelves that hold the electrical components.

Although this is a sturdy unit, as with all such shelf modules it is further stabilized as weight is added to the shelves. You must be careful, however, to avoid overloading the upper shelves and making the unit top-heavy. Keep most books and other heavy items on the lower shelves. Then arrange other items for physical as well as visual balance. It helps to measure everything you plan to store on the shelves before you build the unit and make a rough sketch, rearranging items on paper until you strike the balance that suits you.

Construction Steps

1. Clamp the center panel to a solid surface and use a router and 5/8" straight bit to rout two 3/16"-deep grooves from top to bottom, each vertically centered 2 1/4" from one long edge. Turn the panel over and rout two identical grooves on the other side.
2. On the inside of each side panel, rout an identical groove 2 1/4" from the rear edge; then rout another in each, vertically centered 3" from the front edge.
3. Patch any surface imperfections in all plywood panels with spackling paste, and let stand until paste hardens. Then sand the surfaces with medium-grit and fine-grit sandpaper.
4. Press a 6' metal shelf-support standard into each groove, and use a soft-face mallet or block of wood and claw hammer to tap and seat the standard in the groove.
5. Attach each standard with ring-shank standard nails.

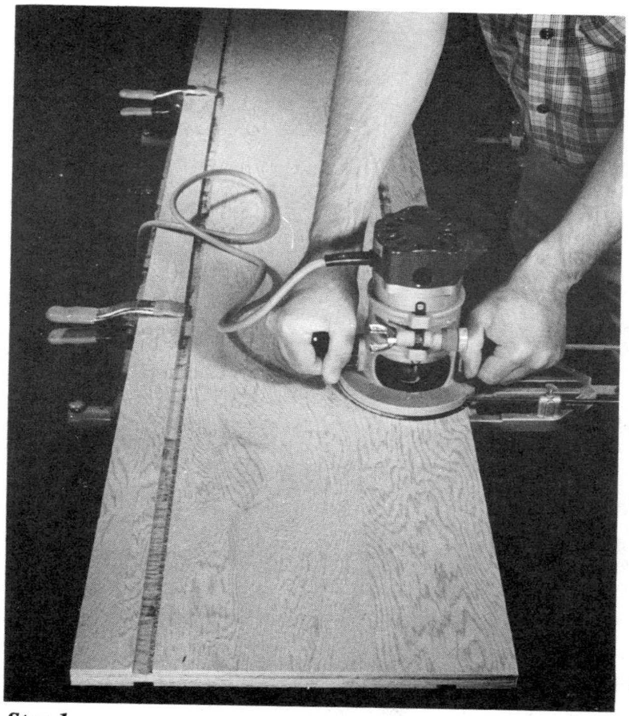

Step 1

Step 8

(These nails are supplied with the shelf supports used with the standards; you can also purchase them separately if you need more. The eight standards will require 104 nails.)

6. With a combination square, scribe a line across the front edge of the center panel $3\frac{1}{2}$" from the top and another $3\frac{1}{2}$" from the bottom.
7. Cut a piece of $\frac{3}{4}$"-square molding to 65" and prenail it with $1\frac{1}{4}$" brads, spaced about 6" or 8" apart.
8. Run a bead of glue down the front edge of the center panel, between the lines scribed in **Step 6.** Then attach the $\frac{3}{4}$"-square molding with brads and countersink the brads, leaving a $3\frac{1}{2}$" notch top and bottom.
9. On the back of the rear panel, scribe a vertical center line; then scribe another vertical line $\frac{3}{8}$" from the right edge and one $\frac{3}{8}$" from the left edge.
10. Scribe a horizontal line across the back of the rear panel $3\frac{1}{8}$" from and parallel to the bottom edge.
11. Use a combination square to scribe a centered line across the top edge of the rear panel and another across the bottom edge.
12. Prenail the rear panel with 1" ring-shank paneling nails, spaced about 6" apart, along each vertical line.
13. On the inside of each side panel and both sides of the center panel, scribe a horizontal line between the shelf standards $2\frac{3}{4}$" from the bottom edges.
14. Cut four shelf cleats from $\frac{3}{4}$"-square molding to $8\frac{1}{2}$". Prenail each with two $1\frac{1}{4}$" brads.
15. Run a bead of glue across each cleat, and attach each to a side or center panel, aligned immediately beneath the lines scribed in **Step 13.** Countersink the brads.
16. Run a bead of glue down the rear edge of the right side panel, butt it to the right front edge of the rear panel, and clamp top and bottom with corner clamps. Then drive and countersink the nails.
17. With the unit standing on the front edges of the side panels, attach the left side panel the same way.
18. Clamp the center panel to the rear panel with two corner clamps, carefully aligning the center panel with the guide lines scribed on the top and bottom edges of the rear panel in **Step 11.** (If you don't have six corner clamps, use one from each side panel.)
19. Loosen the screw on each corner clamp that holds the center panel, leaving the other screw tightly secured to the rear panel. Then slide the center panel out from beneath the unit.
20. Run a bead of glue down the rear edge of the center panel. Carefully slide it back under the unit, align it inside the corner clamps, and clamp tightly in place. Then drive and countersink the nails. See page 158.
21. Turn the unit over to rest on the rear panel, and set it atop a pair of sawhorses or a small workbench. Let stand for about an hour or until the glue sets.
22. Meanwhile, cut two pieces of 1 × 4 to 40". Measure down a broad face of each piece and make a small center mark on each, near the edge.
23. Set a combination square for $\frac{3}{8}$" and make a center

Step 20

mark at each end of the $\frac{3}{4}$"-square molding on the front edge of the center panel.

24. Apply glue to the bottom notch on the front edge of the center panel and to each end of one of the 1 × 4 pieces.
25. Lay the 1 × 4 in position at the bottom of the unit, between the bottom corners, and clamp each corner with a corner clamp. Carefully align the center mark on the 1 × 4 with the mark on the center-panel trim. Then drive two 1$\frac{5}{8}$" paneling nails through the 1 × 4 into the center panel and two more through each side panel into the ends of the 1 × 4. Countersink the nails.
26. Attach the other piece of 1 × 4 to the top front of the unit the same way. Let the unit stand with clamps in place until the glue sets.
27. With a mitre box and backsaw, cut eight pieces of 1" lattice to 19$\frac{1}{2}$". Prenail each piece with three $\frac{3}{4}$" brads, about $\frac{3}{8}$" from the top edge.
28. Run a bead of glue down each piece of lattice and use brads to attach the molding to the front edges of the shelves, flush with the shelf surfaces, creating $\frac{1}{4}$" lips on the shelf undersides.
29. Remove the corner clamps from the unit and stand it on its side on the floor. Then mitre-cut one end of a piece of 1" outside corner molding at 45°, and cut the other end square to fit a rear corner edge of the unit. Then attach the molding to the rear corner edge with glue and $\frac{3}{4}$" brads and countersink the brads.
30. Cut another piece of corner molding, with mitres at each end, to fit the top edge of the unit, and attach it with glue and brads; then countersink the brads.
31. Cut another piece of corner molding to fit the front edge of the unit, with a mitre at the top and a square cut at the bottom, and attach with glue and brads. Countersink the brads.

Step 25

32. Turn the unit over to stand on the trimmed side, and trim the other side the same way.
33. Stand the unit upright, and run a bead of glue along the top edge of each shelf cleat at the bottom of the unit. Lay one of the two untrimmed shelves atop the

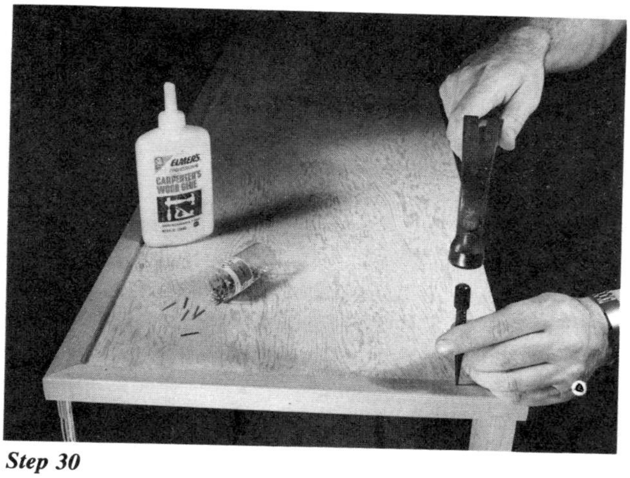

Step 30

cleats in each section of the unit, and press in place. The fit should be snug, so use a block of wood and hammer to gently tap the shelf into position.

34. Drive two 1⅝″ paneling nails through the bottom 1 × 4 into the front edge of each shelf. Then drive two more through the rear panel into the rear edge of each shelf, using the horizontal line scribed in **Step 10** as a guide.

35. Fill all brad and nail holes in the unit and shelf trim with spackling paste. Let stand until paste hardens.

36. If you plan to install electrical equipment in the unit and know where you will put it, drill centered 1″-diameter holes through the rear panel just above where each shelf will be situated.

37. Sand the spackled areas and elsewhere, as required, with medium-grit and fine-grit sandpaper.

38. Clean the unit with a vacuum cleaner to remove all dust, and wipe down shelves with a damp sponge. Then cover shelf standards with strips of ½″ masking tape.

39. Apply two coats of interior latex paint to all surfaces, using a contrasting color on the corner molding, if you wish. Let the unit stand overnight.

40. Move the unit to where it will stand, and install shelves with shelf supports, and your bookcase/entertainment center is ready to use.

Required Tools

Steel tape rule
Combination square
Pencil
Claw hammer
Soft-faced mallet
Nail set
Center punch
Mitre box and backsaw
Two C-clamps
Four to six corner clamps
Putty knife
Paint brush
Electric drill and 1″ bit
Circular saw
Saw and router guide
Pad sander
Router and ⅝″ straight bit

Required Materials

One sheet of ½″ plywood, G1S
Two sheets of ¾″ plywood, G2S
14′ of 1 × 2, clear or patchable
8′ of 1 × 4, clear or patchable
8′ of parting bead
6′ of ¾″-square molding
30′ of 1″ outside corner molding
14′ of 1″ lattice
White glue
Spackling paste
¾″ brads
1¼″ brads
1″ ring-shank paneling nails
1⅝″ ring-shank paneling nails
104 ring-shank shelf-standard nails
Medium-grit and fine-grit sandpaper
One roll of ½″ masking tape
Interior latex paint
Eight 72″ metal shelf-support standards
32 metal shelf supports

Plywood Panels

From two sheets of ¾" plywood, graded A–C or better, cut the following panels:

QUANTITY	SIZE	NOMENCLATURE
2	14¾ × 72"	Side panels
1	14 × 72"	Center panel
10*	14 × 19½"	Shelves

From one sheet of ½" plywood, graded A–D, cut the following panel:

QUANTITY	SIZE	NOMENCLATURE
1	41½ × 72"	Rear panel

*Cut additional shelves, as required, to the same dimensions from leftover ¾" plywood.

33 Four-Drawer File Cabinet

Few of us could get by without at least one small filing cabinet to house all the paperwork and records that accumulate in the course of running a household. Most of us, in fact, learn that our needs for filing space grow continuously and rapidly.

This four-drawer cabinet is a large-capacity unit with heavy-duty, full-suspension drawer slides. It was designed to match the two-drawer cabinet in Chapter 19, and the two make an attractive set for the person who needs plenty of file-drawer space. Drawer assembly is the same for both cabinets.

Construction Steps

1. Cut six 2 × 2 verticals to 57½″. Cut four 2 × 2 horizontals and one 2 × 4 horizontal to 14½″.
2. Mark lines across two of the 57½″ pieces at 15½″, 29″, and 42½″ from the bottom.
3. Prenail each of these verticals with two 8d finishing

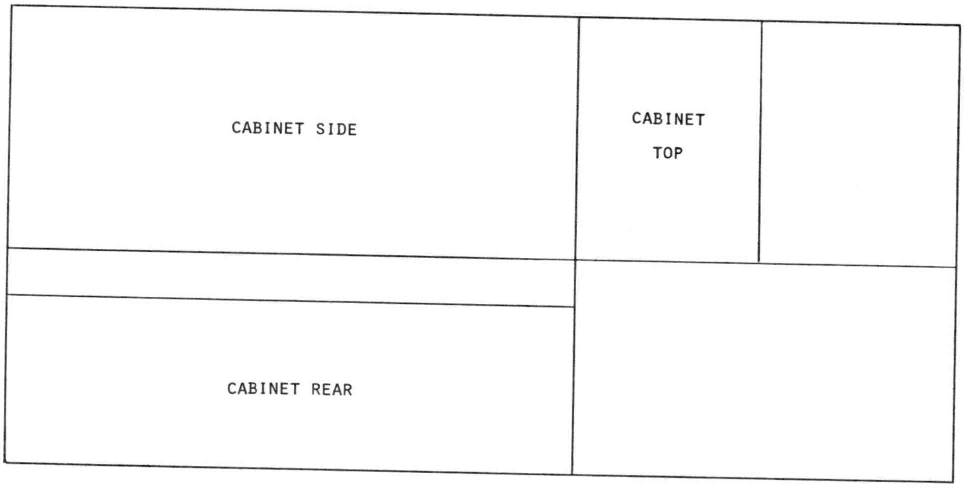

Cutting diagram for first sheet of ½" plywood

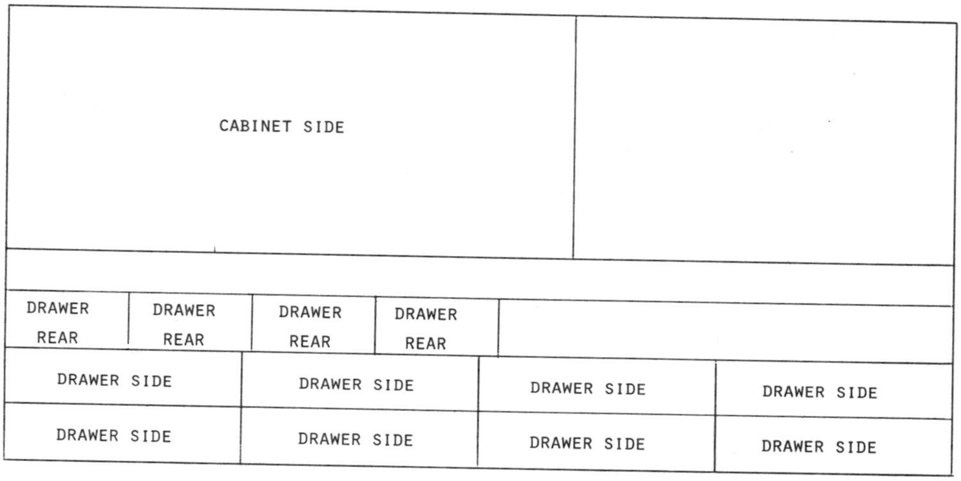

Cutting diagram for second sheet of ½" plywood

nails driven through the side, within 3½" of the bottom; two more above and within 1½" of each line scribed in **Step 2;** and two more within 1½" of the top.

4. Apply glue to the end of a 2 × 2 horizontal, butt it to the top of one of the prenailed verticals, and clamp it with a corner clamp. Glue and clamp three more horizontals to the vertical with their bottom edges aligned with the lines scribed in **Step 2.**
5. Apply glue to the end of the 2 × 4 horizontal, butt it to the vertical—flush with the bottom—and stand the assembly up on the horizontals. Drive and countersink the nails. See page 162.
6. Remove the clamps and attach them to the opposite ends of the 2 × 2 horizontals. Then glue and clamp the other prenailed vertical in place, and drive and countersink the nails.
7. On the outside of each 25½ × 57½" side panel, scribe vertical lines 1½" and 12¾" from the front edge and another 1¼" from the rear edge.
8. Turn the side panels over and on the inside of each, scribe vertical lines ¾" and 12" from the front edge and another ½" from the rear edge.
9. Run a wavy bead of glue down one of the remaining 2 × 2 verticals and clamp it to the inside of the side panel ½" inside the rear edge, using two spring clamps or C-clamps.
10. Glue and clamp another vertical 12" from the front edge. See page 162.
11. Turn the panel over and nail it to the verticals with 1⅝" ring-shank paneling nails. To ensure a proper bond, stagger the nails ¼" each side of the guide lines scribed in **Step 7**.
12. Attach two verticals in the same way to the other side panel.
13. Scribe lines across each of these verticals at 3½", 17", 30½", and 44" from the bottom.
14. Run a wavy bead of glue down the rear edge of the rear vertical on each panel, and run another bead down the ½" lip along the rear edge of each panel.

Step 5

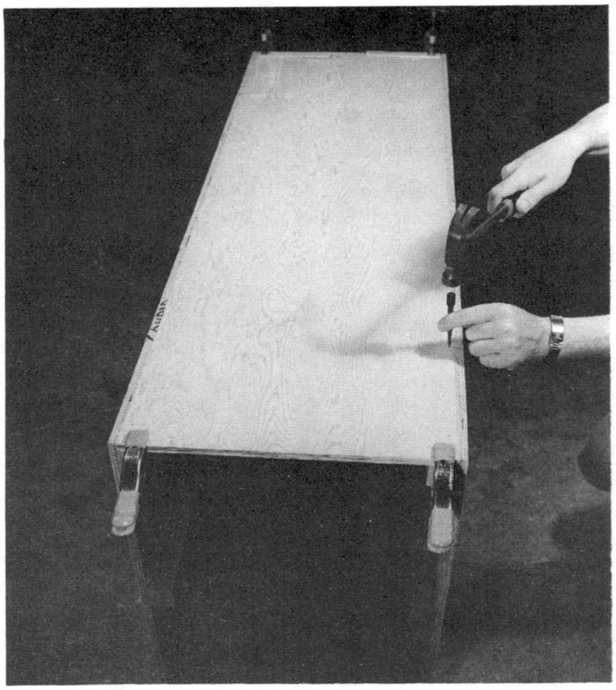

Step 16

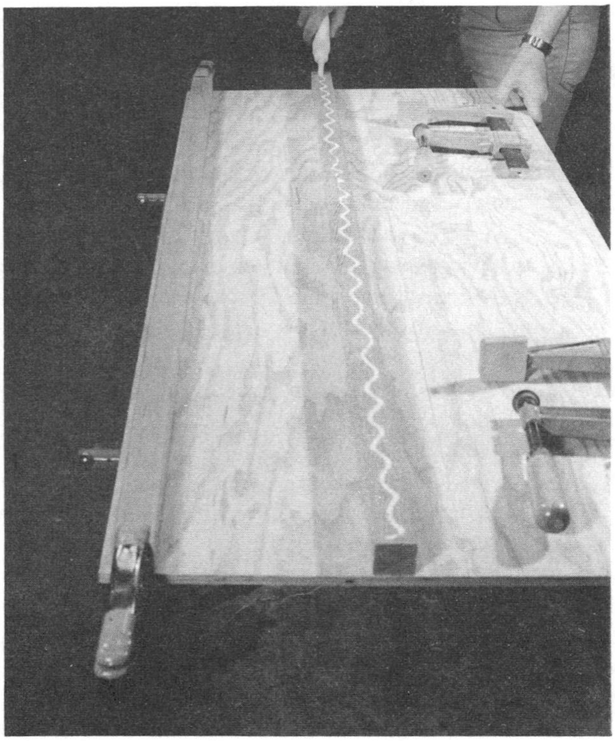

Step 10

Step 19

Step 22

15. Fit the $17\frac{1}{2} \times 57\frac{1}{2}''$ rear panel to the left side panel, and clamp the top corner with a C-clamp or spring clamp. Do likewise with the right side panel.

16. Turn the unit to rest on its front edges, and clamp the bottom corners of the rear and side panels. Then nail the rear panel to the rear verticals with 1″ paneling nails, spaced about 6″ apart. Countersink the nails.

17. Remove the clamps and set the unit upright. Clamp the top rear corners with corner clamps and leave them in place until the glue sets.

18. Apply a thin coat of glue with a paper towel to each side edge of the face frame. Spread the front of the side panels apart slightly and put the face frame in position between them. Align the face frame with the guide lines $\frac{3}{4}''$ from the front edges of the side panels, and clamp both sides top and bottom.

19. Attach the side panels to the face frame with 1″ paneling nails, spaced about 6″ apart and staggered along the guide lines scribed in **Step 7.** Countersink the nails.

20. Remove the C-clamps or spring clamps. Then clamp the top front corners with corner clamps and leave them in place until the glue sets.

21. Turn the unit on its right side and lay a drawer channel marked C-R across the vertical, flush with the front of the face frame, resting against the 2 × 4 horizontal, and aligned with the lines scribed on the verticals in **Step 13.** Using the channel as a guide, mark the vertical for a screw-starter hole. Punch screw-starter holes, and mount the channel with screws provided.

22. Mount another C-R channel, the same way, at each of the next three horizontals.

23. Turn the cabinet over and mount the C-L channels on the left side.

24. Stand the cabinet upright, remove the corner clamps, and apply glue to the top edges of the unit. Then attach the $18\frac{1}{2} \times 25\frac{1}{2}''$ top panel with 1″ paneling nails along each edge and the top horizontal.

25. Cut twelve pieces of parting bead to $12\frac{1}{2}''$ and eight pieces to $22\frac{1}{2}''$.

26. Measure in 2″ from each end of eight $12\frac{1}{2}''$ pieces and mark for a centered hole. Punch a drill-starter hole at each spot. Then drill a $\frac{9}{64}''$-diameter hole at each spot and countersink for #6 screws.

Turn to Chapter 19—"Two-Drawer File Cabinet"—and construct four drawers according to the instructions set forth there in **Steps 27** through **41.**

42. Conceal plywood laminations, fill nail holes, and patch any imperfections with spackling paste. Let stand until paste hardens.
43. Sand all exterior surfaces with medium-grit and fine-grit sandpaper.
44. Clean the cabinet and drawers with a vacuum cleaner to remove all dust. Then apply two coats of interior latex paint to the cabinet exterior and drawer faces. (Drawer faces may be finished in a contrasting color.)
45. When paint has dried, install pulls with mounting screws. Lay drawer bottom atop cleats. Bottoms may be glued to cleats or left unglued.

Required Tools

Steel tape rule
Combination square
Yardstick or large T-square
Pencil
Claw hammer
Nail set
Center punch
Screwdriver
Mitre box and backsaw
Four C-clamps
Four corner clamps
Putty knife
Paint brush
Electric drill and bits, including #6 countersink
Circular saw
Saw guide
Pad sander

Required Materials

Two sheets of ½" plywood, G1S
Half-sheet of ¾" plywood, G1S
Half-sheet of ¼" tempered hardboard
24′ of parting bead
16′ of 1 × 2, clear or patchable
14½" scrap of 1 × 4, clear or patchable
10′ of 2 × 2, standard or better
8′ of 2 × 4, standard or better
White glue
Spackling paste
8d finishing nails
1" ring-shank paneling nails
1⅝" ring-shank paneling nails
⅞" wire nails
16 1 × 6 flathead wood screws
Medium-grit and fine-grit sandpaper
Interior latex paint
Four drawer pulls
Four sets of Model 1300 Knape & Vogt 24" 75-pound-capacity drawer slides
16 self-adhesive drawer/door cushions

Plywood Panels

From two sheets of ½" plywood, graded A–D or better, cut the following panels:

QUANTITY	SIZE	NOMENCLATURE
2	25½ × 57½"	Side panels
1	17½ × 57½"	Rear panel
1	18½ × 25½"	Top panel
8	6 × 24"	Drawer side panels
4	6 × 12½"	Drawer rear panels

From a half-sheet or available scraps of ¾" plywood, graded A–D or better, cut the following panels:

QUANTITY	SIZE	NOMENCLATURE
4	13 × 16½"	Drawer faces

34 Modern Pedestal Desk

For some reason, maybe the big price tags on the commercially available desks, I long considered a modern pedestal desk to be something too complicated for me to build. When I finally began thinking in simpler terms, I found such a desk easy to design and easier to build. After all, a desk is merely a slab of wood atop a pair of pedestals, and the pedestals are no more than simple boxes containing other boxes.

This desk features two large file-size drawers and two shallower stationery drawers, all of which glide smoothly on Knape & Vogt roller slides. You'll want to pick attractive drawer pulls that will coordinate with the paint used on the pedestals, and you might wish to paint the drawer faces and trim a contrasting color, as I did.

For the top, you'll need a solid-core door, and the choice of face veneers is yours. A wide variety of hardwood veneers is available, which can be stained or left natural. I picked senwood for its dramatic grain and stained it lightly with Pen-Chrome English oak stain to bring out the character of the wood.

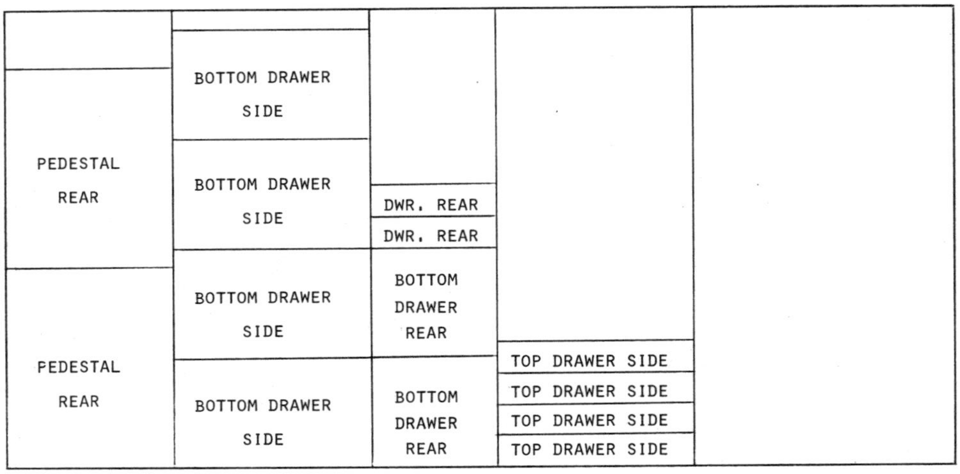

Cutting diagram for $\frac{1}{2}$" plywood

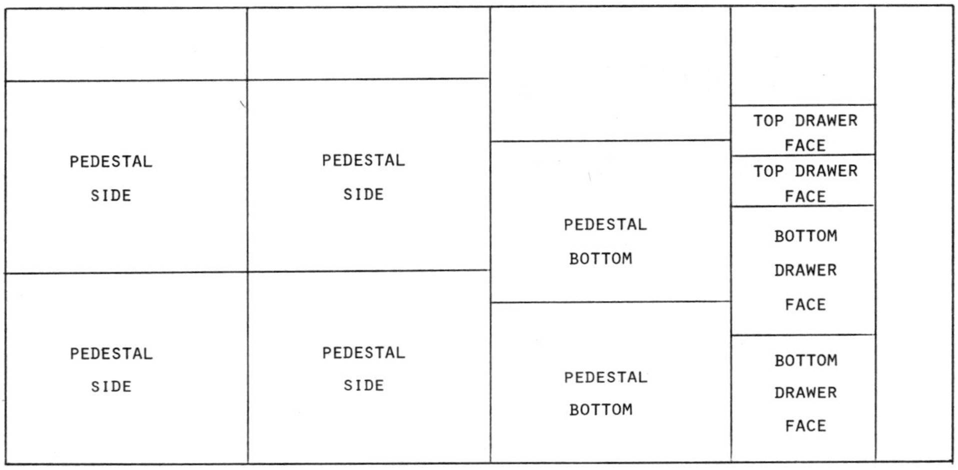

Cutting diagram for $\frac{3}{4}$" plywood

Construction Steps

1. Cut four pieces of $\frac{3}{4}$"-square molding to $20\frac{1}{4}$" and six pieces of 1 × 2 to 14".
2. Use a combination square to scribe a line across each piece of $\frac{3}{4}$"-square $13\frac{1}{2}$" from the bottom.
3. To assemble each pedestal face frame, begin by applying glue to the end of one piece of 1 × 2, butting it to the top inside of a piece of $\frac{3}{4}$"-square molding, clamping the two pieces with a corner clamp, driving two $1\frac{5}{8}$" ring-shank paneling nails through the molding into the 1 × 2, and countersinking the nails.
4. Attach another 1 × 2 horizontal to the bottom of the $\frac{3}{4}$"-square molding the same way. Let stand for about an hour or until the glue sets.
5. Remove the corner clamps. Then glue, clamp, and nail the middle 1 × 2 horizontal with its bottom edge aligned with the line scribed in **Step 2.** Attach the middle horizontal to the other face-frame assembly the same way, and let stand until glue sets.
6. Remove clamps and stand each face frame with horizontals upright; then apply glue to the horizontal ends and clamp top and bottom corners to the $\frac{3}{4}$"-square vertical. Drive and countersink two paneling nails into each horizontal, and leave clamps in place until glue sets.
7. On the bottom of each 17 × $24\frac{3}{16}$" bottom panel, scribe a line $\frac{3}{8}$" from and parallel to each side edge. Mark each line for drill-starter holes at 1" and $8\frac{1}{2}$" from each end.
8. Punch a drill-starter hole at each spot; then drill a $\frac{5}{32}$"-diameter hole at each spot, and countersink for #8 screws.
9. On the inside of each $20\frac{1}{4}$ × $24\frac{3}{16}$" side panel, scribe a line $\frac{3}{4}$" from and parallel to the front edge.
10. On the inside of each 17 × 21" rear panel, scribe a vertical center line. Then scribe short, intersecting, vertical marks at $2\frac{1}{4}$" and $15\frac{3}{4}$" from the bottom.
11. For each pedestal, run a bead of glue down the bottom edge of the right side panel, butt it to the bot-

Step 6

Step 14

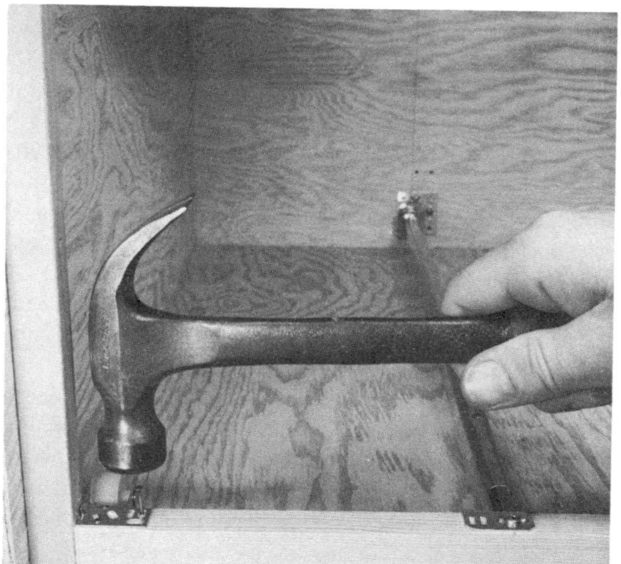

Step 19

tom panel, and clamp each corner with a corner clamp.

12. Drill a $\frac{7}{64}''$-diameter pilot hole through each hole in the bottom panel into the side panel. Then attach the panels with $1\frac{1}{2} \times 8$ flathead wood screws, and remove the clamps.
13. Lay each partially assembled pedestal on its right side. Prenail each face frame with three or more 1″ paneling nails, driven into the right vertical.
14. Run a bead of glue along the bottom and right edges of the face frame; then lay it in place on the inside of the right and bottom pedestal panels, aligned with the lines scribed in **Step 9.** Then drive and countersink the nails.
15. Run a bead of glue down the left side of the face frame and bottom edge of the left side panel; then clamp the left panel and attach with screws, as in **Step 12.**
16. Lay each pedestal face down, and run a bead of glue along the rear edges. Lay the rear panels atop the pedestals and attach with 1″ paneling nails, spaced about 6″ apart. Countersink the nails.
17. Lay the pedestals on their backs, and install two drawer-slide back brackets on each rear panel, aligned with the center line and cross marks.
18. Set the pedestals upright and scribe a center line across the bottom and middle horizontals of the face frame. Then slip the drawer slides into the back brackets. Align the front of the slides with the center lines on the horizontals, and mount with the screws provided or $\frac{7}{8}''$ wire nails.
19. At the bottom corner of each drawer opening, mount a drawer roller with screws or $\frac{7}{8}''$ wire nails.

20. Cut twelve pieces of parting bead to $12\frac{3}{4}''$ and eight pieces to $18\frac{1}{2}''$.
21. Use a combination square to mark the bottom inside edge of each drawer side panel with a short vertical line $\frac{1}{2}''$ from the front and another $1''$ from the rear.
22. Prenail four of the $12\frac{3}{4}''$ pieces and all of the $18\frac{1}{2}''$ pieces with three $\frac{7}{8}''$ wire nails each.
23. Run a bead of glue down the underside of each $12\frac{3}{4}''$ piece and nail each to an $11\frac{1}{2} \times 12\frac{3}{4}''$ or $3\frac{1}{4} \times 12\frac{3}{4}''$ drawer rear panel, flush with the bottom edges.
24. Glue and nail each $18\frac{1}{2}''$ piece along the bottom inside edge of a drawer side panel, positioned $\frac{1}{2}''$ from the front edge and $1''$ from the rear edge.
25. Align the remaining pieces of parting bead side by side and use a combination square to scribe lines across them $2''$ from each end. Then set the square for $\frac{3}{8}''$ and mark the center of each line on each piece.
26. Punch a drill-starter hole at each spot. Then drill a $\frac{9}{64}''$-diameter hole at each spot, and countersink for #6 screws.
27. Scribe a centered horizontal line across the front of each drawer face; then mark each line for drill-starter holes at $5\frac{3}{4}''$ and $8\frac{3}{4}''$ from one end (for standard pulls).
28. Punch a drill-starter hole at each spot, and drill a hole at each spot large enough to accommodate the drawer-pull mounting screws ($\frac{11}{64}''$ diameter is standard).
29. To construct each drawer, start by running a bead of glue down the left edge of the rear panel, butting it to the left side panel, and clamping the two panels at the top with a corner clamp.
30. Drive two $1''$ paneling nails through the side panel into the rear panel on each shallow drawer, and countersink. (Use three nails on the deep drawers.)
31. Glue, clamp, and nail the right side panel to the rear panel the same way, and leave both corner clamps in place.
32. Apply glue to each end of one of the drilled pieces of parting bead and fit it into position, spanning from one bottom front corner to the other, with countersunk holes facing the inside of the drawer. Drive and countersink one $1''$ paneling nail into each end. Glue and nail another piece the same way, between the top front corners, and let the drawer stand with clamps in place until the glue sets.
33. Scribe a horizontal line across the inside of each drawer face, $\frac{3}{4}''$ from the bottom edge on the shallow faces and $1\frac{1}{4}''$ from the bottom on the deep faces. Measure in $\frac{3}{8}''$ from each end and make small marks on each line.
34. Run a bead of glue across the front edges of each drawer assembly and lay it in place on the inside of

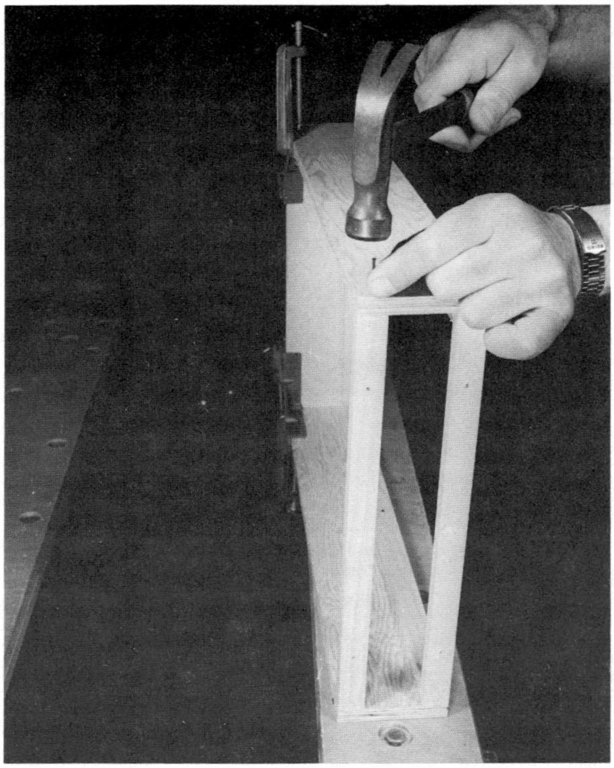

Step 32

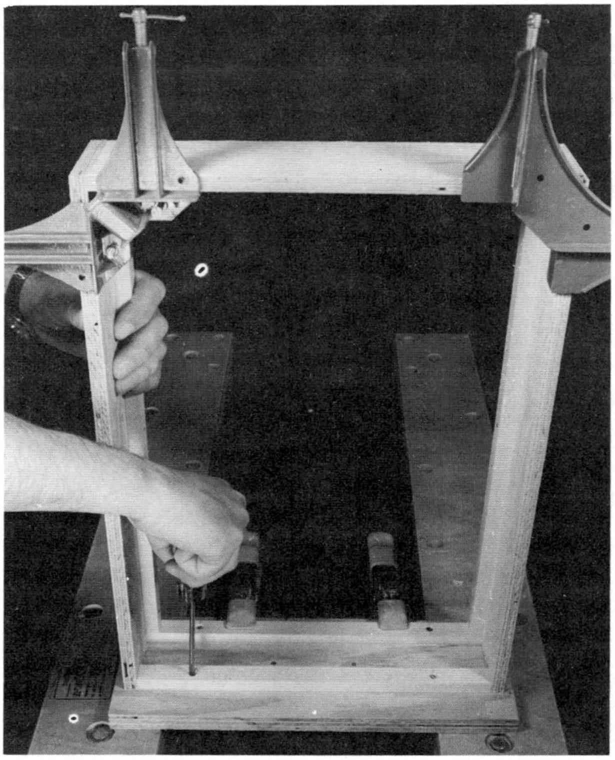

Step 35

a drawer face, aligned with the line scribed in **Step 33,** and set between the cross marks; then clamp with two small C-clamps or spring clamps.

35. Insert a 1 × 6 flathead screw in each hole, tap lightly with a hammer to start, and drive. Then remove the clamps.

36. Scribe a vertical center line across the back of each drawer rear panel. Then align a drawer back roller with the center line, flush with the bottom of the drawer, and attach with the screws provided.

37. For each pedestal, cut a piece of 1″ outside corner molding to fit the left front corner, square at the top and mitred to 45° at the bottom. Then attach it with glue and $^3/_4$″ brads and countersink the brads.

38. Similarly, attach another piece along the bottom edge, and another along the right edge, the last piece cut square and flush with the top.

39. Frame out the rear panel of each pedestal the same way.

40. Fill all brad holes and conceal plywood laminations with spackling paste, and let dry.

41. Sand the pedestals and drawer faces with medium-grit and fine-grit sandpaper.

42. Clean the drawers and pedestals to remove all dust. Then apply two coats of interior latex paint to drawer faces and pedestal exteriors. Use a contrasting color on the faces and corner molding if you wish.

43. When paint has dried, invert the pedestals and attach two leg plates on each—centered front and rear—with the screws provided.

44. Attach the drawer pulls to the faces with mounting screws.

45. Trim the solid-core door to 29 × 69″.

46. Use a mitre box and backsaw to mitre-cut a piece of 1$^5/_8$″ bullnose stop to fit one of the long edges of the desk top.

47. Scribe lines across the outside face of the bullnose stop at $^1/_2$″ and 18$^1/_2$″ from each end and another at the center. Then mark each line for drill-starter holes $^3/_8$″ from the top and bottom edges.

48. Use a narrow-diameter nail set or pin punch (not a center punch) to carefully punch a small, shallow drill-starter hole at each mark. Then drill a $^1/_{16}$″-diameter pilot hole at each spot.

49. Attach the bullnose stop to one long edge of the desk top with glue and 1″ brads, and countersink the brads.

50. Mitre-cut another piece of bullnose stop to fit a short edge. Make a mark and drill this piece at the center and 1$^1/_2$″ from each end, and mount it to a short edge of the top with glue and 1″ brads.

51. Trim the remaining two edges of the top the same way.

52. Fill the brad holes with wood filler and let the top stand until the filler sets.

Step 57

53. Sand the desk top and edges with medium-grit, fine-grit, and extra-fine-grit sandpaper, carefully rounding over any sharp edges and corners. Then polish with #0000 steel wool.

54. Clean all surfaces to remove dust. Then apply the stain of your choice to all surfaces of the desk top as well as to the pedestal legs.

55. Apply a coat of sanding sealer to the desk top and edges and to the pedestal legs. When dry, lightly sand with #400 wet-or-dry sandpaper or #0000 steel wool, and apply two coats of polyurethane varnish, sanding or burnishing between coats.

56. Using a 2″ corner brace as a guide positioned on the inside top edge of each pedestal, 2″ inside each corner, mark for screw pilot holes. Then center-punch drill-starter holes and drill $^9/_{64}$″-diameter holes $^1/_2$″ deep.

57. Mount a corner brace at each location with two $^3/_4$ × 12 panhead sheet metal screws (four braces per pedestal).

58. Lay the desk top upside down on a protected surface (such as a carpeted floor). Set the pedestals upside down on the underside of the desk top, positioned 3″ from each end, with corner molding on the front of the pedestals aligned just inside the bullnose stop on the front edge of the top. Then mark for screw holes, using the corner braces as guides.

59. Remove the pedestals and center-punch drill-starter holes in the desktop underside. Then drill a $\frac{9}{64}$"-diameter hole 1" deep at each spot.

60. Reposition the pedestals and mount them to the desk top with 1 × 12 panhead sheet metal screws.

61. Screw legs into leg plates and set the desk upright.

62. From $\frac{1}{4}$" tempered hardboard, cut four drawer bottoms to $12\frac{5}{8} \times 19\frac{3}{8}$". Either glue them in place atop the cleats in the drawers, or simply lay them on the cleats. Slide the drawers into the pedestals.

Required Tools

- Steel tape rule
- Combination square
- Yardstick or large T-square
- Pencil
- Claw hammer
- Nail set
- Center punch
- Screwdriver
- Mitre box and backsaw
- Two C-clamps
- Two to four corner clamps
- Putty knife
- Paint brush
- Electric drill and bits, including #6 and #8 countersink bits
- Circular saw
- Saw guide
- Pad sander

Plywood Panels

From one sheet of $\frac{3}{4}$" plywood, graded A–D or better, cut the following panels:

QUANTITY	SIZE	NOMENCLATURE
4	$20\frac{1}{4} \times 24\frac{3}{16}$"	Pedestal side panels
2	$17 \times 24\frac{3}{16}$"	Pedestal rear panels
2	$13\frac{1}{2} \times 14\frac{1}{2}$"	Drawer faces
2	$5\frac{1}{4} \times 14\frac{1}{2}$"	Drawer faces

From one sheet of $\frac{1}{2}$" plywood, graded A–D or better, cut the following panels:

QUANTITY	SIZE	NOMENCLATURE
2	17×21"	Pedestal rear panels
4	$11\frac{1}{2} \times 20$"	Drawer side panels
2	$11\frac{1}{2} \times 12\frac{3}{4}$"	Drawer rear panels
4	$3\frac{1}{4} \times 20$"	Drawer side panels
2	$3\frac{1}{4} \times 12\frac{3}{4}$"	Drawer rear panels

Required Materials

- One sheet of $\frac{1}{2}$" plywood, G1S
- One sheet of $\frac{3}{4}$" plywood, G1S
- One solid-core interior door
- Half-sheet of $\frac{1}{4}$" tempered hardboard
- 24' of parting bead
- 32' of $\frac{3}{4}$"-square molding
- 5' of 1 × 2, clear or patchable
- 8' of 1 × 4, clear or patchable
- 24' of 1" lattice
- 24' of $1\frac{5}{8}$" bullnose stop
- White glue
- Spackling paste
- $\frac{3}{4}$" brads
- 1" brads
- $1\frac{5}{8}$" ring-shank paneling nails
- 16 1 × 6 flathead wood screws
- 16 $1\frac{1}{2}$ × 8 flathead wood screws
- 16 $\frac{3}{4}$ × 12 panhead sheet metal screws
- 16 1 × 12 panhead sheet metal screws
- Medium-grit, fine-grit, and extra-fine-grit sandpaper
- #0000 steel wool
- Stain of choice
- Sanding sealer
- Polyurethane varnish
- Interior latex paint
- Four drawer pulls
- Four sets of Model KV1175 Knape & Vogt $22\frac{5}{8}$" drawer slides
- Four 6" table legs with leg plates and screws
- Eight 2" corner braces

35
Base-Cabinet Workbench

A workbench should be rugged and functional, but that doesn't mean it can't be pleasing to look at as well. This base-cabinet bench is as sturdy as they come, provides an abundance of convenient storage space, and is a handsome addition to the workshop.

Although the unit was designed to fit against a rear wall and right side wall, you can easily adapt it to left-wall installation, with the top overhanging the right side. With a few simple modifications, you could even construct it on a long rear wall with no side wall. To do this, attach the right-side horizontals in the same way as the left ones are installed in the plans. You would need two cabinet side panels, instead of one. And the top would be centered on the cabinet, with a 2¼″ overhang at each end.

The plan calls for 24′ of 1 × 2, but you won't be able to get by with the standard eight-footers. Two of the pieces must be slightly longer than 8′, so buy 9′ pieces and a six-footer if you can. If your local lumber dealer won't cut the odd sizes for you, you'll have to get two sixteen-footers cut to nines and sevens, then use the left-overs on other projects.

As usual, you have a number of options: you can paint, stain, varnish, or leave it unfinished. I left my own bench unfinished, which is appropriate for most workshop furnishings. If you decide to finish your unit, you should fill and sand the face frame before attaching the doors. And you'll want to fill and sand the doors and drawer faces and paint them before attaching the hardware.

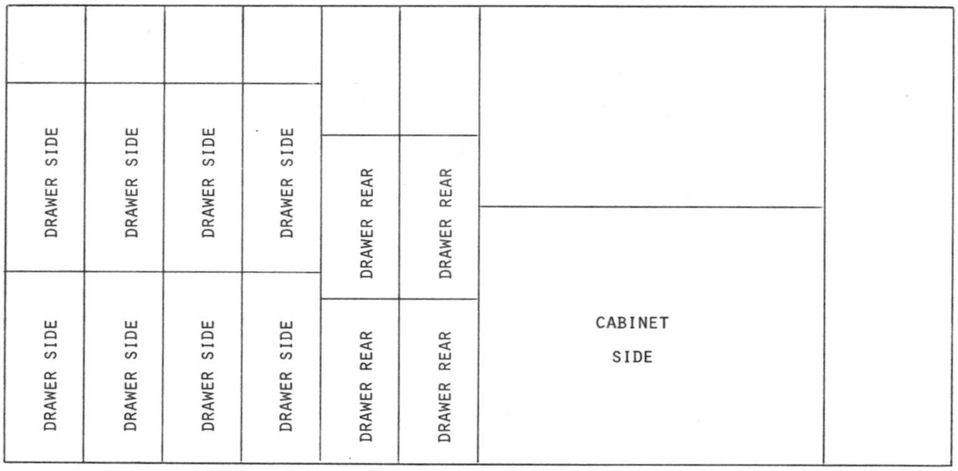

Cutting diagram for ½" plywood

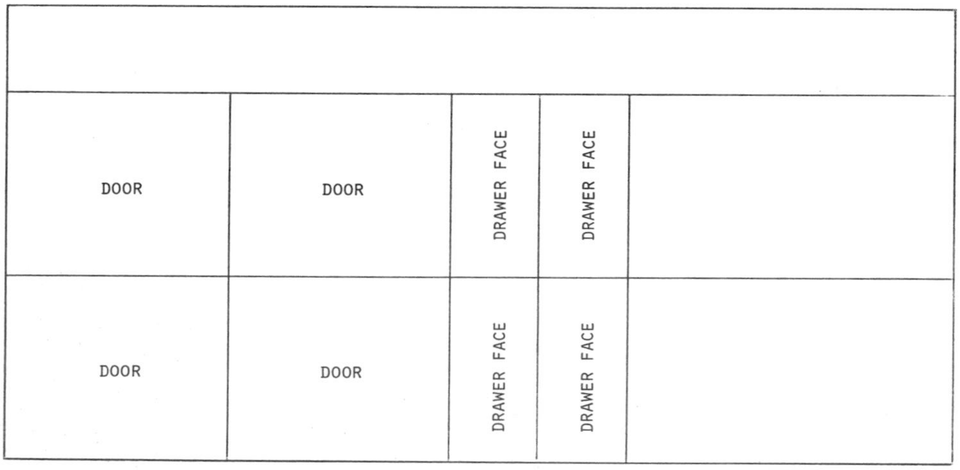

Cutting diagram for first sheet of ¾" plywood

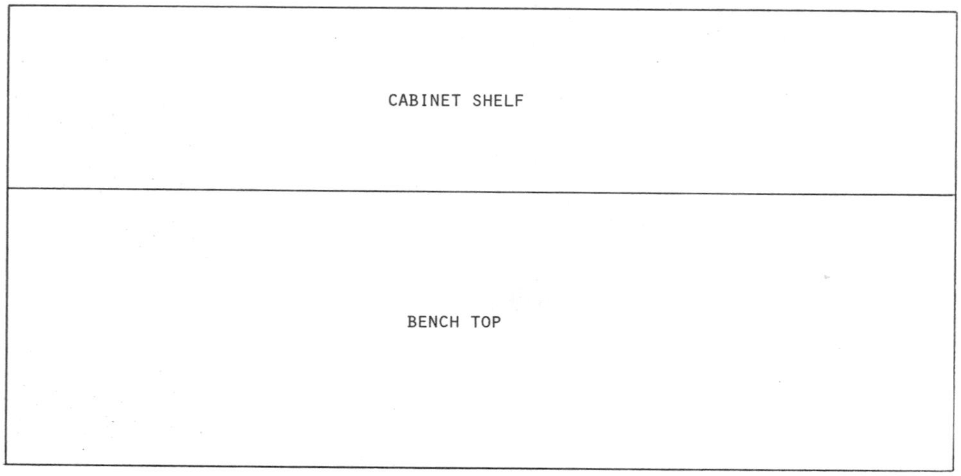

Cutting diagram for second sheet of ¾" plywood

Construction Steps

1. With a mitre box and backsaw, cut a piece of screen molding, with a 45° mitre at each end, to fit one long edge of a drawer face.
2. Prenail the molding with four ¾″ brads. Run a bead of glue down the edge of the drawer face, attach the molding with brads, and countersink the brads.
3. Measure and cut a piece of molding to fit a short edge of the drawer face; then attach it, the same way, with glue and brads.
4. Trim the remaining two edges of the drawer face, as well as all edges of the other three faces, with screen molding.
5. Use the same materials and techniques to trim the edges of the four doors.
6. From 2 × 4 stock, cut five face-frame verticals to 32″.
7. Examine the verticals and lay them out with the best broad faces up. Then, starting with the one on the far right, mark the bottoms with numbers 1 through 5.
8. Turn the #1 vertical to rest with its left narrow face up. Measure down from the top and use a combination square to scribe lines across the narrow face at 8½″ and 10″. Then set the square for ½″ and make perpendicular stop marks on each broad face.

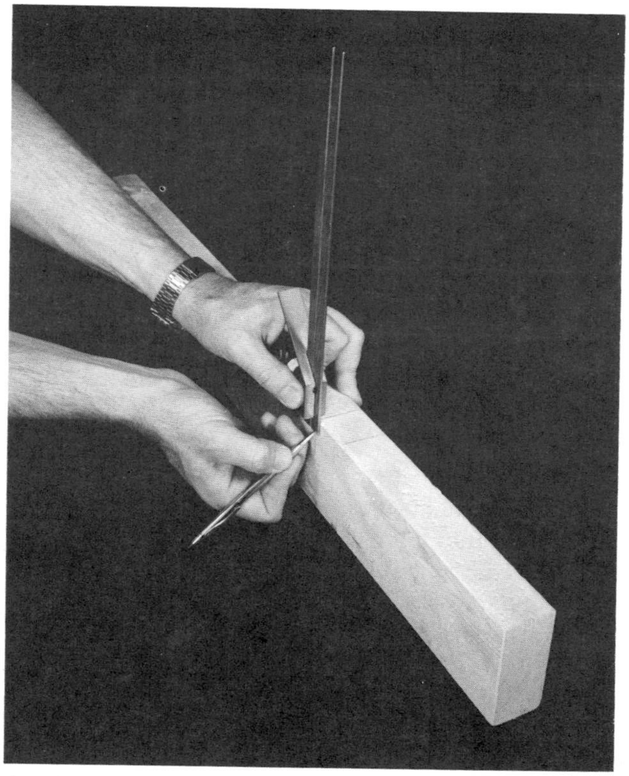

Step 8

Step 12

9. Turn the #5 vertical to rest with its right narrow face up. Scribe lines on this one identical to those in **Step 8**.
10. Scribe identical lines on *both* narrow faces and stop marks on *both* broad faces of each remaining vertical.
11. Use a mitre box and backsaw to make a ½″-deep cut just inside each line scribed across the narrow faces, using the stop lines as depth guides.
12. Use a wood chisel up to 1½″ wide and a hammer to knock out the material between the saw cuts. Then smooth out the dadoes with a wood rasp.
13. From 2 × 2 stock, cut two face-frame horizontals to 91½″.
14. Lay the horizontals best face up, and use a combination square to scribe lines across them at 3½″, 22″, 25½″, 44″, 47½″, 66″, 69½″, and 88″ from one end.
15. Turn the top horizontal top side up, and using the lines scribed in **Step 14** as guides, scribe identical lines across the top face.
16. Turn the bottom horizontal bottom side up, and scribe identical lines.
17. Prenail the top surface of the top horizontal and the bottom surface of the bottom horizontal with two 8d finishing nails between each end and the nearest line. Drive two more nails between each set of lines.
18. Prop the #5 vertical in a corner. Apply glue to the top edge of the #1 vertical. Lay one end of the top horizontal atop the #5 vertical and butt the #1 vertical to the underside of the other end of the horizontal. Then drive and countersink the nails. See page 174.
19. Apply glue to the top end of the #2 vertical, and butt it to the underside of the horizontal, between the first set of lines scribed in **Step 14.** Then drive and countersink the nails.
20. Continue attaching verticals to the horizontal the same way. Then carefully invert the partially assembled face frame.

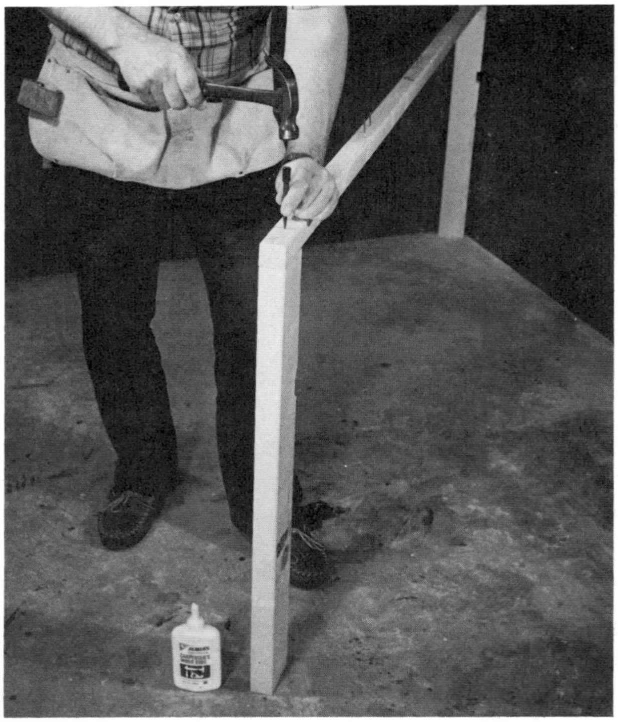

Step 18

Step 22

21. Apply glue to the bottom ends of the verticals. Lay the bottom horizontal in place atop them and drive and countersink the nails.
22. Lay the face frame on the floor and clamp each end with a bar or pipe clamp. Then wrap band clamps around the frame at the #2 and #4 verticals and tighten. Let the frame stand until the glue sets.
23. Measure the distance between the dadoes in the verticals, and cut four 2 × 2 horizontals to fit snugly.
24. Apply glue to the inside of the dadoes and fit the horizontals into them. Use a soft-faced mallet or block of wood and hammer to tap the horizontals into the dadoes.
25. Remove the clamps from the face frame and stand the frame upright. Then toenail a 6d finishing nail through each bottom corner of each drawer opening into the adjacent vertical, and countersink the nails.
26. From 2 × 4 stock, cut four side horizontals to 25½″ and two rear horizontals to 88½″. Then cut another 2 × 4 rear horizontal to 90″ and a 2 × 2 to the same length.
27. Lay one side horizontal on the floor against the side wall, with the rear end butted into the corner of the rear and side walls; then drive two 8d box nails through the horizontal into each stud.
28. Mount another side horizontal, identically, above the first, 35″ from the floor.
29. Measure up the rear wall near the corner and make marks on the wall at 12″, 25″, and 33½″ from the floor. Make identical sets of marks about 4′ and 7′ to the left of those near the corner.

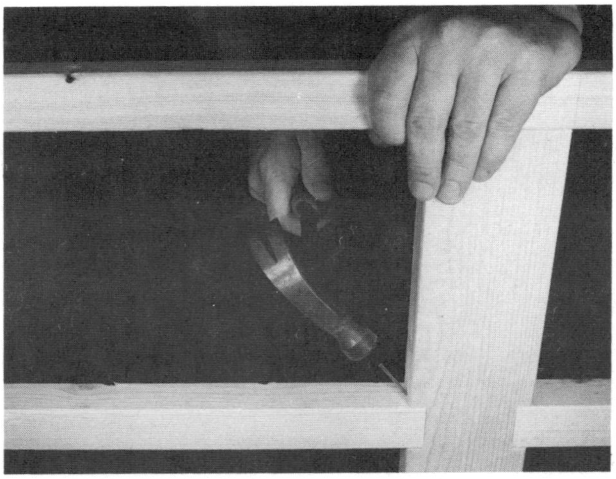

Step 25

30. Scribe lines across the rear horizontals to coincide with the rear-wall studs, and prenail each with two 8d box nails along each line.
31. Position an 88½″ horizontal along the rear wall with the right end butted against the top horizontal on the side wall. Using the top marks made in **Step 29,** align the horizontal 33½″ above the floor, and drive the nails into the studs.

32. Mount a 90″ 2 × 4 horizontal beneath the first and 25″ above the floor, with the right end butted into the corner.
33. Mount the 90″ 2 × 2 horizontal the same way, 12″ above the floor.
34. Butt the right end of the remaining $88\frac{1}{2}$″ horizontal against the bottom side horizontal, and nail it to the studs along the rear wall and floor.
35. Toenail an 8d finishing nail through the top edge of each horizontal into each stud, and countersink the nails.
36. Measure from one end of the 90″ 2 × 4 and make marks on the front face at $12\frac{3}{4}$″, $34\frac{3}{4}$″, $56\frac{3}{4}$″, and $78\frac{3}{4}$″. Then use a combination square to scribe a vertical line across the front face at each mark.
37. Mount four drawer-slide back brackets to the 90″ 2 × 4 with screws provided, each flush with the top of the horizontal and aligned with the lines scribed in **Step 36.**
38. With a mitre box and backsaw, cut six pieces of parting bead to $3\frac{1}{2}$″. Then prenail each with two $\frac{7}{8}$″ wire nails.
39. Lay the face frame on the floor, face down. Measure up from the bottom and, with a combination square, scribe a line across the inside of each end vertical and the center vertical, 12″ from the bottom.

Step 37

Step 34

40. Run a bead of glue down one of the $3\frac{1}{2}''$ pieces of parting bead, and attach it to one of the end verticals on the face frame, aligned immediately beneath the line scribed in **Step 39.** Attach another, the same way, to the other end vertical, and another to the center vertical.
41. Attach each of the remaining $3\frac{1}{2}''$ pieces of parting bead with glue and nails to the three inside verticals, aligned with the top edge of each vertical, where it is joined to the top horizontal.
42. Lay the left door face up on a working surface. Measure 3″ from the right edge and scribe a vertical line from the top down about 10″.
43. Make a cross mark on the line 5″ from the top. Then use a pull as a guide to mark for screw-starter or drill-starter holes.
44. Depending upon which type of pull you're using, center-punch drill-starter holes and drill screw holes, or use a nail set to punch screw-starter holes for the pull.
45. Turn the door over and position a hinge along the left inside edge, 3″ from the top. Use the hinge as a guide to mark for screw-starter holes. Do likewise with another hinge, 3″ from the bottom edge.
46. Punch screw-starter holes for the hinges with a nail set; then mount the hinges with screws provided.
47. On the door that will be hung right of the first door, prepare for mounting the pull the same way, but 3″ inside and 5″ below the top left corner. Then mount the hinges along the right inside edge. Do likewise with the remaining pair of doors.
48. Lay the face frame face up on the floor; then lay the doors in position over the door openings. Arrange the doors so they're centered over the openings, and use the hinges as guides to mark for screw-starter holes.
49. Remove the doors, and punch starter holes in the face frame with a nail set. Reposition the doors, and mount them with hinge screws.
50. Butt one of the remaining $25\frac{1}{2}''$ 2 × 4 side horizontals at a right angle to the bottom rear-wall horizontal, and attach with glue and two 8d finishing nails. Countersink the nails.
51. Similarly, attach the last side horizontal to the top rear-wall horizontal so that the top edge of the side horizontal is $1\frac{1}{2}''$ higher, or 35″ from the floor.
52. Apply glue to the ends of all side horizontals. Then stand the face frame upright and butt it to the horizontals. Drive two 8d finishing nails through each top and bottom corner of the face frame into the respective side horizontal, and countersink the nails.
53. From 2 × 4 stock, cut six shelf and top supports to $25\frac{1}{2}''$.
54. Apply glue to the top edge of each of the three parting-bead cleats located 12″ from the bottom on the inside of the face frame. Then apply glue to the ends of three shelf supports and lay each in place, supported at one end by a cleat and the other end by the 2 × 2 rear horizontal. Drive and countersink two 8d finishing nails through the face frame into each shelf support, and attach the rear of each support to the horizontal with two more nails.
55. The shelf merely can be laid atop the supports and positioned against the rear wall, or it can be perma-

Step 49

Step 52

nently attached with glue and $1\frac{1}{4}''$ brads. In either case, install it now.

56. Use a combination square to scribe a center line across the top edge of each 2 × 2 at the bottom of each drawer opening. Then install a drawer slide and two drawer rollers in each opening, either with screws provided or with $\frac{7}{8}''$ wire nails.

57. Apply glue to the three parting-bead cleats near the top of the face frame and attach the three 2 × 4 top supports with glue and 8d finishing nails the same way as the shelf supports were installed.

58. Apply glue to the sides of the left horizontals and left edge of the face frame. Then attach the cabinet side panel with 1″ paneling nails, spaced about 10″ apart.

59. Cut a piece of 1″ outside corner molding to fit the front left corner of the unit, attach it with glue and $\frac{3}{4}''$ brads, and countersink the brads.

60. Apply a liberal amount of glue to the top of the shelf supports and horizontals and lay the bench top in place, butted into the rear and side walls. Attach the top with 6d finishing nails, spaced about 10″ or 12″ apart along the horizontals and supports, and countersink the nails.

61. Cut a piece of $\frac{1}{4}''$ tempered hardboard to 29 × 96″, and make sure it will fit the top perfectly for a flush fit along the front and left edges. (If your top measurements are slightly off, cut the hardboard about $\frac{1}{4}''$ shorter and narrower, as any gap along the walls will be concealed by the backboards.)

62. Use a notched adhesive spreader to cover completely the bench top with an even coat of panel adhesive. (Be sure to read and heed the adhesive manufacturer's warnings, and, by all means, make sure there is adequate cross-ventilation.)

63. Clean all dust from the hardboard and lay it, smooth side up, atop the bench.

64. Use a J-roller, rolling pin, or hammer and block of wood to seat the hardboard firmly in the adhesive. Check it several times during the first hour to make sure the bond is complete.

65. Cut a piece of 1 × 2 to fit the front edge of the bench top, square at the right end and mitred to 45° at the left end. Then attach the piece with glue and $1\frac{1}{4}''$ brads spaced about 10″ or 12″ apart. Then cut another piece to fit the left edge of the top, install it with glue and brads, and countersink the brads.

66. Cut another piece of 1 × 2 to fit along the rear wall for the length of the top and trim. Mitre-cut the right end, and square-cut or bevel-cut the left end. Attach this backboard along the rear edge of the top by driving and countersinking a 6d finishing nail into each stud. Similarly, attach another piece along the right edge, against the side wall.

67. Scribe a centered horizontal line across each drawer face. Center a pull along each line, and mark for screw-starter or drill-starter holes. Depending upon which type pull you're using, punch or drill the necessary holes.

Step 56

Step 57

68. Turn the drawer faces over, and scribe a horizontal line across each, $\frac{3}{4}''$ from the bottom. Measure in $\frac{7}{8}''$ from each end and make a small cross mark on the line.

69. Cut twelve pieces of parting bead to $17\frac{1}{4}''$ and eight pieces to $18\frac{1}{2}''$. Prenail the $18\frac{1}{2}''$ pieces and four of the $17\frac{1}{4}''$ pieces with three $\frac{7}{8}''$ wire nails each.

70. Lay the remaining eight $17\frac{1}{4}$" pieces side by side and use a combination square to simultaneously scribe a center line across each, as well as lines 2" from each end. Then set the square for $\frac{3}{8}$" and mark the center of each line on each piece.

71. Center-punch a drill-starter hole at each spot; then drill a $\frac{9}{64}$"-diameter hole at each spot, and countersink for #6 screws.

72. Run a bead of glue down each of the prenailed $17\frac{1}{4}$" pieces, and nail to the drawer rear panels, flush with the bottom edges.

73. Similarly, attach the $18\frac{1}{2}$" pieces to the inside bottom edges of the drawer side panels, 1" from the rear edge and $\frac{1}{2}$" from the front.

74. Run a bead of glue down the left edge of a drawer rear panel, butt it to a left side panel, and clamp the top corner with a corner clamp. Then attach the side panel to the rear panel with three 1" paneling nails.

75. Attach the right side panel the same way.

76. Apply glue to each end of a drilled piece of parting bead and position it between the bottom front corners of the drawer (countersunk holes inside), and drive a paneling nail through each side panel into the parting bead. Attach another drilled piece, the same way, between the top corners.

77. Run a bead of glue down the front edges of the drawer, and lay the assembly atop the inside of a drawer face. Align the bottom parting bead immediately above the horizontal line and between the cross marks made in **Step 68.** Lightly clamp the top parting bead to the drawer face with a pair of C-clamps or spring clamps.

78. Insert a $\frac{3}{4} \times 6$ flathead wood screw into each hole in the parting bead, tap lightly with a hammer to start, and drive.

79. Construct three more drawers the same way, and let each stand with corner clamps in place, for about an hour, or until the glue sets.

80. Scribe a vertical center line across the back of each drawer rear panel. Then on each, position a rear roller with the flange aligned with the center line and flush with the bottom edge of the rear panel. Mark for and punch screw-starter holes, and mount the roller with screws provided.

81. Cut four drawer bottoms from $\frac{1}{4}$" hardboard to $17\frac{1}{8} \times 19\frac{3}{8}$". Lay bottoms atop the cleats in the drawers and install the drawers in the cabinet. (Bottoms may be glued to the cleats or left unglued.)

82. Remove all visible pencil marks and layout lines with an eraser. Then attach pulls to the drawers and doors with screws provided.

83. Stick a self-adhesive cork cushion on the face frame near each corner of each door opening, opposite the hinge side. Stick another near each corner of each drawer opening, and your new bench is ready for work.

Step 78

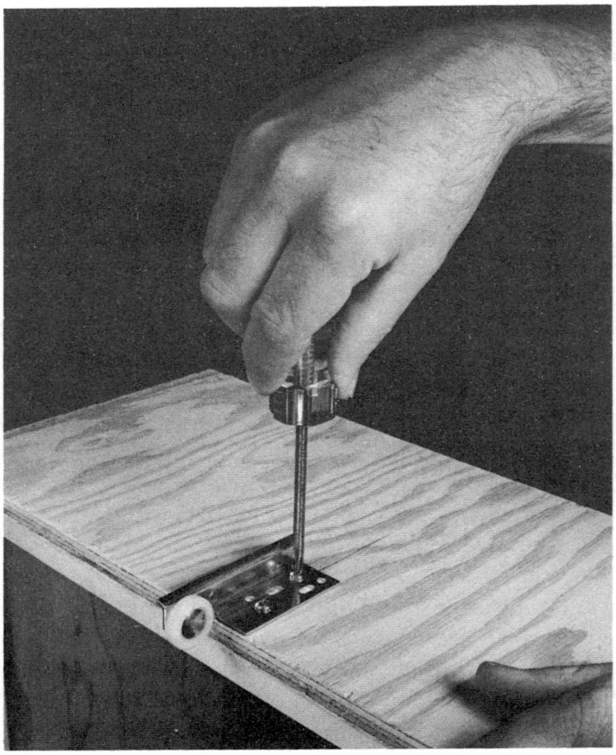

Step 80

Required Tools

- Steel tape rule
- Combination square
- Pencil
- Claw hammer
- Soft-faced mallet
- Nail set
- Center punch
- Screwdriver
- Mitre box and backsaw
- Two C-clamps
- Two 48″ bar or pipe clamps
- Two band clamps
- Two to four corner clamps
- 1½″ or smaller wood chisel
- Wood rasp
- Notched adhesive spreader
- Stud finder
- J-roller
- Electric drill and bits, including #6 countersink
- Circular saw
- Saw guide
- Pad sander

Required Materials

- One sheet of ½″ plywood, G1S
- Two sheets of ¾″ plywood, G1S
- One sheet of ¼″ tempered hardboard
- 32′ of parting bead
- 24′ of 1 × 2, clear or patchable
- 32′ of 2 × 2, standard or better
- 64′ of 2 × 4, standard or better
- 3′ of 1″ outside corner molding
- 56′ of screen molding
- White glue
- One quart of panel adhesive
- ¾″ brads
- 1¼″ brads
- ⅞″ wire nails
- 1″ ring-shank paneling nails
- 8d box nails
- 6d finishing nails
- 8d finishing nails
- 24 ¾ × 6 flathead wood screws
- Eight drawer/door pulls
- Eight self-closing hinges
- Four sets of Model 1175 Knape & Vogt 24″ drawer slides
- 24 self-adhesive drawer/door cushions

Plywood Panels

From two sheets of ¾" plywood, graded A–D or better, cut the following panels:

QUANTITY	SIZE	NOMENCLATURE
1	29 × 96"	Bench top
1	18⅞ × 91"	Shelf
4	19½ × 22½"	Doors
4	9 × 19½"	Drawer faces

From one sheet of ½" plywood, graded A–D or better, cut the following panels:

QUANTITY	SIZE	NOMENCLATURE
4	8 × 17¼"	Drawer rear panels
8	8 × 20"	Drawer side panels
1	27 × 35"	Cabinet side panel

Part

V

Projects from Leftovers

The following twenty projects can be built with the scraps left over from other plywood projects.

36 Workshop Helpmates

Every do-it-yourselfer needs at least one pair of sawhorses, and these will prove more useful and versatile than any others, especially for working with plywood and other sheet stock. If you own a WORKMATE® Work Center and Vise, these handy horses will greatly extend the usefulness of that unit.

The Helpmates, as I call them, will support long boards that are being drilled, sawed, routed, or sanded. They quickly and easily secure 4 × 8′ sheet stock. Material clamps to them with WORKMATE clamp attachments or conventional C-clamps. And, in the spirit of WORKMATE portability and stowability, they break down for carrying to any job site or storing on a shelf or beneath a workbench.

You'll need two pairs of commercial folding sawhorse legs, which are designed to be clamped to pieces of 2 × 4 for sawhorses 30¼″ high. The Helpmates, how-

ever, are made with 2 × 6 stock that gets trimmed for a specific height. If you own or are planning to buy a WORKMATE, you'll want your Helpmates to be of the same height; $31\frac{1}{4}''$ for the Single 23" or Dual 27" models, and $31\frac{7}{8}''$ for the Dual 29" and Clampdown 35" models.

The only materials you probably won't find at your local home-improvement center are the plastic, snap-lock ties that will hold the folded legs of the Helpmates when they're dismantled. These are available at sporting-goods stores, camping centers, and marinas.

You can put your Helpmates together in about an hour by following these simple steps:

Construction Steps

1. Trim two pieces of 2 × 6 to 48" each; then rip each to a width of 4" (for Single 23" or Dual 27" WORKMATE) or $4\frac{5}{8}''$ (for Dual 29" or Clampdown 35" model).
2. Measuring from one end of each 2 × 6, mark the tops for centered lag-bolt holes at 2", 16", 32", and 46".
3. Center-punch a drill-starter hole and drill a $\frac{7}{32}''$-diameter hole at each spot.
4. Trim two scraps of $\frac{3}{4}''$ plywood, G1S, to 5 × 48".
5. Scribe a line down the center of each piece of plywood; then scribe two more lines on each piece, 1" inside each 48" edge.
6. Measuring from one end on each piece of plywood, mark the center line at 2", 16", 32", and 46". Mark the right line at 1", 11", 21", 37", and 47". Mark the left at 1", 6", 16", 24", 32", 42", and 47".
7. Center-punch drill-starter holes at the marks along each line on each piece of plywood.
8. Along the center line on each piece, drill a $\frac{3}{4}''$-diameter hole $\frac{3}{8}''$ deep at each spot. Along the left and right lines, drill $\frac{3}{4}''$-diameter holes all the way through.
9. Drill a $\frac{5}{16}''$-diameter hole through the centers of the $\frac{3}{4}''$-diameter holes along the center line in each piece.
10. Attach each piece of plywood to an altered 2 × 6 with four lag screws and flat washers.
11. Lay the assemblies upside down on the floor, and attach a pair of folding metal sawhorse legs to each. Your Helpmates are now ready to stand upright and go to work.

Optional Steps

12. With a permanent felt-tip marker, trace lines around the sawhorse legs where they meet the 2 × 6. (Lines

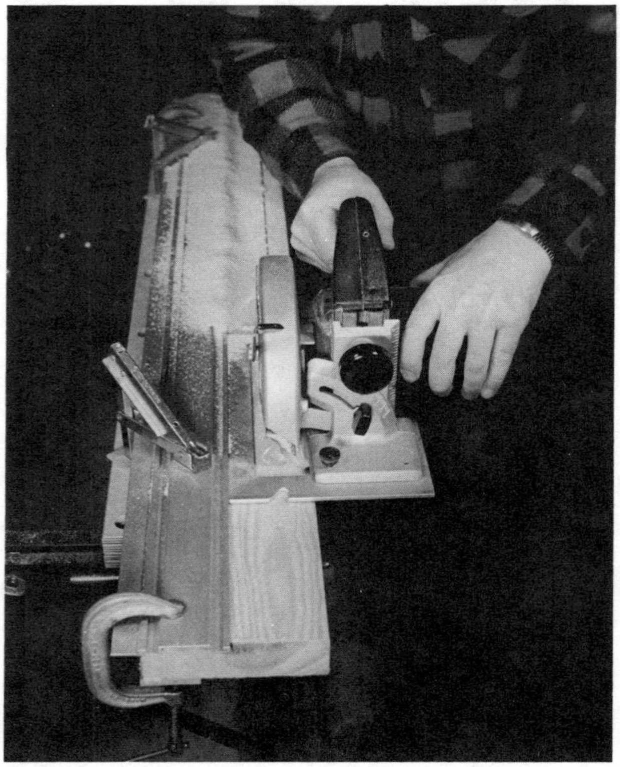

Step 1

Step 3

allow you to position the legs quickly each time you set up your Helpmates.)

13. After removing the legs, with the unit still upside down, measure 12″ down from one end and mark a spot on the side of the 2 × 6 that is 1¾″ from the bottom. Do likewise at the opposite end on the opposite side of the 2 × 6.

14. Position a snap-lock tie on the spot just marked, with the keyed-socket end 1½″ from the mark. Starting at the mark and working toward the bottom edge of the 2 × 6, attach the tie with six staples or double-pointed nails. Attach other ties the same way, two per Helpmate.

15. With the assembly still upside down, mount a 6½″ heavy-duty door pull in the center of each 2 × 6 with the screws provided.

16. Lay a folded set of legs on each side of each assembly and secure with a snap-lock tie. Your Helpmates are now ready to store or carry to the job site.

Step 10

Required Tools

- Steel tape rule
- Combination square
- Yardstick or large T-square
- Pencil
- Claw hammer
- Center punch
- Two C-clamps
- ½″ socket or box-end wrench
- Electric drill and 7/32″, 5/16″, and ¾″ bits
- Circular saw
- Saw guide

Optional Tools

- Permanent felt-tip marker
- Staple gun

Required Materials

- Two 5 × 48″ scraps of ¾″ plywood, G1S
- 8′ of 1 × 6, standard or better
- Eight 5/16″ × 2″ lag bolts
- Eight ¼″ flat washers
- Two pairs of folding metal sawhorse legs

Optional Materials

- Staples
- Four plastic snap-lock ties
- Two 6½″ heavy door pulls with screws

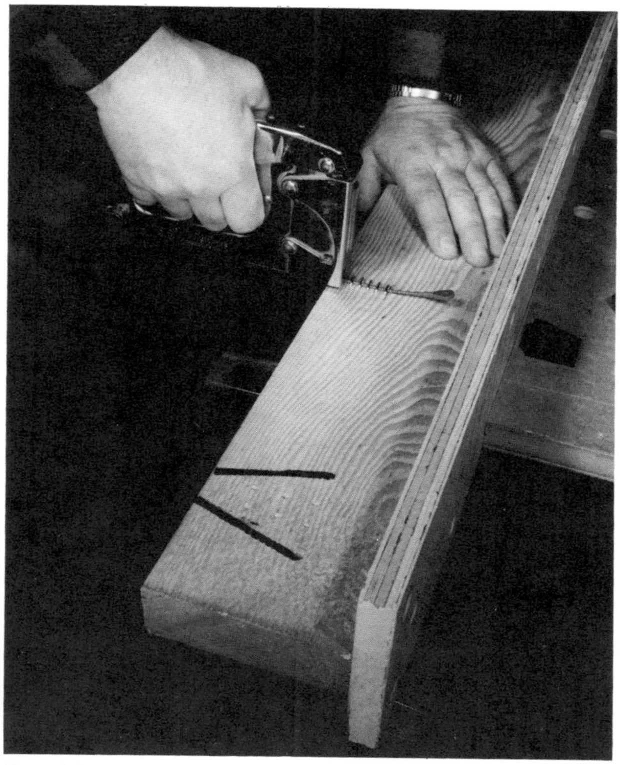

Step 14

37 Bulletin Board

Bulletin boards are useful in the kitchen, study, sewing room, hobby room, or workshop, and they can easily be made to any dimensions. The board can be hung with a single picture hanger, but two hangers, side by side and about 10″ or 12″ apart, will help keep it level. You can also cut four 1″ pieces of self-adhesive foam insulating tape and stick them on the rear of the unit near the corners to keep the board from slipping out of position.

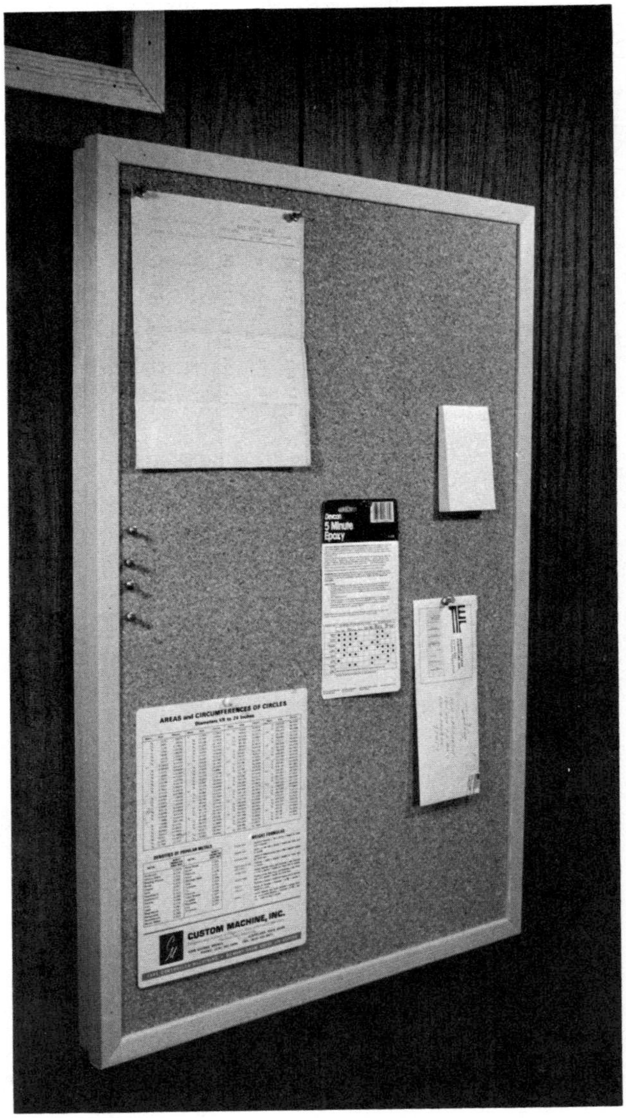

Wall cork is the best material for the face of the board, and it is available in 12 × 24″ sheets or in rolls that can be trimmed to any length. You'll need a handful of push pins for tacking up notes. For convenience, a small memo pad can be stapled to the cork face. And a pen with a self-adhesive holder is another handy item; these are available at most office-supply outlets.

You can stain and varnish the trim or paint it to match the decor of the room where the board will hang. Or you can leave the board unfinished, as I did with the one that hangs in my workshop.

Construction Steps

1. Trim a scrap of ¼″ plywood, any grade, to 24 × 36″.
2. With a mitre box and backsaw set for 45°, cut two pieces of 1 × 2 to 36″ (outside measurement), mitred at each end. Cut two more pieces to 24″, mitred at each end.
3. Apply glue to the end of a 24″ piece and clamp it to a 36″ piece with a corner clamp. Drive two 1″ brads into the mitre joint and countersink the brads.
4. Attach the other 36″ piece to the other end of the 24″ piece the same way.
5. Attach the remaining 24″ piece to the ends of the 36″ pieces, creating a 24 × 36″ frame. Let stand, with clamps in place, until the glue sets.
6. Remove the clamps, and run a bead of glue along the top edges of the frame. Lay the plywood panel atop the frame and secure it with 1″ ring-shank paneling nails, spaced about 10″ apart. Countersink the nails.
7. Turn the unit face down, and measure about 8″ down from each top corner and make a centered mark on the inside of each 1 × 2 side piece.
8. Punch a screw-starter hole at each spot with a hammer and nail set. Then drive a ¾″ eye screw into each hole.
9. Cut a length of picture-hanging wire to about 36″. Run about 4″ or 5″ of one end through one of the eye screws. Double the tag end back on the wire and wrap it in tight coils. Secure the opposite end of the wire to the other eye screw the same way.
10. Set the unit face up, and spread a thin, even coat of panel adhesive over the entire face with a notched adhesive spreader.
11. Position three 12 × 24″ sheets or one 24 × 36″ sheet of wall cork atop the adhesive and press firmly in place by hand. Then use a J-roller, rolling pin, or hammer and block of wood to seat the cork in the adhesive.

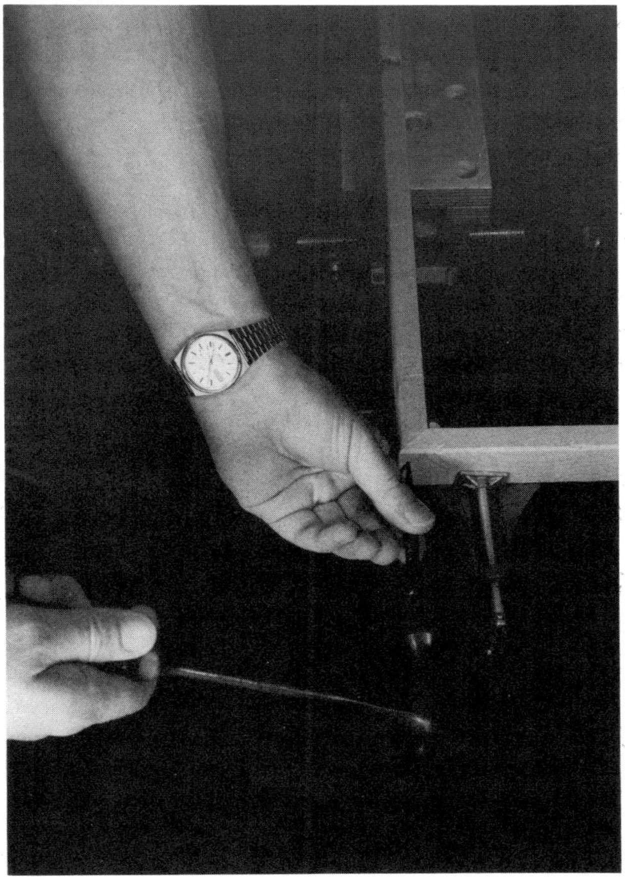

Step 3

Step 9

12. With a mitre box and backsaw, cut a piece of 1″ outside corner molding, with a 45° mitre at each end, to fit a 36″ edge of the unit. Run a bead of glue down the inside of the molding and attach it with three 1″ brads. Countersink the brads.

13. Measure and cut another piece of corner molding to fit one of the 24″ edges, and attach it with glue and three 1″ brads. Trim the remaining two edges the same way.
14. If you plan to paint the trim and frame, fill the nail holes with spackling paste, let dry, and sand with medium-grit and fine-grit sandpaper.
15. Mask the edges of the cork with 2″ masking tape. Apply two coats of interior latex paint and let dry.

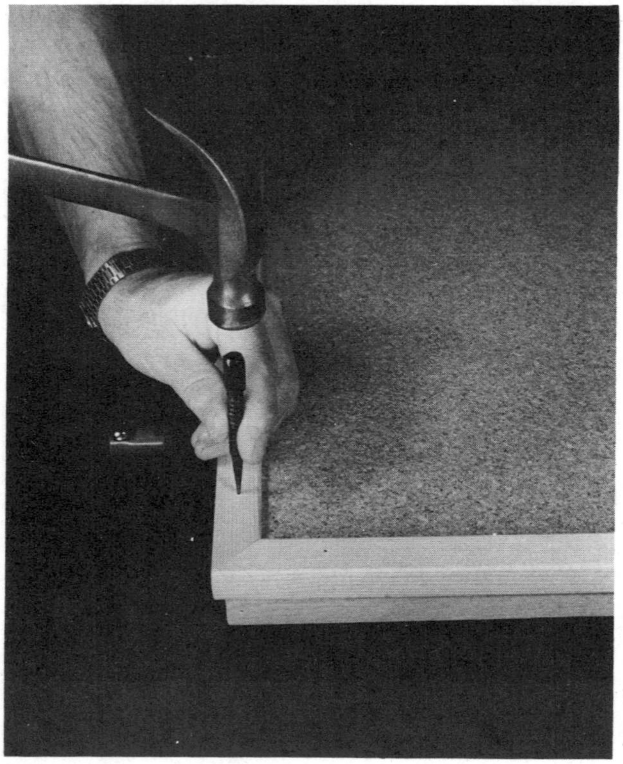

Step 13

Required Tools

- Steel tape rule
- Combination square
- Pencil
- Claw hammer
- Nail set
- Two C-clamps
- Two to four corner clamps
- Wire cutters
- Notched adhesive spreader
- J-roller
- Circular saw
- Saw guide

Required Materials

- One 24 × 36″ scrap of 1/4″ plywood, any grade
- Three 12 × 24″ sheets of wall cork
- 12′ of 1 × 2, standard or better
- 12′ of 1″ outside corner molding
- White glue
- Panel adhesive
- 1″ brads
- 1″ ring-shank paneling nails
- Two 3/4″ eye screws
- Medium-grit and fine-grit sandpaper
- 36″ of picture-hanging wire
- Two picture hangers
- Push pins

Optional Materials

- Spackling paste
- Interior latex paint
- One roll of 2″ masking tape
- 3 × 5″ memo pad
- Pen with self-adhesive holder

38
Once-Around Cribbage Board

Commercially made cribbage boards are usually strictly functional and designed so the players must go around the board twice during the scoring process. The board featured here is large and easy to use. It's finely finished, and you need only go around once during a game.

Although you can use any good-one-side $\frac{3}{4}''$ plywood to make this project, I recommend a hardwood plywood that you can finish naturally. I made ours out of a scrap of oak plywood, left over from another project, and finished it naturally with spray urethane varnish.

The most important part of the project is the drilling process. If you don't have access to a drill press, you should use a drill-press attachment or drill guide for your electric drill to assure that the holes will be perfectly perpendicular and all of the same depth . You will also need a Stanley No. 105 wood-boring bit for smooth, splinter-free holes.

If you have cribbage-playing friends, keep this project in mind for gift-giving occasions.

Construction Steps

1. Trim a scrap of ¾″ plywood to 12 × 22″.
2. Measuring from one 22″ edge, mark for and scribe lines parallel to that edge at (A) 2⅛″, (B) 2⅞″, (C) 4⅛″, (D) 4⅞″, (E) 6″, (F) 7⅛″, (G) 7⅞″, (H) 9⅛″, and (I) 9⅞″.
3. Run a steel tape rule between lines A and B, and mark each for drill-starter holes at 3″ and 5″, 6″ and 8″, 9″ and 11″, 12″ and 14″, 15″ and 17″, and 18″ and 20″; then, between each of those sets of marks, make additional marks at ½″ increments, so that each line has six sets of five marks, with the sets spaced 1″ from one another.
4. Similarly, mark line pairs C and D, F and G, and H and I.
5. At the end of the board where you started making marks, mark lines A, D, F, and I, 2″ from the end.
6. Measuring from the same end, mark line E at 3″, 3½″, 4″, 4½″, 5″, 10¼″, 10¾″, 11¼″, 11¾″, 18″, 18½″, 19″, 19½″, and 20″.
7. With a center punch and hammer, make a drill-starter hole at each spot marked.
8. With a drill press or electric drill and drill-press attachment or drill guide equipped with a Stanley No. 105 ⅜″ wood-boring bit, drill a ⅜″-deep hole at each spot.
9. With a mitre box and backsaw, cut a piece of screen molding to 22″ (outside measurement), mitred at each end.
10. Prenail the molding with four ¾″ brads. Run a bead of glue along the underside; then attach the molding to a 22″ edge, and countersink the brads.
11. Mitre-cut one end of a piece of screen molding and fit it to a 12″ edge of the board with the mitred end joined to the piece already attached. Mark the opposite end and mitre-cut it to fit. Attach it with glue and three brads, and countersink the brads.
12. Measure, mitre-cut, and attach screen molding to the remaining two edges the same way.
13. Fill the brad holes with wood filler and let the board stand until the filler hardens.
14. With medium-grit sandpaper, sand a length of ⅜″ dowel rod smooth until it will fit into a ⅜″-diameter hole.
15. With a mitre box and backsaw, cut four 2″ pegs from the dowel rod. Sand any rough edges with medium-grit paper.
16. After the wood filler has hardened, sand all surfaces of the board and round over sharp corners with medium-grit and fine-grit sandpaper. Then polish the top and trim with extra-fine grit paper.
17. Clean all dust from the board with a vacuum cleaner. Then apply two light coats of spray urethane varnish.
18. Stain the pegs for contrast, and let dry.

Step 6

Step 11

Required Tools

- Steel tape rule
- Yardstick or large T-square
- Pencil
- Claw hammer
- Nail set
- Center punch
- Mitre box and backsaw
- Two C-clamps
- Putty knife
- Electric drill with guide or drill-press attachment
- Stanley No. 105 $\frac{3}{8}$" wood-boring bit
- Circular saw
- Saw guide
- Pad sander

Required Materials

- One 12 × 22" scrap of $\frac{3}{4}$" hardwood plywood
- 6' of screen molding
- 1' of $\frac{3}{8}$" dowel rod
- White glue
- Wood filler
- $\frac{3}{4}$" brads
- Medium-grit, fine-grit, and extra-fine-grit sandpaper
- Stain of choice
- One can of spray urethane varnish

39
Quick and Simple Magazine Rack

One way to store magazines and keep them orderly and handy is in magazine racks that you can build from scraps. These racks, made from $\frac{1}{2}$″ or thicker plywood, can be made quickly with simple tools. They are best suited for use in bookshelves or atop small shelf units. Since the standing height of each rack will be $10\frac{1}{2}$″, it will fit on just about any shelf. Rack width and finish is a matter of the builder's choice.

Construction Steps

1. Cut a face piece of $\frac{1}{2}$″ or thicker plywood to a height of 11″ and the width of your choice.
2. From the same material, cut two right triangles with $5\frac{1}{4}$″ bases, $9\frac{1}{4}$″ heights, and $10\frac{1}{2}$″ hypotenuses.
3. Sand the face piece with medium-grit and fine-grit sandpaper.
4. Cut a piece of $1\frac{5}{8}$″ bullnose stop to a length equal to the width of the face piece; then prenail it with $1\frac{1}{4}$″ brads, spaced about 10″ apart.

5. Run a bead of glue down the bullnose stop and attach it to the bottom edge of the face piece, creating a lip to hold the magazines.
6. Lay the face piece down on a flat surface and glue the hypotenuse of each triangle to the back, flush with the bottom edge and about 4″ inside one end, using hot-melt glue and a glue gun or Weldwood Touch-n-Glue.
7. Conceal the plywood edges and fill brad holes with spackling paste, and let stand until the paste hardens.
8. Sand spackled areas with medium-grit and fine-grit sandpaper, and wipe away dust with a damp sponge.
9. Apply two coats of interior latex paint to the rack and let dry.

Required Tools

- Steel tape rule
- Pencil
- Claw hammer
- Nail set
- Two C-clamps
- Putty knife
- Paint brush
- Circular saw
- Saw guide
- Pad sander

Optional Tool

- Electric glue gun

Required Materials

- One scrap piece of 1/2″ or thicker plywood, 11″ wide and 36″ long or longer
- 2′ or more of 1 5/8″ bullnose stop
- White glue
- Hot-melt glue or Weldwood Touch-n-Glue
- Spackling paste
- 1 1/4″ brads
- Medium-grit and fine-grit sandpaper
- Interior latex paint

Step 2

Step 6

40
Handy Lap Desk

For those of you who, like me, find it difficult to sit still and listen to the stereo or watch TV without simultaneously doing something constructive, here's a project that should interest you. It's a simple lap-size desk that allows you to relax in your favorite chair while seeing to various business, household, or workshop paperwork.

The top is roomy enough to handle pads of paper, notebooks, bills, and the like, while the interior neatly houses paper clips, pens and pencils, a pocket calculator, ruling instruments, sketch pads, stationery, and similar items.

With a few scraps of plywood and lath, and odds and ends you'll probably find in the shop, you can put the desk together in about an hour. Put a couple of coats of paint on it, and use it the same evening.

Construction Steps

1. Trim a scrap of $\frac{3}{4}$″ G1S plywood to 16 × 18″. Then, from available scraps of $\frac{1}{2}$″ G1S plywood, cut a bottom panel to 13 × 15″, a back panel to 4 × 15″, a front panel to 2 × 15″, and two side panels to 4 × 14″.

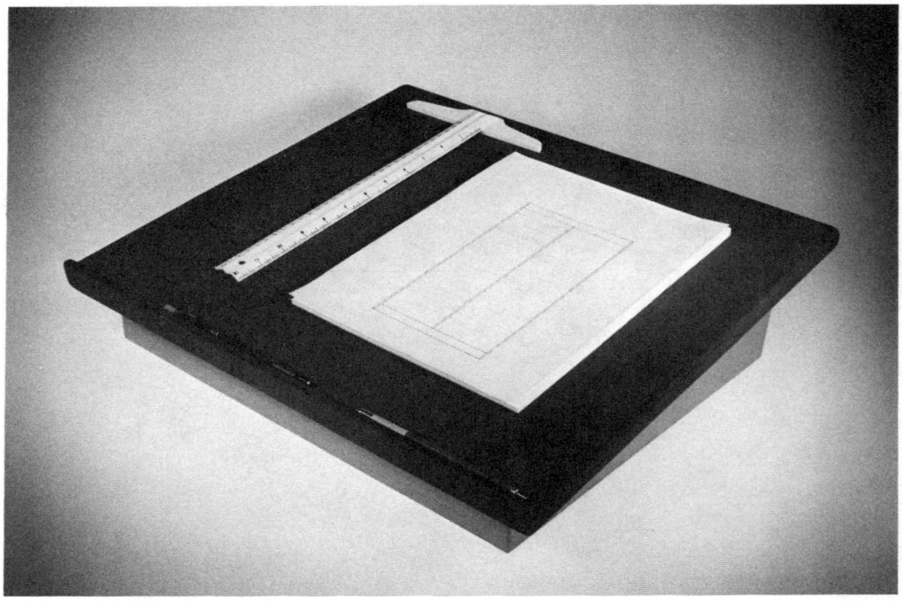

Lap desk has roomy top with pencil ledge.

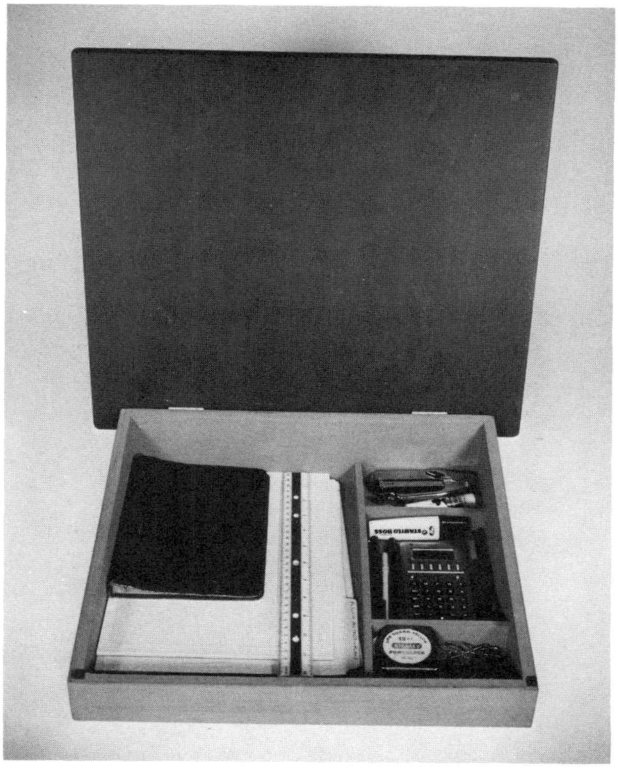

Hinged top opens to reveal spacious storage area

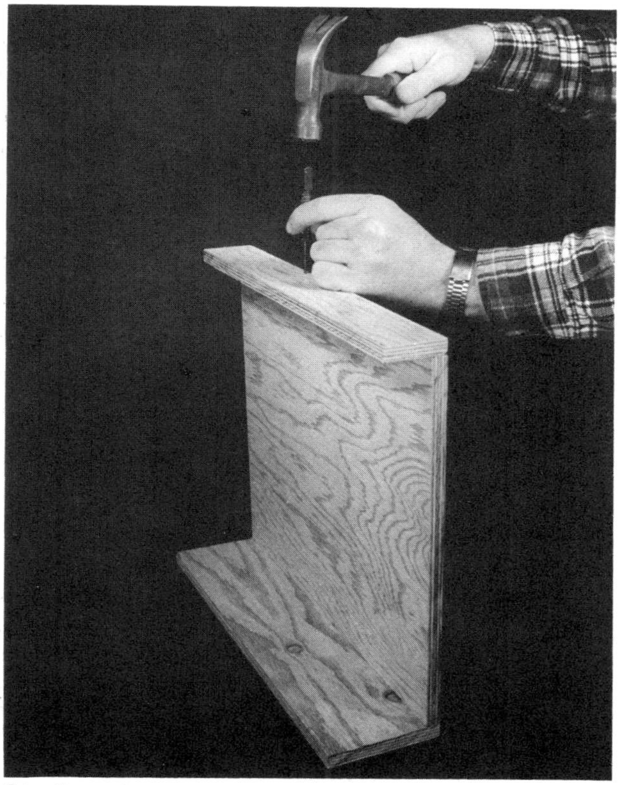

Step 9

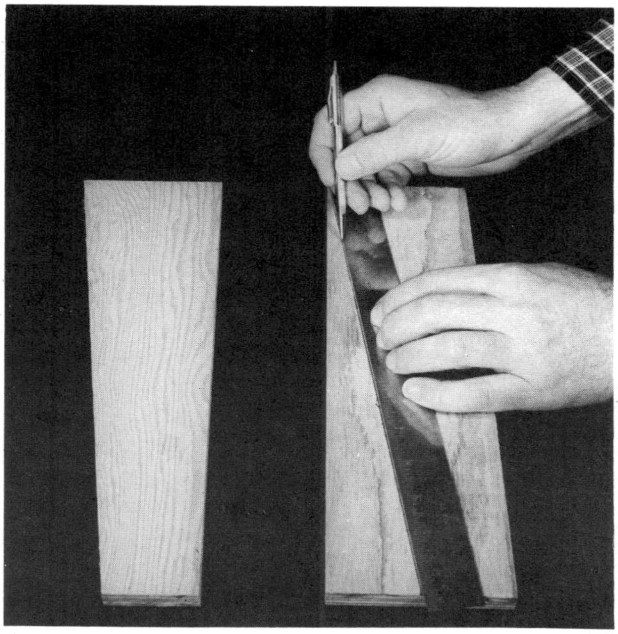

Step 10

2. With a mitre box and backsaw, cut a piece of screen molding to fit one 18″ edge of the 16 × 18″ desk top, mitred at each end. Prenail the molding with four $\frac{3}{4}$″ brads.
3. Run a bead of glue down an 18″ edge of the desk top; then attach the molding with brads, and countersink.
4. Cut two more pieces of screen molding to fit the 16″ edges of the top, each mitred at one end and cut square at the other end to fit flush with the corners.
5. Glue and nail each piece of molding to a side edge with four brads, and countersink.
6. Cut a piece of 1″ lattice to $18\frac{1}{2}$″, and prenail it with four $\frac{3}{4}$″ brads.
7. Run a bead of glue down the remaining edge of the top and attach the lattice with brads, making sure it is flush with the underside of the top, creating a $\frac{1}{4}$″ lip or pencil ledge.
8. Prenail the 4 × 15″ rear panel with four 1″ brads along the bottom edge. Then run a bead of glue along a 15″ edge of the 13 × 15″ bottom panel and butt the rear panel to the bottom panel. Drive and countersink the brads.
9. Similarly, prenail the 2 × 15″ front panel and attach it to the front edge of the bottom panel.
10. Measure down one 4″ edge of each 4 × 14″ side panel and make a mark at 2″. Then scribe a line connecting that mark with one corner of the other 4″ edge.
11. Use a circular saw to cut along the scribed line on each side panel, creating a tapered panel that is 4″ at the rear and 2″ at the front.

12. Prenail each side panel with two 1″ brads along the rear edge, three along the bottom edge, and two more along the front edge.
13. Connect each side panel with glue and brads, and countersink the brads.
14. Cut a piece of 1″ lattice to $12^{15}/_{16}$″ and two more pieces to 5″ each.
15. Scribe lines across the longest piece of lattice 3″ from each end. Apply glue to one end of each short piece; then butt each to the larger piece at the scribed lines. Clamp with corner clamps, and let stand until the glue sets.
16. Use a rasp or Stanley Surform Shaver to taper the rear edge of the rear panel to match the taper of the side panels.
17. Fill all brad holes, conceal plywood laminations, and patch all imperfections with spackling paste, and let the unit stand until the paste hardens.
18. Sand all surfaces with medium-grit and fine-grit sandpaper and remove dust with a vacuum cleaner.
19. Lay the desk top face down and position the desk base upside down on the top panel, centered with the top panel extending $1^1/_4$″ on all sides.
20. Position hinges at the rear of the desk, against the rear panel, each 2″ from the nearest corner.
21. Using the hinges as templates, mark for screw-starter holes on the underside of the desk top and on the rear panel.

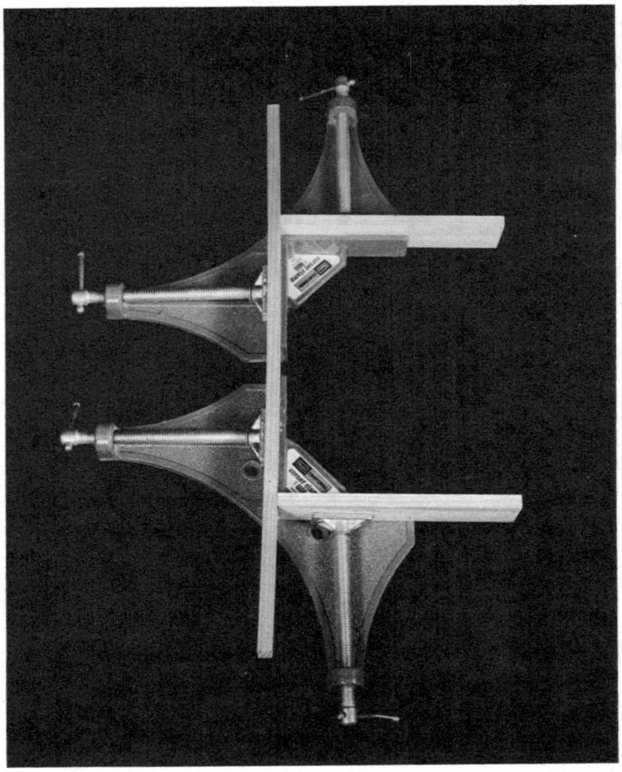

Step 15

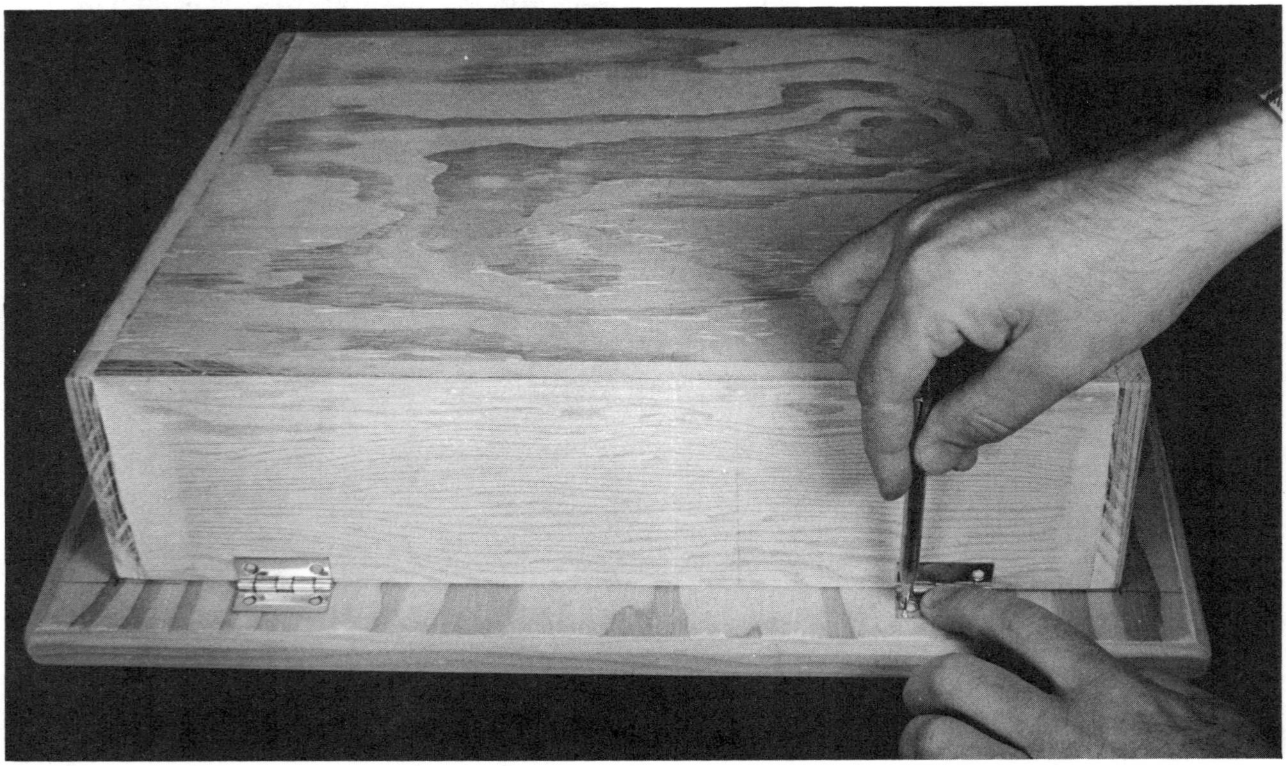

Step 21

22. Use a nail set to punch a screw-starter hole at each spot marked.

23. Run a bead of glue along the bottom edges of the lattice assembly as well as along the ends of the short lattice pieces. Then press the assembly into position on the inside of the desk base, butted to the front, rear, and right panels. Let stand until the glue sets.

24. Apply two coats of interior latex paint to all surfaces.

25. When the paint is dry, attach the top to the base with hinge screws.

26. Press a self-adhesive cork cabinet-door cushion in place at each top front corner of the desk base, and your lap desk is ready to use.

Required Tools

Steel tape rule	Two C-clamps
Yardstick or carpenter's square	Two corner clamps
Pencil	Wood rasp or Stanley Surform Shaver
Claw hammer	Putty knife
Nail set	Paint brush
Center punch	Circular saw
Screwdriver	Saw guide
Mitre box and backsaw	Pad sander

Required Materials

Two 4 × 14″ scraps of ½″ plywood, G1S
One 13 × 15″ scrap of ½″ plywood, G1S
One 4 × 15″ scrap of ½″ plywood, G1S
One 16 × 18″ scrap of ¾″ plywood, G1S
3½′ of 1″ lattice
6′ of screen molding
White glue
Spackling paste
¾″ brads
1″ brads
Medium-grit and fine-grit sandpaper
Interior latex paint
Two 1½″ hinges
Two self-adhesive cabinet-door cushions

41 Correspondence Trays

These correspondence or file trays are a must for any desk top for sorting and containing paperwork. They need not be restricted to the home office, den, or study, though. They're equally useful in the kitchen for holding recipes and coupons; in a child's room, they organize magazines, notebooks, homework, and other school papers. And in the workshop, they can be used to file plans and diagrams, tool manuals, and how-to magazines.

Best of all, they can be built quickly from leftovers and cost you next to nothing.

Construction Steps

1. From scraps of 3/4″ G1S plywood, cut two bottom panels to 11 × 14″ each. Then from available scraps of 1/4″ G1S plywood cut four side panels to 4 × 14″, and two rear panels to 4 × 11 1/2″.

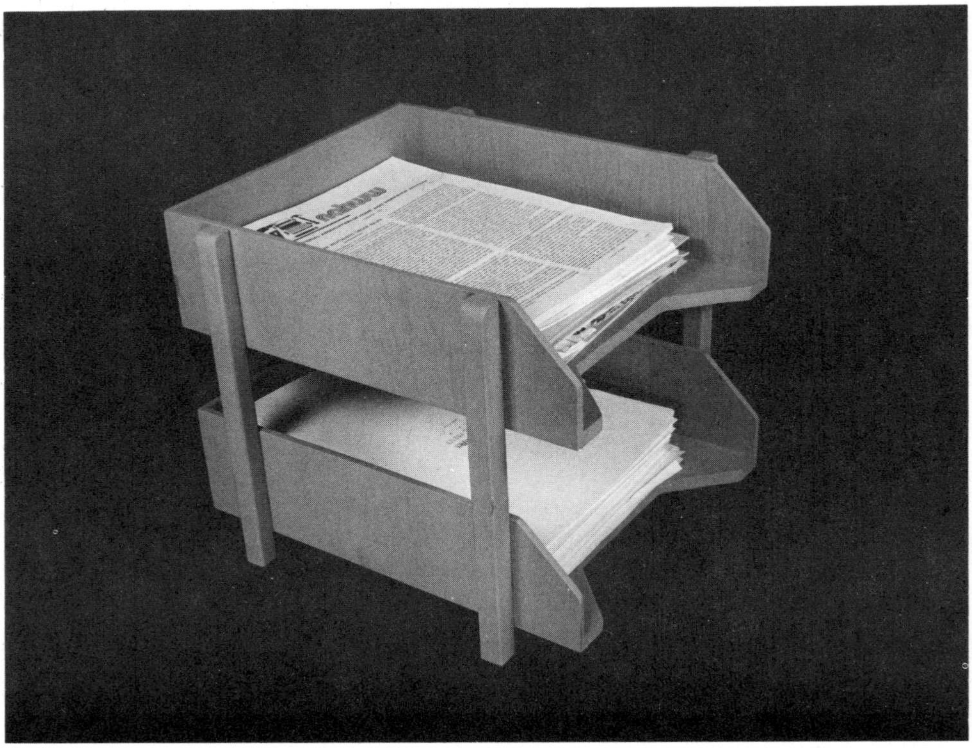

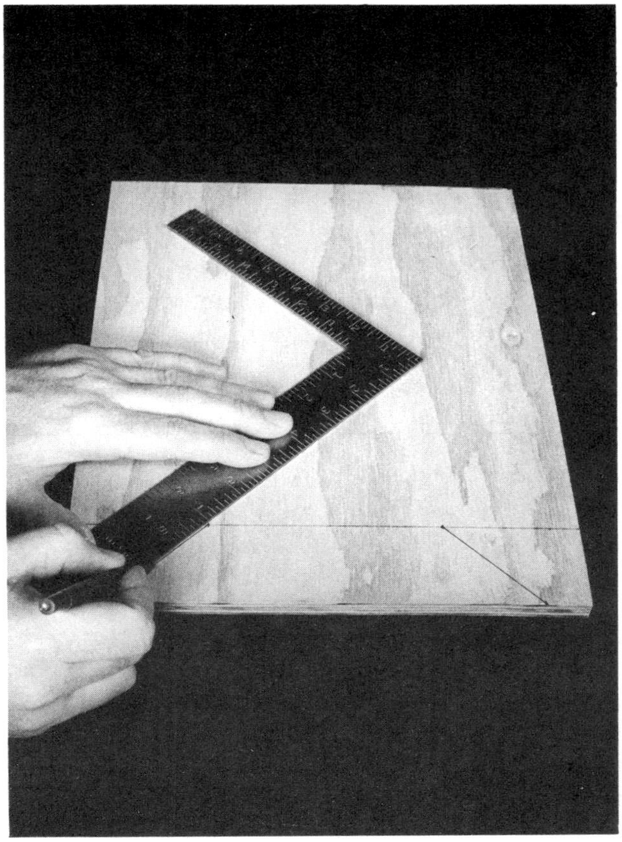

Step 4

Step 6

2. On the underside of each 11 × 14″ bottom panel, scribe a line 2″ from and parallel to the front edge.
3. Mark a point B on the line 3″ from the left end and another point C 3″ from the right end. On the front edge of each panel, mark a point A 2″ from the left end and another point D 2″ from the right end.
4. Scribe lines connecting points A and B and points C and D. Then use a sabre saw to cut from point A to B to C to D on each panel.
5. Measure down 2″ on one 4″ edge of each side panel and make a mark. Then use a mitre box and backsaw set at 45° to cut the top front corner off each panel with the saw set at the 2″ mark.
6. Prenail the bottom edge of each side panel with four ¾″ brads; then attach them to the side edges of the bottom panels with glue and brads, and countersink the brads.
7. Prenail each rear panel with two brads along the side edges and three along the bottom edge.
8. Run a bead of glue along the rear edges of each tray, and attach the rear panels with brads; countersink the brads.
9. Fill brad holes, gaps in the plywood laminations, and any imperfections with spackling paste, and let trays stand until paste hardens.
10. Sand the trays with medium-grit and fine-grit sandpaper.
11. Scribe two lines across the outside of each side panel 2″ and 12″ from the rear.
12. Cut four pieces of ¾″-square molding to 12″; then scribe lines across all four sides of each piece 1″ from one end.
13. Prenail the inside of each side panel with two ¾″ brads located approximately ⅜″ inside the lines scribed in **Step 11.**
14. Run a bead of glue across one side panel of one tray, inside the line nearest the front.
15. Press one of the 12″ uprights in place, aligned with the front line on the side panel, with the lower end of the upright extending 1″ beneath the bottom of the tray.
16. Carefully turn the unit over and lay it on a bench top; then drive and countersink the brads.

17. Attach the rear upright along the rear line on the side panel the same way.
18. Run a bead of glue across the corresponding side panel of the other tray, just inside the scribed lines.
19. Press the top tray in place with the upright tops flush with the top of the side panel. Carefully invert the unit and drive and countersink the brads.
20. Attach the remaining two uprights to the other side panels the same way.
21. Fill all brad holes and any other surface imperfections with spackling paste and let the unit stand until the paste hardens. Then sand spackled areas with medium-grit and fine-grit sandpaper.
22. Clean the trays to remove dust; then apply two coats of interior latex paint, and let stand until paint dries.

Step 17

Required Tools

Steel tape rule
Ruler or carpenter's square
Pencil
Claw hammer
Nail set
Mitre box and backsaw
Two C-clamps
Putty knife
Paint brush
Circular saw
Saw guide
Sabre saw
Pad sander

Required Materials

Four 4 × 14" scraps of 1/4" plywood, G1S
Two 4 × 11½" scraps of ½" plywood, G1S
4' of 3/4"-square molding
White glue
Spackling paste
3/4" brads
Medium-grit and fine-grit sandpaper
Interior latex paint

42
Small-Bird Chalet

One of the best ways to use up scraps of exterior plywood is to turn them into birdhouses. The birds they will attract will give you many hours of enjoyment. Moreover, there's no better project for teaching a youngster how to work with tools and wood.

Birds come in a variety of sizes and shapes, and so must their nesting sanctuaries. This particular one was designed for small birds, such as wrens, warblers, nuthatches, and chickadees.

The rear of the house is attached with screws only, which facilitates easy removal. You should take the house down each winter, remove the rear panel, and clean the house thoroughly. Every couple of years it will probably need a fresh coat of paint, too.

For best results, hang the house from 8′ to 15′ above ground level. If possible, make sure there is an ample supply of tiny twigs, bits of straw, and other nest-building materials nearby.

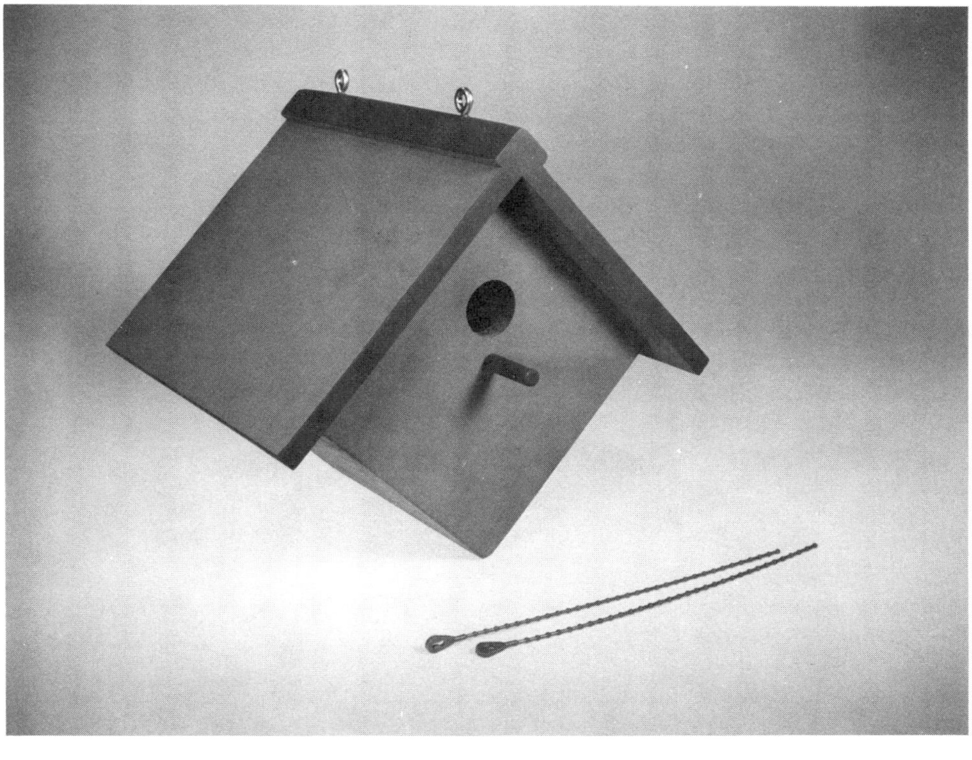

Construction Steps

1. From a 6″-wide scrap of ½″ G1S exterior plywood, cut one piece to 6 × 6″ and another to 6 × 6½″.
2. From a 6½″-wide scrap of the same plywood, cut two 6½″ squares.
3. Cut another piece of the same type of plywood to 8 × 9″ and one more to 7½ × 9″.
4. Place a ruler across one of the 6½″-square pieces, from corner to corner. Mark a spot 3″ from one corner and another 4¼″ from the same corner. Center-punch a drill-starter hole at each spot.
5. Drill a 1¼″-diameter hole through the panel at the top spot marked and a ⅜″-diameter hole beneath that one.
6. Run a bead of waterproof glue along one edge of the 6 × 6″ piece and butt it to the 6 × 6½″ piece along one of the 6″ ends, forming an el. Attach the two pieces with three 1″ brads, creating the birdhouse floor.
7. Run a bead of glue along the front edges of the floor assembly. Lay the drilled house front atop the glued edges and attach it with 1″ brads.
8. Scribe a line ¼″ from and parallel to each bottom edge of the 6½ × 6½″ rear panel. Make a mark on each line 1″ from the top edge. Center-punch a drill-starter hole at each mark and where the two lines intersect.
9. At each spot, drill a 9/64″-diameter hole and countersink for #6 screws.
10. Attach the rear panel to the bottom assembly with three 1 × 6 flathead wood screws. (Do not use glue.)
11. On the outside face of each floor panel, scribe a line 1″ from and parallel to the top edge. Mark for and punch three drill-starter holes along each line; then drill a ¼″-diameter ventilation hole at each spot.
12. To construct the roof assembly, run a bead of waterproof glue down one long edge of the 7½ × 9″ panel, butt it to the 8 × 9″ panel, and clamp each end with a corner clamp. Drive and countersink three 1″ brads. Let stand until glue sets.
13. Cut a piece of 1″ outside corner molding to 9″. Run a bead of glue along the inside, and press it into position along the peak of the roof assembly. Nail it in place with four 1″ brads, and countersink.
14. Measure in 2″ from each end of the roof assembly and punch a screw-starter hole at each spot with a nail set.
15. When the glue has set, remove the clamps from the roof assembly; then scribe a line down each side of each roof panel 1¼″ from and parallel to the front edge. Scribe another line on each panel perpendicular to the first and 1¼″ from the bottom edges.
16. Run a bead of glue along the top edges of the front

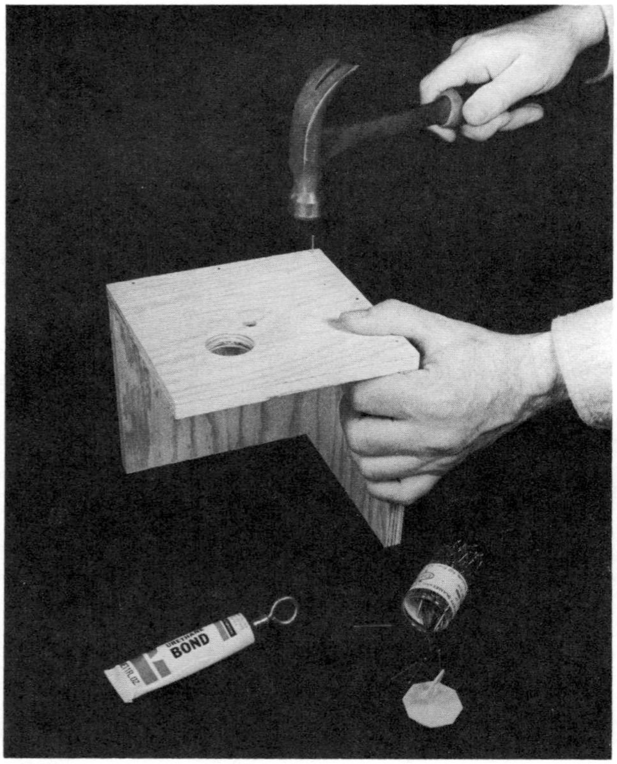

Step 7

Step 11

Step 17

and floor panels, stopping ½″ short of the rear to prevent seepage to the rear panel.

17. Put the roof assembly in place atop the house, allowing a 1″ overhang front and rear. Then nail it in place with 1″ brads along the lines you scribed in **Step 15.** Countersink the brads.
18. Cut a piece of ⅜″ dowel rod to 2″. Apply glue to the inside of the ⅜″-diameter hole in the front panel. Then twist the dowel into the hole until it is firmly seated.
19. Fill all brad holes and gaps in the plywood laminations with wood filler, and let the house stand until the filler hardens.
20. Sand the entire unit with medium-grit sandpaper.
21. Wipe away all dust, and apply two coats of exterior latex paint. Paint the trim a contrasting color if you wish.
22. Insert a 1″ eye screw into each hole in the roof peak, and hang the house from a tree branch with heavy cord or two plastic snap-lock ties.

Required Tools

Steel tape rule
Ruler or small carpenter's square
Pencil
Claw hammer
Nail set
Center punch
Screwdriver
Mitre box and backsaw
Two C-clamps
Two corner clamps
Putty knife
Paint brush
Electric drill and bits, including #6 countersink
Circular saw
Saw guide

Required Materials

One 6 × 6″ scrap of ½″ exterior plywood, G1S
One 6 × 6½″ scrap of ½″ exterior plywood, G1S
Two 6½ × 6½″ scraps of ½″ exterior plywood, G1S
One 7½ × 9″ scrap of ½″ exterior plywood, G1S
One 8 × 9″ scrap of ½″ exterior plywood, G1S
9″ scrap of 1″ outside corner molding
2″ scrap of ⅜″ dowel rod
Waterproof glue
Wood filler
1″ brads
Three 1 × 6 flathead wood screws
Two 1″ eye screws
Medium-grit sandpaper
Exterior latex paint
Heavy cord or two plastic snap-lock ties

43
Large-Bird Nesting Box

Here's another birdhouse for your property, but this one was designed to attract the larger birds, particularly flickers and various woodpeckers. In some areas, it might also house small owls.

The best way to hang this house without damaging the tree is with two elastic tie-down cords, which you'll find in a variety of lengths at sporting-goods stores, discount stores, and camping centers. Simply buy two cords long enough to fit around the tree where you'll hang the house.

To keep the house attractive to birds, take it down once a year, remove the floor, and clean the house. Hang it again in the early spring, and provide fresh nesting material each year. Every couple of years, give it a fresh coat of paint.

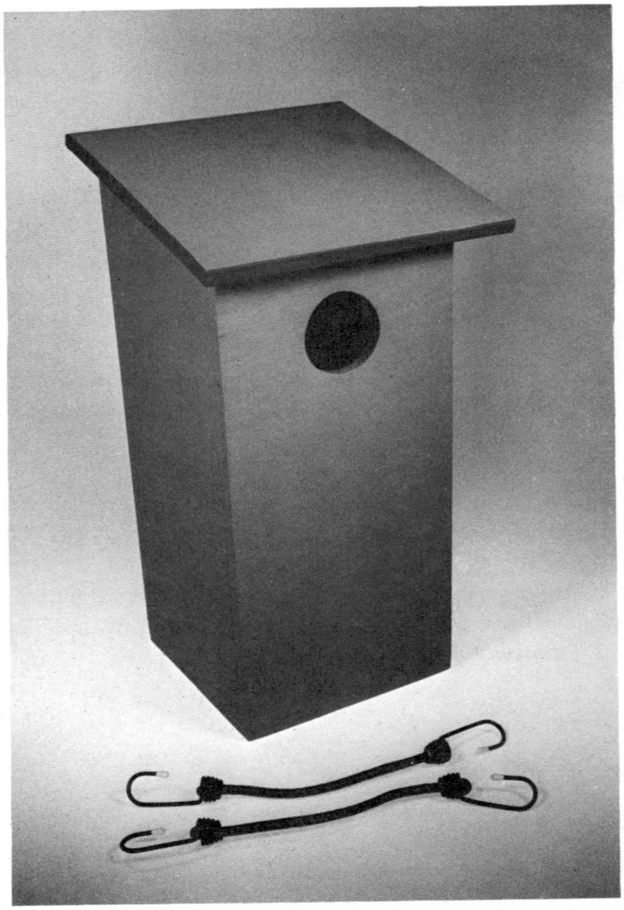

Construction Steps

1. On two pieces of ½″ G1S exterior plywood, 7″ wide and at least 18″ long, measure 18″ up one long edge and make a mark. Measure up the opposite edge and make a mark at 16″. Then scribe a line across each panel connecting the marks.
2. With a circular saw, cut the tops of these two pieces off at an angle, along the lines you just scribed.
3. Now cut a front panel to 8 × 16″ and a back panel to 8 × 18″ from scraps of the same plywood.
4. Cut a floor to 8 × 8″ and a roof to 10 × 10″ from the same type of plywood.
5. On the front panel, scribe a line parallel to and 3¼″ from the top edge. Make a mark at the center of that line.
6. With a compass set for a 1¼″ radius and the point at the center mark on the line, scribe a 2½″-diameter circle.
7. Inside the circle, drill a ⅜″-diameter hole to accommodate a sabre-saw blade; then cut the circle out with a sabre saw.
8. Turn the front panel face down and use a wire brush to score the inside of the panel, horizontally, from the bottom of the hole down. (The ridges created will aid the fledglings' exit when it's time for them to climb out.)
9. Run a bead of waterproof glue down the front edge of one of the side panels. Butt it to the inside edge of the front panel, and drive four 1″ brads through the front panel. Countersink the brads.
10. Attach the other side panel to the front panel the same way.
11. Run a bead of glue down each rear edge of the side panels, and attach the rear panel with four brads along each side. Countersink the brads.
12. On the house floor, mark a spot ¼″ inside each corner and another centered ¼″ inside each edge. Center-punch a drill-starter hole at each spot; then drill a $\frac{9}{64}$″-diameter hole at each spot and countersink for #6 screws.
13. Attach the floor with 1 × 6 flathead wood screws. (Do not use glue.)
14. On the outside of each side panel, scribe a line 1″ from and parallel to the top edge. Mark for and center-punch four drill-starter holes along each line; then drill a ¼″-diameter ventilation hole at each spot.
15. Use a wood rasp or Stanley Surform Shaver to trim the top edge of the front panel to an angle that matches that of the side panels.
16. On the roof, scribe a line 2⅛″ from and parallel to the front edge. Scribe two more lines—each 1¼″ inside and parallel to a side edge.

Step 6

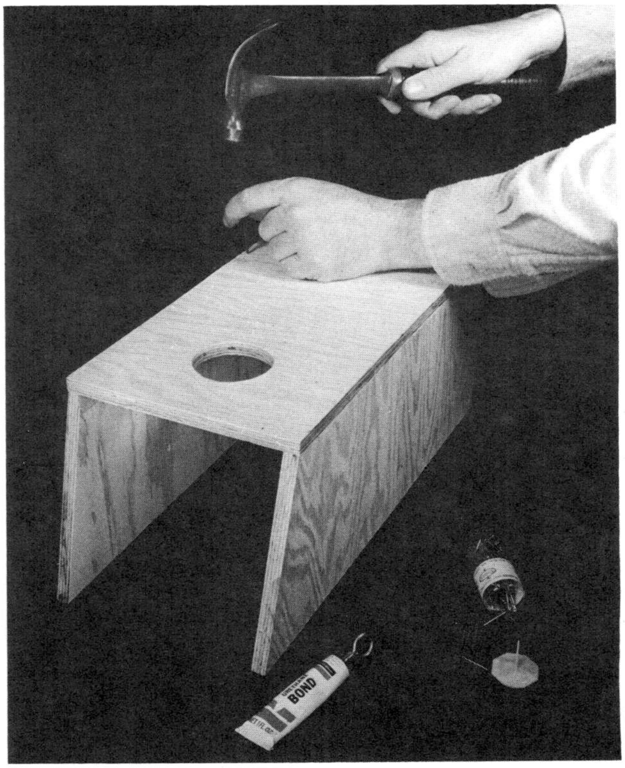

Step 10

17. Run a bead of glue along the top edges of the house, and attach the roof with 1″ brads. Make sure the roof is flush with the rear edge and overhangs 1″ on each side, leaving a front overhang of about 1¾″.
18. Fill all brad holes and gaps in the plywood with wood filler and let stand until the filler hardens.
19. Sand the house with medium-grit sandpaper, and wipe away all dust.
20. Apply two coats of exterior latex paint, and let dry.
21. Use a nail set to punch a screw-starter hole in each corner of the rear panel. Locate the top holes 1″ below the top edge and ¼″ inside the side edges, and bottom holes 1″ above the bottom edges and ¼″ inside the side edges.
22. Insert a 1″ eye screw in each of the punched holes.
23. For flickers and woodpeckers, put enough coarse sawdust and wood shavings inside the house to provide a layer of about four inches.
24. Attach the house to the trunk of a tree with two elastic tie-down cords, from 10′ to 20′ above ground level.

Step 14

Step 17

Required Tools

Steel tape rule
Ruler or small carpenter's square
Pencil
Claw hammer
Nail set
Center punch
Screwdriver
Two C-clamps
Wood rasp or Stanley Surform Shaver
Putty knife
Paint brush
Compass
Wire brush
Electric drill and 9/64″, 3/8″, and #6 countersink bits
Circular saw
Saw guide
Sabre saw

Required Materials

Two 7 × 18″ scraps of ½″ exterior plywood, G1S
One 8 × 16″ scrap of ½″ exterior plywood, G1S
One 8 × 18″ scrap of ½″ exterior plywood, G1S
One 8 × 8″ scrap of ½″ exterior plywood, G1S
One 10 × 10″ scrap of ½″ exterior plywood, G1S
Waterproof glue
Wood filler
1″ brads
Eight 1 × 6 flathead wood screws
Four 1″ eye screws
Medium-grit sandpaper
Exterior latex paint
Two elastic tie-down cords

44
Handy Tool Tote

If you're just starting out as a do-it-yourselfer you'll need something to keep your tools in, and this simple tote should prove ideal. If you're an experienced woodworker, or as your tool collection grows and is housed in a large chest or along a pegboard wall in the shop, you'll still find your tool tote handy for carrying tools to job sites beyond the workshop. The tote would also be an excellent aid to the gardener in the family.

If you're introducing a youngster to tools and woodworking, this is an excellent first project.

Construction Steps

1. From scraps of ½″ plywood, any grade, cut a tote bottom to 10 × 24″, two sides to 5 × 24″, and two ends to 10 × 10″.
2. On an end piece, measure 4″ down from a top corner and make a mark on a side edge. Measure 4″

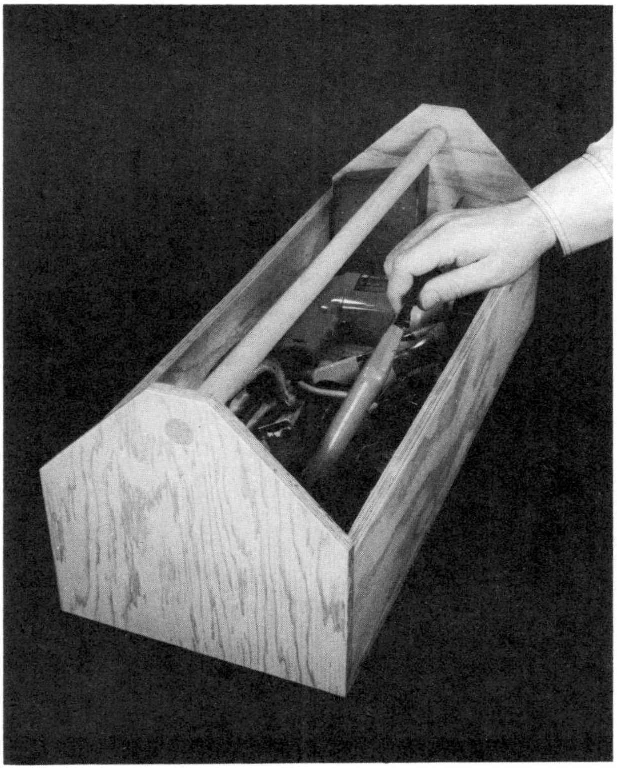

from the same corner across the top edge and mark another spot. Join the two spots with a straight line; then duplicate the process at the opposite top corner.

3. Scribe a vertical center line about $1\frac{1}{2}''$ down from the top edge of the end piece. Mark a short intersecting line $1\frac{3}{16}''$ down from the top edge, and punch a drill-starter hole there.
4. Put the marked end panel atop the other end panel, and clamp them to the edge of a workbench with one top corner extending beyond the bench edge. Use a circular saw to cut the corners off the two panels along the line scribed in **Step 2.** Readjust the two panels and remove the opposite top corners the same way.
5. Readjust the two panels, keeping them aligned, so that the top edge extends beyond the bench edge and clamp them securely. Now drill a $\frac{3}{4}''$-diameter hole through both panels at the spot marked and punched in **Step 3.**
6. Cut a piece of $\frac{3}{4}''$-diameter dowel rod to 25″. Then sand it smooth with medium-grit and fine-grit sandpaper.
7. Apply a light coat of glue to each end of the dowel rod and insert each end into a hole in one of the end panels so the dowel is flush with the outside face of the panel.
8. Drive a 1″ brad through the center of the top edge of each end panel into the dowel rod; then countersink the brads.
9. Run a bead of glue along the edge of one end of the bottom panel. Butt it to the bottom of one end panel, and join the two pieces with three 1″ brads.
10. Glue and nail the opposite end panel to the bottom panel the same way, and countersink the brads.
11. Run a bead of glue along the bottom edge and both end edges of a side panel. Slip it into place on one side of the tote, between the two end panels, and secure with two 1″ brads through each end panel and three more through the bottom panel.
12. Attach the other side panel the same way, and countersink all brad holes.
13. Fill brad holes and gaps in the plywood laminations with wood filler and let stand until the filler hardens.
14. Sand, as required, with medium-grit and fine-grit sandpaper. Clean the tote to remove dust.

Step 10

Step 8

Required Tools

- Steel tape rule
- Ruler or small carpenter's square
- Pencil
- Claw hammer
- Nail set
- Two C-clamps
- Putty knife
- Electric drill and 3/4″ bit
- Circular saw
- Saw guide

Required Materials

- Two 10 × 10″ scraps of 1/2″ plywood, any grade
- Two 5 × 24″ scraps of 1/2″ plywood, any grade
- One 10 × 24″ scrap of 1/2″ plywood, any grade
- 25″ of 3/4″ dowel rod
- White glue
- Wood filler
- 1″ brads
- Medium-grit and fine-grit sandpaper

45 Desktop Book Trough

If you have to rise frequently from your desk chair and walk to the bookcase to get the dictionary, thesaurus, or Zip-code directory, or if such books are cluttering your desk top in teetering stacks, what you need is a book trough. The one featured here is made of scraps of $\frac{3}{4}''$ plywood. It goes together quickly, and will hold more than a half-dozen of your often-used reference books.

Construction Steps

1. From $\frac{3}{4}''$ G1S plywood scraps, cut two end panels to $6 \times 8\frac{1}{2}''$, a bottom panel to $4 \times 15''$, and a rear panel to $7 \times 15''$.
2. Prenail the rear panel with four $1\frac{1}{4}''$ brads along one $15''$ edge.
3. Run a bead of glue down one $15''$ edge of the bottom panel; then butt the rear panel to the bottom panel, and drive and countersink the brads.

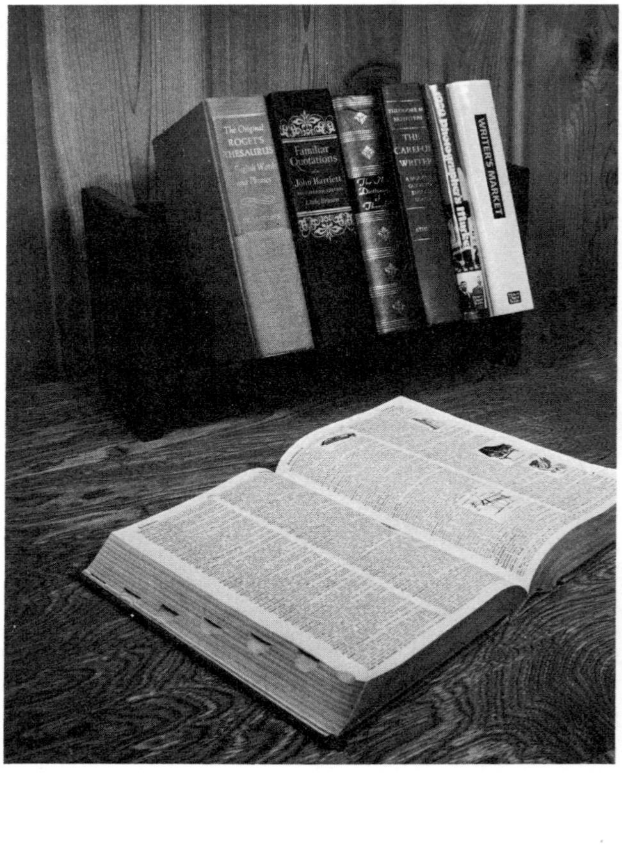

4. Cut two pieces of ¾″ quarter-round molding to 15″; then prenail each with three 1″ brads.
5. Run a bead of glue down one of the 15″ edges of the partially assembled trough. Then attach a piece of prenailed molding with brads, rounded edge on the outside, and countersink the brads.
6. Attach the other piece of molding, the same way, to the other 15″ edge.
7. Lay an end panel on a flat working surface. Then measure 1¾″ down from the top right corner and make a mark on the edge. Measure down 6″ from the top left corner and make another mark.
8. Now stand the partially assembled trough on end atop the end piece. Align the rear panel with the mark on the right edge and the bottom panel with the mark on the left edge. (The bottom corner of the assembly should be flush with the bottom edge of the side panel.) Now trace lines onto the side panel along the bottom edges of the assembly.
9. Invert the assembly and run a bead of glue down the edges. Turn it over and position it on the side panel, carefully aligning it with the lines you scribed in **Step 8.** Press firmly and let it stand for fifteen minutes.
10. Carefully lift the assembly and side panel and invert. Attach the side panel with three 1¼″ brads and countersink the brads.
11. Run a bead of glue along the edges at the opposite

Step 8

Step 6

Step 11

end of the assembly. Then set the unit in an upright position on a flat surface. Press the other side panel in place; then stand the unit on end and attach the side panel with brads, and countersink the brads.

12. Fill all brad holes, patch any imperfections, and conceal plywood laminations with spackling paste. Let the trough stand until paste hardens.
13. Sand all surfaces with medium-grit and fine-grit sandpaper, and clean to remove all dust.
14. Apply two coats of interior latex paint and let dry.

Required Tools

Steel tape rule	Circular saw
Pencil	Saw guide
Two C-clamps	Mitre box and backsaw
Putty knife	
Paint brush	

Required Materials

Two 6 × 8½″ scraps of ¾″ plywood, G1S
One 4 × 15″ scrap of ¾″ plywood, G1S
One 7 × 15″ scrap of ¾″ plywood, G1S
30″ of ¾″ quarter-round molding
White glue
Spackling paste
1″ brads
1¼″ brads
Medium-grit and fine-grit sandpaper

46
Triangle Game

Here's a game that's fun for kids and grown-ups as well. It's easy to learn but difficult to master. It can be made from small scraps of any good-one-side $3/4''$ plywood, but hardwood plywood looks best. And since this is such a simple project, requiring little material, you might want to make several; they're great stocking stuffers at Christmastime.

To play the game, simply fill the holes with all the available pegs, leaving one hole (any hole) vacant. The object is to jump the pegs, one at a time, checker style, and remove the jumped pegs until you can make no more jumps. In a perfect game, only one peg is left on the board.

Luckily for you, the game is a lot easier to make than it is to play.

Construction Steps

1. On a scrap of $3/4''$ G1S or better plywood that measures 10″ square or larger, scribe a vertical center line.

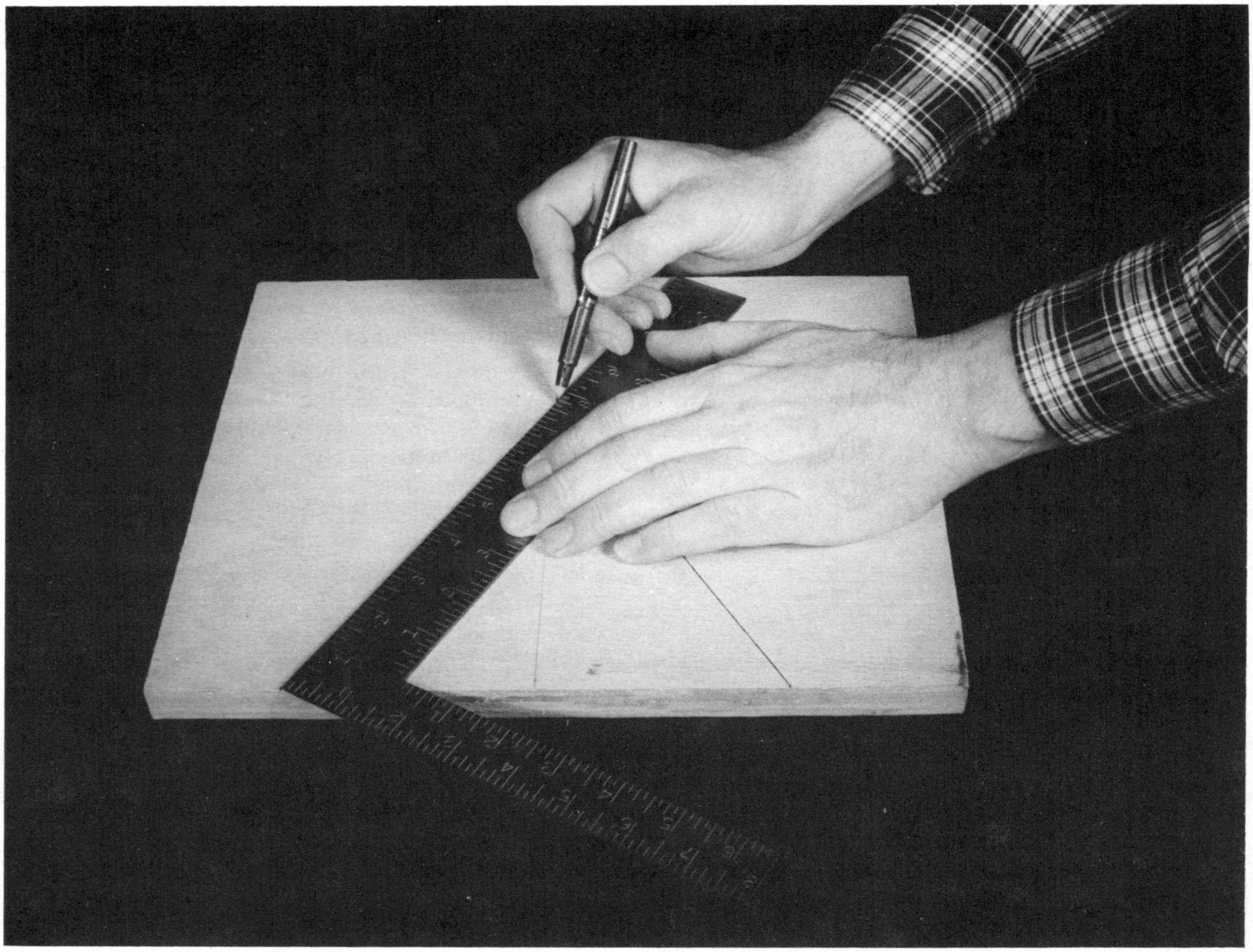

2. Along the bottom edge, measure 3⅞" from each side of the vertical line and make a mark.
3. Set one end of a small square or ruler on the edge mark right of the center line and swing the ruler so that its 7¾" mark touches the center line. Scribe a line connecting the edge mark with the center line.
4. Do likewise with the mark on the left side of the center line.
5. With a circular saw, cut along the scribed lines, creating an equilateral triangle with 7¾" sides.
6. On the face of the triangle, scribe a pencil line ½" inside and parallel to each side, creating an internal triangle with 6" sides.
7. Position a ruler along the base line of the internal triangle with the 0" mark at the left corner and the 6" mark at the right corner. Now mark for drill-starter holes at 1½", 3", and 4½".
8. Do the same on the other two sides of the internal triangle.
9. Now align your ruler above the base line of the internal triangle with the 0" mark aligned with the first pencil mark above the left corner and the 4½" mark aligned with the first pencil mark above the right corner. Now mark spots at 1½" and 3".
10. Move the ruler up to the next set of marks on the internal triangle's sides, aligning left and right marks with the ruler's 0" and 3" marks. Mark a spot at 1½".
11. With a center punch and hammer, make a drill-starter hole at each mark made as well as at each corner of the internal triangle.
12. With a drill press or an electric drill and drill-press attachment or drill guide, use a Stanley No. 105 ⅜" wood-boring bit to drill a ⅜"-deep hole at each spot punched.
13. Sand the edges and surfaces of the triangle smooth with medium-grit and fine-grit sandpaper; then clean it with a vacuum cleaner to remove all dust.
14. Stain the triangle or leave it natural; then apply two light coats of urethane spray varnish to all surfaces, and let dry.
15. Use medium-grit sandpaper to smooth a piece of ⅜"

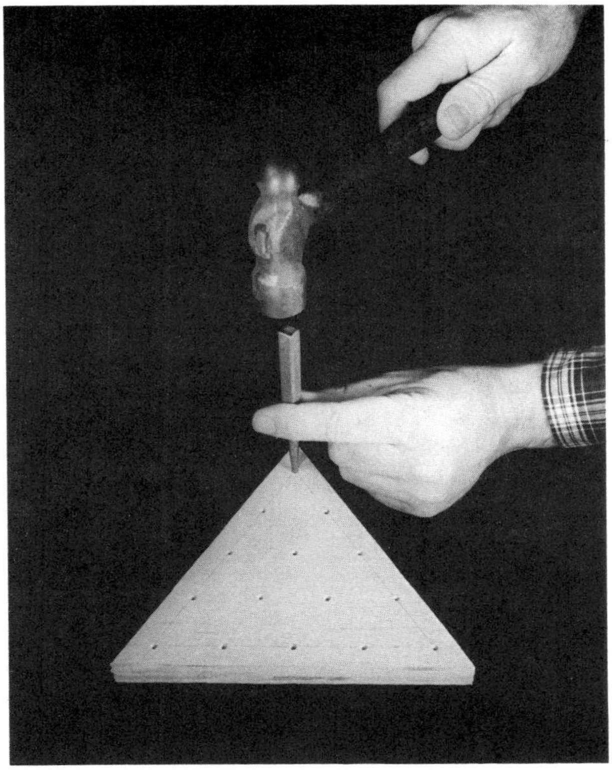

Step 11

dowel rod and slightly reduce its diameter so it will fit into the 3/8″-diameter holes.

16. With a mitre box and backsaw, cut fourteen pegs from the dowel rod to 1½″ each.
17. Lightly sand the rough edges of the pegs with medium-grit sandpaper. Then stain the pegs or leave them natural.

Required Tools

Steel tape rule
Ruler or small carpenter's square
Pencil
Claw hammer
Center punch
Mitre box and backsaw
Two C-clamps
Electric drill with guide or drill-press attachment
Stanley No. 105 3/8″ wood-boring bit
Circular saw

Required Materials

One 10 × 10″ or larger scrap of 3/4″ plywood, G1S
2′ of 3/8″ dowel rod
Medium-grit and fine-grit sandpaper
Stain of choice
One can of urethane spray varnish

47 Pair of Bookends

As anyone with a personal library knows, bookends always seem to be in short supply. And if you have shopped for them recently, you know they don't come cheap. But you can make all the bookends you need, quickly and easily, from scraps of $\frac{3}{4}''$ plywood.

Unadorned, these bookends will certainly serve their purpose. But by simply affixing any of a number of knickknacks, collectibles, or ornamental items to their bases with epoxy glue, you can make them real eye catchers.

You can use any good-one-side plywood for the project and finish the bookends with the paint of your choice. Or you can use hardwood plywood and finish them naturally. Simply follow these easy steps, and add a dash of imagination to create handsome bookends that will complement your library or make fine gifts for good friends.

Construction Steps

1. From a scrap of 3/4″ plywood between 4 and 6″ wide and at least 24 1/2″ long, or from several suitable scraps, cut four pieces to 6″ lengths with a mitre box and backsaw.
2. At one end of each piece, measure in 1″ from each side edge and make a pencil mark on the front edge. Then, with the mitre box set for a 45° cut, and using the pencil mark for a guide, cut the corners off one end of each piece, leaving square corners at the opposite end.
3. Prenail the rear (squared) underside of two pieces with three 1 5/8″ ring-shank paneling nails each.
4. Run a bead of glue along the rear edge of each remaining piece. Butt each glued edge to a prenailed piece; then drive and countersink the nails, creating two L-shaped bookends.
5. Fill open flaws, as necessary, using spackling paste if bookends will be painted, or wood filler if they will be finished naturally. Let stand until paste or filler cures.
6. Sand all surfaces, except rears and bottoms, with medium-grit, fine-grit, and extra-fine-grit sandpaper, carefully rounding over sharp corners and edges as you sand.
7. Apply the finish of your choice: two coats of paint, or stain and two coats of polyurethane varnish.
8. Attach four self-adhesive cork cabinet-door cushions to the bottom of each bookend, and the set is ready for use; or attach decorative items with a small amount of epoxy glue, according to the manufacturer's directions.

Required Tools

Steel tape rule
Pencil
Claw hammer
Nail set
Mitre box and backsaw
Putty knife

Required Materials

One 4 to 6 × 24 1/2″ scrap of 3/4″ plywood, G1S
White glue
1 5/8″ ring-shank paneling nails
Spackling paste or wood filler
Medium-, fine-, and extra-fine-grit sandpaper
Finish of choice
Eight self-adhesive cabinet-door cushions

Optional Materials

Two bookend ornaments
Epoxy glue kit

Step 2

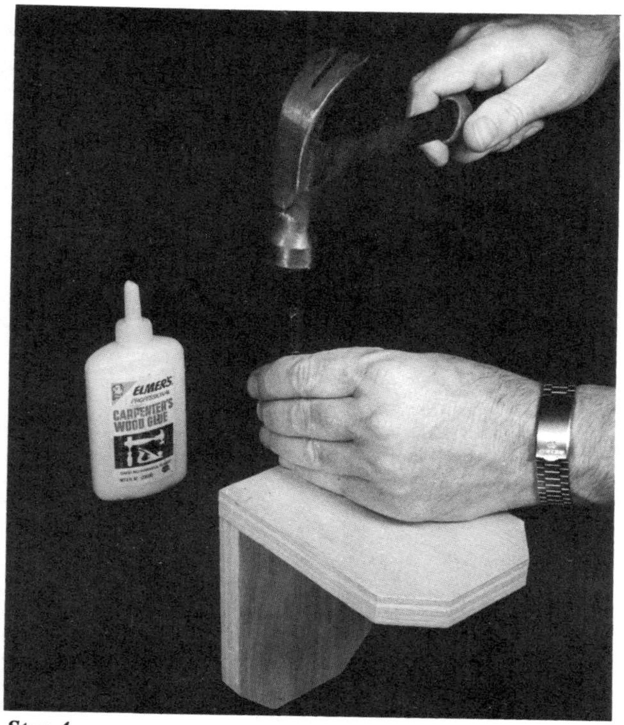

Step 4

48 Simple Wine Rack

Bottles of wine should be stored on their sides in order to keep the corks wet and expanded against the inside of the bottlenecks, providing a perfect seal. The wine rack featured here can be put together during an evening in the shop.

Ideally, wine should be kept in a cool, dry, and preferably dark room. In the absence of a wine cellar, dark area of a basement, or a cool pantry, you can put your wine rack on the floor of a closet, and you need not paint or varnish the rack.

If, for some reason, you plan to keep the rack in view, patch and fill plywood edges, brad holes, and open defects with spackling paste or wood filler. Sand the plywood panels to a fine finish before attaching them, and finish sand them after filling the brad holes.

If you consume wine only occasionally, you might not need more than a single tier that will hold four bottles. The single tiers also fit easily on shelves. Or you can make the simple 2 × 2 uprights that were designed to support three tiers and form a rack that will hold a case of wine.

Incidentally, unlike most wine racks, the single tiers and the top tier of the three-tier rack will accommodate magnum-size bottles.

Construction Steps

1. For each tier of the rack, cut ten 4 × 4″ squares from available scraps of 1/2″ plywood—thirty in all for the three-tier rack.
2. For each tier, cut two pieces of 3/4″-square molding to 30 1/4″ and two more to 7″—six each for the three-tier rack.
3. Set a combination square for 3/4″ and use it to scribe a line across each end of each piece of 3/4″-square molding.
4. Set the square for 3/8″ and scribe lines on the adjacent sides of the molding, perpendicular to those scribed in **Step 3.**
5. With a mitre box and backsaw, make a crosscut 3/4″ from each end of each piece of molding, using the lines scribed in **Step 3** as guides. Cut to a depth of 3/8″, using the lines scribed in **Step 4** as stop marks.
6. With a hammer and 3/4″ or wider wood chisel, remove the material from the ends of the molding, creating end-lap notches. Smooth the notches, as necessary, with a narrow wood rasp.
7. Prenail each plywood square with two 1″ brads. Position one about 1/2″ inside one corner and the other about 1/2″ inside the opposite diagonal corner.
8. Run a thin bead of glue across the underside of a plywood square, diagonally from corner to corner, opposite the brads.
9. Center the square horizontally on one of the long pieces of 3/4″-square molding, 1″ from one end; then drive and countersink the brads.
10. Attach another square the same way next to the first. Continue attaching squares for a total of five. Then attach five more to another length of molding.
11. Apply glue to each end lap of the two short pieces of molding, join them at right angles to the end laps in the long pieces with squares attached, and lightly clamp each joint with a C-clamp. Let stand until the glue sets, and one tier is ready for use or finishing.
12. If you plan to build the three-tier rack, assemble two more tiers the same as the first. Then cut four pieces of 2 × 2 to 17 1/4″.
13. Scribe lines across each 2 × 2 at 3″, 3 3/4″, 9 1/4″, 10″, 15 1/2″, and 16 1/4″ from the bottom.
14. With a mitre box and backsaw—or circular saw, table saw, or radial-arm saw set for a 3/4″-deep cut—crosscut along each line scribed in **Step 13** to a depth of 3/4″.

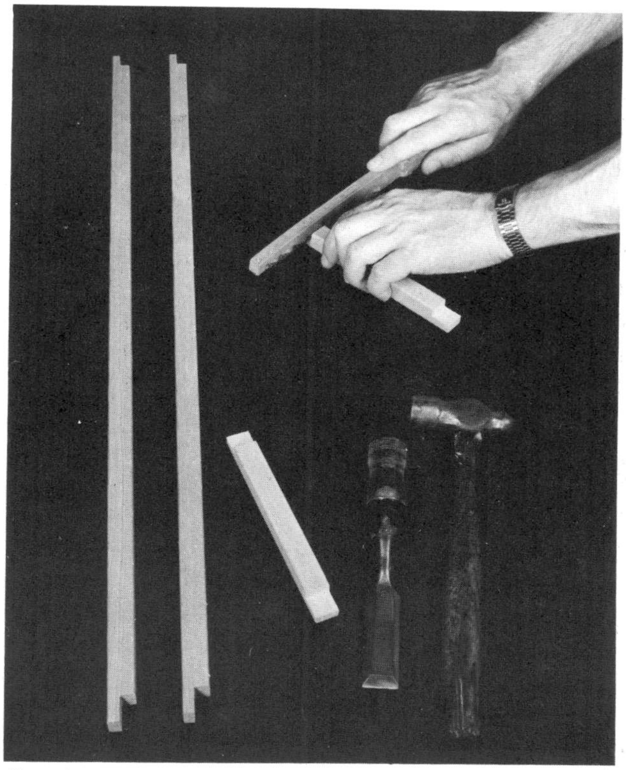

Step 6

Step 11

15. Use a hammer and ½″ wood chisel to knock out the material between the cuts, creating three ¾″-deep and ¾″-wide dadoes in each piece of 2 × 2. Use a narrow rasp to smooth the dadoes.
16. Apply glue to the inside of the bottommost dadoes in two of the 2 × 2 uprights. Press the end of a tier frame into the dadoes with corners fitting flush. Drive one or two 1¼″ brads through the tier frame into each upright. Attach the other two tiers, the same way, in the remaining dadoes.
17. Apply glue to the dadoes in the remaining two uprights, and attach them to the opposite ends of the tier frames with brads. Let the rack stand until the glue sets and it's ready for use or finishing.

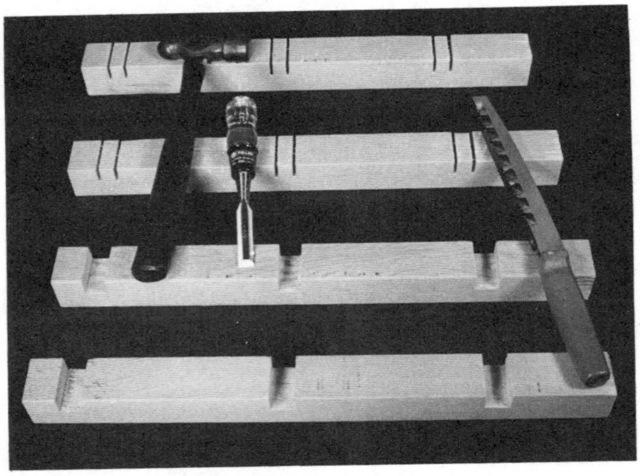

Step 15

Step 16

Required Tools

- Steel tape rule
- Combination square
- Claw hammer
- Nail set
- Mitre box and backsaw
- Two C-clamps
- ½″ wood chisel
- ¾″ or larger wood chisel
- Wood rasp
- Circular saw
- Saw guide

Required Materials

- 30 4 × 4″ scraps of ½″ plywood, G1S
- 18′ of ¾″-square molding
- 6′ of 2 × 2, standard or better
- White glue
- 1″ brads
- 1¼″ brads
- Medium-grit sandpaper

49
Easy-up Utility Shelves

Narrow strips of plywood from three to six inches wide, left over from various projects, often end up in the trash heap, simply because there's nothing else to do with them. Before you discard such scraps, take a look at this simple project and evaluate your utility-shelving needs. Chances are, you'll start saving these pieces and putting them to good use.

Strips of $\frac{1}{2}''$ or $\frac{3}{4}''$ plywood as narrow as three inches are perfect for shelves that will hold a variety of small parts in the workshop. They are ideal, too, for storing canned goods in a single rank along a pantry wall. Wider shelves, of course, will hold larger cans, bottles, and boxes. You can cut the shelves to any length, and trim

the edges with 1″ lattice to create a lip that will keep jars and bottles from toppling off.

The shelves go up with utility brackets that come in a range of sizes from 3 to 14″, the smaller of which will prove most useful for this project. Brackets are mounted to the underside of the shelves with wood screws and to the wall studs with nails, although you could use 1½″ wood screws instead of nails, if you prefer.

Stud-mounting provides support every 16″, which should prove more than adequate. With ¾″ stock, you can plan to have your shelves overhang the end brackets up to about 10″. Don't extend them any more than 6″, though, if you are using ½″ plywood.

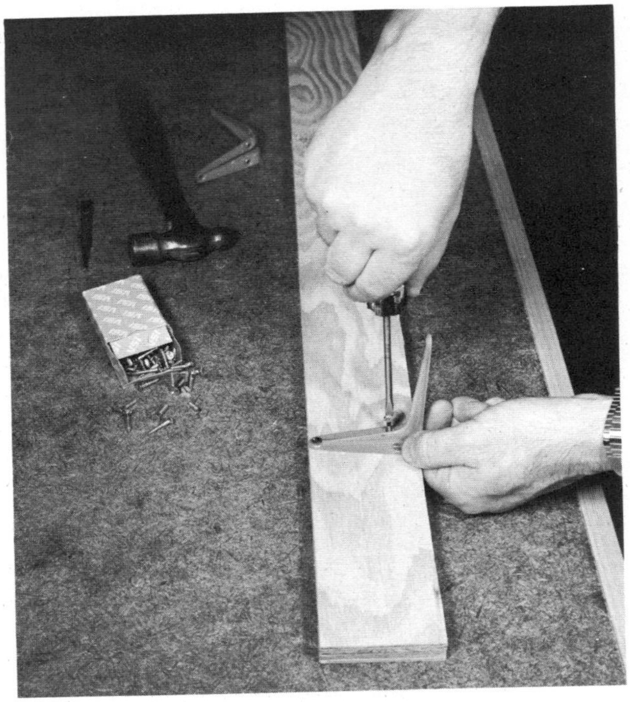

Step 6

Construction Steps

1. Use a stud finder to locate the studs in the wall where you plan to install the shelves; then, for ease of assembly, lightly mark the stud locations on the wall with a pencil.
2. Measure the wall to determine how long the shelves should be and how many you will need.
3. From suitable scraps of ½″ or ¾″ plywood, any grade, and in widths from 3″ to 6″, cut shelves to the desired length.
4. Lay the shelves face down, and scribe lines across each to coincide with the studs in the wall where they'll be mounted.
5. Align a utility shelf bracket along each line, with the rear of the bracket flush with the rear edge of the shelf, and use the bracket as a guide to mark for screw-starter holes.
6. Punch a screw-starter hole with a nail set at each spot marked, and attach each bracket to the shelf with three ½ × 6 flathead wood screws (for ½″ plywood) or ¾ × 6 screws (for ¾″ plywood).
7. With a mitre box and backsaw, cut a piece of 1″ lattice to fit each end of each shelf; then attach the pieces to the shelf ends with glue and two ¾″ brads each. Lattice should fit flush with the bottom of the shelf, creating a lip along the top edge.
8. Cut lengths of lattice to fit the front edges of the shelves, and attach them with glue and brads, spaced about 6″ apart. Countersink the brads.
9. Position each shelf so the brackets align with the wall studs, and mount with two 8d box nails driven through each bracket into its respective stud. If you are mounting more than one shelf, start with the lowest one and work up.
10. To mount additional shelves above the first one, cut two scraps of wood (e.g., 1 × 2, 2 × 2, 2 × 4) to a length that coincides with the planned shelf-to-shelf distance. Then for quick shelf alignment, prop the second shelf above the first atop the two scraps of wood. For different spacing between subsequent shelves, simply trim the scraps to the right length or cut others.

Required Tools

Steel tape rule
Combination square
Pencil
Claw hammer
Nail set
Mitre box and backsaw
Stud finder
Screwdriver
Two C-clamps
Circular saw
Saw guide

Required Materials

Any available scraps of 3″- to 6″-wide ½″ or ¾″ plywood, any grade
3″ to 6″ utility shelf brackets (one required for every 16″ of shelving)
Three ½ × 6 or ¾ × 6 flathead wood screws per bracket
Two 8d box nails per bracket required
1″ lattice, as required for each shelf
White glue
¾″ brads

50 Workshop Plan Stand

If you have ever built anything by following the step-by-step instructions in a magazine or book, you know that the volumes have a tendency to slam shut, according to Murphy's First Workshop Law, at precisely the wrong moment. So you have probably acquired the habit of propping the publications open with any tool that's handy and heavy enough to do the job. And from this practice you've likely learned Murphy's Second Workshop Law: "The tool you pick to prop open a magazine or book will be the very tool needed for the next construction step."

Well, you can outsmart Murphy by buying a couple of cheap clipboards, gathering a few scraps of wood together, and building a plan stand that will hold any book or magazine open, at a convenient angle, for ready reference.

Construction Steps

1. Trim a scrap of 3/4″ plywood, any grade, to 15 × 20″.
2. Scribe a line across the plywood 3/4″ from and parallel to one of the 20″ edges. Then mark the center of the line.
3. Clamp a clipboard to a solid surface with a pair of spring clamps or C-clamps. Use another C-clamp to depress the clip to relieve the spring tension.
4. Put a drop of oil on each rivet holding the clip to the board, and use a 13/64″-diameter bit to drill through each rivet. Remove the other clip the same way.
5. Center a clip on the left side of the center mark on the line scribed in **Step 2,** and use the rivet holes as guides for marking for screw-starter holes on the line. Do the same on the right side of the center mark. Then punch screw-starter holes with a nail set and hammer.
6. Squeeze a clip open between thumb and forefinger, and mount it to the face of the stand with two 1/2 × 8 sheet metal screws. Mount the other clip the same way.
7. Cut two scraps of 2 × 4 to 10 1/2″, each mitred to 45° at one end.
8. Measure down 1″ from the top (mitred) end along the rear narrow edge of each piece of 2 × 4, and prenail each with a 1 1/2″ brad.
9. Lay the face of the stand face down on a flat surface. Apply glue to the mitred edge of each 2 × 4, opposite the brad, and position each in a top rear corner of the face piece. Drive and countersink the brads.
10. Carefully stand the unit upright to rest on the 2 × 4 legs. Then drive two 6d finishing nails through the face into each leg, and countersink the nails.
11. Let the unit stand until the glue sets.

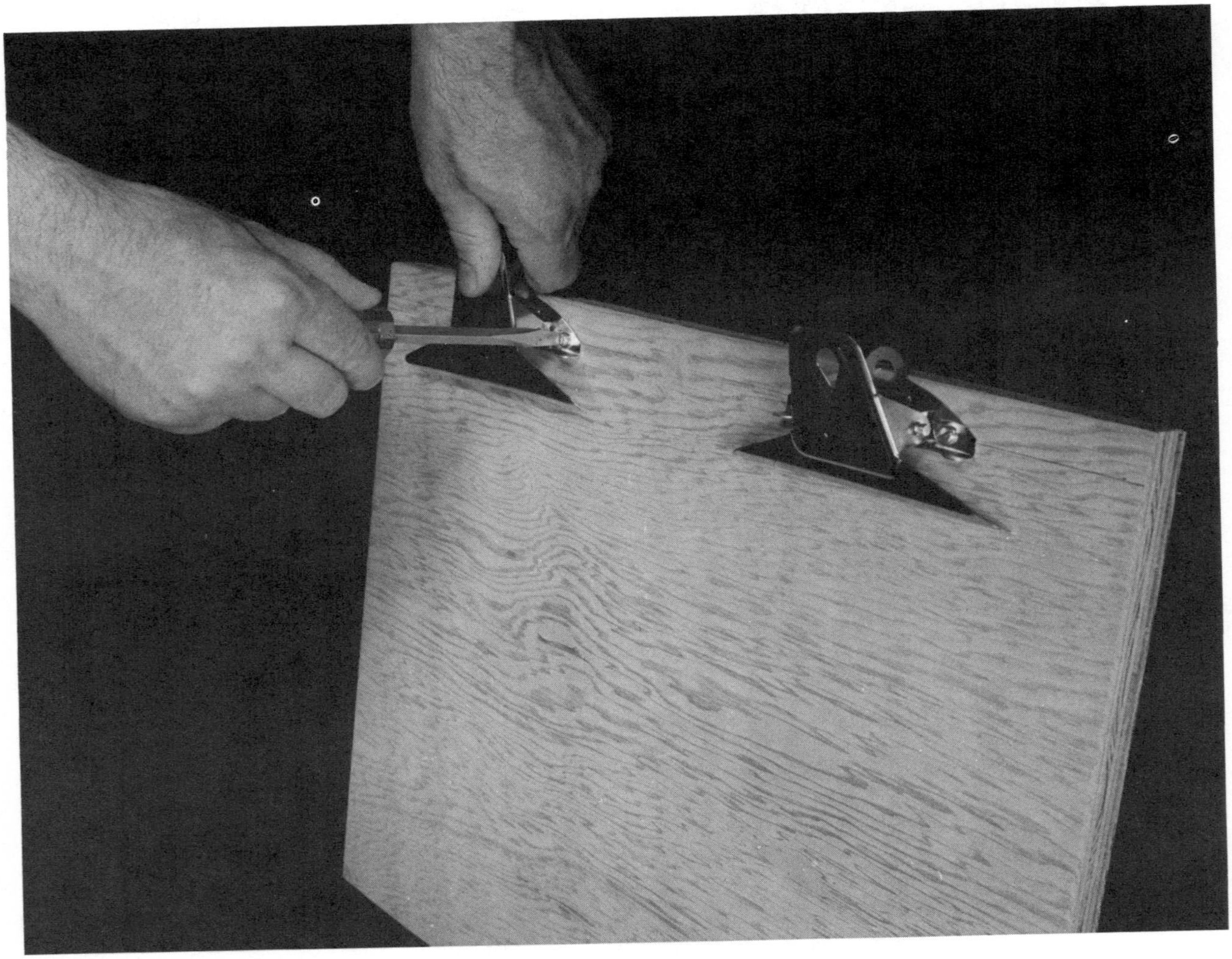

Step 6

Step 10

Required Tools

- Steel tape rule
- Yardstick or large T-square
- Pencil
- Claw hammer
- Nail set
- Mitre box and backsaw
- Three C-clamps
- Electric drill and $^{13}/_{64}$″ bit
- Circular saw
- Saw guide

Required Materials

- One 15 × 20″ scrap of ¾″ plywood, any grade
- 21″ scrap of 2 × 4, standard or better
- White glue
- 1½″ brads
- 6d finishing nails
- Four ½ × 8 panhead sheet metal screws
- Lubricating oil
- Two clipboards

51 Stereo Speaker Elevators

While small stereo speaker cabinets fit well in shelf units or can be hung on a wall, large speaker units often end up on a floor, for lack of a more convenient place to put them. But a floor, especially a carpeted one, will alter and deteriorate the quality of the sound. For top performance, speakers should be elevated above floor level. The units featured here will provide the necessary elevation and ensure superior sound reproduction.

Since the elevators are no more than short tables, the same principles can be employed in other projects as well. You can use plywood scraps of suitable size to make table tops of any dimensions and simply cut the legs to the appropriate lengths.

To make the speaker elevators shown, just follow these easy steps:

Construction Steps

1. Measure the base width and length of your speaker cabinets, and cut two scraps of 3/4″ or thicker plywood 1 1/2″ shorter in width and length. (Shorter dimensions are to allow for trim thickness.)
2. With a mitre box and backsaw, cut a piece of 1 × 3 to a 45° angle at one end. Lay it in place along one edge of one of the plywood panels, and mark for another mitre cut at the opposite corner. Cut to fit.
3. Prenail the 1 × 3 trim with three or more 1 1/4″ brads, placed 3/8″ to 1/2″ from the top edge, depending on plywood thickness.
4. Run a bead of glue along the edge of the plywood panel, attach trim with brads, and countersink the brads.
5. Continue attaching 1 × 3 trim the same way, until all four edges of each panel have been trimmed.
6. Fill brad holes and surface imperfections with wood filler if you plan to finish the elevators naturally, or with spackling paste if you plan to paint.
7. Before cutting a 50″ length or suitable scraps of 2 × 2 into legs, sand all edges with a pad sander and medium-grit and fine-grit sandpaper. (Don't round over the corners.)
8. Use a mitre box and backsaw to cut 2 × 2 stock into eight 6″ legs.
9. Round over the bottom edges of each leg with medium-grit and fine-grit sandpaper.
10. Sand tops and trim with medium-grit and fine-grit sandpaper.
11. Turn the tops upside down, and lay them on a bench top. Apply glue to the top of a leg and to the top inch of the two sides that will come in contact with the 1 × 3 trim. Press in place in one corner of the top assembly, and lightly clamp with a C-clamp.
12. Attach the remaining legs to the corners of the top assemblies, and let the units stand until the glue sets.
13. Round over the edges of the legs with medium-grit and fine-grit sandpaper.
14. If you plan to paint the units, they're ready for cleaning and painting. If you will finish them naturally, hand-sand them with extra-fine-grit sandpaper and #400 wet-or-dry sandpaper; then clean them to remove all dust.
15. Apply the finish of your choice.

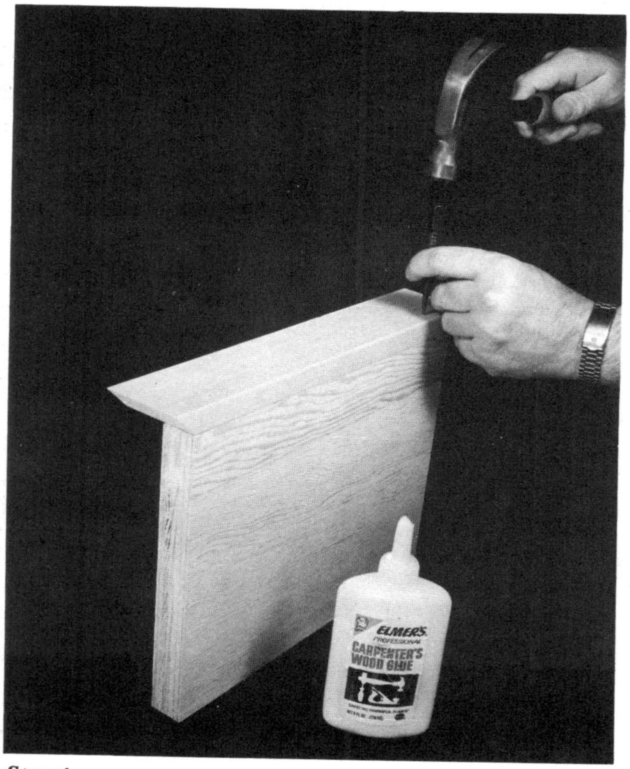

Step 4

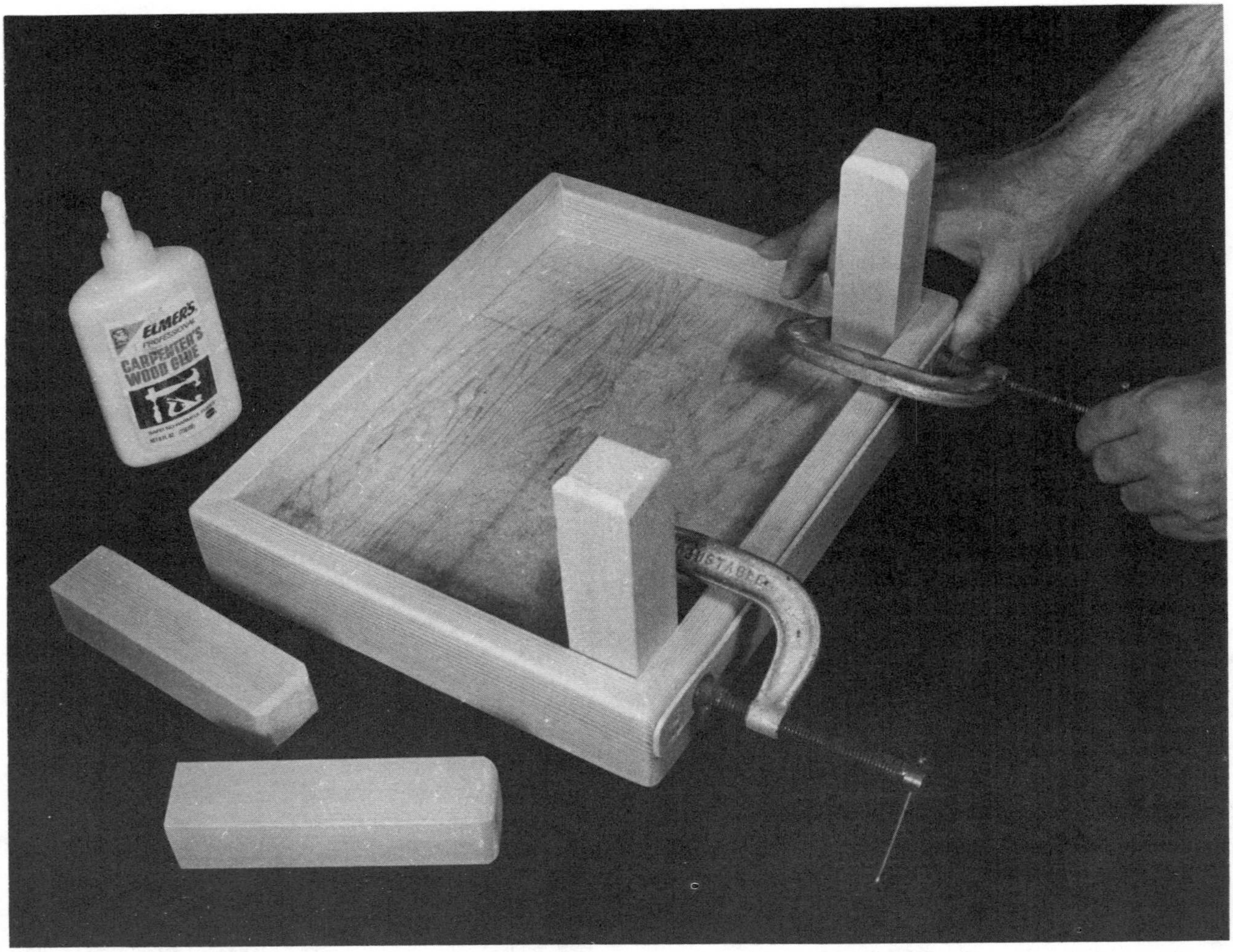

Step 12

Required Tools

Steel tape rule	Two to eight C-clamps
Pencil	Putty knife
Claw hammer	Circular saw
Nail set	Saw guide
Mitre box and backsaw	Pad sander

Required Materials

Suitable scraps of $\frac{3}{4}''$ or thicker plywood, G1S
1 × 3 trim, clear or patchable, as required
50″ of 2 × 2, clear or patchable
White glue
Wood filler or spackling paste
$1\frac{1}{4}''$ brads
Medium-grit and fine-grit sandpaper
(For natural finish) Extra-fine-grit and #400 wet-or-dry sandpaper
Stain and varnish or paint of choice

52 Spice or Small-Parts Rack

Here's another project that will use up some of those narrow scraps of $\frac{3}{4}''$ plywood. And since the unit is small, you'll probably have enough molding and hardboard scraps to complete the project, without having to shop for materials.

If you need something to conveniently store spices and herbs in the kitchen, this unit will hold about a dozen and a half jars. If you need more space, add a shelf or two, or increase the width, to a maximum of about 24″.

The rack is equally useful in the workshop, where it will keep all those little plastic containers and boxes of brads, screws, washers, and other small parts organized and right at your fingertips. Again, you can alter the dimensions to fit your needs.

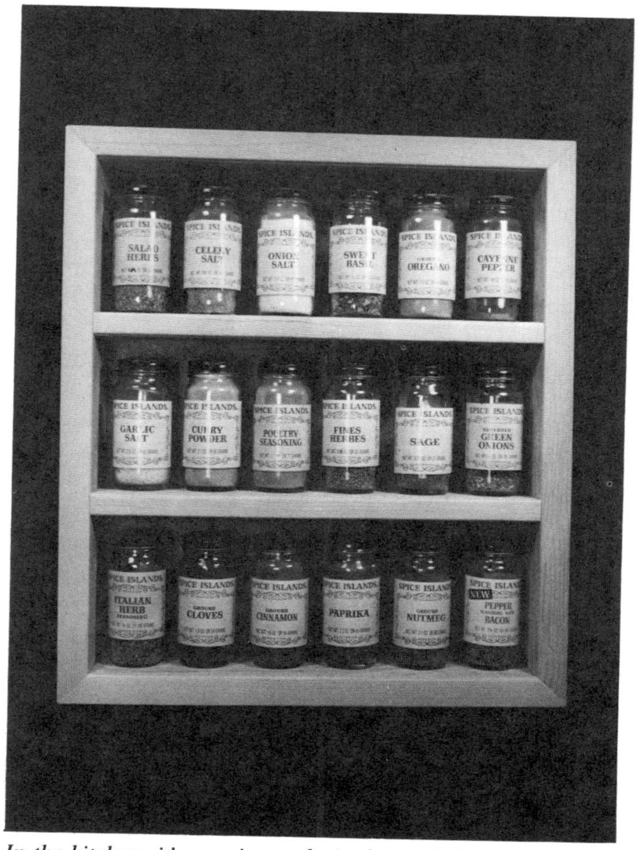

In the kitchen, it's a spice rack; in the workshop, it's a small-parts rack

If you're building the unit as a spice rack, you might want to paint it to match or contrast with the kitchen decor. In that case, fill the brad holes, conceal the plywood laminations with spackling paste, and sand to a fine finish before painting. If you have some hardwood plywood scraps, however, you might prefer to finish the rack naturally. In that case, use a scrap of ¼″ hardwood plywood for the rear panel and fill brad holes with wood filler before finishing or colored putty after. Take the wood down to an extra-fine finish and polish with steel wool before giving the rack two coats of polyurethane varnish.

If the rack will be used in the workshop, you might want to leave it unfinished, as I did with mine.

Construction Steps

1. From 3″-wide scraps of ¾″ G2S plywood, cut two verticals to 18″ and four horizontals to 14″.
2. Measuring from the bottom end of the 18″ verticals, mark each at 5¾″ and 11½″; then use a combination square to scribe a line across each piece at each mark.
3. Apply glue to the end of a 14″ horizontal, butt it to the bottom inside of a vertical, and clamp with a corner clamp.
4. Attach another horizontal, the same way, to the top inside of the vertical. Then stand the unit up on the horizontals and drive two 1⅝″ ring-shank paneling nails into the bottom horizontal and two more into the top one.
5. Remove the bottom corner clamp and use it to glue and clamp another horizontal to the vertical 5″ above the bottom, aligned above the first line scribed in **Step 2.** Then drive two paneling nails through the vertical into the horizontal.
6. Move the clamp back to the bottom corner. Remove the top clamp and use it to attach the remaining horizontal with glue and two paneling nails, aligned above the second line scribed in **Step 2.** Then return the clamp to the top corner.
7. Turn the unit over, with horizontals upright, and apply glue to the ends. Clamp the remaining vertical to the top and bottom horizontals with corner clamps, and attach the verticals with paneling nails, as above. Let the unit stand with clamps in place until the glue sets.
8. Trim a scrap of ¼″ tempered hardboard to 15½ × 18″.
9. Set the unit rear side up, and run a thin bead of glue along the rear edges. Spread the glue with a paper towel to keep seepage to a minimum.
10. Lay the hardboard atop the unit, smooth surface down, and nail it to the unit with ⅞″ wire nails.

Step 6

Step 13

11. Turn the unit to rest on its back, and remove the corner clamps. Use a mitre box and backsaw to cut a piece of 1″ outside corner molding to fit one edge, mitred at each end.
12. Attach the molding with glue and three ¾″ brads, and countersink the brads.
13. Measure and cut molding and attach it, the same way, to the remaining three sides.
14. Cut two pieces of screen molding to 14″. Run a bead of glue down the rear of each, attach to the front of each untrimmed shelf with three ¾″ brads, and countersink the brads.

15. Mark the top and bottom sections of the rear panel for centered drill-starter holes, and center-punch starter holes. Then drill an $^{11}/_{64}$″-diameter hole at each spot.
16. Fill brad holes and conceal plywood laminations and surface imperfections with spackling paste (if you plan to paint) or wood filler (if you plan to finish naturally or leave the unit unfinished), and let the unit stand until the filler hardens.
17. Sand, as required, with medium-grit and fine-grit sandpaper; then use a vacuum cleaner to remove all dust.
18. If you plan to paint, apply two coats of aerosol paint of your choice. For a natural finish, use spray urethane varnish. Or leave unfinished for use in the workshop.
19. Hang the unit with two $1\frac{1}{2} \times 8$ oval-head screws and finish washers, driven into the wall studs. (If you can't attach the rack to studs, use $2\frac{1}{2}$″ toggle bolts and finish washers instead.)

Required Tools

Steel tape rule	Two C-clamps
Combination square	Two to four corner clamps
Pencil	Putty knife
Claw hammer	Electric drill and $^{11}/_{64}$″ bit
Nail set	Circular saw
Center punch	Saw guide
Screwdriver	
Mitre box and backsaw	

Required Materials

Two 3×18″ scraps of ¾″ plywood, G2S
Four 3×14″ scraps of ¾″ plywood, G2S
One $15\frac{1}{2} \times 18$″ scrap of ¼″ tempered hardboard
6′ of 1″ outside corner molding
2½′ of screen molding
White glue
Spackling paste or wood filler
¾″ brads
1⅝″ ring-shank paneling nails
⅞″ wire nails
Two $1\frac{1}{2} \times 8$ ovalhead wood screws
Two #8 finish washers
Medium-grit and fine-grit sandpaper
One can of spray paint or urethane varnish
Stain of choice for natural finish

53
Space-Efficient Corner Table

Corners in many houses and apartments go unused, mainly because furnishings just don't fit into them. If you have corners going to waste in your home, consider adding a few simple three-legged tables that you can build from scraps.

These tables can be made from any scraps of good-one-side $^3/_4$″ plywood measuring 12 by 12″ or larger. You can paint them, antique them, or finish them naturally. They're ideal for house plants, candles, statues, and other decorative items. They also can be custom-built to hold stereo speakers. Make them any height you want by picking the appropriate-length legs.

The following steps describe the assembly of a 15-by-15″ table made from a scrap of oak plywood, trimmed with oak 1 × 2, lightly stained with Pen-Chrome English oak stain, finished with Watco Natural Danish

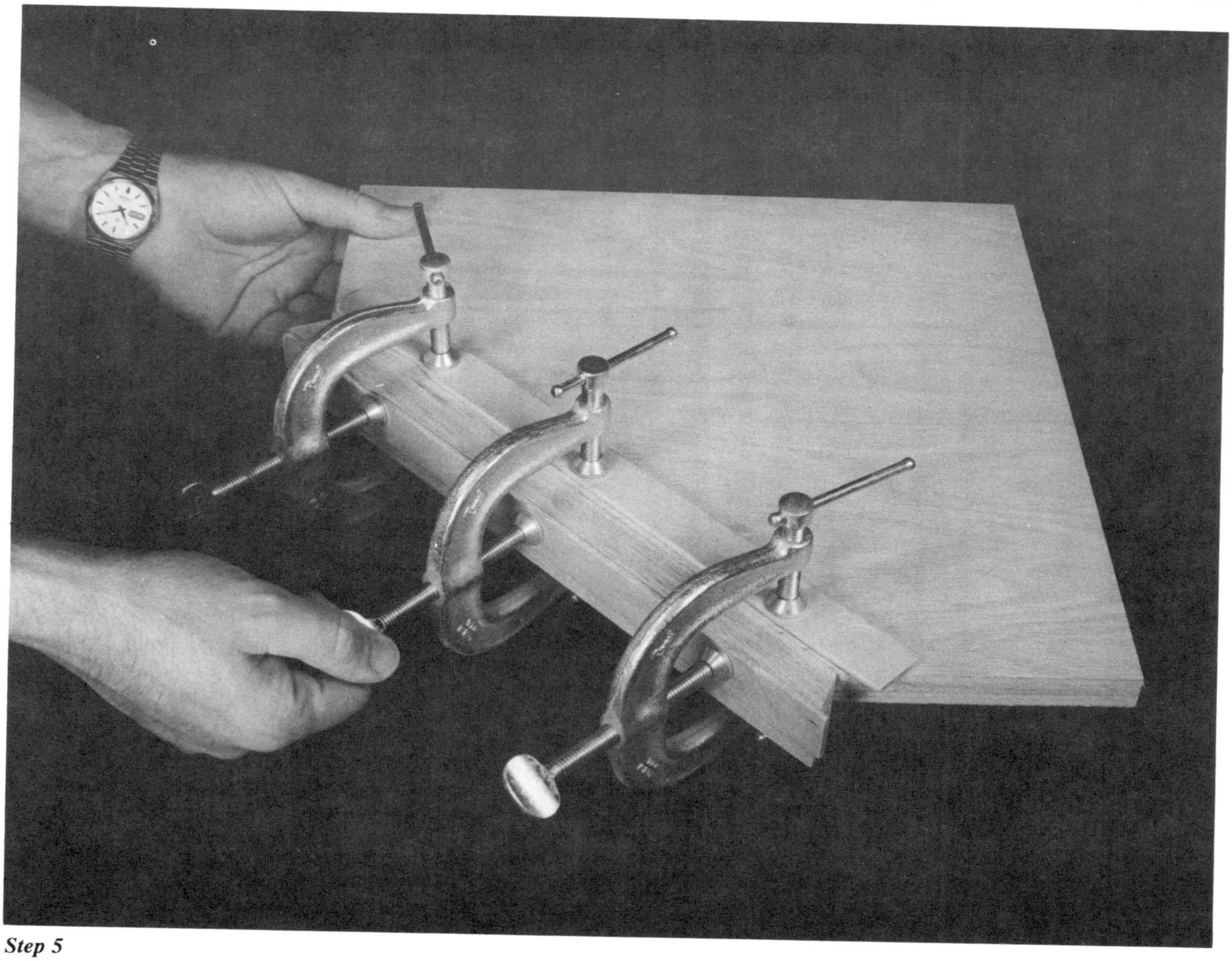

Step 5

Oil, and waxed. Trim was attached with glue and edge clamps, and no fasteners were used. If you don't own edge clamps and don't want to buy them, attach the trim with glue and brads, countersink the brads, and fill the holes. If you're painting, fill with spackling paste; for a natural finish, fill with wood filler or colored putty or wax sticks.

Construction Steps

1. Trim a suitable scrap of hardwood plywood to 15 × 15″.
2. Measure along the right front edge 5″ from the right corner and make a mark. Measure along the left front edge 5″ from the left corner and make another mark. Then scribe a line connecting the two marks.
3. Cut along the line scribed in **Step 2** with a circular saw to remove the front corner.
4. Set your mitre box for a 22½° cut and cut one end of a piece of 1 × 2 hardwood (species to match plywood). Hold the piece in place along the front edge and mark for a second cut. Mitre-cut the other end to 22½° to fit.
5. Run a bead of glue along the top inside edge of the 1 × 2, press it in place along the front edge, and clamp with three edge clamps. Let stand for about an hour, or until glue sets.
6. Cut two pieces to fit the short, angled portions of the front edge, each mitre-cut at one end at a 22½° angle to fit the first piece of trim attached, and at 45° to fit the corner. Glue and clamp each piece with two edge clamps, and let stand until the glue sets.
7. Cut two more pieces of 1 × 2 to fit the right and left rear edges, each mitred at 45° at each end. Glue and clamp each piece in place with three or four edge clamps, and let stand until glue sets.
8. Sand the top and edge trim with a pad sander and medium-grit, fine-grit, and extra-fine-grit sandpaper, rounding over sharp edges and corners as you sand.

9. If you plan to varnish, hand-sand with extra-fine-grit paper. If you plan an oil finish, follow that with #400 wet-or-dry sandpaper, and polish with #0000 steel wool.
10. Sand legs, as required, to an extra-fine finish.
11. Turn the table top upside down on a flat working surface. Position one leg plate against the trim at the rear corner. Position each of the other two against the trim, midway between the 90° and 45° front corners. Using the plates as guides, mark for screw-starter holes.
12. Punch screw-starter holes with a nail set, and mount the leg plates with the screws provided.
13. Screw the legs into the plates, and clean the table to remove dust.
14. If you plan to stain, turn the table upside down, apply the stain of your choice to the legs and underside, and wipe dry with paper towels. Set the table upright, and stain the top and trim. Let the table stand until stain dries.
15. Apply the finish of your choice and let stand until dry.

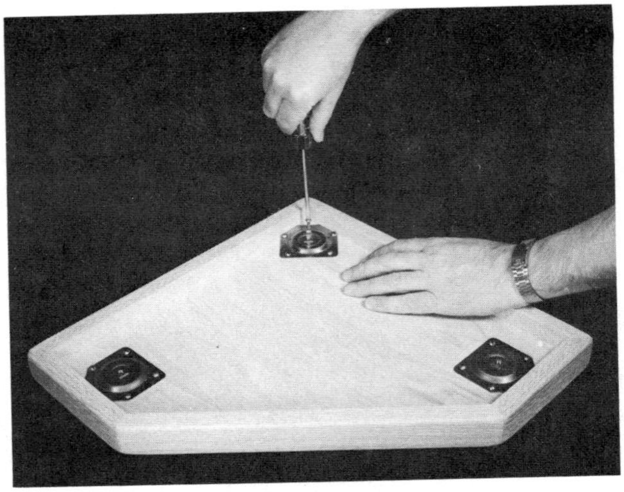

Step 12

Required Tools

- Steel tape rule
- Yardstick or carpenter's square
- Pencil
- Claw hammer
- Nail set
- Screwdriver
- Mitre box and backsaw
- Two C-clamps
- Four edge clamps
- Paint brush
- Circular saw
- Saw guide
- Pad sander

Required Materials

- One 15 × 15″ scrap of ¾″ hardwood plywood, good or better
- 5′ of 1 × 2 hardwood to match the plywood
- White glue
- Medium-grit, fine-grit, extra-fine-grit and #400 wet-or-dry sandpaper
- #0000 steel wool
- Stain of choice
- Polyurethane varnish or oil finish
- Three 12″ table legs with straight plates

54 Sturdy Step Block

When I grew weary of hauling out the stepladder or traipsing upstairs to borrow my wife's stepstool whenever I needed to reach something, I decided to build a step block that I could keep in my workshop for such purposes. It went together in less than an hour with scraps I had lying about the shop, and it has proved handy in numerous ways.

With the step block, I'm able to reach anything in the shop, including the top items on my highest storage shelves and all trim and lumber in my overhead storage racks. When I'm working near the floor—such as when I'm changing a tire on my truck or repacking the wheel bearings on my boat trailer—I no longer squat or kneel; I sit comfortably on the step block. And when I'm standing at the bench for long periods, I relieve back strain by propping one foot on the step block.

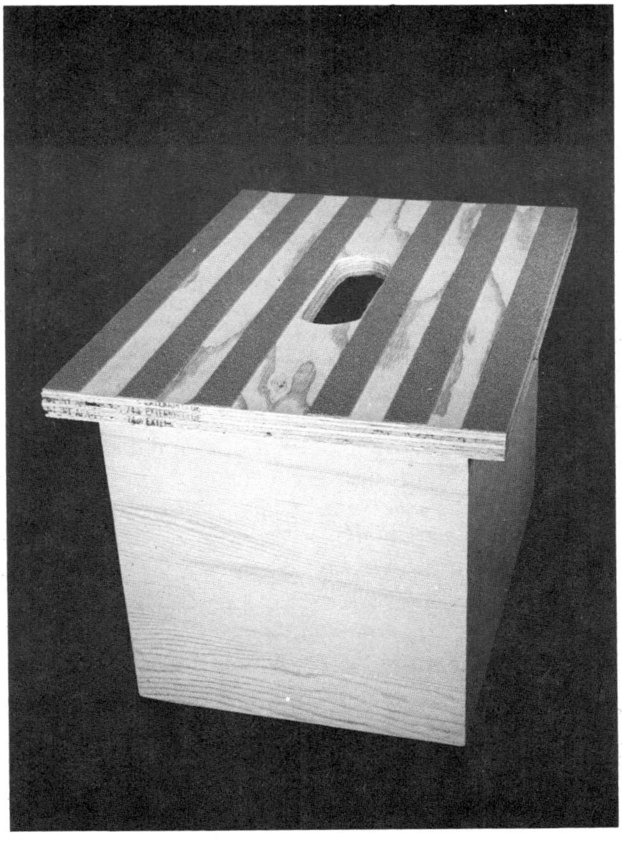

The compact block fits conveniently in the base cabinet of my workbench. Its hand hole makes it easy to grasp and move to wherever I need it. Strips of tread tape ensure good footing.

Construction Steps

1. From available scraps of $3/4''$ plywood, any grade, cut two side panels to $10 \times 12''$ each, two end panels to $9\frac{1}{2} \times 10''$ each, and a top panel to $11\frac{1}{2} \times 15\frac{1}{2}''$.
2. Trim two scraps of 2×4 to 12″ each.
3. On the top panel, scribe a center line parallel to each $15\frac{1}{2}''$ edge. Measure in 6″ from each end, and mark the line for drill-starter holes.
4. Center-punch a drill-starter hole at each spot, and drill two $1\frac{1}{2}''$-diameter holes in the top panel.
5. Scribe a line connecting the top edge of one hole with the top edge of the other. Scribe another line connecting the bottom edges of the holes.
6. Use a sabre saw to cut out the material between the holes, along the lines scribed in **Step 5.**
7. Run a wavy bead of glue down a broad face of a 12″ piece of 2×4; then nail a side panel to it with $1\frac{5}{8}''$ ring-shank paneling nails, so the top edge of the panel is flush with the top edge of the 2×4. Attach the other side panel to the other 2×4 the same way.
8. Run a bead of glue down one end of a side panel and the end of the attached 2×4; then butt an end panel to it and attach it with three paneling nails.
9. Attach the other side panel to the end panel the same way.
10. Turn the unit over and attach the remaining end panel with glue and six paneling nails.
11. Scribe a line across the top panel $2\frac{1}{2}''$ from and parallel to one $15\frac{1}{2}''$ edge and another $2\frac{1}{2}''$ from the other $15\frac{1}{2}''$ edge. Mark each line at the center and at 3″ from each end. Then mark the center line scribed in **Step 3** at $1\frac{3}{8}''$ from each end.
12. Prenail the top panel with a paneling nail at each spot marked on the parallel lines.
13. Apply glue to the top edges of the unit, including the 2×4's. Lay the top panel atop the unit, and adjust it for a 1″ overhang along all sides; then attach it with the paneling nails.
14. Cut six strips of 1″ tread tape to $15\frac{1}{2}''$ each. Remove the backing and stick a strip along each long edge of the top panel, another along each side of the hand hole, and each of the remaining strips between the first two sets.

Step 6

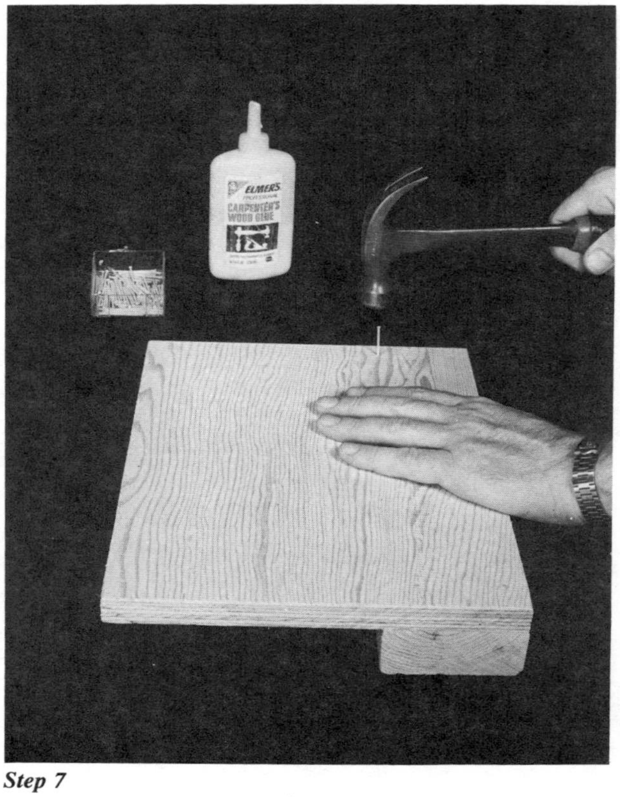

Step 7

Step 10

Required Tools

Steel tape rule
Yardstick or carpenter's square
Pencil
Claw hammer
Center punch
Two C-clamps
Electric drill and $1\frac{1}{2}''$ bit
Circular saw
Saw guide
Sabre saw

Required Materials

Two $10 \times 12''$ scraps of $\frac{3}{4}''$ plywood, any grade
Two $9\frac{1}{2} \times 10''$ scraps of $\frac{3}{4}''$ plywood, any grade
One $11\frac{1}{2} \times 15\frac{1}{2}''$ scrap of $\frac{3}{4}''$ plywood, any grade
2' of 2×4
White glue
$1\frac{5}{8}''$ ring-shank paneling nails
8' of 1"-wide Scotch-Tred self-adhesive tread tape
Medium-grit sandpaper

55
Shoeshine Box

Here's a handy little storage container that will hold all your jars and cans of shoe polish, saddle soap, neatsfoot oil, buffing rags, brushes, and extra shoe and boot laces. The lid is fitted with a shining block that also serves as the lid's handle.

The narrow box will fit conveniently in a kitchen or bathroom cabinet or on the floor of a closet. When you need to put a quick shine on shoes or boots, pick the appropriate polish, and prop your foot atop the shining block. This practical item will use up a few of your plywood scraps and less than an hour of your time.

Construction Steps

1. From available scraps of ¾″ plywood, G1S, cut a top panel to 6 × 12″ and two end panels to 6 × 9″.
2. From scraps of ½″ plywood, G1S, cut two side panels to 9 × 13½″.
3. Trim a scrap of ¼″ tempered hardboard to 6 × 12″.
4. Cut a scrap of 2 × 4 to 11″ and a scrap of 1 × 4 to 8″.

5. At each end of the 2 × 4, measure in from each corner along the short edge, and make a mark at 1″. Do the same on the 1 × 4, *at one end only*.
6. With a backsaw and mitre box set for 45°, use the marks made in **Step 5** as guides, and cut off all four corners of the 2 × 4 and the corners at one end of the 1 × 4.
7. Apply glue to one broad face of the 1 × 4, and sandwich it to the 2 × 4, matching the trimmed corners of the 1 × 4 with those at one end of the 2 × 4; then clamp with two C-clamps and let stand until the glue sets.
8. Cut four pieces of parting bead to 12″; then prenail each with three 7/8″ wire nails.
9. Scribe a line across and 3/4″ from the top long edge of each side panel. Then make a mark 3/4″ inside each edge on each line. Make corresponding marks inside the bottom corners.
10. Run a bead of glue down one of the pieces of parting bead, and attach it to a side panel, flush with the bottom edge, 3/4″ from each end. Attach another, the same way, to the other side panel.
11. Run a bead of glue down another piece of parting bead, and attach it to a side panel, 3/4″ from the top edge and 3/4″ from each end, using the lines scribed in **Step 9** as guides. Attach the remaining piece to the other side panel the same way.
12. Run a bead of glue down a side edge of an end panel, butt it to a side panel, and clamp the top corner with a corner clamp.
13. Attach the other end panel to the opposite end of the side panel the same way. Then turn the unit to stand on the end panels, and drive three 1″ ring-shank paneling nails through the side panel into each end panel.
14. Invert the unit, and run a bead of glue down the edges of the end panels. Lay the remaining side panel in place, and attach with three 1″ paneling nails at each end.
15. Set the unit upright, and run a bead of glue down the top side of each bottom cleat. Lay the hardboard bottom panel in place, put several heavy objects on it, and let stand until the glue sets.
16. Remove the clamps from the shining block assembled in **Step 7.** Then, with the block secured in a vise or clamped to a bench, round over all corners and top edges with a belt sander and medium-grit belt or pad sander and medium-grit sandpaper. Then hand sand, as necessary, to remove any sharp edges.
17. Scribe a centered line down the underside of the top panel, parallel to each 12″ edge. Then measure in 3″ from each end of the line, and mark for a drill-starter hole.

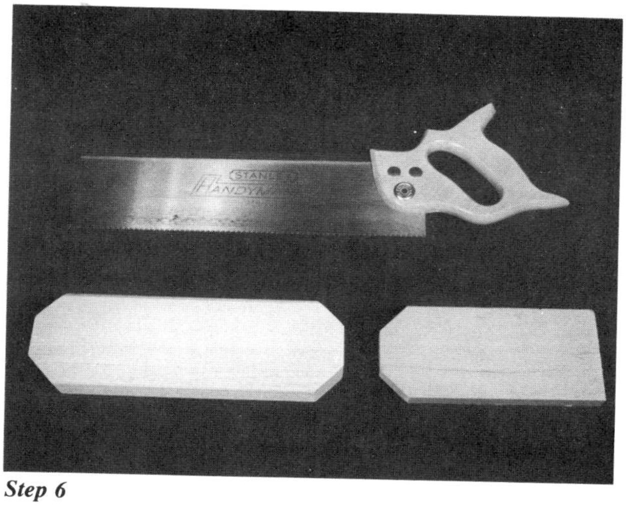

Step 6

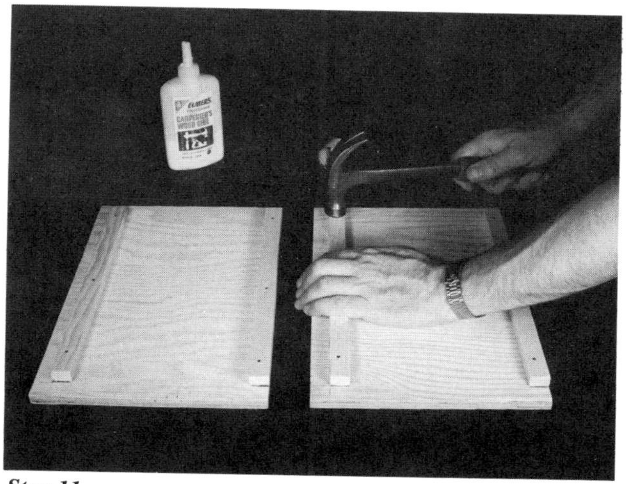

Step 11

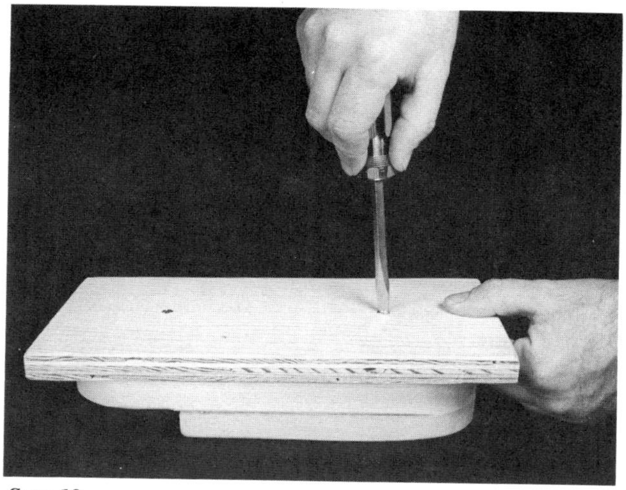

Step 19

18. Center-punch a drill-starter hole at each spot. Then drill $^{11}/_{64}$"-diameter holes and countersink for #8 screws.
19. Apply an ample amount of glue to the underside of the shining block, and center it on the top of the top panel. Carefully invert the top-panel assembly, and use a scratch awl to make screw-starter holes through the holes drilled in **Step 18.** Then attach the shining block with two $1\frac{1}{2} \times 8$ flathead wood screws. See page 239.
20. Stand the box on one end, and center a utility pull on a side panel, 2" from the top edge. Use the pull as a guide to mark for screw-starter holes.
21. Punch screw-starter holes with a nail set, and mount the pull with screws provided.
22. Invert the unit, and mount another pull on the other end panel the same way.
23. Fill your shoeshine box with shoe-care and cleaning materials, and set the top assembly in place atop the parting bead.

Step 21

Required Tools

Steel tape rule
Ruler or carpenter's square
Pencil
Claw hammer
Scratch awl
Nail set
Center punch
Screwdriver
Mitre box and backsaw
Two C-clamps
Two corner clamps
Electric drill and $^{11}/_{64}$" and #8 countersink bits
Circular saw
Saw guide
Belt or pad sander

Required Materials

Two $9 \times 13\frac{1}{2}$" scraps of $\frac{1}{2}$" plywood, G1S
One 6×12" scrap of $\frac{3}{4}$" plywood, G1S
Two 6×9" scraps of $\frac{3}{4}$" plywood, G1S
One 6×12" scrap of $\frac{1}{4}$" tempered hardboard
4' of parting bead
One 8" scrap of 1×4, standard or better
One 11" scrap of 2×4, standard or better
White glue
1" ring-shank paneling nails
Two $1\frac{1}{2} \times 8$ flathead wood screws
Medium-grit sandpaper
Two utility door pulls with screws

Customary to Metric System Conversion Table

Inches		1	2	3	4	5	6	7	8	9	10	11		
Feet	Centi-meters	2.54	5.08	7.62	10.16	12.70	15.24	17.78	20.32	22.86	25.40	27.94	Fractional Equivalents in.-cms.	in.-cms.
1	30.48	33.02	35.56	38.10	40.64	43.18	45.72	48.26	50.80	53.34	55.88	58.42	1/16 = 0.15875	1/8 = 0.31700
2	60.96	63.50	66.04	68.58	71.12	73.66	76.20	78.74	81.28	83.82	86.36	88.90	3/16 = 0.47625	1/4 = 0.63500
3	91.44	93.98	96.52	99.06	101.60	104.14	106.68	109.22	111.76	114.30	116.84	119.38	5/16 = 0.79375	3/8 = 0.95250
4	121.92	124.46	127.00	129.54	132.08	134.62	137.16	139.70	142.24	144.78	147.32	149.86	7/16 = 1.11125	1/2 = 1.27040
5	152.40	154.94	157.48	160.02	162.56	165.10	167.64	170.18	172.72	175.26	177.80	180.34	9/16 = 1.42875	5/8 = 1.58730
6	182.88	185.42	187.96	190.50	193.04	195.58	198.12	200.66	203.20	205.74	208.28	210.82	11/16 = 1.74625	3/4 = 1.90500
7	213.36	215.90	218.44	220.98	223.52	226.06	228.60	231.14	233.68	236.22	238.76	241.30	13/16 = 2.06375	7/8 = 2.22250
8	243.84	246.38	248.92	251.46	254.00	256.54	259.08	261.62	264.16	266.70	269.24	271.78	15/16 = 2.38125	1 = 2.54000
9	274.32	276.86	279.40	281.94	284.48	287.02	289.56	292.10	294.64	297.18	299.72	302.26		
10	304.80	307.34	309.88	312.42	314.96	317.50	320.04	322.58	325.12	327.66	330.20	332.74		
11	335.28	337.82	340.36	342.90	345.44	347.98	350.52	353.06	355.60	358.14	360.68	363.22		
12	365.76	368.30	370.84	373.38	375.92	378.46	381.00	383.54	386.08	388.62	391.16	393.70		
13	396.24	398.78	401.32	403.86	406.40	408.94	411.48	414.02	416.56	419.10	421.64	424.18		
14	426.72	429.26	431.80	434.34	436.88	439.42	441.96	444.50	447.04	449.58	452.12	454.66		
15	457.20	459.74	462.28	464.82	467.36	469.90	472.44	474.98	477.52	480.06	482.60	485.14		
16	487.68	490.22	492.76	495.30	498.84	500.38	502.92	505.46	508.00	510.54	513.08	515.62		
17	518.16	520.70	523.24	525.78	528.32	530.86	533.40	535.94	538.48	541.02	543.56	546.10		
18	548.64	551.18	553.72	556.26	558.80	561.34	563.88	566.42	568.96	571.50	574.04	576.58		
19	579.12	581.66	584.20	586.74	589.28	591.82	594.36	596.90	599.44	601.98	605.52	607.06		
20	609.60	612.14	614.68	617.22	619.76	622.30	624.84	627.38	629.92	632.46	635.50	637.54		

Example:
(1) To convert 13 feet 6 inches to centimeters, read along line 13 under feet and under column 6 inches read 411.48 cms. To reduce to meters move decimal point two spaces to left; thus, 4.1148 meters is the answer.

Meter = 100 Centimeters = 39.37 Inches